Coinage in the Northumbrian Landscape and Economy, *c*.575–*c*.867

Tony Abramson

BAR British Series 641

2018

Published in 2018 by
BAR Publishing, Oxford

BAR British Series 641

Coinage in the Northumbrian Landscape and Economy, c.575–c.867

ISBN 978 1 4073 1653 6

COVER IMAGE *York gold shilling, Paulinus 627-33, Abramson collection.*

Printed in England

BAR
PUBLISHING

BAR titles are available from:

BAR Publishing
122 Banbury Rd, Oxford, OX2 7BP, UK
EMAIL info@barpublishing.com
PHONE +44 (0)1865 310431
FAX +44 (0)1865 316916
www.barpublishing.com

For JRA

Acknowledgements

I am grateful for the assistance of the following, without whose support this study, which is based on my thesis, would not have been possible:

- Bernard Abramson for data manipulation.
- Ben Abramson for IT support.
- Jane Abramson for putting up with my numismatic obsession.
- Dorothy Bonser for giving me her late husband's archive of detector finds.
- James Booth for advising on the integrity of the numismatic discourse.
- Ron Bude for unpublished data on his analysis of the *sceattas* of Eadberht and Ecgberht
- David Haldenby for advice on artefactual finds from Cottam and Cowlam.
- Alan Morton for support and guidance on his DMAP software.
- Mary Garrison for providing a medieval historical perspective to the study and specifically for discussions on the interpretation of the York Gold Shilling.
- Michael Metcalf and Rory Naismith for their guidance on the narrative.
- Julian Richards, Andy Woods and Steve Roskams, for guidance on my original thesis.
- The late Liz Pirie for her remarkable dedication to compiling the corpus of *styca*s in her *Coins of the Kingdom of Northumbria.* Moreover, without access to her prodigious archives on *styca*s, which were so nearly discarded had I not intervened, this work would have been considerably impoverished. Feisty and obdurate she may have been, as well as misguided in her classification, but, hopefully I have resurrected Michael Metcalf's hope that her work, ultimately, would be ground-breaking. I also thank YNS for funding the recovery of part of her archive from The National Museum of Scotland. Thanks also to Allen Martin for giving me the remainder of the Pirie archive.
- Trevor Russell Smith for proof-reading and checking consistency.
- Sarah Wightman for assistance with format editing.
- Chris Myers for his assiduous typesetting.
- Paul and Bente Withers of Galata Press Limited for retrieving and releasing Liz Pirie's corpus *gratis*.
- Andy Woods for many helpful suggestions such as periodization of the Anglian coinage of Northumbria.
- The many detectorists who have volunteered information and generously provided images.
- All other individuals and institutions who have kindly granted me permission to use their images.

Contents

PART TWO: ANALYSIS AND INTERPRETATION

Databases and datasets supporting this study are available to download from www.barpublishing.com/additional-downloads.html

List of Figures

List of Graphs

List of Plates

List of Tables

Preface

Numismatic dating conventions of the era, as used in this study, are based on changes in metal and coinage reforms, such that the early Anglo-Saxon period is from *c.* 575 to *c.* 750, the date of the transition to broad penny in the south of England; the middle period is to the reform of Eadgar in 973 and the late Anglo-Saxon period to the Norman Conquest. Archaeological and historical conventions differ from this, as do the divisions used in the Viking and Anglo-Saxon Landscape and Economy Project (*VASLE*) from where the artefact database used in this study is drawn.

Although, the term 'early penny', favoured by Blackburn and Naismith, avoids linguistic difficulties, *sceat, sceatt* and *sceatta* are now, for better or worse, embedded in the language and literature,[1] and I have been as guilty as any in their misuse. In this volume I use *sceat* for the singular, and *sceattas* for the plural.

Periods are shown in square brackets e.g. [4a].

All coin images are from the author's collection, housed at the Fitzwilliam Museum, Cambridge, unless indicated.

Images are not reproduced to scale. Gold shillings, *sceattas* and *stycas* all have flans of around 11mm in diameter.

Illustrations are grouped either by chapter, period or region.

Reference to 'artefacts' excludes coins.

Databases and datasets supporting this study are available to download from www.barpublishing.com/additional-downloads.html. See also *Table 4, Dataset Sources*.

Metadata are given in the introduction to the online resources.

[1] Naismith (2014c). See also Hines (2014) and Naismith (2017).

List of Abbreviations

AA	*Archaeologia Aeliana.*
AASE	Wilson, D. M. (ed.) (1976) *The Archaeology of Anglo-Saxon England.* London: Methuen.
ADS	Archaeology Data Service, Department of Archaeology, University of York.
AJ	*Archaeological Journal.*
APC	Archaeological Planning Consultancy.
Archibald Festschrift	Cook, B., and Williams, G. (eds.) (2006) *Coinage and History in the North Sea World, c.* AD *500–1250: Essays in Honour of Marion Archibald.* Leiden: Brill.
ASC	Garmonsway, G. N. (trans.) (1953) *Anglo-Saxon Chronicle.* London: Dent & Sons.
ASGC	Sutherland, C. H. V. (1948) *Anglo-Saxon Gold Coinage in the Light of the Crondall Hoard.* London: OUP.
ASSAH	*Anglo-Saxon Studies in Archaeology and History.*
AY	Archaeology of York.
BA	British Academy.
BANS	British Association of Numismatic Societies.
BAR128	Hill, D., and Metcalf, D. M. (eds.) (1984) *Sceattas in England and on the Continent: The Seventh Oxford Symposium on Coinage and Monetary History.* B. A. R. British Series. 128. Oxford: B. A. R.
BAR180	Metcalf, D. M. (ed.) (1987) *Coinage in Ninth-Century Northumbria: The Tenth Oxford Symposium on Coinage and Monetary History.* B. A. R. British Series. 180. Oxford: B. A. R.
BM	(Trustees of the) British Museum.
BNJ	*British Numismatic Journal.*
BNS	British Numismatic Society.
Bonser archive	The private archive of Michael Bonser, recovered by the author and now at the Fitzwilliam Museum, Cambridge.
c.	(law) code.
CA	*Current Archaeology.*
CASSS	*Corpus of Anglo-Saxon Stone Sculpture.* www.ascorpus.ac.uk/.
CBA	Council for British Archaeology.
CCH	*The Fitzwilliam Museum's Checklist of Coin Hoards from the British Isles, c. 450–1180.* http://www-cm.fitzmuseum.cam.ac.uk/dept/coins/projects/hoards/.
CCI	*Celtic Coin Index.* www.celticcoins.ca/about.php.
CKN	Pirie, E. J. E. (1996) *Coins of the Kingdom of Northumbria, c. 700–867, in the Yorkshire Collections: The Yorkshire Museum, York, the University of Leeds, the City Museum, Leeds.* Llanfyllin: Galata.
CR	The *British Numismatic Journal's* 'Coin Register'. See Abramson 2011b.
CUP	Cambridge University Press.
DAN	Grierson, P. (1979) *Dark Age Numismatics: Selected Studies.* London: Variorum.
DMAP	Mapping software designed specifically for producing Distribution and Coincidence Maps in Microsoft Windows®.
DMV	Deserted medieval village.

DNB	Matthew, H. C. G., and Harrison, B. (eds.) (2004) *Dictionary of National Biography*. New ed. Oxford: OUP. www.oxforddnb.com/.
EH	Bede (1969) *An Ecclesiastical History of the English People.* Edited and Translated by Colgrave, B., and Mynors, R. A. B. Oxford: Clarendon Press.
EHD	*English Historical Documents.*
EcHR	*Economic History Review.*
EMC	*Corpus of Early Medieval Coin Finds*, a database of single finds of coins minted AD 410–1180 found in the British Isles. Established and maintained by the Fitzwilliam Museum, Cambridge. http://www-cm.fitzmuseum.cam.ac.uk/dept/coins/projects/hoards/
EMMH	Naismith, R., Allen, M., and Screen, E. (eds.) (2014) *Early Medieval Monetary History: Studies in Memory of Mark Blackburn*. Farnham: Ashgate.
EMN	Petts, D., and Turner, S. (eds.) (2011) *Early Medieval Northumbria: Kingdoms and Communities, AD 450–1100*. Turnhout: Brepols.
FLO	Finds Liaison Officer. See PAS.
HER	Historic Environment Records (sometimes referred to as Sites and Monuments Records), which may be held by District or County Councils or Unitary Authorities. www.algao.org.uk.
JBAA	*Journal of the British Archaeological Association.*
JMP	*Jaarboek voor Munt- en Penningkunde.*
LCAS	*Lancashire* and Cheshire *Antiquarian Society.*
MEC	Grierson, P., and Blackburn, M. A. S. (1986) *Medieval English Coinage, Cambridge, I: The Early Middle Ages (5th–10th Centuries).* Cambridge: CUP.
Med Arch	*Medieval Archaeology.*
N	North, J. J. (1994) *English Hammered Coinage*. 3rd ed. London: Spink.
NC	*Numismatic Chronicle.*
NH	*Northern History.*
OJA	*Oxford Journal of Archaeology.*
OUP	Oxford University Press.
P&U	Pestell, T., and Ulmschneider, K. (2003) *Markets in Early Medieval Europe: Trading and 'Productive' Sites, 650–850.* Macclesfield: Windgather.
PAS	Portable Antiquities Scheme. The *Department of Portable Antiquities and Treasure*, within the British Museum, was formalised under the Treasure Act, 1996.
PASE	*Prosopography of Anglo-Saxon England.* www.pase.ac.uk.
Pirie archive	Material collected from the National Museum of Scotland and the Fitzwilliam Museum, Cambridge, by the author, and now stored at the Leeds Museum Depository Centre.
PSAS	*Proceedings of the Society of Antiquaries in Scotland.*
R&M	Rigold, S. E., and Metcalf, D. M. (1984) A Revised Check-List of English Finds of Sceattas. In BAR128, pp.245–68.
RBN	*Revue belge de numismatique et de sigillographie.*
RCHME	Royal Commission on Historical Monuments in England.
RN	*Revue numismatique.*
RNS	Royal Numismatic Society.
SASH	*Studies in Early Anglo-Saxon History.*
SCBI	Sylloge of the Coins of the British Isles.

SEMSS	Graham-Campbell, J., Sindbæk, S. M., and Williams, G. (eds.) (2011) *Silver Economies, Monetisation and Society in Scandinavia,* AD *800–1000*. Aarhus: Aarhus Universitetsforlag.
SEVA	Graham-Campbell, J., and Williams, G. (eds.) (2007) *Silver Economy in the Viking Age*. Walnut Creek: Left Coast Press.
SiEMC	Abramson, T. (ed.) (2008–14) *Studies in Early Medieval Coinage*. 3 Volumes. Woodbridge: Boydell & Brewer; London: Spink.
SL	Sceatta List. See Abramson 2012d.
SMA	Society for Medieval Archaeology.
SNC	*Spink's Numismatic Circular*.
Stenton	Dolley, R. H. M. (ed.) (1961) *Anglo-Saxon Coins: Studies Presented to F. M. Stenton on the Occasion of His 80th Birthday*. London: Methuen.
T&S	Metcalf, D. M. (1993–94) *Thrymsas and Sceattas in the Ashmolean Museum, Oxford*. RNS Special Publication. 276. 3 Volumes. London: RNS.
TCWAAS	*Transactions of the Cumberland and Westmoreland Antiquarian and Archaeological Society*.
TDGNHAS	*Transactions of the Dumfriesshire and Galloway Natural History and Antiquarian Society*.
TRHS	*Transactions of the Royal Historical Society*.
xlxs	Microsoft Excel Worksheet.
YAHS	Yorkshire Archaeological and Historical Society.
YAJ	*Yorkshire Archaeological Journal*.
YAT	York Archaeological Trust.
YMT	York Museums Trust.
YN	*Yorkshire Numismatist*.
YNS	Yorkshire Numismatic Society.
YPS	Yorkshire Philosophical Society.
YUAP	York University Archaeological Publications.
VASLE	Richards, J. D., Naylor, J., and Holas-Clark, C. N. J. (2008) *The Viking and Anglo-Saxon Landscape and Economy Project* http://intarch.ac.uk/journal/issue25/2/toc.html.

Abstract

This study describes the evolutionary process of monetization in Northumbria. It shows how the uses and functions of coinage grew as the face-value of coins fell.

Part One describes the numismatic and historical background to the phases of Northumbrian coinage. A broad overview is given on theories of markets and money from the different perspectives of anthropology, archaeology, economics, monetary history and numismatics. Consideration is also given to land use and law and comparisons drawn to neighbouring polities. These approaches are synthesized leading into a definition of terms and a characterization of northern monetization.

A numismatically-based phasing has been created. This presents 10 periods, some subdivided, chronicling the progression of northern monetization from the gold shilling, through the silver early-penny to the base *styca*, unique to Northumbria.

A new and significant interpretation of the York gold shilling is given, which overturns the conventional view that the York issue was late in the gold coinage. It is now seen as at the forefront. Analysis of *sceattas* largely follows conventional lines. The focus is on the introduction and growth of the copper-alloy *styca*. Research into *stycas* was confounded by Pirie's taxonomy, in her otherwise commendable *Coins of the Kingdom of Northumbria* (1996). The digitization of Pirie's catalogue, presented and discussed in Part Two, removes this impediment to research. The database is augmented by information from online and informal sources to give comprehensive detail on *c.* 8000 coins.

A second database of finds of portable antiquities has been extracted from The Viking and Anglo-Saxon Landscape and Economy Project (*VASLE*), compiled at the Department of Archaeology, University of York by Richards, Naylor, and Holas-Clark, in 2008. This has been updated from the Portable Antiquities Scheme's finds database.

In Part Two, after considering the constraints on the reliability of the evidence, the quantitative methodology is described. The databases are interrogated in a variety of ways to create datasets, tables, graphs and maps. Statistical tools are developed for analysing and comparing individual sites within regions. A numerical synthesis of coin- and artefact-rich locations facilitates comparisons between regions by the creation of the ratio *co-occurrence* (the proportion of locations with both coins and portable artefacts to those with only the latter), measures of coin mix, by age and metal and correlations with Roman and normal distributions of finds.

Case studies of the economically active regions of Northumbria are grouped under the headings York and its environs, the 'Central Lowlands', the Yorkshire Wolds, Beverley and Holderness, the Vale of Pickering, Bernicia and the north. These are supported by descriptions of finds of coins in association with artefacts, assessed on a parish basis.

The work is copiously illustrated throughout.

The primary conclusion is that Northumbria benefitted increasingly, both monetarily and fiscally, as the face-value of coins fell. Secondary conclusions include:

- a strong episcopal presence in York exemplified by Paulinus's gold shillings at the forefront of English monetization;
- Northumbrian coin production was erratic;
- the Yorkshire Wolds were more highly monetized than the surrounding lowlands indicating a more enterprising culture;
- *styca* hoards represent episcopal expropriations and
- there were significant changes in settlement and economy in the Central Lowlands.

Northumbrian monetization reflected northern independence, innovation and enterprise.

PART ONE

AIMS AND BACKGROUND

1

Introduction

'In the coming decades, greater emphasis will probably be placed on the wider economic and social implications to be drawn from the use of coinage. To contribute to these debates further work should be done on interpreting the pattern of single-finds, comparing them with other artefact distributions and historical data.'

Mark Blackburn (2011, 596).

The period *c*. 575–*c*. 867 saw several major changes: in governance and religion, in rural settlement patterns, the emergence of urban communities and of an economy which demonstrates evolving domestic and Continental trade linkages. The development of coinage is an integral part of these processes and coin recovery can help us ascertain the territorial extent and volume of coin use. However, to date too little attention has been paid to the distinctive gold, silver and especially base coinage of Northumbria in the seventh to ninth centuries, its unique characteristics and its place within the broader contemporary economic and social context.

The Northumbrian landscape exhibits a patchwork of settlements with complex linkages to interconnected exchange networks ranging from kin-based subsistence communities to towns featuring hinterlands, production, labour specialisation and long-distance trade. Settlements were formed under varying topological, agricultural, economic and social circumstances and their impact is conventionally assessed by reference to functional spheres of influence—legal, administrative, economic, fiscal, cultural, religious and defence.[2] Tribute, links between separated estate holdings, patronage, obligation and tradition have previously been seen as the determining factors in transforming settlement patterns.[3]

There is scope to consider the northern material in a similar manner to the southern, especially as regards the balance of power in the north as Northumbrian *sceattas*[4] and *stycas*[5] name kings and archbishops whilst *sceattas* elsewhere are predominantly anonymous.

The most recent contribution to our understanding of Northumbrian coinage in the landscape is to be found in the work of Naylor,[6] but this study presents a more granular analysis of a substantially larger database.

Exploitation requires an economic surplus and this is the key to understanding how settlement hierarchies developed. Surplus can remain at the domestic level, be gifted, donated or used for votive, funerary or compensation purposes, be consumed by tribute in labour, goods or services, be extracted by tax and rent or be exchanged for other consumables or 'capital' goods. All of this can be accomplished in markets without the benefit of a medium of exchange, as was the case in England in the period now narrowed to *c*. 470[7]–*c*. 570, when no medium is archaeologically visible; which does not exclude commodity money. However, the presence of coinage facilitates exchange chiefly both as a medium and also as an accounting mechanism and store of wealth.

The environmental and human factors which may have influenced economic activity are explained in addressing the core question: To what extent was Northumbrian economy monetized? Before proceeding some definition of terms and scope is necessary. Northumbria is essentially the territory remaining after the defeat of Ecgfrith at Nechtansmere in 685,[8] after which Aldfrith brought stability—and silver coinage—to the realm. The study also considers the earlier gold shillings of York and Northumbrian coins found elsewhere. Monetization in the narrow, practical sense used in this study refers to the *re-introduction* of coinage.[9] At the simplest level, this occurs when coins are used to settle regular daily transactions—the purchase of dietary staples and other necessities. Monetization is here characterized by the proximity of finds of coins and portable artefacts, demonstrating that the use of coin as a medium of exchange, even when there is only one denomination, has permeated throughout society, rather than fulfilling only the needs of a social, mercantile or religious élite.

Assemblages of diagnostic material contain coins, metallic artefacts including copper-alloy dress accessories, ceramics, building materials, stonework and biological remains. In a network of settlements, different distributions of such artefacts require explanation and the use of coins for exchange, rather than other purposes, must be established. Northumbria may be a special case in

[2] Perring (2002, 12–16).

[3] Perring (2002, 16–27).

[4] Silver *denarius* or proto-penny essentially modelled on Merovingian prototypes. The origins of the word *sceat* are discussed by Hines (2014, 7–17).

[5] The Northumbrian base metal successor to, and of the same module as, the *sceat*, first introduced under Eanred sometime after 810 (whereas Southumbrian coinage followed Pepin the Short's initiative in introducing the broad penny in the 750s).

[6] Naylor (2002, 2004 and 2007).

[7] See section 4.1.

[8] Woolf (2006, 182–201).

[9] There is a paucity of literature on monetisation *per se* and what exists generally refers to the classical world where Howgego (1995), Tye (2001), Cribb (2004) and Schmandt-Besserat (2008) have made valuable contributions.

view of its distinctive coinage and particularly the phased evolution of its silver early-pennies into the unique base-metal *styca* currency.

Particular emphasis is placed on the *styca* coinage which is represented by a wealth of both hoard and single-find material.[10] However, possibly due to its generally unprepossessing appearance, this coin has not always been fully appreciated as an economic driver.[11] As the sole denomination it would have been used for transactions of different frequencies—routine daily transactions, the regular payment of dues, and for more substantial occasional transactions such as tribute payments and the transfer of estates and people to church establishments known as 'bookland'.[12] Both economic and political factors, such as internecine rivalry, are explored as possible contributors, not only to driving down the intrinsic value of the sole denomination to a more generally useful level, but also to erratic coin production in the north.

The primary aim of this study is to assess, in the context of other artefacts, the extent and nature of monetization during the seventh to ninth centuries, when coin use varied geographically, temporally and by transactional type. Monetization provides *prime facie* evidence of economic, technical and intellectual recovery after the dislocation of the Roman withdrawal.

Given the extent to which recent finds and new interpretations improve understanding of early Anglian Northumbria, several objectives, are pursued in support of the primary aim. These constitute pre-requisites to monetization in that an economic and political infrastructure is needed to provide a stable platform for a viable and appropriate medium of exchange. Sufficient and necessary conditions include a clear hierarchy with authority vested in responsible officials whose roles in administering the monetary and fiscal functions of state are distinct and effective. Moreover, the public must have confidence in both the organisation and the coinage if it is to operate efficiently.

Distributional factors and trading advantages may cause divergent degrees of penetration in different areas. Political instability and exogenous influences may disrupt steady production.

The objectives of the study include:

1. Evolution: To establish to what degree the evolution of the Northumbrian coinage was steady, to what degree erratic and to assess the relationship between the advancement of Northumbrian coinage and political and economic developments.
2. Power: To describe how Northumbrian coinage reflects the exercise and balance of power, specifically between church and state.
3. Regional Differences: To expose significant regional differences, and metro-centricity, in coin use.
4. Expropriation: To demonstrate the role of coinage in surplus expropriation by the authorities.
5. Settlement Patterns: To show how the varying mix of coins indicates different trading and settlement patterns and networks.

Part One describes the context of the numismatic and artefactual evidence. Chapter two discusses relevant contributions to the theory of monetization, including those to market models, from various related disciplines. Previous work based on analysis of artefactual data from PAS is also considered, and, in brief, the evolution of monetization in comparable neighbouring polities. This leads into a definition of terms and economic characterisation in chapter three, which proposes a hypothesis of monetization. Part One of the study is completed by the presentation of a numismatic periodization, based on the historical background in chapter four.

Part Two introduces the data describing how it has been assembled, then proceeds to analyse this in the context of the landscape and economy. Chapter five commences with a discussion of the various constraints on the integrity of the evidence before introducing the quantitative and qualitative methodological frameworks. Chapter six presents the data analyses and several analytic tools are applied by site, within a regional structure, in light of the objectives set above. The results of conventional numismatic analyses are summarised. In chapter seven the case studies are described.

In the practical, second part of this study, the quantitative methodology is to assemble a dataset compiled from existing archaeological records primarily of coins and secondarily, artefacts and to facilitate interrogation.[13] Sources include Pirie's *Coins of the Kingdom of Northumbria* (*CKN*),[14] the *Corpus of Early Medieval Coin Finds* (*EMC*) and *Sylloges of the Coins of the British Isles* (SCBI), the Portable Antiquities Scheme (PAS), the *Viking and Anglo-Saxon Landscape and Economy Project* (*VASLE*) and informal,[15] as well as antiquarian sources. This approach includes assessment of material that may have eluded formal recording. Mapping is used to reveal

[10] Found both within and beyond Northumbria.
[11] *The Tenth Oxford Symposium*, 1987, focussed considerable attention on the 'wretched styca' (Brooks, *BAR* 180, 1987, 398); *MEC* described 'the least respected Anglo-Saxon coin' (1986, 298). The change in attitudes was marked by Yorke, who stated: 'The styca could be seen as evidence of efficient royal control of the economy and a sensitive response to changing circumstances rather than as evidence of decline.' (1990, 97).
[12] Wormald (2006, 153–58). In his letter of 731 to Ecgberht, Bede complained about the removal of land from taxation and people from service (9).

[13] The ultimate objective is to make the database available online, perhaps as part of *EMC* or similar.
[14] Pirie's *CKN* (Galata, 1996), was not part of *SCBI* and is therefore not in *EMC*.
[15] The most significant being Elizabeth Pirie's archive now in the City of Leeds Museum Depository.

spatial and temporal patterns in the development and use of coinage, subject to detecting bias. Significantly, I have digitized Pirie's corpus of *stycas* in *CKN*, which is the major achievement of the work presented here. It is collated with the other sources into a comprehensive database, providing a versatile tool, easily searched and sorted, for interrogation and investigation.

A numismatic-based phasing is developed. Finds at coin-rich sites have been collated according to the periods defined so that this age-profile gives a fresh perspective on site comparisons.

The qualitative analysis involves the comparison of numismatic and artefactual finds at coin-rich sites and *wics* within Northumbria. Evidence of the ready availability of coinage, whether or not local, in proximity to other artefacts, is taken as indicative of economically active sites. Sites are grouped regionally facilitating comparisons between regions.

Differences, whether of type, period or volume between selected sites are identified. The corpus of material is arranged by location and date then interrogated to establish if the presence of coinage is associated with particular types of other artefacts. The result is a fuller understanding of monetization in early medieval Northumbria, and the place of gold, silver and base-metal coinage in the contemporary social landscape. Coinage contributes to key debates in early Anglo-Saxon history: the development of towns and emporia; the rôle of 'productive' sites; the 'minster debate' and the rôle of the church.

Research has shown that there are *wics* in Southumbria which provide comparative templates for evaluating monetization in the north.[16] These include *Hamwic* which is considered in detail. Finds at Rendlesham, Heckington, Royston and Sledmere are tabulated as exemplars, at *Dataset 15, Wic Comparison 1. Dataset 20*, tabulates finds at *Gipeswic* and *Lundenwic*. Again, credit is due to Pirie for compiling an archive of site reports.

These methodologies are combined to produce tabulations and maps of artefactual and numismatic find-spots. An expedient indicator, *co-occurrence* is the ratio of the number of locations with both artefacts and coins to those with just artefacts. While this is a pragmatic measure, its use as a comparative tool is justified in chapter 6.

Minor numismatic findings are given at section 6.4.3 and the general conclusions in chapter eight, closing with suggestions for future research.

[16] Scull (1997, 280–89). Hill and Cowie (2001, 85).

2

Perspectives on Monetization

> 'Imagining the past is the business of the historian and historical novelist, but sometimes the past springs more readily to life at the sight of something small and ephemeral with nothing—no other minds—standing between you and it.'
>
> Ian Jack, *The Guardian*, 5 April 2014.

This chapter provides a synopsis of prevailing thinking on the evolution of markets and money in its various forms. It discusses, from a variety of perspectives, the economic and numismatic foundations for an understanding of monetization on which the practical work of the study is built. As a discipline, monetization is a relatively unexplored branch of numismatics with strong links to economics. It has barely been touched upon previously in relation to Anglo-Saxon Northumbria. The first part of the chapter introduces the key thinkers who have influenced the debates about markets and monetization and in the second half of the chapter the previous literature on the development of coinage in Northumbria, and the Northumbrian economy, is introduced and discussed.

2.1 Anthropology

Polanyi[17] developed two meanings of the term 'economic' separating, on the one hand, the mechanisms for allocating scarce resources from, on the other, the methods by which humans make their living using natural resources to best satisfy physiological and psychological needs.[18] The neo-classical approach to economics assumes perfect knowledge, mobility, rationality, self-interest and the maximisation of 'utility'. These concepts facilitate analysis but are open to challenge as, at best, normative rather than positive,[19] and at worst, necessarily extreme. Anthropologists and archaeologists refer to the neo-classical approach as formalism.[20]

An alternative or complementary methodology, substantivism, was proposed by Polanyi.[21] This does not rely on rationality and scarcity but explores human interaction in social and natural environments. His are general propositions, not universal; they accommodate the wide spectrum, divergences and inefficiencies, of human preferences and constraints, and the vagaries of nature. Polanyi's substantivism viewed economics as indivisible from 'culture'.

Polanyi described three mechanisms by which the institutions of society combine to enable economic activity; multiple individual exchanges constituting a market, symmetrical reciprocal behaviour in a community and redistribution from a centrally administered accumulation.[22] There are evolutionary, transformative, aspects to each of these mechanisms such that they are dynamic not static. The formalists, in asserting the ubiquity of the quest for gain, condemn this as romantic, relativist ideology.[23]

Skre was succinct on these issues: '...in every society, prehistoric as well as medieval and modern, the pure market (where every transaction is dictated *only* by an economic rationality) never existed and does not even do so today, any more than gift exchange free of economic consideration.'[24] He commended avoidance of simplistic descriptions and use of terms 'that reveal variations and characterize complexity in past economies, as well as the manner in which they are interwoven with the rest of society.'[25] Naismith argued that the choice between substantivist and formalist is not binary either between or within societies.[26]

It may be that substantivism answers the case in societies at an early stage of economic development, making use of commodity money, while a formalist approach is more relevant to societies generating surplus resources to support specialisation in circumstances where complex transactions require a medium of exchange, unit of account and store of value.

Two concepts borrowed from Polanyi are perhaps relevant here. First, the 'ports of trade' concept can be summarized as 'sites at which travelling merchants and other traders would gather, for which political authorities—whether monastery, city or empire—guaranteed the security of business, organised a judicial system, and provided facilities of anchorage, debarkation and storage.'[27] This is a version of the familiar discussion of *wics*, and, more recently, minster sites, which will be explored further in respect of Northumbria.[28]

---

[17] Karl Polanyi, anthropologist (1886–1964). Dale (2010, 1–18).

[18] Polanyi (2001, ch. 4, esp. 48–50).

[19] In economics, 'what ought to be' rather than 'what is'.

[20] Dale (2010, 109–14).

[21] Dale (2010, 90–108).

[22] Polanyi (2001, 50–52). Hann and Hart (2011, 14). Skre (2011, 67). Dale (2010, 117–23).

[23] Dale (2010, 123–27, 240–46).

[24] Skre (2011, 80). The market exchange mechanism is constrained by social convention: "In Viking-age and medieval Scandinavia, an open display of greed would have been dishonourable." Also see Skre (2008, ch. 9).

[25] Skre (2011, 85).

[26] Naismith (2012, 26).

[27] Polanyi (1977, 95). He acknowledged that such 'ports' need not be coastal. See also, Hodges (1988, 52–55).

[28] Initially, Hodges over-emphasised the role of kings. (Naismith, 2012, 33). Levison (1946, 4–14) discussed *mercimonium*, which is how

Second, his distinction between general- and special-purpose money, relating respectively to subsistence commodities and luxury objects, resonates with the gold-silver-brass progression of Northumbrian coinage as its societal penetration increased.[29]

Polanyi's substantivism, strengthens the tools available for analysing the process of monetization. The most significant criticism of his approach[30] relates to his reliance on broad generalisations resulting particularly in an overstatement of the prevalence of reciprocity and redistribution, which together with market exchange, constitute his 'forms of integration' in primitive societies.[31] This is exacerbated by his failure to recognise fully the importance of friction (competition, conflict, power and exploitation) in creating dynamism and risk-taking—as is evident in Northumbrian dynastic rivalry.

2.1.1 The Historical Perspective

According to Pirenne,[32] the tribes invading the Western Roman Empire maintained the Roman institutions: 'All the features of the old economic life were there: the preponderance of Oriental navigation, the importation of Oriental produce, the organization of the ports, of the tonlieu[33] and the imposts, the circulation and the minting of money, the lending of money at interest, the absence of small markets, and the persistence of a constant commercial activity in the cities, where there were merchants by profession.'[34] This continued until disrupted by the Islamic invasion of the Mediterranean. Europe was then deprived of trans-Saharan gold supplies and its coinage was transferred to a silver standard.[35] Pirenne believed that the instrument of change after Charlemagne's expansionist rule was the Viking incursions which ultimately resulted in a more urban society.[36]

Grierson emphasised the non-monetary use of coin—for fines, tribute, and gifts,[37] and supported Pirenne's view of a dismal post-Islamic period with a dearth of coinage and trade. However, the wealth of metal-detecting finds and archaeology in the main trading settlements demonstrates the vibrancy of this era. Spufford's account of diminishing gold use in Europe is described at section 4.2.5.3,[38] but absence of any mention of Pirenne by Spufford is indicative that the discussion had moved on.[39] Naismith described the variety of forms of giving,[40] and having analysed payments in Anglo-Saxon charters dated before *c.* 900, noted the prevalence of precious metal, particularly gold, and gifts as means of payment for land. Pennies 'were primarily a currency for more mundane purposes concentrated below the élite.'[41] In view of the substantial volume of coinage in the early Anglo-Saxon period, Naismith downplayed the rôle of gift-giving by the élite and advocated a more flexible approach recognising the versatile nature of currency.[42]

Scott's 2012 resurrection of Pirenne's thesis gave evidence of architectural and intellectual activity to demonstrate that far from the 'Barbarian' invasion of the Western Empire having a catastrophic effect, it was virtually seamless (*Figure* 1). The Gothic hordes were only too keen to be assimilated into Roman ways.

According to Pirenne, in the late sixth and early seventh centuries: 'the Ostrogoths, Visigoths, Vandals and Burgundi were governed in the Roman manner. There was hardly a trace, or none at all, of 'Germanic principles'. Under the new kings the old system of government survived, though doubtless in an imperfect form. There was only one novelty: service in the army was gratuitous, thanks to the distribution of land. The State was relieved of the terrible war budget which had formerly crushed the people.'[43] Tenure, taxation, trade and the organisation of the great estates were unchanged,[44] though the Franks regarded themselves as immune from land tax, which is no longer referred to by the seventh century.[45] 'Language, religion, institutions and art were entirely, or almost entirely, devoid of Germanism.'[46] Even the Merovingians shared aspects of *Romanitas*: they were absolutist, secular and exercised fiscal governance.[47]

The decay, albeit erratic, in the gold content of the Anglo-Saxon coinage through the mid-seventh century,[48] is less likely the outcome of any domestic intention to extend monetization than the consequence of distant geo-political events adversely affecting the flow of gold from its sources in North Africa, through the Mediterranean,[49] (though Germanic and Roman treasuries were well stocked).[50]

commercial markets were referred to in contemporary documents.

[29] Polanyi's work on Dahomey concluded that the society's stability was, in part, due to its stratified economy, which extended to different types of money. This is not uncontested. Dale (2010, 172–81).

[30] Dale (2010, 246).

[31] Hann and Hart (2011, 14). Skre (2011, 67).

[32] Henri Pirenne, historian (1862–1935).

[33] A *tonlieu* is a tax on market fair stallholders.

[34] Pirenne (2001, 116).

[35] Spufford (1988, ch. 7).

[36] Pirenne (2001, 240). Scott (2012, 195–98).

[37] Grierson (1959, 123–40). Alms-giving was probably as important as gifts. Alms-giving was manifest in the emission of the rare 6-penny ELIMOSINA offering piece of Alfred the Great, demonstrating how kingship responded to social need.

[38] The impact of Islam on the metrology and volume of Carolingian coinage is disputed. The high-volume estimates of Metcalf (1965 and 1967) were rejected by Grierson (1967), whose emphasis was on the social rather than economic use of coinage, stressing gift exchange rather than monetary mechanisms.

[39] Pirenne is not mentioned either by Wood (2008) or Grierson and Blackburn (*MEC*, 1986).

[40] Naismith (2012, 262).

[41] Naismith (2012, 273).

[42] Naismith (2012, 276).

[43] Pirenne (2001, 54).

[44] Pirenne (2001, 76).

[45] The Gallo-Romans gradually shifted to Frankish allegiance to take advantage of this immunity (Pirenne, 2001, 193).

[46] Pirenne (2001, 142).

[47] Pirenne (2001, 58 and 136–39).

[48] Williams and Hook (2013, 55–70).

[49] Scott (2012, 171–72). Pirenne (2001, 157).

[50] Pirenne (2001, 59–60). Pirenne argues that the abundance of gold was the result of trade, specifically in slaves (111–13). Spufford (1988, 49).

Pirenne noted the absence of gold and professional merchants from Merovingian Francia, these and the absence of loans, define an economic recession. Jews 'constituted the only economic link which survived between Islam and Christendom, or, one may say, between East and West.'[51]

The twin pincer movements of the Vikings and Muslims around the Mediterranean shared a common purpose. Muslims had an insatiable demand for white-skinned eunuchs and concubines. The slave trade was the key component in international commercial activity, the extent of which can be assessed by, for example, the enormous hoards of Islamic dirhams deposited in Gotland by the Rus.[52]

Around the time that the trans-Saharan gold route to Europe was blockaded, the imported *tremisses* were replaced by native gold shillings. With diminishing gold stocks in the West, the alloy deteriorated to as little as 4 per cent in the 660s.[53] Within 10 years, a silver standard was adopted and there is a consequent, substantial, enlargement of the volume of coin in circulation as silver was mined and available within Europe. Slaves were a major export in this specie flow, in which the Vikings colluded in satisfying Islamic appetites;[54] The ripples washing onto the Northumbrian shore were not merely qualitative and quantitative; in the 780s, Northumbrian *sceattas* abandoned figurative, animal designs, though a more positive explanation may be that the new inscriptional type shifted responsibility for the integrity of the coinage to the named moneyer.[55]

[51] Pirenne (2001, 174), though his suggestion that Jews were 'numerous everywhere' is misconceived.

[52] Other sources of this wealth may have included tribute, trade in furs and other products, and gift exchange. Gaimster (2007, 123–33). Spufford (1988, 51) notes the disparity in the ratio of gold to silver between Francia at 1:12, Byzantium at 1:6 (in C7th rising to 1:7 in C10th) and an Arab ratio at 1:10 (presumably showing arbitrage) such that, during the currency of the slave trade, gold flowed west.

[53] This was at the northern frontier of the economic system. In Merovingian Francia, there was a discrete step, by 670, from good quality gold to high purity silver. Hines and Bayliss (eds.) (2013) presented a scientific chronology based on analysis of graves and grave goods which brings the initiation of primary *sceattas* into the 660s. Archibald (2013, 493–515) disputed this but not convincingly. The move to silver in England may have preceded that in Merovingian Francia. Identification of varieties Cii and Ciii of the York gold shilling (37), preceded by the uninscribed varieties B and Ci, and the tentative proposal that the reverse inscription of the Crondall (Hampshire) and Tangmere (West Sussex) specimens of the gold shilling of Eadbald of Kent reads Mellitus, thereby dating the issue to *c.* 619–24, shift the commencement of Anglo-Saxon native coinage earlier by the same extent as Bayliss and Hines's publication shifted back its cessation.

[54] Pirenne (2001, 98–100), in describing the 'abundant circulation of gold' describes how British slaves would be shipped from Marseilles as return cargo for incoming spices, silk and papyrus. A slave could be ransomed for 12 solidi.

[55] The moneyer was likely to have been a wealthy court official, who would neither have engraved the dies nor hammered the coins.

2.2 Archaeology

In the same year as he co-published a rebuttal of the work of Pirenne,[56] Hodges postulated a trade and exchange model involving three types of settlement. Type A comprises temporary, gateway, boundary communities, usually at coastal 'beaching-places', hosting a seasonal, small-scale fair for the exchange, with foreign traders, of prestige goods as part of a regional exchange system.[57] Type B is a permanent urban community with native artisans and alien traders engaged in long-distance travel. These may co-exist.[58] Type C exhibits greater diversification, production and regional governance.[59] Hodges described primary *entrepôts* for gathering sellers, or their produce, for shipment to emporia. Loveluck and Tys challenged Hodges' model for its failure to recognise what is now known as the North Sea trading zone with its common early-penny currency.[60]

Hodges favoured the spatial patterns described by Smith[61] ranging from simple networks and bounded exchange systems to solar, dendritic[62] and interlocking 'central-places' but, again, the dissonance between general theory and specific application should discourage over-extending hypotheses. As a concession to this, in attempting to define the nodal points of Smith's networks, Hodges discussed nucleated settlements, ports-of-call, urban complexes and market-places in terms of 'bundles of criteria', offering a selection of broad yardsticks.[63]

In his *Primitive and Peasant Markets*, Hodges deduced that 'the concept of marketing at its most primitive was selectively introduced to English kings about AD 600. Dendritic central-place markets functioned first as gateway communities for administering the distribution of prestige goods, before becoming monopolistic centres for controlled regional/territorial production. Drawing upon Carolingian technology and economic experience the pre-conditions for a commercial take-off pre-date the Viking assault.'[64]

Hodges, despite acknowledging Hart's warning that anthropological definitions may seem 'mindbogglingly… reductionist',[65] shared the compulsion of economic anthropologists to devise ever more complicated models.[66]

[56] Hodges and Waterhouse (1983).

[57] Skre (2008, 340), pointed out that Hodges use of 'gateway community' differs from its use by Hirth (1978).

[58] Hodges (2012, 97).

[59] Hodges (1989, 51–52).

[60] Loveluck and Tys (2006).

[61] Smith (1976, 309–74), which, being based on work in modern Guatemala (Hodges (1988, 22), should not be generalized. Hodges cited Colin Renfrew.

[62] Smith referred to a 'trunk-and-branch' pattern (Hodges, 1988, 20), whereas 'root-and-branch' would have been both more evocative and accurate.

[63] Hodges (1989, 21).

[64] Hodges (1988, 90).

[65] Hodges (1988, 2 and 15).

[66] Does the use of a logarithmic rank-size rule advance understanding? (Hodges, 1988, 26).

Skre attempted to cut through anthropological conjecture: 'The connections between society, cultural social norms and economy are so complex that the absolute linkages between specific combinations of the basic conditions cannot be postulated. Each individual economic history has to be examined empirically.'[67]

Of Gerald Dunning, Hodges wrote: '(he) planted the seed of long-distance trade, in the form of imported ceramics, as the key to understanding Middle-Saxon England... with long-distance trade being the stimulus to culture process.'[68] Hodges characterized the new emporia as large, planned sites located beyond Roman ruins, with no ecclesiastical presence, yielding rich finds of *sceattas* and imported pottery. These 'non-places'[69] are not mentioned in the historic record, Hodges suggested, because regal and ecclesiastical authorities may have had a contempt for trade. For example, in York, *Eoforwic*[70] was well away from the Roman remains but was already in decline before the *micel here* arrived.

The surge in metal-detected finds since the first publication of *Dark Age Economics*, indicating, for example, that the volume of *sceattas* in circulation must be measured in millions,[71] led Hodges to a revision of this standard work. He considered that the intervening debate had focussed too much on the élite, neglecting the household as the core component. The transition from gift exchange to money is accompanied by a crystallization of fixed and moveable property rights. Hodges, in common with most anthropologists, failed to recognise that gift exchange and reciprocity are social not economic constructs.

Hodges noted an intensification of Frankish agriculture from the late sixth century with numerous storage pits showing the extent of cereal production.[72] At this time, rotational field usage is evident. These changes were accompanied by an increase in material culture, specifically ceramics. England saw migration from small farmsteads to new villages with fenced enclosures and field boundaries demonstrating the increased awareness of property.[73] There is a shift of emphasis from pastoralism to stock farming, which would have required an increase in salt production and transportation. Infields were more intensively farmed, and the marginal outfield only used in times of need. Clearly, these changes are part of a systemic progression, demonstrating a degree of planning, driven by the desire to increase tribute but also constituting an agrarian revolution. The material culture is most evident at monastic sites and minsters,[74] whereas evidence of peasant culture, other than increased numbers of storage pits, is more likely to have biodegraded.[75]

As a Marxist alternative to the trading model, Wickham proposed an agrarian model whereby the élite were sustained by rents not taxes.[76] The latter form of surplus extraction is termed the tributary mode of production and the former, the 'feudal' mode.[77] This marked the transfer from Roman fiscal demands to sustain the army, to Germanic land use. Charters from this time onwards, such as the *Tribal Hidage*,[78] were likely to make assessments in land. Military service was a further form of tribute essential to the survival of the sub-kingdom. Tension arose within the tributary mode as landlords were taxed by the state in the form of the food-render or *feorm*.[79] Alienation of *bookland* alleviated the tension but transferred the economic initiative to rentiers.[80]

Criticism prompted Hodges to offer a further model—the ritual economy—a major component of which is 'materialisation' meaning the physical manifestation of ideas, specifically religious ideas.[81] He noted that inalienability is a characteristic of the gift which distinguished it from commodity money. Not only did the Church gain very substantial economic power through receiving gifts of land but it exerted profound influence over a rude peasantry willing to surrender its economic surplus for psychological security. There was less of an exchange of real for virtual in the taxed peasantry's expectation of protection from the state. Hodge's ritual economy is also referred to as the 'shrine franchise' whereby gift-giving bought salvation.[82] This brought enormous wealth to the Church. As Hodges stated: this 'involved the mobilisation of resources on a massive scale, and simultaneously it stimulated a sudden and important spike in the procurement of materials [iron, stone, *spolia*,[83] etc.] to supply the ritual rhetoric of the *renovatio*.' He described an accompanying materialisation of artistic and material culture corresponding to that under Aldfrith a century earlier.

The clergy were the architects of urbanisation. The later eighth and ninth centuries, the Carolingian *renaissance*, saw the arrival of monastic cities. By this time, monks were barred from manual labour. The rôle of monasteries became administrative—managing productive lands and policing the acts of kings.

[67] Skre (2008, 335).
[68] Hodges (2008, 117).
[69] After Agué (1995). 'Like modern airports and shopping malls.' Hodges (2008,116).
[70] If it be at, or neighbouring, Fishergate.
[71] Op den Velde and Metcalf (2003, 74–75 and 2009, 123).
[72] Hodges (2012, 49).
[73] Hodges (2012, 50).
[74] This is contradicted by the findings at section 7.6.6.
[75] Hodges (2012, 51). Loveluck and Tys (2006).
[76] Wickham (2005, 56 and 2009, 186–87). See section 2.7.
[77] See section 2.8, on the law codes of Ine, §70.
[78] *Dumville (1989, 225–30).*
[79] This explains why the aristocracy sponsored minsters. Saunders (2001, 9).
[80] Saunders (2001, 11).
[81] Hodges (2012, 15) stated: '...the Church as an agent of change is most definitely the elephant in the room...' As he managed to describe materialisation without referring to early-penny iconography despite being a contributor to *SiEMC*1 (2008, 113–18), perhaps his elephant spotting is deficient.
[82] Hodges (2012, 67–68).
[83] Reworked building material.

2.3 Land Ownership

Land ownership is crucial to power relations in the medieval period. Some of the early written laws necessitated a reeve collecting produce to render to the king.[84] He and his entourage would need to be peripatetic to benefit from this, until monetization facilitated greater efficiency.

As trading centres became established in the seventh and eighth centuries, there was symbiosis between the king offering protection and patronage, and the render of tolls generated from trade. Reeves were responsible for administering these tolls and the royal estates or *villae*.

In early Anglo-Saxon Northumbria, pre-existing British strongholds, at Bamburgh, Carlisle, Catterick, Driffield, Yeavering and York, remained the focal points of continued economic, administrative, royal and religious activity. At Lindisfarne, Bamburgh, Catterick and Easby, religious communities distanced themselves from the centre sufficiently to retain monastic detachment,[85] However, in the period under study a new institution, the minster, stimulated economic activity.

Monasteries are enclosed, contemplative communities following a defined regimen, whereas Blair, in his seminal work on this subject, defined 'minsters' in terms of hierarchical communities of religious devotees engaged with the economic and pastoral life of their parish.[86] However, he disavowed a 'minster model' of pastoral care as inflexible, though the 'central and enduring importance of minsters in local religious life' remains.[87] He dismissed the view that the British and Roman Christian traditions were in stark contrast: 'In the melting-pot of early insular culture, influences from many sources re-combined and a wide range of alternatives was on offer.'[88] The diversity of early-penny iconography confirms this. The 'minster debate' of the 1990s attempted to reconcile the introspection necessitated by monastic life with the pastoral care demanded of minsters.[89] Morris warned against regarding all minsters as of uniform foundation when there was 'a dissimilarity in their origins which makes it hard to conceive of them as products of any coherent campaign,'[90]

Blair viewed religious communities as an economic catalyst.[91] Minsters differed from monasteries in terms of tenure; they could be adopted and endowed privately by aristocrats and monarchs.[92] Conversion spread downward in society at a rate that may have been inhibited only by the gradual political crystallization of the Anglo-Saxon sub-kingdoms.[93]

Morris regarded liminality as significant in the life and location of parish churches, illustrating this with the moor-side positions of the Ryedale 'constellation' of religious houses including Lastingham,[94] Kirkdale and Middleton. Taken with Old Malton, Kirkby Misperton, Appleton-le-Moors, Hovingham, Stonegrave. Gilling East, Crayke and Coxwold,[95] these fit the model of 'clusters and dependencies' articulated by Foot,[96] who also commented: 'Minsters occupied a liminal space between the society of the secular aristocracy from which most of their professed members were drawn and the ecclesiastical society of the Christian church.'[97]

From *c.* 650 'royal patronage fuelled a monastic boom',[98] but, other than in Kent, there was a paucity of small local churches unlike in Ireland or Gaul. It was more likely the impact of the arrival of Theodore of Tarsus in Canterbury in 669, his Neapolitan dean Hadrian, together with the second generation of, now native-born, bishops, Chad, Wine and Wilfrid, rather than the Synod of Whitby or the devastating plague of the same year, that facilitated this boom.[99] Minsters were now sited in more congenial locations as the austerity of the early conversion phase gave way to Theodore's more institutional management and those seeking liminality now evangelized on the Continent.[100]

Blair associated this surge with economic activity in north-west Europe: 'a mass currency in silver…emerged during *c.* 670–690. But again, the fact that the monastic culture blossomed so spectacularly in Bernicia, with a thoroughly old-fashioned wealth-base and essentially no coinage, suggests that the financial and cultural stimulus of the new economy does not explain the phenomenon on its own.' He also noted: 'Although Northumbria had a fine silver coinage from the 730s, the distribution of single finds suggests that coins did not circulate north or west of Whitby during the early-penny era.'[101] Despite inexplicably overlooking Aldfrith's *sceattas* and the imported coinage before Eadberht's reign, and early-penny finds in the north-west (e.g. Whithorn), Blair's conclusion stands: monarchs wished to demonstrate that they had thrown off all vestiges of paganism; they sought havens for their royal ladies, such as Ælfflæd of Whitby, in 'double houses'; monasticism offered novel means of deploying land. There is historic evidence of substantial land-grants in the last 30 years of the seventh century, following the Northumbrian precedents of Oswy in 654/5 and Alhfrith to Wilfrid *c.* 660,[102] who

[84] See for example, Laws of Ine 70. §1 ((section 2.8 and *Table* 1).
[85] Morris (1989, 118, 128–39). Manby, Moorhouse and Ottaway (2003, *figures* 37 and 40).
[86] Blair (2005, 3). Morris (1989, 128–39).
[87] Blair (2005, 5).
[88] Blair (2005, 5).
[89] Foot (2006, 287–91).
[90] Morris (1989, 122, 130 and 134). Morris (2011, 174–79). Foot (2009, *figure* 11). Pirie (1996, *figure 1*).
[91] Blair (2005, 6).
[92] Foot (2006, ch. 3).
[93] Blair (2005, 51).
[94] Of the brothers Cedd, Chad, Cynebill and Caelin.
[95] Morris (1989, 116 and *figure 26,* p.122).
[96] Foot (2006, 278).
[97] Foot (2006, 347).
[98] Blair (2005, 75).
[99] Blair (2005, 79).
[100] Morris (1989, 123–24).
[101] Blair (2005, 84 and *fn.* 29).
[102] Blair (2005, 85–87 and 95).

was uninhibited in transforming Ripon from a monastic community to a secular minster.[103]

Northumbria remained at the heart of developments, 'in the marchlands of the confrontation'.[104] Bede's own houses of Monkwearmouth and Jarrow, founded by Benedict Biscop, aided by Coelfrith, in 674 and 680/1, respectively, had the material support of king Ecgfrith.[105] Royal and ecclesiastical interests converged temporarily, but early in the eighth century Bede perceived that founders' motivations had been corrupted.[106] The land-grants bestowed inalienable food-rents on minsters controlled by their sponsors, an incestuous fiscal mechanism.

At the end of the seventh century, as the English Church grew rich and produced masterpieces of literature and architecture, what Bede regarded as a corrosive form of land-tenure—*bookland*, which freed the founder from religious and secular duties—was embraced by the lower aristocracy and smaller minsters proliferated, there being at least two hundred by the end of the eighth century.[107] Shortly before his death in 734, Bede fulminated about the subversion of the monastic culture in his famous letter to Ecgberht, and no doubt this applied equally to the other kingdoms.[108] Bede's ire is reserved not for fiscal manipulation but for the failure of the family minsters to meet his standards of observance and their compromised integrity having accepted patronage.[109] After all, he had tolerated 30 years of Aldfrith's dissolute and incompetent successors. However, despite Bede's narrow perspective and sweeping condemnation, this transfer of capital assets was economically dynamic. It injected previously dormant wealth into the economy, which, dispersed widely both geographically and socially, was the springboard for a 'take-off into sustained growth'.[110] While Bede complained that land that may have supported young warriors had been eliminated. Many of Bede's proposed reforms were, in fact, eventually implemented in the *Clofesho* canons of 747, including extending the authority of bishops over private minsters.[111]

Blair associated the flowering of the minsters with the era of the early-penny coinage. Though other forms of wealth were not extinguished with the demise of the southern *sceat*, there is a prolonged recession in the third quarter of the century. However, the more successful minsters were economically, the more they were treated as financial pawns. While this 'largely hidden transition' caused their decline in the ninth century, they survived as religious centres.[112]

The basic unit of territorial organisation seems to have been a 'province' or *regione*, comparable to the hundred, which was measured in hides responsible for generating food-renders to the king. These territorial divisions may have been suitable for the minsters to dispense pastoral care.[113] This provided a link between royal and aristocratic land management and ecclesiastical pastoral care, as evidence by the widespread collection of *churchscot*.[114] Blair based his conceptual framework on this: 'it must have been as easy to know who owed churchscot to which minster as to know who owed food-rent to the royal vill.'[115] These were reciprocal arrangements whereby the former gave security and the latter 'sacramental ministrations, preaching and pastoral care.' Itinerant kings and their retinues travelled within manageable bounds to consume the food-rent.[116] On the ground, it was local priests who gave solidity to this arrangement and perhaps this is consecrated in the stonework at Otley,[117] Hovingham,[118] Northallerton, Aldborough and Dewsbury (*Figure* 2).[119] *Sceattas* were a versatile source of propaganda for them, but were intentionally far from unambiguous iconographically.

The presence of a mother-parish would have given structure to the governance and care of these provinces[120] and one would expect this to be reflected in the material culture. The significant accumulation of styli at Flixborough, sited below a limestone escarpment overlooking the Trent, suggests a minster.[121] Each may have propagated satellite communities,[122] many of which await discovery, probably of the nature of the ritual-based networks in Hodge's revised model. In siting minsters, consideration was given to sacral,[123] topographical and economic considerations, as Blair stated: 'as many minsters grew into centres of economic exchange, and eventually into proto-towns, their topographical advantages would prove decisive.'[124] Clearly, the renders to minsters involved travel of the producer not the consumer as with peripatetic kings on their food-circuits. Indeed, an increased level of estate management was necessary to

[103] Morris (1989, 131).
[104] Muir (1987, 95). For example, that the major reconciliation between Christian factions should have been staged at Whitby is significant. Note that most monasteries were often sited near harbours, as liminal coastal sites and to facilitate movement and supply. Sawyer (2013, 70), Spratt and Harrison (1989, 63).
[105] Alcock (2003, 83). Blair (2005, 88).
[106] Blair (2005, 91).
[107] Sawyer (2013, 72).
[108] Blair (2005, 99–104).
[109] Blair (2005, 106–07). This seems a little hypocritical.
[110] Rostow (1963).
[111] The Council of 816 warned bishops that they could not take control of minsters to sate their greed as their interests had become 'as much gastronomic as religious', Blair (2005, 131). Bailey tentatively advances Hertford as a candidate for the unidentified *Clofesho*. Keynes (1994, 14–17).

[112] Blair (2005, 133–34).
[113] Blair (2005, 154–55).
[114] See Laws of Ine, §4 (section 2.8 and *Table* 1).
[115] Blair (2005, 157).
[116] Blair (2005, 252).
[117] Wood (1987). Blair (2005, 165).
[118] Morris (1989, 121).
[119] Morris (1989, 138).
[120] Blair (2005, 160).
[121] Blair (2005, 206–09).
[122] Blair (2005, 212).
[123] Blair (2005, 191–95). See Abramson (2012a, 93), re Lastingham (Morris, 2005). See also Op den Velde and Metcalf, 2009 47, accepting my interpretation of Metcalf's 'mixed grill' as a disguised cruciform device.
[124] Blair (2005, 185).

sustain the conspicuous if not rapacious, consumption[125] of minsters.[126] The centrality of this institution, with its diversely resourced hinterland, encouraged a dynamic economic escalation where technology could be exploited to produce surplus.[127] By 716, Monkwearmouth and Jarrow had nearly 600 'brethren', a significant workforce,[128] which, supplemented by specialization and more intensive agrarian and industrial production, signifies an economic arrangement, which, if replicated throughout the landscape, was arguably well beyond the capability of a travelling king to manage.

Coin finds at minster sites indicate the wealth generated. Aesthetically pleasing artefacts (including Series Q *sceattas*, probably the product of an East Anglian minster),[129] show that the wealth was crafted into luxuries. 'Pottery, small finds, and especially coins indicate catchment zones on different scales: rather as late medieval England had hierarchies of markets, so the bigger sites may constitute a layer between the long-range trade of the emporia and the inter-regional and local trade of the lesser ones.'[130]

Offering sanctuary and refuge conceivably jeopardised the internal sanctity of minsters. Economic activity inevitably exacerbated this, initiating conflicts at various levels, but this is an unavoidable symptom of urbanisation and it is the commercial aspects of early Anglo-Saxon life which are of chief concern in this study. Indeed, the secular and sacral—the checks and balances of royal and ecclesiastical spheres of influence—responded to both the dynastic friction and countervailing stability evident in Northumbria's political dynamic.

To summarize, specific aspects of the disciplines of anthropology, history and archaeology can be drawn upon to explain the development of markets. These provide a broad framework, wherein particular studies and hypotheses lead towards a consideration of monetization in sixth- to ninth-century Northumbria. The major contributions to analysis of the evolution of different forms of money, explanations of transitions to more sophisticated and versatile forms, and why reversions occurred, will now be assessed. These include Davies on the evolution of money and coinage, Einzig on terms of reference and Metcalf's application of distributional analysis to identifying the sources of ninth-century coinage in England.

2.4 Economics

The evolution of money and coinage has been a minority interest among economists, let alone historians. There are several stages of development to consider—the use and forms of barter and commodity money in early exchange,[131] the emergence and purposes of primitive currencies,[132] representational currencies, the growth of banking in ancient civilisations and the transmission of all these advances. These stages need not be sequential; there will be significant overlap. However, it is necessary to limit the scope to what may be relevant to the *re-emergence* of coinage in Anglian Northumbria.

What is opaque in Polanyi is pellucid in Davies.[133] The obscure becomes obvious—possibly because Davies is better anchored in factual evidence. Davies lists 10 micro- and macro-economic functions of money[134] (though the list omits some abstract aspects such as propaganda, iconography and *remembering*[135]) concluding that 'money is eminently fungible'.[136] Jevons characterized money as essentially having cognizability, utility, portability, divisibility, indestructability, stability of value and homogeneity.[137] Beyond this characterisation, Davies' definition is: *money is anything that is widely used for making payments and for accounting for debts and credits.* This is simplified, in the present study, to: that which is accepted in resolution of indebtedness. *Resolution* is preferred, due to its legalistic connotations, over *redemption*, even though the religious loading of this word appeals in view of the ecclesiastical iconography and source of many coins of the period and the significance of spiritual redemption.

Relevant in this context is Bede's commendation of Aidan: 'he distributed gifts of money (*pecuniarum*) which he received from the rich, either, as we have said, for the use of the poor or for the redemption (*redemptionem*) of those who had been unjustly sold into slavery,'[138] though as Aidan died in 651, the precise form of *pecuniarum* is uncertain

[125] Veblen (1899).
[126] Blair (2005, 256).
[127] Blair (2005, 253).
[128] Blair (2005, 255).
[129] Hutcheson suggested this is Bawsey (2009, 5).
[130] Blair (2005, 260).

[131] See definitions of commodity money (section 2.5) from Einzig (1949, 346), and Skre (2011, 80). Cribb (2004, 7–9), gives an early example of the use of grain in making payments under a 3rd millennium BC Mesopotamian law code.
[132] The numismatic and anthropological use of 'primitive' differs. Use of primitive currency distinguishes peasants from primitive man.
[133] Glyn Davies, economist (1919–2003).
[134] Davies (1994, 27). Compared to Polanyi's exchange, standard, store and payment, Davies had unit of account, measure of value, medium of exchange, means of payment, standard of deferred payment and store of value as specific functions and liquid asset, resource allocation mechanism, causative factor in the economy and controller of the economy as general functions. The subsets of economic transactions, settlement of commercial and fiscal obligations, exemplify, but are not, functions.
[135] Hann and Hart (2011, 96).
[136] Davies (1994, 29).
[137] Davies (1994, 46). There are other ways of expressing the same value set, for example, Hodges (1988, 103) quoted Harris's portability, divisibility, convertibility, generality, anonymity and legality. Few such descriptions distinguish adequately between hard and soft money (Sehgal chs 4 and 5). As an early non-metallic form of currency, bovine (and even equine) currencies may be more divisible than is obvious. As recently as last century, the Kirghiz used horses with sheep as subsidiaries and lambskins as small change. The ancient association persists in language—other than *pecus*/pecuniary—the Welsh 'da' means good as an adjective and both 'goods' and 'cattle' as a noun. Davies (1994) inherently favours the Welsh example, though there are many others (e.g. *feoh*/fee). Davies (1994, 42–43).
[138] Bede (1969, III, 5).

as gold coin may be an inappropriate medium for these purposes. Bede's use of 'money' seems anachronistic; the correct translation is *wealth* as shown in his example of the alms donation by Aidan of a horse gifted him by King Oswin,[139] and in Bede's description of the frugality of Colmán and his predecessors (664): 'They had no money but only cattle: if they received money from the rich they gave it to the poor'.[140]

In introducing his discussion of barter, Davies suggested that 'we know more about barter's complementary co-existence with money than we do about barter in those long, dark, moneyless ages of prehistory',[141] and, as a result, the disadvantages of barter are exaggerated by such as Jevons.[142] The vast array of primitive monies is illustrated in Quiggin[143] and described in Einzig. Einzig attributed the overstatement of the inconvenience of barter to a failure to realise that in a small community, with a limited range of produce, expectations are constrained.[144] Primitive currency marked an evolutionary step from barter to an intermediary artefact, conventionally held in such social esteem as to hold the trust of both sides in a prestige transaction. Typical of such human and social transactions would be those involving a bride or slave, compensation for injury or death, protection, conspicuous ornamentation or ritual ceremony.

There were no discernible primitive monies in England between the final Roman and early Anglo-Saxon coinages.[145] From the repertoire of economic tools, this leaves barter and commodity money as mechanisms to catalyse English exchange, at least during the period *c.* 470–*c.* 570, if not a further 60 years on each side.

2.5 Monetary History

Einzig defined primitive money in a sufficiently elastic way as to accommodate the remarkable variety of such monies, their circumstances and uses: 'a unit or an object conforming to a reasonable degree to some standard of uniformity, which is employed for reckoning or for making a large proportion of payments customary in the community concerned, and which is accepted in payment with the intention of employing it for making payments.'[146]

He argued that many communities chose their staple product as their currency. His analysis would have benefited from a differentiation between *commodity* and *primitive* monies. In current parlance, the former is regarded as a local staple product and extracting this subset from the broader definition of primitive money clarifies both concepts. He gave a reasonable definition of commodity money: 'It seems probable that when the growing diversity of goods and services and the advancing division of labour made the use of a medium of exchange increasingly necessary, the object chosen as an intermediary was very often not a favourite medium of barter but the ready-made medium of payment which was already widely used in the community for non-monetary purposes.'[147] Skre characterized a society most suited to use commodity money as consisting of households self-sufficient in essentials with a surplus of storable necessities and the ability to exchange subsistence produce with others in times of need; an occasional demand for specialist tools and materials; and an absence of long distance traders.[148] Commodity money is very likely to have played an important rôle in the post-Roman and early Anglo-Saxon periods. Money became more sophisticated with the need to minimise search and transactions costs.[149]

Einzig recognised some social functions of money not previously raised—ornamentation, ceremonial, religious, matrimonial, and political by which he meant judicial. His social theory of money placed him in the substantivist camp.[150]

2.6 Numismatics

The seminal *Thrymsas and Sceattas in the Ashmolean Museum*[151] by Michael Metcalf, former Keeper of the Heberden Room at the Ashmolean Museum, Oxford, gave a profound insight into the evolution of different types and their geographical distribution.

Noting the lack of documentary evidence in relation to ninth-century monetization, Metcalf warned that this 'has been a matter of historical controversy for the last 30 years and continues to be so...Archaeological evidence of inter-regional transfers of goods does not lend itself very well to quantification and has tended to focus attention on high-status objects.'[152]

Metcalf cautioned that the paucity of historical evidence sets the bar high for numismatic arguments which have to be 'not just possible but inescapable. This is what gives the debate its special flavour', each step must be rigorous without incoherence or ambiguities and with a sufficiency of material to be statistically valid.[153]

In the *Epilogue* to *BAR* 180,[154] Brooks highlighted the significance of the volume of production of *stycas*, warning of the risk of extrapolating from die numbers.

[139] Bede (1969, III, 14).
[140] Bede (1969, III, 26).
[141] Davies (1994, 9–10).
[142] Jevons (1875, ch. 1) on the inefficiency of the 'double coincidence of wants'.
[143] Quiggin (1949).
[144] Einzig (1949, 342–42).
[145] There were few in the Iron Age. Van Arsdell (1989, 5–3).
[146] Einzig (1949, 317).
[147] Einzig (1949, 346).
[148] Skre (2011, 80).
[149] Skre (2011, 82–83).
[150] Of monetary theories, he stated: 'By concentrating on a relatively narrow aspect of the subject, however, they all miss the substance.' (1949, 489).
[151] Metcalf (1993–94, vols 1–3).
[152] Blackburn and Dumville (1998, 169–70).
[153] Blackburn and Dumville (1998, 170).
[154] *BAR* 180 (1987, 397–401).

He contrasted the known high survival rate with a more cautious view of the scale and function of *stycas*: 'unless archaeologists can demonstrate that this distinctive brass coinage did provide a great fillip to the Northumbrian economy' the minimalist view that the coins merely served the aristocracy must be considered. He concluded that the 'great leap forward' only came with the silver penny issued by the Vikings of York.[155]

In response, Metcalf, despite describing Brooks' scepticism as 'invincible', set out to demonstrate as 'inescapable', independent of arguments on volume, that the pervasive topography of finds, devoid of any obvious pattern of privileged use 'is strong prima facie evidence of widespread monetisation at ordinary social levels'. Clearly, for this view to prevail, 'randomness is all'.[156]

Metcalf illustrated the age-distribution of the 450 single finds to show the decline in production in the ninth century.[157] Only a handful are from north of the Humber. The longevity of circulation is compensated for, in this representation, by the transfer of a third of the finds to the next period.[158] This is a crucial assumption, for it is both the date and durability of the coins that are diagnostic. Durability may be determined by condition, but this is not a sure guide when coins have been deposited in chemically active soil.

Metcalf regarded the downward trend throughout the ninth century as contrary to expectations in the light of increasing Viking incursions. A more sudden monetary retreat in the face of the threat may be anticipated, but the picture is one of steady, long-term deterioration.[159] Metcalf analysed this on a geographical basis to find that it is the mints south of the Thames that were in decline, suggesting a reaction to the growing Viking assaults. This decline did not significantly affect Mercia. That this trend represents a loss of confidence with a likely compensating increase in commodity exchange and informal credit, is beyond conclusive proof. Metcalf's regression analysis of mints and polities indicated not only that there was a broad mix of coins generally, but also that Canterbury (the dominant mint in the first half of the ninth century), Rochester and London were far more involved in long-distance trade than those mints in East Anglia or Wessex, which served a more local function.[160] These mints were not royal power bases but ports of convenience where incoming currency could be recycled.[161]

Two special cases were considered. The first is that of Carolingian finds, where, for example, finds at York fall into the 'window of opportunity' prior to Viking emissions of pennies. The second case is that of *stycas* found south of the Humber-Mersey line, where the widespread distribution—coastal, estuarine, riverine and inland—is well beyond areas of immediate Northumbrian influence such as the Irish Sea coast and south Yorkshire/north Lincolnshire and confirms the dissemination in my dataset described below, *Map 1*.

Without relying on die productivity, in response to Brooks' scepticism, Metcalf made persuasive arguments in favour of widespread ninth-century monetization, not restricted to a privileged élite, even if the west of England is typically under-represented.[162]

Metcalf's well-argued assumptions on the sources of different early-penny varieties, provided the foundations for site interpretation according to the mix of varieties present.[163] While an element of this Metcalfian analysis remains speculative, it is employed extensively in the case studies in the second part of this study.

While the work of Metcalf is key to the present study, it is important to place it in the context of numismatic and artefactual studies of sixth- to ninth-century England, if not the North Sea trading area, in general and Northumbria in particular.

Festschrifts (*C&H*, *EMMH*) and occasional symposia have encapsulated current research. Notable are *BAR* 128 (1984) and 180 (1987)[164] as well as the author's biennial *International Symposium in Early Medieval Coinage* (2006–16, *SiEMC* 1–3). Lyon's *SCBI* 68 summarizes current scholarship on *stycas*.

Naismith gave an excellent summary of the landmarks in numismatic literature[165] while Blackburn and Metcalf have been prolific, notably the latter's *T&S*, which updated the corpus very substantially.[166] Gannon shone a bright light on the Conversion Period iconography.[167]

For the seventh-century gold, Sutherland is the point of embarkation.[168] Abdy and Williams catalogued most gold finds but was not illustrated.[169] On the gold shilling of York, Abramson (2019) will supersede Naylor and Allen.[170]

The relative proliferation of finds during the metal-detecting era render earlier literature on *sceattas* of limited value. Essentially, modern scholarship commenced with Rigold's classification, a paradigm of brevity.[171] Metcalf, Blackburn and Gannon have been notable contributors and

[155] *BAR* 180 (1987, 399).
[156] Blackburn and Dumville (1998, 171).
[157] Metcalf (1998b, 167–97).
[158] This method was devised by Blackburn (1989 and 2003, 21 *fn.*)
[159] See Abramson (2012b, 113).
[160] Metcalf (1998a and b, 2003, 40–42).
[161] Blackburn and Dumville (1998, 179–84).

[162] For example, the fertile Severn Basin is devoid of coin.
[163] Metcalf (1993–94, parts II–IV).
[164] This focussed on the *styca*. The contributions are summarised in Abramson (2012d Supplement, 3–4).
[165] *MEC* vol. 8 (2017, 42–43 and 65–67), even if too prescriptive on derivation of terms.
[166] Metcalf (1993–94).
[167] Gannon (2003).
[168] Sutherland (1948).
[169] Abdy and Williams (2006).
[170] Naylor and Allen (2014).
[171] Rigold (1977).

the author has provided accessible identification guides and discussion fora.

Booth's landmark contribution to *The Seventh Oxford Symposium*,[172] provided a clear and well-reasoned taxonomy for Northumbrian *sceattas* at the start of the metal-detecting era and has remained the standard reference since.

Op den Velde's collaborations with Metcalf provided a major source for Low Countries' coinage, Coupland is eloquent on Merovingian and Carolingian material, and *SEVA* (*Silver Economy in the Viking Age*) and *SEMSS* (*Silver Economies, Monetisation and Society in Scandinavia,* AD *800–1000*) provide copious information on Scandinavian development. Naismith's work on Southumbrian numismatics is significant.[173]

In discussing the source of the more common elements in Series J (types 36, 37 and 85, *SL*18–20, *Figure* 34), Metcalf stated: 'York is the home of Series J, which has had a history of misinterpretation',[174] though Booth was more sceptical,[175] as was Archibald.[176] Naylor[177] promoted Lindsey as the source, but Metcalf refuted this.[178] Naylor used regression analyses to favour northern or central Lincolnshire, arguing that Mercian interests in exporting commodities, notably salt and wool, would have been aided by local minting, but undermined the argument by noting that Lindsey had no *wic*.[179] However, the source(s) of the main varieties of Series J remain unresolved and the likelihood that they differ in origin should be considered. Metcalf speculated that the facing heads (type 37), emulating the *denier* of Reims,[180] represented King Coenred and John of Beverley. One of the Fishergate Series J finds is a previously unrecorded/unremarked variety (now *SL18*–25, type 85). These types may favour a source north of the Humber, while a pristine specimen of type 36, with a 7/8[ths] profile, plausibly the prototype, was found at Castle Donington, Leicestershire.

As regards Northumbrian *stycas*, while Adamson's illustrations of 944 Hexham *stycas* remains helpful, Lyon initiated recent analysis.[181] He mapped out the chronological foundations of the coinage, after studying the accumulation in the Yorkshire Museum particularly in respect of the Hexham hoard in comparison to the St. Leonard's Place and Bolton Percy (1846) hoards. Die links enabled him to establish the members of Eanred's 'Group A' moneyers and to show that only these and the coins of Eanbald II date to before 837, when Wigmund succeeded Wulfsige.[182] Lyon identified Eardwulf as the dominant moneyer of Æthelred II's restoration,[183] suggested that Osberht's output was limited in duration early in the reign and observed that the emissions of Wulfhere (succeeded 854) by his sole moneyer Wulfred, in style and execution were neater than Osberht's and closer to Æthelred II's.[184] He favoured a date not before 830 for the appearance of silver-alloy coins and only a short interval after the death of Eanbald II before the base emissions were produced on a large scale in the last two or three years of Eanred's reign. Northumbria's 829 capitulation at Dore is here regarded as separating Eanred's emissions.

Lyon also suggested, on stylistic grounds, that engravers worked, on both obverse and reverse dies, for several moneyers—an important demarcation of functions, as in most narratives there is a presumption that the *monetarius* financed, engraved and struck the coins whereas these rôles would have been separate and hierarchical. *Sceattas* of different moneyers for Æthelred I may well have been engraved by the same hand and this practice seems to have continued into later periods.

Pirie was prolific in exploring a complex field, but the flawed taxonomy of her *magnum opus* left a difficult legacy.[185] Pagan's review of *CKN* engaged with Pirie's eccentricity.[186] Pirie committed herself to building an unparalleled corpus of *stycas* but her classification was subject to a lively debate.[187] While it was clear that close attention to Northumbrian orthography was necessary, her undue emphasis on epigraphy and central motifs created a keenly contested arrangement based on her 'phases and groups' which Pirie was adamant should be published but she denied herself *Sylloge* endorsement, despite Metcalf's plea that 'this is purely a didactic problem'.

In early June 1987, Metcalf again wrote to Pirie regretting her decision to withdraw the *Sylloge* volume on the basis that she would prefer the work to be unpublished rather than appear in an emasculated form. He made an articulate, reasoned if frank argument, referring to her denial of the separation between Æthelred II's first and second reign moneyers[188] and the lack of evidence for *ateliers* other than

[172] Booth (1984, 71–111).

[173] Naismith (2011 and 2012).

[174] Metcalf (1993–94, 341, 351 and 357).

[175] Booth (1997b, 16).

[176] Evans and Loveluck (2009, 404).

[177] Naylor (2006, 159–70).

[178] Abramson (2008, 160–66) and (2011, 25–29).

[179] Moreover, repeated Northumbrian and Mercian vying over the wealthy Lindsey may have rendered it an unstable site for a mint (Ulmschneider, 2000, 102–03).

[180] Of the type found near Bridlington (*Figure* 33). Metcalf (1993–94, 344).

[181] Lyon (1957).

[182] *Dataset* 3, tab 5.

[183] Also see Pagan (1997, 276).

[184] Lyon does not remark on the fact that Wulfhere's obverses are indeed neat, but the reverses are not. The case for a different engraver is stronger than that for a different mint, given how few *stycas* of Wulfhere were produced.

[185] Pirie's *CKN* (1997).

[186] Pagan (1997, 274–82).

[187] Abramson (2012d Supplement, 1–6) described the controversy surrounding Pirie's 'phases and groups' and their publication. In 2011–12, the two parts of her archive (left at—as opposed to bequeathed to—the Fitzwilliam Museum and the National Museum of Scotland) were re-united. [My gratitude to the Yorkshire Numismatic Society for funding this.] This archive, now consolidated, is stored at Leeds Museum's depository.

[188] There could be no overlap due to the absence of silver from Eardwulf's emissions, although in Metcalf and Northover's *The Northumbrian royal*

York. He argued that she had failed to separate die-cutting from die-use. He did try to find a way to accommodate her unconventional name forms: they 'need be no hindrance to the reader grasping any arguments that you have to make.' Metcalf diplomatically balanced harsh criticism with justified praise: 'You have invested an enormous amount of skill and devotion and effort into the Yorkshire *stycas*, and the results of your numbering and illustrating the dies, and presenting the die-chains, will be to make the *styca* series one of the show-pieces of medieval numismatics, with enormous potential for future research. That's why it is a public as well as private tragedy if you perversely throw it all away.'

Pirie appeared to have compromised temporarily but, by May 1990, in a joint letter Metcalf and Blackburn felt obliged to express concerns that the *Sylloge* was not the proper forum for a 'radical new arrangement'.[189] They defined the conventional orthography in detail, but this proved counterproductive.[190] No *Sylloge* was produced, in view of the justifiably hostile stance of the *Sylloge* Committee, but *CKN* was published privately in 1996.[191]

Pirie's treatment of *sceattas* was naïve in comparison to Booth's well-structured corpus. She chose to distinguish between Northumbrian *sceattas* and *stycas* based on design rather than metal content. She regarded the inscriptional *sceattas* as a departure in the 780s, such that the named moneyer *sceattas* of Æthelred I are catalogued as *stycas* despite there being no perceptible change in metallurgy—and even though the controversy over whether this was an innovation of Ælfwald I or Æthelred I remained—and remains—unresolved. Her Phase I covered both inscriptional *sceattas* and Eanred's silver-alloy issues, here divided into Periods N8 and N9. Lyon suggested that the move to base metal was due to the Mercians inhibiting supplies of Welsh silver.[192] Might submission to King Ecgberht of Wessex at Dore in 829 have caused not just a loss of prestige but also of silver supply? This event conceivably divides Periods N9 and N10a.

Furthermore, Pirie had overstated the significance of apparent die links in the later, chaotic period of *styca* manufacture, when, as Booth pointed out, the proximity of die-cutters working together daily in the same workshops 'seems to offer the only plausible explanation for the promiscuous sharing of dies which is such a prominent feature of the coinage'.[193] One cannot assume that non-current dies are retired—they are heavily and randomly re-used.

While Pirie's *styca* corpus is invaluable, what her classification added to Lyon's exposition was confusion. It is also undoubtedly to Booth that credit is given for having already publishing the first comprehensive corpus of the silver issues (690–796), crucially, setting this in a proper historical context, and also for publishing silver and brass coins from the first Northumbrian 'productive site' to see the light. His work is seminal.[194]

2.7 Land Use

Land use and management are the key economic factors of production in the period under review and were influenced considerably by geomorphology. Sheep-rearing took place in the dry chalk Wolds, where droveways evince transhumance, but other uplands were agriculturally marginal. The more fractured northern uplands of the Yorkshire Moors and Pennines, gave opportunity for mineral extraction with arable farming restricted to the broad valleys, but other than close to the great monasteries and on routes between them, activity was inhibited by terrain and climate,[195] while lowlands were largely given over to cereals and cattle. This pattern of usage facilitated different forms of land management. Landowners in York exercised control over the vast managed estate of the Central Lowlands,[196] similarly Beverley with its hinterland, and Ryedale with its numerous religious houses in elongated parishes, while pasturalism in the Wolds encouraged greater mobility.

Modern scholarship with a substantial emphasis on the post-Roman economic transformation of Northumbria includes Hunter-Blair, Marsden, Cramp, Higham, Hansen and Wickham, Manby, Moorhouse and Ottaway, Rollason, Smith, Wormald, Pryor, Woodman, and Higham and Ryan.[197] Hyer and Owen-Crocker and Banham and Faith focussing respectively on material culture and agriculture, are practical economic studies but relate substantially to later periods.[198]

Though the evidence for demographic and economic change in the post-Roman era remains slender, the century-long numismatic discontinuity after Patching (section 4.2.5.1) is indicative of a declining need for a ready medium. Retrenchment probably implies agricultural withdrawal to the most fecund land and produce. Bede provided evidence of a network of administrative *regiones,* based on royal

coinage in the time of Æthelred and Osberht there is the speculation not only that such an overlap occurred but that concurrent moneyers could have been "high silver" or "low silver" issuers, but Eardwulf's silver free emissions are a significant step change—a difference of kind not degree.

[189] Pirie archive.

[190] Pirie (1988, 5) tried to justify her stance that 'the standard Northumbrian elements are not those of West Saxon usage.' In response, Smart (1997, 69–72) argued for a system that is orderly and explicable—there being no attempt "to suppress the distinctive northern character"!

[191] By Galata Print, Llanfyllin, who generously provided me with proofs capable of digitization.

[192] Lyon (1957, 229), but see *fn.* 663, Naismith (2012, 247).

[193] Booth (1997b, 26).

[194] Booth (1984, 1987 and 1997b).

[195] Muir (1987, ch. 1).

[196] Defined in Ch. 2.2.

[197] Hunter-Blair (1956), Marsden (1992), Cramp (1995), Higham (1993, 1999), Hansen and Wickham (2000), Manby, Moorhouse and Ottaway (2003) Rollason (2003), Smith (2006), Wormald (2006), Pryor (2010, 209–34), Woodman (2012), and Higham and Ryan (2013, 20–178).

[198] Hyer and Owen-Crocker (eds.) (2011) and in Banham and Faith (2014), the economic outcomes are characterized at section 3.2.

estate centres, often at former Roman sites.[199] Though by Bede's time the Humber Estuary was regarded as a political frontier, 'Elsewhere in eastern England the river-systems became the centres rather than the boundaries of the first Germanic settlements.'[200]

Loveluck endorsed the theory of a catastrophic event in the mid-530s,[201] which had a generational impact; societal change was inevitable.[202] This may have facilitated the territorial expansionism of the Idings, replacement of gift exchange by élite coinage and receptivity towards conversion. What has previously been referred to as 'multiple estates' seen by Blair as *regiones*, the basic unit of resource collection,[203] could be episcopal as much as regal. That, from the ninth century, these formed the basis of a pervasive, reciprocal, arrangement between nobles, clergy and peasantry—'feudalism'[204]—is now regarded as an anachronistic construct.[205]

One of the major developments in the 1980s, which led to new thinking about Northumbrian economics, was the identification of so-called 'productive sites', a term favoured by numismatists, where metal detector users had found significant numbers of artefacts and coins, on otherwise unrecognised sites. Pioneering research was achieved by Booth and Blowers in 1983 on the 'Sancton' (South Newbald) material, where they recognised the possibility of a move of 'productivity' from North Ferriby to a possible emporium or royal site at 'Sancton'.[206] The first paper to be published by a metal detectorist, Haldenby, related to Cottam.[207] This assiduous detectorist then published further papers in association with Richards, which extended to Cowlam and environs.[208] This series of publications[209] revealed an evolving understanding of interrelationships between widespread and dispersed settlements, being dependencies of a single estate, and the progression from Anglo-Saxon to Anglo-Scandinavian culture. Richards concluded that the Wolds, used for upland grazing, were depopulated and that by middle Anglo-Saxon times sub-rectangular 'Butterwick-type' enclosures were established for economic, craft and administrative purposes.[210] Local markets, being dependencies of lowland estates, acquired specialisms in resource provision, but became nucleated villages in the disruption of Scandinavian settlement.

Several conferences addressed 'productive sites', emporia and markets. Blackburn and Metcalf organised an Oxford symposium to ensure that numismatic and archaeological approaches were systematic.[211] A conference held in York, in September 1991, considered the nature of emporia.[212] Papers from the Oxford conference of 2000[213] were published in Pestell and Ulmschneider (*P&U*) and focussed on the treatment of the accumulating evidence from 'smaller, less well-documented trading places'[214] some of which had attributes of permanence—'central places, acting as foci not simply for trade and exchange, but production, consumption…administration and justice.'[215] Blackburn compared the age profile of coin losses to the norm[216] and Metcalf used regression analysis to identify distribution patterns.[217] The nature of 'productive sites' was tempered by Richards' view that they were not special—the 'productive' aspect was predicated by detecting activity, rather than similar economic function. In comparing Wharram Percy and Cottam, he found the density of finds to be variable, with no reason to view them as markets or central places. Such sites were part of a continuum and were better 'seen in the context of the evolution of the Anglo-Saxon kingdoms, the development of lordship and a tributary economy.'[218]

Richards demonstrated the use of traditional and emerging archaeological techniques in again comparing Wharram Percy and Cottam, the former revealed by Beresford's attention to deserted medieval villages (*DMVs*) and the latter identified by 'Butterwick-type' cropmark enclosures associated with metal-detected finds.[219] He concluded that 'sites are not so much invisible as hitherto unrecognised.'[220] Leahy focussed on the rich assemblage of metal-detected finds from South Newbald which he contrasted with other local sites to provide an age profile of activity.[221] The characteristics of the South Newbald, such as the location, abundant coinage and lack of domestic material, led him to speculate that the site was a fair or market, although a minster could have been present. He warned against 'a single, simple, identification.'[222]

Ulmschneider, comparing Lincolnshire and Hampshire, produced the first full-length study of the early medieval period to have been based on metal detector finds but did not draw on PAS data.[223] In attempting to establish

[199] Hall (2003, 171). (Blair (2005, 154).
[200] Myers (1986, 174).
[201] Loveluck (2003, 154). Keys (1999, 254–72). Gunn and others (2000). Gräslund and Price (2015).
[202] Analogous to the recovery after the Black Death, Zeigler (1998, 240–59).
[203] Blair (2005, 154 and *fn.* 77).
[204] Bloch (1961).
[205] Brown (1974) and Reynolds (1974).
[206] Booth and Blowers (1983, 139–45).
[207] Haldenby (1990, 1992, 1994).
[208] Haldenby and Richards (2009, 2010), Richards (1999a, 2000), and Richards and others (2013). These were the first metal-detected sites in Northumbria to be subject of an archaeological excavation.
[209] Culminating in Richards and others (2013, 201–71).
[210] Richards and others (2013).
[211] Blackburn and Metcalf (1989, unpublished)
[212] 'Wics and Emporia: The Pre-Viking Trading Centres of Europe'. See Hill and Cowie (2001).
[213] 'The Archaeology of Inland Markets Fairs and "Productive" Sites', Worcester College, Oxford, December 2000.
[214] *P&U* (2003, 1).
[215] *P&U* (2003, 8).
[216] Blackburn (2003, 20–36).
[217] Metcalf (2003, 37–47).
[218] Richards (1999b, 79).
[219] Richards in Geake and Kenny (2000), the result of a student conference University of York Archaeological Society, June 1995.
[220] Richards (2000, 27–41).
[221] Leahy (2000). Covered by Booth and Blowers (1983, 139–45) and Booth (1987).
[222] Leahy (2000, 51–82).
[223] Ulmschneider (2000).

the economic centrality of minsters, she avoided a deterministic approach by assessing two different areas, archaeologically and topographically, using an early commencement date. She used topographical analysis to minimise find-spot imprecision and to survey 'the strategic positioning of sites within the landscape'.[224] She concluded that find-spot inaccuracy is unlikely to distort the overall distribution pattern, that there is differential wealth distribution and that 'productive sites' are not just a northern phenomenon.[225] She differenced 'productive sites' from *wics* chiefly in the inland location and strong inter-regional and local trading links of the former, which exploit their hinterland to create wealth through the use of skilled labour with 'the presence of a strong ecclesiastical element'. The church acquired, perhaps in return for spiritual support for kings, large, well-resourced, estates and provided regular meeting places, giving impetus to a resurgent economy.[226] She regarded 'a disparity in sources, recovery and recording' as explaining perceived differences between the two areas of study, the greatest difference being the absence of a *wic* in Lincolnshire.[227]

Detecting led to a major expansion of the artefactual record, *via* PAS. One of the first studies to attempt to make use of this new evidence for Northumbria was undertaken by Naylor, based on his 2002 PhD research.[228] However, given the modest sample size the results are unreliable. Naylor overlaid finds of coins, pottery, stoneware and metalwork in two study areas of middle Saxon England—Yorkshire (Area 1) and Kent (Area 2)—to assess and compare rural involvement in trade and the relative influence of royalty and the church therein. For the coinage, Naylor set out a periodization[229] to facilitate comparisons to regional norms. For Yorkshire, he deduced from the coin loss pattern, especially for eastern Yorkshire after the mid-eighth century, that all settlements were within fifteen kilometres of sites identified as markets, and that these networks were integrated. Stone finds indicated widespread movements, but pottery was less diagnostic. Long-distance trade was also apparent from coin loss but Naylor discerned 'an attempt to restrict much of the monetised trade in the Vale of York/Humber estuary to Fishergate and then to the productive sites across Area 1.'[230] His general conclusions were that evidence for attributing 'productive sites' to minsters was 'flimsy',[231] and that royal involvement focussed on extraction of tolls, mainly levied on 'bulk, utilitarian items and raw materials' more than luxuries. Markets were sited to optimise royal revenues.[232]

[224] Ulmschneider (2000, vi–vii and 3).
[225] Ulmschneider (2000, 101–02).
[226] Ulmschneider (2000, 103–05).
[227] Ulmschneider (2000, 107).
[228] Naylor (2004).
[229] Naylor (2004, 22 and Appendix 1).
[230] Naylor (2004, 80–82).
[231] Naylor (2004, 133).
[232] Naylor (2004, 134).

Naylor's study of Deira followed Blackburn in discerning trends in patterns of coin loss.[233] Naylor selected sites with 10 or more coin finds and compared these to a regional mean as suggested by Reece.[234] Naylor identified increasing volume of coinage, if cyclical, with some sites showing long-term activity. He regarded the *sceat* as signifying long-distance trade, but with redirection of activity, under royal influence, to the internal economy, and a reduction in trading activity in the second half of the eighth century, *sceat* production declined leading to the *styca* as a cash currency.

Naylor revisited the origins of English emporia, in the light of recent data on portable antiquities, emphasising the importance of coastal zones.[235] The southern emporia seem to have arisen from undistinguished origins in the early eighth century, as shown by significant growth in the coin assemblage. Activity in York, and its Ouse-Humber traffic, saw an apparent decline, evident from the fewer finds of secondary issues compared to primary *sceattas*, in contrast with a significant increase in the Yorkshire Wolds. Naylor suggested curtailment was due to growing Mercian power. He concluded that monetization is not homogeneous through time or between locations and that the association of emporia and royal power may have been overstated.

Naylor proposed an alternative to the conventional view of the hinterlands of emporia in terms of traded goods and coinage by suggesting a more nuanced view taking account of different types of hinterland.[236] This included the immediate 'impact' zone of the emporium, the 'productive' area providing raw materials, the 'subsistence hinterland' from which produce was procured and the region under the 'social' influence of the emporium.

Scull and Naylor demonstrated that Primary *sceattas* as grave goods in coastal southern and eastern England indicated greater monetization, though whether this is tributary or commercial cannot be determined.[237] It is clear that the transition from gold took place a decade or two prior to the numismatic convention.

Smith also made use of metal-detected data but assessed Deiran economic history under the conventional headings of production, distribution and consumption.[238] Various types of subsistence and specialist production are evident: thrown pottery at Whitby and Otley; widespread textile manufacture with numerous spindle-whorls and loom-weights as evidence; smithing at Fishergate and Wharram Percy from both ore and scrap.[239] Working in copper alloy is regarded as a specialism of Wharram Percy, linked to supply of material for *styca* production: 'The

[233] Naylor (2007). Blackburn (2003).
[234] Reece (1987).
[235] Naylor (2012).
[236] Naylor (2016).
[237] Scull and Naylor (2016) building on Hines and Bayliss (2013).
[238] Smith (2006).
[239] Smith (2006, 110–18).

rarity of working copper alloy in Anglo-Saxon England means that their presence at Wharram is particularly significant.'[240] Smith also made some useful observations about the use of glass. All Deiran sites with glass-working also have evidence of metalworking.[241] For example, decorative glass rods are found at Kirkdale in association with metalworking, suggesting production of decorative mounts and enamelling.[242] Chemical analysis shows that virtually all glass is recycled Roman glass and Smith suggested that there may be an analogy for copper alloy and iron.[243] Haldenby and Richards mentioned non-ferrous metals at Cottam.[244] Loveluck cited iron-smelting at Elmswell near Driffield suggesting that the wealth generated by this financed coin production.[245] Craft production included metal-working at Beverley, Fishergate and Wharram Percy as well as widespread use of antler, fur and leather.

An invaluable database, *VASLE*, was created by Richards, Naylor and Holas-Clark, based on two data-streams: a national dataset of finds dated from *c.* 700 to 1050; and a sites dataset of finds from over 65 'productive sites', including data from Historic Environment Records (HER) and excavation reports.[246] Extensive data cleansing was required to standardise, or indeed introduce, classification and address generic dating issues. For the purposes of the present study, the sites dataset was purged of non-metallic items and those of insecure or early date. The data was periodized and allocated by parish. *VASLE* coinage data has not been used as it is superseded by the dataset created in this study.

VASLE was one of the first studies to make research use of the PAS database. There is a growing body of work using PAS data to evaluate landscape archaeology, settlement and economic development. These include Chester-Kadwell (2009), Bevan (2012), Brindle (2014), Leonard (2015) and Daubney (2016). Robbins noted seven 'stages' of sampling bias in PAS data: 'burial/loss, preservation, survival, exposure, recovery, reporting, and recording' and how these are influenced by choices made throughout this process.[247] She concluded that granting of permissions, site targeting, site proximity, group searching and FLO availability are the major influences on the completeness and accuracy of recording.[248]

2.8 Law

A survey of early English customary and formal legal remedies for abuse and resource exploitation, and the control of the emerging social framework, illustrates the emphasis and direction of early codifications of law and its symbiotic relationship with money. Not only do laws increasingly reflect commercial activity but penalties are progressively denominated in money rather than commodity money, mirroring the evolution of coinage and its growing penetration into daily activity.

The earliest surviving Anglo-Saxon law codes are the Kentish codes of Æthelberht (ninety laws, 602–23), Hlothere, possibly the king at the time of the Series A and B *sceattas*, and Eadric (sixteen laws, *c.* 685), and Wihtred (twenty-eight laws, *c.* 695). Ine of Wessex (688–726) also codified 76 laws early in his reign, probably by 695 (see *Table 1*).[249]

In practical terms, it is evident from Æthelberht §54, 55, 70 and 72, *Table 1*,[250] that a shilling consisted of 20 *sceattas*. The revival of the term '*sceatt*' by antiquarians is anachronistic as it was applied to a denomination whose name is unknown but was not current until more than half a century after Æthelberht's death.[251] In Ine's laws, there were increasing numbers of rules governing trading practices and mobility, e.g. §25. If the trader was found to be in possession of stolen property, he would pay the unusual fine of 36 shillings. The intention seems to be to discourage trade outside towns, for instance, §39 restricted movement between districts without permission. Protection and appraisal of agriculture, livestock and woodland is governed by Ine §40, 42–44, 46, 49 and 55–60, wherein, for example, §55 and 58 give specific valuations.[252] Here, and in Ine §59 and 69, unusually, value is denominated in *pæninga*.

Having briefly described references to money in Southumbrian law, some interpretation with reference to the power, structure of the codes, monetary penalties and nomenclature is informative.

The comparative *gyldes* due to monarchs and the episcopacy in Æthelberht's code demonstrates a balance of power in favour of the latter. Wihtred's decrees were vested with the authority of the Church—in return for granting the Church immunity from taxation (§1). By this time the Church and monarch appear to be of more comparable authority and Alfredian law strengthened the monarch's relative power.[253]

Æthelberht's code does not approach a cohesive, let alone comprehensive set of principles and penalties. Roebuck

[240] *Ibid.* 119.
[241] *Ibid.* 119.
[242] *Ibid.* 140. Hall (2003, 179).
[243] *Ibid.* 145.
[244] Haldenby and Richards (2010). NB: there are many scraps of lead at 'Site B' near Pocklington.
[245] *Ibid.* 119 and Loveluck (1996, 44–46). Workings were probably of a far larger scale at Ryther.
[246] Richards, Naylor and Holas-Clark (2008).
[247] Robbins (2012).
[248] Robbins (2012).

[249] See Attenborough (1922 (2012 reprint), 1–61), Oliver (2002), Roebuck (2008, 1–126).). Hill and Cowie (2001, 111–12). Also see http://archive.org/stream/lawsofearliesten00grea#page/4/mode/2up
[250] Referring to the relative compensation for the loss of thumbs, big toes and their nails. (Attenborough, 1922 [2012], 11–15)
[251] Oliver (2002, 82–83). Conventionally, the early medieval silver to gold ratio by weight is taken to be a median value of 1:12. Spufford (1988, 51). The average weight for a gold shilling is around 1.30g, and for a primary *sceat* around 1.10g. See also Naismith (2014c, 275–77).
[252] See Walbers (2012, ch. 5, 235–99, esp. 289–92), giving some common values e.g. a sheep costs 1 shilling = 4 (or 5) pence.
[253] Attenborough (1922 [2012], 65, Alfred §3).

Table 1: Early Anglo-Saxon Law

A. Æthelberht's code includes:	**B. Wihtred's code includes:**
10: If a man lies with a maiden belonging to the king, he shall pay 50 shillings compensation.	27: If a slave steals, and is released, 70 shillings…
14: If a man lies with a nobleman's serving maid, [he shall pay] 12 shillings compensation.	28 If a man from afar, or a stranger, quits the road, and neither shouts, nor blows a horn, he shall be assumed to be a thief, and as such may be either slain or put to ransom. (Same as Ine 20)
16: If a man lies with a commoner's serving maid, [he shall pay] 6 shillings compensation; if he lies with a slave of the second class, [he shall pay] 50 sceattas [compensation]; if one of the third class, 30 sceattas.	**C. Ine's code includes:**
54: If a thumb is struck off, 20 shillings (§1–5 list compensation for each finger)	7. §2: A ten-year old child can be [regarded as] accessory to a theft.
55: For the nail, 1 shillings	4: [Be ciricsceatte] Church dues shall be rendered at Martinmas.
58, §1: If the blow is received with uplifted hand, a shilling shall be paid.	14: He who is accused of belonging to a band of marauders shall clear himself with an oath of 120 hides, or pay corresponding compensation.
59: If [the blow] leaves a black bruise outside the clothes, 30 sceattas shall be paid as compensation.	19: A member of the king's household, if his wergeld is 1200 shillings, shall be allowed to swear for 60 hides, if he is a communicant.
70: If a big toe is struck off, 10 shillings	25: If a trader [makes his way into] the interior of the country and [proceeds to] traffic, he shall do so before witnesses.
71: For each of the other toes, [a sum] equal to half that laid down for the corresponding fingers shall be paid.	37: If a commoner has often been accused of theft and is at last proved guilty, either in the ordeal or by being caught in the act of committing an offence, his hand or foot shall be struck off.
72: If a big toe nail is knocked off, 30 sceattas.	49. §3: If pannage is paid in pigs, every third pig shall be taken when the bacon is three fingers thick…
73: If a freeborn woman, with long hair, misconducts herself, she shall pay 30 shillings as compensation.	59. §1: For every labourer a man has he shall pay six weys [of barley] as 'barley-rent'.
75: The compensation to be paid for the violation of the mund[1] of a widow of the best class, [that is, a widow of the nobility] shall be 50 shillings.	55: An ewe with her lamb is worth a shilling until a fortnight after Easter.
§1. For violation of the mund of a widow of the second class, 20 shillings; of the third class, 12 shillings; of the fourth class, 6 shillings.	58: The horn of an ox is worth 10 pence. Here, and in Ine 59 & 69, unusually, value is denominated in *pæninga.*
77: If a man buys a maiden, the bargain shall stand, if there is no dishonesty.	60: allows for hire of a yoke of oxen to be recompensed in fodder.
§1. If however there is dishonesty, she will be taken back to her home, and the money returned to him.	70. §1: specifies the payment for every 10 hides, to be paid as food rent, on the death of one of the lord's men: 10 vats of honey, 300 loaves, 12 ambers of Welsh ale, 30 ambers of clear ale, 2 full-grown calves or 10 wethers, 10 geese, 20 hens, 10 cheeses, a full amber of butter, 5 salmon, 20 pounds of fodder and 100 eels.

[1]Attenborough interprets this as guardianship or possibly, the marriage price of a widow.

argued that it is misleading to call them codes as that implies they were systematic: 'they are a heterogeneous collection of edicts.'[254] However, certain themes can be identified[255] and one may assume that these were based on social occurrence and commercial experience.

The monarch was peripatetic, constantly on the move to collect renders,[256] assert authority and dispense justice in which legislation on violence against the person and property predominate. Other than the many rules concerning homicide, Æthelberht's laws (*dooms*) §33–76 relate to very specific injuries. Policing and enforcing such minutiæ, may have been impossible, indicating that this was as much a code of behaviour, and a record of specific incidents, as a juridical scheme. The *dooms* preserve honour,[257] social stratification and other social conventions, such as slavery.

The specificity of judgments imply that the foundations of English legislation were in case law from the beginning. Certainly, these codes are in the Germanic tradition and

[254] Roebuck (2008, 105).
[255] Oliver (2002, 36).
[256] Oliver (2002, 86).
[257] Oliver (2002, 90).

'they stand boldly at the watershed between orality and literacy'.[258] Although the codes are from the southern kingdoms it is reasonable to assume that northern England followed similar legal constructs and practices.[259]

The codes of Hlothere (670–85) and Eadric (685–86) extended existing law, again demonstrating the process of building legislation on case law, but now with more emphasis on process and responsibility,[260] mediation and arbitration.[261] There is an escalation of compensation with (what we would now regard as) civil offences attracting the penalties previously reserved for criminal charges. These inflated penalties seem disproportionate to the meagre volume of coin then in restricted circulation.[262]

Again, the overriding impression of Ine's laws,[263] are that they were, in fact, specific judgments, which had been recorded as case law. The circumstances described are not common occurrences to be policed but rulings handed down by the king presiding over his court when presented with a particular prosecution. This impression is reinforced by the random, unstructured, nature of the legislation. There is little pretence at systematic organisation or prioritisation; law not built on principle must be characterized as weak.

However, there is more evaluation of certain activities and obligations other than *wergeld.* This contrasts with the seemingly more structured Salic law,[264] initiated by Clovis I (*c.* 466–511), with its emphasis on inheritance. Sawyer argued that as Clovis's successors claimed hegemony over part of southern Britain for most of the sixth century, there are similarities between Frankish and Kentish laws.[265]

Contemporary Merovingian gold *solidi* and *tremisses* were an élite currency not present in England in great numbers, so one may surmise that there was a mechanism in practice for converting penalties to commodity money.[266] According to Hines 'a comparison of the coin evidence we have from the fifth- to seventh-centuries in England with that for collections of small pieces of gold and silver bullion argues firmly against a widespread and large-scale use of hack-silver and -gold currency in this period.'[267] Hines proceeded to state that finds of weights, scales, pans and touchstones are evidence of weighing small quantities of metal. However, these equally could be for testing the weight of coins in circulation as suggested by Scull's investigation of grave finds of weights of this period (including Barton-on-Humber) showing that they cluster at two points 1.30–1.33g and 1.50–1.58g. The former equate to *tremisses.*[268] Equating the shilling to the *tremisses* leaves the *sceat* as a unit of account. However, this equivalence is not undisputed.[269]

Note the *wergeld* of 30,000 coins paid by King Wihtred of Kent in 694 to King Ine of Wessex in compensation for the death of Mul, the brother of Ine's predecessor Cædwalla, who had been killed during a Kentish rebellion in 687. It is implausible that, in 694, these were gold shillings; perhaps they were silver *sceattas.*[270] Hamwic was an active trading centre in Ine's day controlling the local *sceat* of Series H, for which there are numerous dies, though it stretches credulity, despite Metcalf's estimate of production[271] that such a sum was in coin.

Inhibitions on trade (e.g. Ine §39) may have facilitated the management of estates, resulting, for example, in the veneer of finds in the Central Lowlands, implying metro-centricity.

In the case of Ine §19 above, the apparently very substantial *wergeld,* 1,200 shillings, being four times the Kentish penalty, demands explanation. Either the Kentish shilling is worth four Wessex shillings (the conventional view), or, with the elapse of time, the penalty has increased as the gold content of the circulating medium has declined.[272] We know this deterioration occurred, though it was not linear.

The use of the term *sceatta,* meaning dues, is incorporated in *Ciricsceatta,* for example in Ine §4. The etymology of '*sceat*' and its derivatives is explained in considerable detail by Hines.[273] Naismith refers to I Æthelræd (978–1013 and 1014–16), *c.* 3,[274] which regulates exchanges by barter. This confirmation of the continued use of non-monetary exchange, can certainly be applied retrospectively. There are numerous examples of non-monetary penalties in Ine's laws: §14, 19, 37, 49, 59, 60, and particularly 70 which specifies the payment for every 10 hides, to be paid as food rent, on the death of one of the lord's men, *Table 1.* Not only does this encapsulate the tributary mode of surplus extraction but it provides a window on the rich variety of produce commonly available.

Numismatically, ignoring nomenclature, we are presented with three problems. First, the gold and silver coinages did not overlap, there was a gradual transition from the former to the latter, such that penalties in terms of two

[258] Oliver (2002, 25–36) demonstrated orality from linguistic grounds.
[259] It is worth noting that many of the laws and the structure of compensation are not dissimilar to pre-biblical codes e.g.: http://www.historyfiles.co.uk/KingListsMiddEast/MesopotamiaEshnunna.htm
[260] Hlothere and Eadric §15: A host has responsibility for a stranger's behaviour.
[261] Roebuck (2008, 125).
[262] See above on the relative values of shillings of Kent and Wessex.
[263] Preserved by attachment to the law code of Alfred the Great (871–99)
[264] Drew (1991). *Pactus Legis Salicae* 209 and 216–25.
[265] Sawyer (2013, 46–47).
[266] Roebuck (2008, 107).
[267] Hines (2010, 162).
[268] Scull (1990, 183–215). At the Richard Hall Symposium, 12st February 2016, Gareth Williams argued convincingly that English weights were not standardized but were merchant-specific. See *fn.* 1081.
[269] Hines (2010, 154–56).
[270] Garmonsway (1953): '694. In this year the Kentishmen came to terms with Ine and gave him 'thirty thousands' because they had burnt Mul to death.' Also: *MEC* (1986, 186). [Michael Metcalf *pers. comm.*]
[271] See *Case Study 1—York and its environs new.*
[272] Hines (2010, 159–61). *MEC* (1986, 157).
[273] Hines (2014, 7–17) which concluded: "'sceatta'…is a neologism some 200 years old now and long enough established to be counted an acceptable term."
[274] Naismith (2012, 290 *fn.* 228) (Liebermann I, 220).

denominations are paradoxical. Second, the circulation of gold, probably expanded during the seventh century—as the gold content declined the penetration beyond the wealthy élite may have grown—but these penalties extend well beyond the social élite. Third, the volume of recovered gold, especially relating to Æthelbert's reign is relatively minute—there is less than a handful of 'man-worths'[275] for the entire seventh century with only the Crondall (Hampshire) hoard approximating to this size.[276] We must assume that most gold was recycled. However, the recovered volume of *sceattas* does bear a better proportionality to the scale of fines enacted. Perhaps these penalties should not be taken too literally but as equivalences.[277]

The legal framework, described above, indicates that coinage was as much an institution of governance as the law itself, providing the foundation for the southern development of a *burh* system with strategically sited, fortified, commercial, administrative, minting and religious centres. Documentation survived better in the south but it would not be unreasonable to assume that northern judicial practices were not far removed from southern legislation.

A different perspective on monetisation in Northumbria may be gained by a review of the production and use of coinage in neighbouring Southumbria. Frankish coinage is not considered as there was no comparable lapse in production after the end of the Roman Empire, but the use of the *sceat* in Jutland can be contrasted with Northumbria, though the monetization of the remainder of Scandinavia from the tenth century is outside the scope of this study.[278]

2.9 Southumbria

In the period of study, when polity boundaries were fluid, the evolution of northern and southern English coinage were asynchronous.[279] The York gold shilling had greater longevity and better organisation than its southern counterparts, with the possible exception of Eadbald's coinage, but the southern primary early-penny phase is earlier and longer, if less literate. The secondary early-penny phases overlap for less than two decades, parting company with the introduction of the southern broad penny. The uniquely Northumbrian *styca* compounds the separation. However, a comparison of north and south, at these points of departure, is relevant.

The historical background of Southumbria has been thoroughly discussed in the numismatic literature, including Blackburn, North, Blackburn and Dumville, *C&H,* Naismith, *EMMH* and *MEC,* so will not be repeated here.[280]

The process of the early Anglo-Saxon re-introduction of coinage in the seventh century, initially emulating Merovingian types, shows control in the north is stronger in the gold and primary early-penny coinages. The main southern *wics* account for the more substantial trading varieties—for example, Series R, Ipswich, H, Hamwic—but other than identifying the 'official issues', which were themselves heavily imitated, the organisation of the huge variety of smaller, often eclectic, emissions remains uncertain. What is clear, is that during the last 10 years of the Southumbrian *sceattas,* in the 740s, there was a significant debasement.[281] Economic activity could have gradually declined due to Merovingian control of the Frisian *emporia.* Metcalf reminds us that 'the purchasing power of silver in eighth-century England was more like that of gold today...Probably, the monetary sector of the economy did not reach so far down into low-value transactions.'[282]

Naismith's perceptive analysis of the coinage of the southern English kingdoms covering the period, 757–865, when the northern and southern coinages diverged, is informative.[283] Its relevance here is constrained not so much because Northumbrian designs converged into a single type at least a century before Southumbrian uniformity[284] nor because the south was more fractured, but more because it was the unique, high-volume, low-denomination, *styca* that catalysed northern monetization.

There seems to have been a delay between Offa's early reformed coinage,[285] whose output 'remained trifling',[286] and the introduction of the main volume of the light coinage, which probably lasted from around 782 to its replacement by the heavy coinage from 792.[287] Coins were minted in East Anglia,[288] London and Canterbury, which issued both royal and episcopal coins as well as Kentish

[275] A *manwyrþ* (Lendinara, 1997, Appendix A, *hapax legomena,* 224), *manbot* or *wergeld* of 100 shillings. Charles-Edwards (1997, 175–77). Possibly, *sceattas* were merely the unit of account measuring the extent of the blood feud. Paying cash would not have had the desired 'negative interaction' (Charles-Edwards (1997, 172). Lendinara (1997, 217) suggested there was sufficient gold coin in circulation but Scull and Hines (Discussion 241–42) rightly dispute this. Ausenda (242) stated 'wergilds are fixed in some kind of unit of account (242).

[276] *MEC* (1986, 126).

[277] Alcock (2003, 122–23), regarding the seventh century: 'If blood was shed during an annual hosting...a lot of money must have changed hands every year.' Alcock felt that the church's tempering of the drive for blood vengeance would be ineffectual.

[278] See Skre (2008, 2011 and 2015) for Scandinavian monetisation beyond the range of this study.

[279] Southumbrian phasing has been aligned with Northumbrian in *Dataset 1, Periodization.*

[280] Blackburn (ed.) (1986). North (1994). Blackburn and Dumville (1998). *C and H* (2006). Naismith (2010, 2011, 2012 and 2017).

[281] Blackburn (2003, 35). Metcalf (2009, 5).

[282] Metcalf (2009, 6).

[283] Naismith (2012).

[284] Arguably as late as the lunettes coinage of the mid-ninth century. Lyons and Mackay (2007, 71).

[285] Metcalf (2009, 10) persisted in Chick's assertion (1997, 56) that the early coins inscribed MANG, are the work of a moneyer of this extraordinary name, rather than a contraction of *Merciorum Anglorum,* as I believe, although Metcalf later admits that Mang is an 'improbably named moneyer'.

[286] Metcalf (2009, 30).

[287] Metcalf (2009, 8–9). Chick (2011, 188).

[288] The precise whereabouts are uncertain; there may have been one or two mints.

coins for 10 years after Offa lost the battle of Otford in 776. The heavy coinage in the last four years of Offa's reign sets a southern precedent for both metrology and use of the three-line reverse.[289]

In comparison, the northern early-penny coinage continued with its minimal and conservative iconography; there is no sense of further convergence of its symbolic, administrative and economic rôles; these were already convergent. As with the southern coinage 'Stability was surely the primary message.'[290] The joint regal/episcopal issues of the north commence before those of the Archbishops of Canterbury, Jaenberht and Æthelheard, and their Mercian overlords, Offa and Coenwulf.[291] When the moneyers' names do appear in the north from Ælfwald I onwards (admittedly a couple of decades after moneyers have become responsible for the integrity of the coinage in the south)[292] they are not known to have any influence beyond the operation of the mint. Clearly, the Northumbrian monarchs did not exploit, for their own purposes, symbolism in their coinage—there is no portraiture[293]—though the cult of the cross is as ubiquitous in the north as the south.[294] There is no evidence that the northern monarchs profited overtly from production of *sceattas*. In the 30 years between Eadberht's death in 758 and Æthelred I's named-moneyer coinage, both northern and southern coinages show signs of distress.[295] There was no profit from minting to be had in the lean years after Lindisfarne and one struggles to imagine that the manufacture of *stycas* was a lucrative source of mint revenue.[296,297]

Judging by the continuing scarcity of southern gold shillings, this was an élite coinage, though volumes increased and became better organised with the reduction of gold content.[298] Prolific sites, such as Rendlesham and Coddenham, show that usage focussed on major commercial or administrative locations, though single losses are thinly but widely spread. *Graph 1* illustrates the chronological dispersal of finds at the main sites with the wics skewed to early usage and only Flixborough, as would be expected, showing *styca* finds.

The proportion of Frisian *sceattas* (such as the Series E Kloster-Barthe types) circulating in England falls from around a fifth of the total volume in the Primary phase,[299] which indicates a healthy balance of payments surplus mainly generated by exported wool, until around 740, when there is a paucity of secondary Frisian emissions (the Series E Franeker types).[300] This implies either a drastic reduction in trade or more effective recycling. The latter is more probable in Northumbria and East Anglia where inscriptions on the reformed coinages of Eadberht and Beonna, respectively, indicate regal monetary control and the number of finds implies buoyant trade.

Blackburn demonstrated comparable patterns of peak coin use in the first half of the eighth century with a steep and prolonged decline for the broad penny, at Hamwic (129 coins, *Graph* 1.2), Tilbury (146), Royston (near, 95), Bawsey (124), South Lincolnshire (Heckington/Garwick, 141) and Hollingbourne (39).[301] He associated this pattern, and the deterioration of the early-penny alloy in the second quarter of the eighth century, to variations in Continental silver supplies.[302]

Tight monetary control may be responsible for the near absence of Offa's coinage from Northumbria, other than the Aiskew, North Yorkshire, hoard including fifteen pennies of Offa and his contemporaries.[303] In contrast, in Southumbria, secondary *sceattas* are heavily intermingled as were the subsequent broad pennies,[304] constrained only slightly by political boundaries.[305] Whereas numerous locations could have acted as early-penny mints (or were possibly temporary bases for peripatetic moneyers), after the mid-eighth century, mints (both regal and ecclesiastical) were consolidated in York, Ipswich, London, Canterbury, Rochester and Southampton/Winchester.[306]

The link between the demise of the Southumbrian early-penny coinage and the introduction of Offa's broad penny may be provided by the Middle Harling hoard of proto-pennies of Beonna of East Anglia (749–60), which also contained some late *sceattas*.[307] Archibald argued that Beonna's small module coins date from towards the end of his reign, which seems to indicate a rich vein of minting in otherwise distressed circumstances. Together the English emissions from now on 'establish a tradition of explicit royal patronage that survives to this day.'[308]

[289] North (1994, 26).
[290] Naismith (2012, 66).
[291] An interesting point on iconography, is that portraits of kings are in profile and ecclesiastical figures (Wulfred of Canterbury, Wigmund of York) are typically facing. This shows what Naismith (2012, 68) referred to as 'serene disconnection.' See also Naismith (2014b).
[292] Ignoring what may be moneyers' names on some southern *sceattas*.
[293] The enthroned/genuflecting Archbishop Ecgberht aside.
[294] Wood (2008).
[295] *Fn.* 281.
[296] Though this low denomination 'widow's mite' meant that even the relatively poor could be taxed in coin.
[297] Woodman (2012, 40, *fn.* 101) implied that the archbishops profited from *stycas* issued analogously to what is prescribed in Æthelstan's law §14.2 (Attenborough, 1922 [2012], 135).
[298] Metcalf (1993–94, 29–84)
[299] Metcalf (2003, 40)
[300] The inclusion of a coin attributed to Milo of Trier, dates the Goting Kliff hoard from the island of Föhr, which is largely composed of Franeker types, to *c.* 748–*c.* 750. Metcalf (2009, 16). The Series E Franeker types, constituted a substantial issue, though significantly smaller than the Kloster-Barthe phase.
[301] Blackburn (2003, 26–29).
[302] Blackburn (2003, 34–35).
[303] Found 2006. Chick (2010 no. 140e 124), note especially, for its exquisite preservation, the penny of Cynethryth, PAS YORYM-731473. This hoard must have been a purse lost by a traveller and does not necessarily imply circulation of Offan pennies in the north.
[304] To be clear, not *sceattas* and pennies with each other.
[305] Metcalf (2009, 30). The coins of Jænberht, Archbishop of Canterbury, are largely restricted to south of the Thames.
[306] Naismith (2102, 7).
[307] Archibald. Note that a Wilræd coined for both Beonna and Offa. Metcalf (2009, 21).
[308] Naismith (2012, 8).

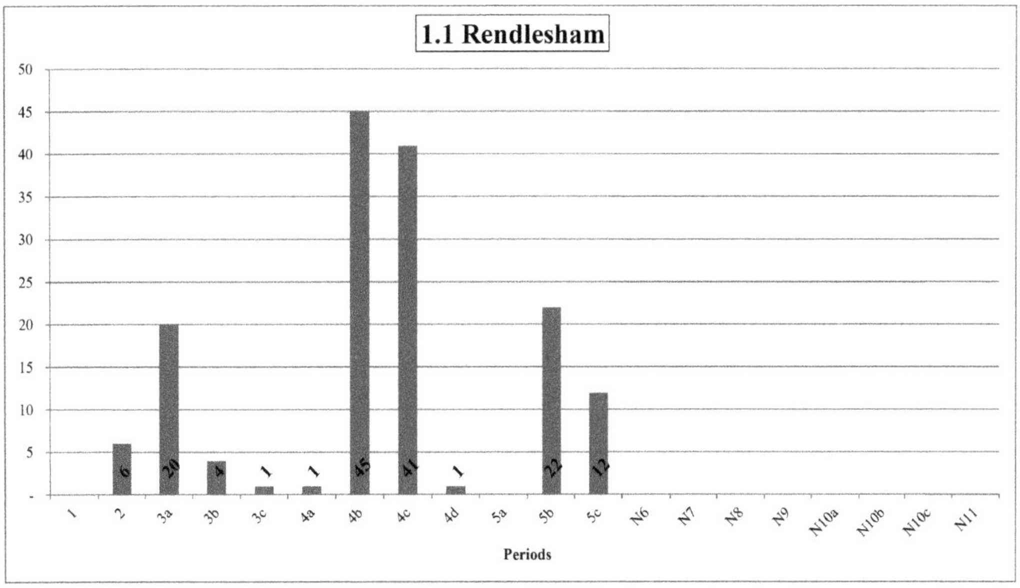
1.1 Rendlesham
50
45
40
35
30
25
20
15
10
5
-
6
20
4
1
1
45
41
1
22
12
1
2
3a
3b
3c
4a
4b
4c
4d
5a
5b
5c
N6
N7
N8
N9
N10a
N10b
N10c
N11
Periods

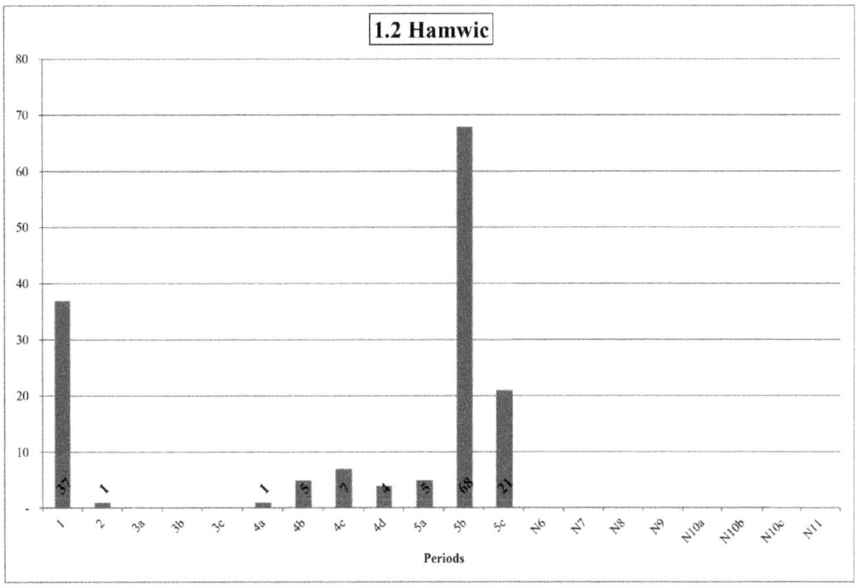
1.2 Hamwic
80
70
60
50
40
30
20
10
-
37
1
1
5
7
4
5
68
21
Periods

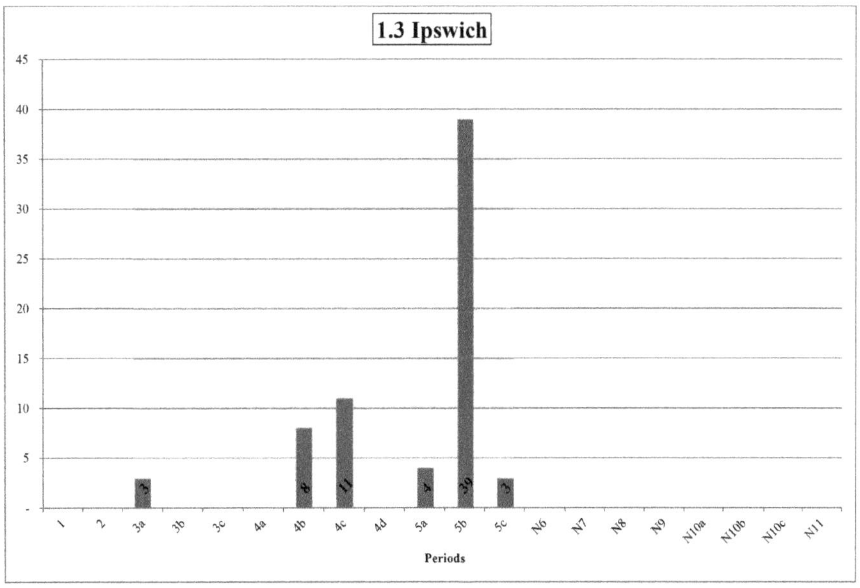
1.3 Ipswich
45
40
35
30
25
20
15
10
5
-
3
8
11
4
39
3
Periods

Graphs 1

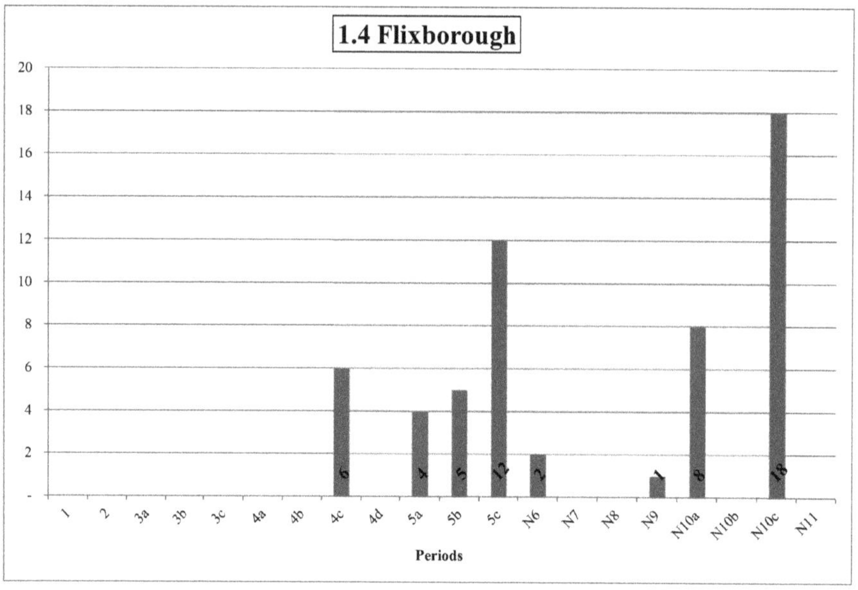

Graphs 1: Site finds by period arranged regionally by weighted average of peak activity, Southumbria i. Sources: *Datasets 1* and *8*. Numerical axis varies.

Whereas, in England, Merovingian coin finds are scarce, widely scattered and from a broad variety of mints, Carolingian coins are very rare.[309] Similarly, English coins are rare in Carolingian Francia, showing a limited level of cross-channel trade during what appears to be a recession,[310] from *c.* 750 to *c.* 782, if not to the end of Offa's reign.[311] Presumably, foreign coins were rapidly recycled.

Aspects of southern monetization are mentioned below but there is little more to be gained by further investigation of the southern coinages itself after Offa because a second point of departure—the introduction of the *styca*—renders comparison unproductive, though the question of interchangeability of southern penny and northern *styca* remains.

Further insight into the process of monetization may be gained by study of the process on the near Continent, in those countries not monetized from Roman times but which may be regarded as participating in the North Sea trading zone.

2.10 Scandinavia

The above review of Southumbrian monetization, gives some insight to the process in England. While trading partners in Francia and Scandia were both influential, the former remained monetized throughout the period under review; a contrast between the latter and Northumbria may be instructive.

From the eighth century, southern Scandinavia is characterized by the development of several trading and manufacturing centres, equivalent to the Southumbrian wics. Ribe is discussed below as *sceattas* are present here but not at other sites such as Hedeby or Birka.

Ribe is among the seven eighth/ninth-century nodal points identified by Sindbæk for having a long-distance, material culture including glass and ceramic sherds, beads, Badorf- and Tating-ware, and fragments of Mayen-basalt quernstones in common with the other nodal points he identified.[312]

Importation by regular travellers distinguishes these sites from local markets. 'The conceptualisation of spatial, social or economic relations as a network, continuously being formed by a heterogeneous assemblage of actors, offers a more organic approach to prehistoric trade and its location than the previous perspectives that assigned agency in advance to external force or internal social process.'[313] Later, royal supervision led to fortification, mints and seats of administration (*cf.* the English burhs).[314] Secure nodal points, 'of an incipient urban character'[315] occur where topography requires trans-shipment and storage—here long-distance traders could meet.

The recent numismatic work on the Ribe site is largely that of Feveile.[316] The exceptional dendrochronology and artefact-rich stratification has significance well beyond this site. The attribution of Series X, known, perhaps

[309] *Plate 3ii, figure* 10.
[310] Allowing that modern vocabulary is admissible.
[311] Metcalf (2009, 18). To what extent the mutual trade embargo in the 790s, following unsuccessful marriage discussions involving the offspring of Offa and Charlemagne, contributed to this is unknown. Naismith (2012, 36–37).

[312] Sindbæk (2007, 119–32).
[313] Sindbæk (2007, 120).
[314] Sindbæk (2007, 128). He also mentioned that Badorf-ware occurs on contemporary sites in England (121).
[315] Sindbæk (2007, 129).
[316] *Graph* 3.2, illustrates the chronological dispersal of finds.

inaccurately,[317] as the 'Wodan/monster type', to Ribe, is incontrovertible.[318]

Feveile's chronology showed Series X to have been in use throughout the eighth century—confirming what numismatists had long suspected.[319] Northumbria and Denmark, therefore, shared a common currency in the second half of the eighth century—as did Southumbria and Francia with the broad penny.[320] However, the rarity of *sceattas* outside Ribe and in the hinterland, unlike Northumbria where distribution is widespread, shows that Denmark was not fully monetised economy—and that it was limited to trading transactions in the town. Insular copies of Series X occur in Northumbria and elsewhere. Indeed, through its coinage Ribe may have been a source of silver to its trading partners. The demise of Series X may not be unconnected with the attack on Lindisfarne and consequent loss of commercial confidence.

For the Vikings, trading and raiding were not serial, but rather parallel, activities. Their energetic expansionism, to both east and west, facilitated by superior vessels, rested on a domestic economy, the nature of which has been subject to much scholarship.[321] The impact on Northumbria was profound.[322] Commencing around 825,[323] and peaking in the 890s, hoarded Islamic dirhams mark the extent of the exchange of northern furs, honey, amber but especially slaves (northern Russians, Franks and predominantly Slavs) for silver dirhams in the *kufic* script.[324]

Arguably, hacksilver is more versatile than coinage, even that of low denomination, despite the inefficiency of constantly weighing bullion. This, and the Viking lack of minting experience, help explain the suspension of Northumbrian monetization in 866/7. Initially, the Vikings were generally careless of the premium value that coins and jewellery, when intact, held above the bullion value of the components. Such premium value reflects the confidence of the holder in the case of *fiat* money and the skill of execution in the case of jewellery—it is a work of artistry. As Myrhe pointed out,[325] artefacts have symbolic as well as functional purposes. Feveile described the Hogbrogard hoard of hacksilver,[326] indicating that wealth was now stored in this form and may have been used for barter. Perhaps, such was the extent of Viking plunder that they need not be concerned with aesthetic subtleties and all silver artefacts were tossed into the *hacksilver* trove to be reduced to bullion when required. It was only with permanent settlement that the Viking perspective changed.

This comparative overview of developments in Southumbria and Scandia, finalises the description of the theoretical background to Northumbrian coinage. To complete Part One of this study, a hypothesis of monetization is presented below and consideration given to the historical and economic context of the evolution of the coinage to introduce a periodization. A more practical approach is pursued in Part Two through the compilation and analysis of recorded finds and their locations.

2.11 Synthesis

The main formative propositions drawn from the first part of this chapter include Hodges' ritual model with temporal and spatial continuity of settlement and Skre's post-substantivism. To this can be added Blair's promotion of minsters as economic drivers. These rest, literally, on more solid ground than the earlier debates concerning substantivism and formalism, embeddedness and Mediterranean power struggles. The formation of primitive and peasant markets is not of direct relevance as this is a study of the *re*-commencement of coinage in an area previously fully monetized by the Romans.[327]

Indeed, what remains of relevance to Northumbria from this high-level theorising? 'Top-down' models cannot cater adequately for the subtleties of local circumstances; the picture is inevitably more complex than can be condensed into a unified theory; there is no binary choice between substantivism and anachronistic formalism.

To recapitulate the first part of the chapter, use of the remaining stock of Roman coinage declined as barter became prevalent, especially rurally. Before the end of the fifth century, coinage was absent, and transactions were settled in barter with deficiencies remedied by informal credit. The élite may have participated in gift exchange but this involved social obligation not economic advancement. Reciprocity, the currency of co-operation, probably played a key rôle in sustaining travellers but the obligation was as much communal as personal. Such social obligation would have diminished as coinage increasingly led to economic activities being treated as priced transactions. That prices replaced values is not to be underestimated in terms of social relationships.

[317] Gannon (2016).
[318] Feveile (2008, 63). *Pers. comm.* Michael Metcalf to Mike Bonser, 18th October 1992: 'In Stockholm I was very rudely attacked by Professor Brita Malmer over the attribution of Series X to Ribe.'
[319] Feveile (2008, 58) showed that other than the 216 *sceattas* found at Ribe, 87 in the Föhr hoard and 10 at Dankirke (probably two small hoards), only between one and three *sceattas* were found at six other archaeological sites.
[320] Though differences in the mean weight of surviving specimens of the English penny and Merovingian *denier* implies that these would only have exchanged by weight not tale.
[321] *P&U* (2003). *SEVA* (2007). *SEMSS* (2011). Blackburn (2011).
[322] *Graph 2* illustrates the chronological dispersal of finds at three Viking sites—clearly dominated by *stycas*.
[323] Coinciding with the Hedeby coinage but of vastly greater volume.
[324] To *c.* 800, over half of the dirhams come from the mints of Baghdad and Tehran. After Kabul fell to the Moslems, Tashkent and Samarkand are the main mints, with Merv featuring until *c.* 870 (Metcalf, 1997, 295). Spufford (1988, 65). 80–90 per cent of hoarded dirhams in Scandinavia are tenth and early eleventh century (Metcalf 1997, 316). It has been demonstrated that armlets and hacksilver consist of ninth- and tenth-century dirhams. Metcalf (1997, 329).
[325] Myhre (1993, 184–204).
[326] The 61st International Sachsensymposion, held in the Museum Sønderjylland Arkæologi Haderslev, 11–16 September 2010.
[327] There was no Brigantean Iron Age coinage.

The second part of the chapter not only describes the literature on which this study builds but also briefly summarizes recent studies based on PAS data, showing that it can be deployed effectively, beyond type analyses, in characterising sites and identifying change over time. Moreover, clusters of sites can be grouped regionally to give meaningful interpretations despite the biases in the data.

This validates the methodology of the current study, which builds on previous studies chiefly by interrogating two largely underutilised datasets—*CKN* and *VASLE*. It parallels and strengthens existing scholarship by evaluating these datasets of coins and portable artefacts by parish, grouped regionally (*Map* 2), in a chronological framework, while acknowledging limitations. The propinquity of a medium of and artefacts for exchange demonstrate monetization within and between settlements.

2.12 Illustrations—Chapters 1 and 2

Figure 1: The pseudo-Imperial *tremissis* and its imitations. Left: Anastasius (491–518) gold *tremissis*, Constantinople. Sear 8.[328] Centre: Theoderic, King of the Ostrogoths (493–526), gold *tremissis* in the name of Anastasius, Rome. MEC 114–15. Ex Goodacre, 1986. Right: Lombards: gold *tremissis*, in the name of Maurice Tiberius (582–602); perhaps Milan or Pavia. MEC 301–04. Found near Driffield[329] (All courtesy James Booth)

Figure 2: Sculpture: Dewsbury and Otley

[328] *Curio* 9, YNS Newsletter June 2014

[329] Also illustrated at *Figure* 6.

3

Hypothesis

'The nitty-gritty of the individual coin finds may strike the reader as being of limited general historical interest. That idea is over-hasty. Short-cuts in the monetary interpretation of the sceattas, based on a selective reading of the evidence, can lead to errors of judgement and sometimes even a loss of common sense.'

Michael Metcalf (2011, 14).

Having synthesized various perspectives on monetization in chapter 2, this chapter provides a practical definition of terms, an economic characterisation and, for Northumbria, a hypothesis of monetization.

3.1 Definition of Terms

Money is here regarded as that which is accepted in resolution of indebtedness. It is multi-functional, fungible and increasingly virtual. It includes barter, coinage, bullion and credit. Coin is pragmatically characterized as a subset of hard money[330] typically on a small flan, authorised and authenticated by *imprimatur*.

As coins were introduced, prices were applied to increasingly inexpensive and common goods, services and skills. This was a gradual process of monetization as coin penetrated further into economic life with the steady long-term fall in value of the sole circulating denomination. In a non-monetary society, the wayfarer relied on social reciprocity, a communal obligation. It may be assumed that there was a consequent decline in such reciprocity as obligations became quantified in money terms, and it is only in this sense that there was a shift from substantivism to formalism, otherwise the latter should be regarded as a construct of capitalism. The impact on social relationships, and empowerment (rather than democratization), as prices replaced values, are candidates for future research.

For the purposes of this study, a narrow, practical definition of monetization is used, as more abstruse renderings tend to suffer from circular reasoning. It is a long-term process commencing with the élite use of coins and resulting in their use to settle regular daily transactions—the purchase of dietary staples and other necessities. It is characterized by close physical association of coins with portable artefacts and occurs when the use of coin, as a medium of exchange has percolated through all levels of society rather than satisfying just the substantial or special transactions of the social or religious élite, or in settling the trading accounts of merchants.

[330] 'Hard' as opposed to 'virtual'.

An economic definition of *wics* is preferred: they provide the necessary commercial, fiscal, monetary and judicial conditions for trade but these cover a spectrum and need not be homogenous—there may have been more controlled sites for processing or redistribution. *Sceattas* catalyse economic activity within and beyond such market places.[331]

3.2 The Early Medieval Economy

The provisional conclusions in previous chapters, concerning the economic anthropological context characterising late antiquity and early medieval England in general, and Northumbria in particular, can be summarized as follows:

Those relating generally to the economy and the nature of kingship include:

- England was insular but not isolated with well-established internal and external routes.[332] Tribal, coastal-inland and long-distance exchange is evident in the material culture before coinage.
- The potential for economic surplus from agriculture is manifest, at an early stage. There is no reason to believe that economic surplus from agriculture failed after the Romans departed. At a later stage, the material culture of the minsters evinced managed, even manipulated, the distribution of wealth.
- Successive waves of migration,[333] which sometimes involved 'decapitation' of the ruling élite, at least politically, or varying degrees of 'creative destruction',[334] characterize English history. The results of the 'Anglo-Saxon model', typified by a high level of innovation, judged broadly on the basis of long-term wealth creation, and the accumulation of social capital and governance, was economically successful.[335]
- Specialization, a signifier of surplus,[336] is present from an early stage.
- Art forms, also a signifier of surplus, including illuminated manuscripts and early medieval literature,[337] are present, often at a high level of achievement.

[331] Verhulst (2000, 110–13) characterised coastal *emporia* on the major Continental rivers emphasising the greater longevity of the former Roman cities. These *emporia* coincided with Frankish unity, 720–840. (Wickham, 2000, 347).

[332] Including Iron-Age trackways and Roman roads.

[333] Later, outward during colonization and industrialization.

[334] Schumpeter (1942).

[335] Though exploitative.

[336] Both settlement and capitalism are characterised by specialization.

[337] Hamer (1970). This includes not only the illuminated manuscripts but also the work of Cædmon, Stephanus, Bede and Alcuin.

As regards coinage and money:

- There is a near absence of archaeologically-visible 'primitive' monies.
- Special purpose issues exist but are of no direct economic significance, though they may be indicative of political or cultural affiliations. Coinage, in its various uses, probably remained familiar from Biblical parables, in folk memory and from Continental, especially Merovingian use, despite the century-long discontinuity.
- Gift exchange and reciprocity exist but have little bearing on the penetration of media of exchange.
- The high and fixed early Anglo-Saxon denominations would have necessitated the continuation of commodity money, barter and informal credit.
- The economic motivations to monetize are both commercial and fiscal.

In Naismith's view, there was a significant monetary component in the early Anglo-Saxon economy, though it was not fully monetized: he speculated that perhaps less than half of all transactions were satisfied in currency and possibly far less in the mid-eighth and mid-ninth centuries: 'Coins, to put it bluntly, were not indispensable. They were a convenience, not a necessity, and their absence could be sustained by the economy.'[338] On the other hand, he acknowledged that there was a substantial circulating stock of coin, the product of efficient mints, and that the volume of loss cannot be attributed to élite gift-giving and merchants trading luxuries.

3.3 Hypothesis of Monetization

The synthesis of formative propositions at section 2.11 can be complemented by a hypothesis of monetization. Northumbria follows a simple model of re-emerging monetization in three phases, the degree of penetration being dependent on metal type. In this *Olympic* regime of gold, silver and bronze, the first phase is characterized by the élite use of precious metal, the second by the mercantile use of intrinsic-value metal and the third, and final, stage by the domestic use of base alloy.

3.3.1 Élite Use of Gold

As agrarian practices were managed to produce surplus, commodity money or barter was likely to have been used regularly in the lower echelons of the root-and-branch network. Commencing probably by the late third quarter of the sixth century, imported gold coins were being lost in Northumbria. Recoveries to date have been largely of Merovingian *tremisses* but one can expect further Byzantine and other (e.g. Lombardic or Visigothic) discoveries.[339] By the fourth quarter of the sixth century, at the hub, the élite would have routinely used imported gold *tremisses*, but not always for monetary purposes. By mid-seventh century, Anglo-Saxon gold shillings,[340] commodity money and barter would have been in use simultaneously, in a stratified monetary system.

In conventional numismatics,[341] the relatively high gold content of the York shilling has placed its start before the mid-seventh century. My research anchors this firmly between 627 and 633. Transactional use may not have been the predominant purpose of gold coins—alternative uses include gift exchange, taxation, propaganda, votive and funerary offerings, ornamentation and ostentatious display.

Around the final quarter of the seventh century, as the trans-Saharan gold supply waned, the denominational value of the gold shilling had been reduced intentionally by managed dilution of the gold content. The gradual reduction in the precious metal content, which gives broad structure to the chronology of these emissions,[342] results, around the 670s,[343] in the 'pale-gold' shillings of Pada and Vanimundus, containing as little as 4 per cent gold.[344] This decline is inversely proportional to, and a consequence of, the growing volume of circulating medium. Merovingian gold production was truncated before such dilution.

3.3.2 Mercantile Use of Silver

Currency uniformity required for entry to the North Sea trading zone led to the replacement of the pale-gold shilling by the silver *sceat*. Recent scientific discussion on the chronology of grave goods has resulted in this replacement being advanced to the 660s,[345] arguably predating the Merovingian move to the silver *denier*.

Recovery statistics show that, as silver entirely replaced gold, recovery statistics show that a step change occurred in production. However, the intrinsic value of the *sceat* remained relatively high. Even were one to surmise, as a working assumption, that it equated perhaps to a day's pay (at minimum wages, *fn.* 801), the equivalent today would be around £50, with no small change to facilitate transactions.

The *sceattas* of the north—in Northumbria, Frisia and Denmark—are sustained into the early ninth century. The mercantile early-penny coinage continued in the south until Offa reformed the currency by introducing the broad

[338] Naismith (2012, 291).

[339] Meols and Rendlesham among other sites have produced low-denomination Byzantine coppers and Yapham and Rendlesham counterfeit tremisses implying monetisation.

[340] The Bulmer Beck daisy reverse gold shilling is Southumbrian (*Figure* 11).

[341] Williams and Hook (2013, 55–70).

[342] The reduction is non-linear, varying with such factors as gold supply and source, and the assaying technology (X-ray fluorescence) not wholly reliable in that an atomic surface measurement may not be representative.

[343] Hines and Bayliss (2013, 509–12).

[344] Williams and Hook (2013, 55–70).

[345] Hines and Bayliss (2013, 509–12). See *fn.* 53. The debate between the conventional numismatic chronology and the Baynesian carbon-dating of inhumations does not impinge directly on the coinage of Aldfrith as his regnal dates are accepted. However, the southern coinage is now regarded as relatively earlier.

penny, following Carolingian precedent.[346] However, Offa's initial issues were of light broad pennies and the heavier, broader pence were not issued in significant numbers until later in his reign,[347] following what seems to be an economic depression. Thus, it may not have been so conspicuous that Northumbria did not follow suit but retained the small module *sceat* as did Frisia and Denmark. There is presently only slight evidence of mixing of the northern and southern currencies.

If the *sceat* represents a day's pay, barter, credit and commodity money would still have been required by the peasantry and for small transactions. Gold is virtually absent from the eighth century to the fourteenth.

In the case studies which follow, in considering numismatic accumulations recovered from individual sites, the interpretation of both local and long-distance trading relationships rests largely on the sources of the *sceattas* in the circulating medium. The identification of sources has chiefly been achieved by Metcalf, in *T&S*. The greater the mix of varieties, the broader the potential trading connections *allowing for condition* i.e. only pristine coins can be thought to have come reasonably directly from source. This is assumed throughout, but the evidence must be treated cautiously. Moreover, one must be mindful that long-distance trade was not the sole driver, 'the wealth that under-pinned large-scale demand was essentially the wealth of the landowning aristocracy.'[348]

3.3.3 Domestic Use of Base Metal: Copper Alloy

The 793 Viking raid on Lindisfarne led not only to loss of life and accumulated wealth,[349] but also to a breakdown of social[350] and particularly commercial confidence, after generations of North Sea trade. The subsequent break in Northumbrian coinage,[351] until re-introduced by Eanred, possibly between two and four decades later, indicates a long-term recession. The absence of northern Annals from the start of the ninth century leaves the timing of Eanred's reformed coinage, eventually evolving to the base *styca*, unrecorded. There can be no doubt that this small value 'widow's mite', given the random mix and widespread distribution of finds in rural and urban sites of varying regal, ecclesiastical, mercantile and secular status and function, in Northumbria and well beyond, in hoards and as single finds, represented full monetization at all levels of northern society. That the single most prolific *styca* moneyer, Monne, produced more coins than all 11 'Group A' moneyers of Eanred's initial silver-alloy period (*Dataset 3. 'Group A' Moneyers*) may indicate that the take-off into 'sustainable' monetization in the north occurred only when silver was replaced by zinc in the alloy. Indeed, the author favours the view that Eanred's silver-alloy issues were an attempt to perpetuate the *sceat* with the *styca* proper commencing only with the complete replacement of silver.

Presumably, this occurred only after a further lengthy cessation in production, given that only Æthelweard of the 'Group A' members survived credibly to the brass phase.[352] This moneyer, produced coins for Eanbald II but was more prolific for Wigmund, implying that he enjoyed both Episcopal favour and longevity.

It may be assumed that informal credit was necessary, for economic lubrication, during lapses in coin production. This need for credit may have increased when the silver emissions were discontinued and receded when production in brass was commenced. Implicit in an ongoing use of credit is a degree of trust between debtor and creditor. This need for economic confidence was not removed by the introduction of a *fiat*, i.e. brass, currency, but transferred to a different, vertical, axis—between state and subject. It would not be difficult to envisage, *post hoc,* an agrarian economy, subject to exogenous shock, wherein a period of recovery of up to three decades or more—a working lifetime in early medieval times—is the norm. The periodicity in *Table 2* falls into this cyclical pattern with the years of famine, exceeding those of plenty (181 to 77). Perhaps the recovery phase was prolonged as credit sources were also fractured by shock. In the absence of historic records, this is difficult to demonstrate. Northumbria was a kingdom of high literacy, especially among an established clerical class, many of whom resided at minsters, which provided local economic foci—and, presumably, a degree of protection for the necessary documentation of estate management. It is inconceivable that recording of transactions,[353] and any consequent indebtedness, was absent, but it may have been palimpsestic. In other circumstances, such recording of credit had led to banking.[354]

To push speculation one small step further, given the absence of a denomination higher than this 'widow's mite' it is not surprising that large hoards were accumulated, possibly in ecclesiastical treasuries. However, for high value transactions, which continue among the élite whatever the situation for the average subject, it is impractical for huge quantities of *stycas* to be deployed.

[346] Chick (2010, 32).
[347] Around the time of the Viking attack on Lindisfarne.
[348] Wickham (2005, 819).
[349] The potential of Lindisfarne as a target may have been evident from the extent of its animal husbandry. *Fn.* 1335.
[350] Garrison (2001, 21) contrasted the volume of Alcuin's surviving writings, protected in Charlemagne's court, with that of his York predecessors, presumably plundered or destroyed. After the catastrophes of 796—the murder of Æthelred (18th April), the magnates' desertion of Osbald (18th May), the deaths of Archbishop Eanbald, Offa (26th July) of Mercia and his heir Ecgfrith—Alcuin moved his library from York to Tours (24), which in itself would have exacerbated Northumbria's loss.
[351] Whether dating from 793 or Æthelred I's murder in 796.
[352] Cynewulf and Eadwulf may also have minted later.
[353] Garrison recorded examples from the court of Charlemagne by Einhard (1999, 94–95).
[354] Davies (1993, 70–73). Garrison suggested that such records may have been ephemeral though some 'voices from the garbage dump'—wax-tablets or rune-sticks—may recover what was not intentionally preserved. (1999, 70–71).

Table 2: Northumbrian Minting Activity and Inactivity

Mint activity	Relative inactivity/ importation	Years (approx)		Reason
627–33		6		York gold shilling
	633–85		52	gold/silver interval
685–704		19		Aldfrith
	704–37		33	Incompetent succession
737–58		21		Eadberht's *renovatio*
	758–88		30	Third quarter C8 recession
788–93		5		Ælfwald & Æthelred I
	793–825?		32	post-Lindisfarne depression
825?–829?		5		Eanred's silver-alloy
	829?–837?		7	post-Dore interval
837?–867		39		Base stycas
	867–94		27	*micel here*
Totals		77	181	

Might contemporary local imitations of the *solidus* of Louis the Pious serve a rôle in high value transactions?[355]

Returning to hard fact, there is such a profusion of *styca* finds that they often fail to be registered by less scrupulous finders,[356] which may result in statistical distortion. Finds occur on numerous archaeological sites, both locally and often beyond Northumbria, *Map 1.*[357]

To summarize, the coinage shows a sequence of metals; there were no parallel issues in different metals. However, this mono-metallism was not entirely by design. When silver replaced gold, coin may have lost its attraction as an élite object for social and ritual use; when copper alloy was current, there was little precious metal to be had. This is borne out by the paucity of eighth-century finds of gold coin and of ninth-century finds of gold and silver coin.[358] Does this paucity reflect the real situation and more broadly, is the picture reconstructed from finds representative? Monetization was both an urban-led process wherein the *sceat* was integral to trade in York and a royal-led process requiring coin for court transactions.[359]

Some mention needs be made of the monetary situation in Northumbria after the fall of York. While the Viking presence would have deterred some traditional economic activities, others would have been stimulated by the requisites of the *micel here. Graph 2* shows loss of Period N10 *stycas* at Viking camps; Torksey and Littleborough are strongest in Period N10a, though the latter falls off far more sharply, and London is stronger in Period N10c. It is plausible that after a period of disruption, economic activity may have resumed, even at a higher volume, but without coined money. The Vikings were rich in looted precious metal, but probably did not feel the need to use formalized, coined money until raiders settled as traders broadcasting their new-found faith. Hack-silver and -gold sufficed as fungible bullion at least until the adoption of the broad penny in the mid-890s, although a dual economy operated considerably longer as demonstrated by the hack-silver content in such hoards as that found in the 'Vale of York' hoard.[360] In rural areas, pre-existing commodity monies had most likely continued in use alongside *stycas*, and would now have persisted in their absence. It would be an exaggeration to describe this as de-monetization; economic exchange was sustained but probably with little use of coin—there are a few finds of pennies and *deniers*—for 25 years. Northumbria had witnessed such cyclical disjuncture previously, *Table 2* and had improvised successfully.

Having now established a hypothesis of monetization, the next chapter creates the chronological framework for the subsequent data analysis.

[355] Grierson (1951, 11), Andrews (1988, 71–72), Blackburn (2007). Coupland (paper presented at Leeds IMC, July 2016). See section 6.4.2.1. The consensus is that these are Viking imitations of Frisian origin.

[356] Such as the purported 430 *stycas* found in recent years at Bolton Percy [*pers comm.* C. Best].

[357] Pirie (1996, 18). See also PAS mapping at http://tracemedia.co.uk/lostchange/

[358] Abdy and Williams (2006) and Blackburn (2007). On the other hand, when gold was replaced the unit volume and probably total value of the circulating medium increased. When copper-alloy *stycas* circulated, silver was available. These indicate intentional monetary policy.

[359] But the operation of a primitive quantity theory of money in the hinterland is facilitated only by a lower denomination. Irving Fisher's 1911 equation, MV=PT, signifying an equivalence between the quantity of money current (M) allowing for its velocity of circulation (V) and the number of transactions (T) expressed in average prices (P), is arguably more applicable to unsophisticated monetary regimes than to modern systems.

[360] Agar (2011, 121–34)

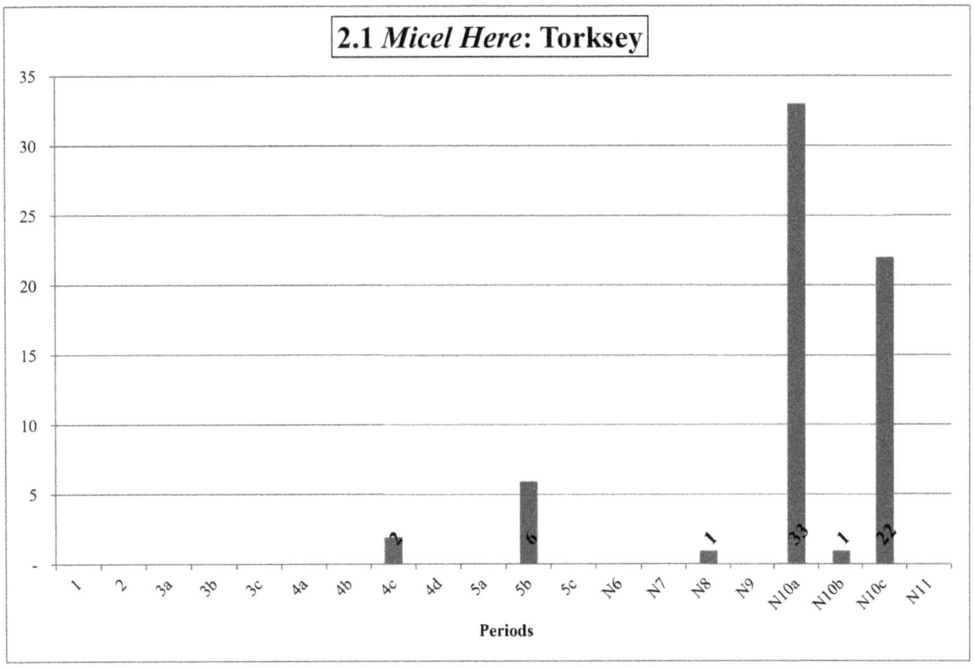

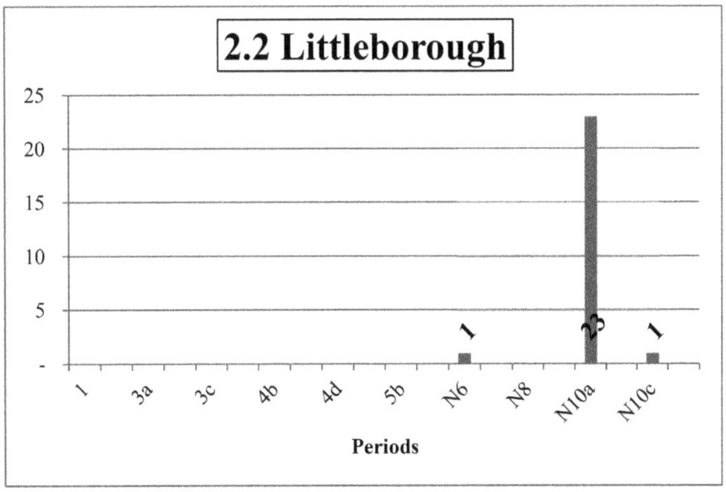

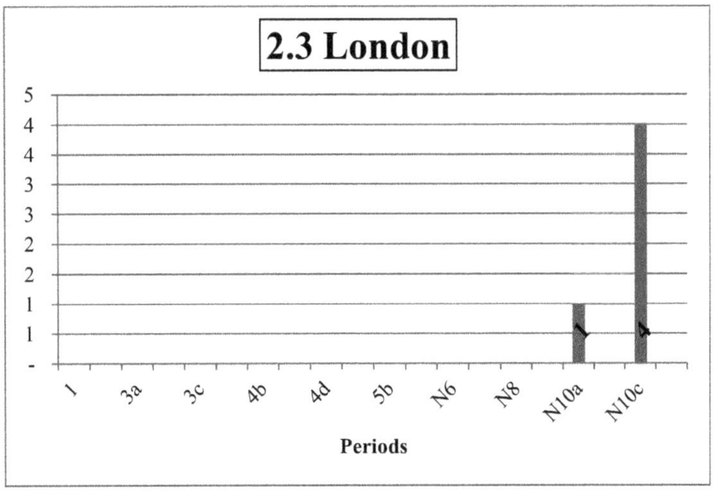

Graphs 2: Site finds by period arranged regionally by weighted average of peak activity, Southumbria ii. Sources: *Datasets 1* and *8*. Numerical axis varies.

4

Historical Framework for Northumbrian Monetization

'... barter introduced the use of money ... for a convenient place from whence to import what you wanted or to export what you had a surplus of being often at a distance, money necessarily made its way into commerce ...'

Aristotle, *Politics*[361]

Having developed a theoretical approach to monetization in Northumbria, and reviewed the situation in neighbouring polities, this chapter revises the periodization, as previously set out by Naylor,[362] in order to illustrate the way coinage complements the historical record for Northumbria, adding both texture and colour. Coinage is a versatile medium which operates well beyond the purely functional sphere, it constitutes an historical document, has decorative and sacral dimensions, is a major channel of political and religious propaganda and is rich in metaphor. However, in this study, it is coinage as a component of material culture which is the major concern.

This chapter starts with a periodization for Northumbrian coinage, based on the historical framework, with a focus on the alternating periods of mint activity and inactivity, *Table 2*.[363] Production is addressed at a denominational level, for gold, silver and base coinages separately showing how a coin of fixed module depreciated over time from noble to base metal in inverse relation to its utility. How the periodization established below is integral to the quantitative and qualitative methodologies is discussed in the introduction to Part Two, where an analytical resource, the database, is developed, which enables the periodic table to be populated by location, *Dataset 1*, giving an insight to coin use. Abstracted from this within the dataset are correlations to the normal distribution, a chronological analysis by region, a ranking of sites by the number of finds and an indication of the longevity of settlements.

4.1 Periodization

The arrangement proposed here builds on previous work by Sutherland, Metcalf, Abdy and Williams, and Blackburn, who have defined the phases of the gold coinage; Naylor and Allen are the most recent to focus on the York gold shilling. Rigold, Booth and Metcalf have contributed to classification of the northern *sceat*. Lyon and Pirie have led studies of the Northumbrian *styca*. Other contributors to the field are mentioned in chapter 2.[364]

[361] 384–22 BC. Quoted from Cribb (2004, 80).

[362] Naylor (2002, 239, Appendix 1).

[363] Kelleher (2012, 34) used the criteria of national re-coinage and weight reduction for medieval periodization.

[364] Sutherland (1948), Metcalf (1993–94), Abdy and Williams (2006). Blackburn (2007). Naylor and Allen (2014). Rigold (1977). Booth (1984). Metcalf (1993–94). Lyon (1957).

Reece defined and assessed the main phases of Romano-British coinage.[365] He argued that, at the end of the occupation, there was no point in locals producing copies to supplement the copper coin supply as there was no state authority to guarantee its exchange for precious metal—the copper coin was a token currency based on confidence not intrinsic value.[366] This is not a watertight argument as small denominational coins, such as Roman siliqua, seem to have facilitated exchange even in the absence of a governing authority.

To add definition to the successive phases of Northumbrian coinage and currency,[367] Reece's precedent of introducing 'easy stages' is followed.[368] The periods selected may be transitional or major phases, and some are sub-divided, though this approach must be used with caution as periods may overlap or, indeed, exhibit discontinuity. The current state of knowledge better supports periodization based on the date of issue rather than the period of use or time of loss. The former is more certain and the latter more subject to conjecture.[369] Moreover, it is local supply of currency which facilitates monetization—demand for coinage in the absence of local supply will draw coinage from elsewhere, but the specie flow is likely to be irregular and unreliable.

Dataset 1. Periodization gives the chronology of the successive phases as the local coinage evolved, briefly describes the current type and shows the comparative situation for Southumbria. This progression is explained in full below. The coinages current north and south of the Humber are similar to the end of the primary phase, allowing for Aldfrith's reign, 685–704, which constitutes the northern primary phase, to be contained within the somewhat longer southern primary phase, from the 670s to *c.* 710. The *lacunæ* which are apparent in the northern emissions,[370] and the consequent inflows filling these *vacua*, are not seen in the south, which makes the southern scheme simpler, especially with its far earlier migration to the broad penny. The southern broad penny did not emerge fully-formed but evolved through a couple of steps. *Sceat*-like coins were issued by Beonna of East Anglia[371] and possibly also by Offa[372] before his light penny averaging

[365] Reece (2002, 13–360).

[366] Reece (2002, 62–66).

[367] I differentiate here between native coinage and imported currency.

[368] Reece (2002, 13)

[369] See also *fn.* 742 and 743.

[370] *Table 2.*

[371] Archibald (1985 and 1995); the latter included the 1984 find at Whithorn (C13, Efe). Also Metcalf (1993–94, 601–07).

[372] Metcalf (1993–94, 608), Chick (2010, 31). Northover's electron probe micro-analysis in Metcalf (1993–94, 609–79) showed that Offa's pennies, which were of high purity, were not composed (in the main) of recycled *sceattas*.

1.16g[373] was issued possibly in the late 770s.[374] The heavy penny was inaugurated with Æthelheard's appointment to the See of Canterbury in 793, reflecting (though only partially) a change in the metrology of the Frankish coinage.[375] Indeed, the Offan light penny was more aligned in weight with the northern *sceat* than the Frankish *denier*—perhaps the contrast was insufficiently stark to entice the north to follow.

Table 2 summarizes the alternating periods of activity at the York mint. Short bursts of production, covering only 30 per cent of the entire period under review, are separated by prolonged inertia. The periodic scheme of arrangement shown at *Dataset 1*,[376] is inevitably a simplification of the gradual and erratic decline in precious metal content, from noble to base, of a coin of fixed module over two and a half centuries. The silver-alloy emissions of Eanred are regarded here as an erstwhile attempt to resurrect the *sceat*, albeit it in the absence of sufficient silver.[377] Eanred's base *styca*, issued after an undefined, possibly lengthy, interval, is a continuation of this monetization process. Within each of the gold, silver and copper-alloy phases, the periodization of Northumbrian coinage relies upon an historically-derived sequence of Northumbrian rulers, *Dataset 1, Periodization.* In the sections which follow, therefore, a brief outline of the Northumbrian regnal and ecclesiastical succession is presented, before the periods of coin production are introduced.

4.2 Gold: Periods 1–3

Described here are the sub- and post-Roman, imported Merovingian, early Anglo-Saxon, local York and Southumbrian gold coinages.

4.2.1 The Migration Period[378]

> 'Kann uns zum Vaterland die Fremde werden'[379]
>
> Wilhelm Levison (1946, *vii*)

Blair saw 'the ethnic (and presumed linguistic) melting-pot of the Migration Period, culminating in a 'common "Anglo-Saxondom" of material culture' by the late sixth century, and a linguistically distinct *gens Anglorum* by the time of Bede.[380] According to Levison 'a vigorous civilization grew up in a receptive soil, in which the mingling of native and foreign elements yielded a rich harvest.'[381] However, much of post-Roman, early Northumbrian history to the late sixth century remains conjectural.[382]

Bernicia and Deira can be compared to the territories of the Brigantes and Parisii.[383] The division was resilient.[384] Bernicia (Brynothic *Brynaich* 'Land of the Mountain Passes')[385] originally stretched north to include the former Scottish county of East Lothian. Ida (reigned 547–59),[386] the son of Eoppa, was first king of Bernicia, which was largely coastal, with a capital at Bamburgh Castle (Welsh *Din Guardi*). His descendants are referred to as the 'Idings'.

According to Wood,[387] 'Bede talks of the kingdom, region or people of the *Deiri* or the *Bernicii*: that is, he sees the northern kingdom as being divided between two peoples, rather than as being two set regions.[388] Indeed he tends to refer to it as the *provincia, regnum* or *gens Northanhymbrorum*, rather than as a geographical entity called Northumbria.[389]'

Higham discussed the evolving nature of *imperium* at this time: 'An Æthelfrith warrior king of *c.* 600 was far removed from the coin-minting, tax-collecting, church-founding, law-issuing, synod-presiding kings of late seventh- and eighth-century England.'[390]

4.2.2 The Conversion Period

> 'the Christian conversion of Anglo-Saxon England had a disastrous effect on the survival of material for archaeological analysis'
>
> Richard Bailey (1974, 146)

While some earlier *tremisses* have been found in England, the focus here is on the historical background to the issuing of coin in Northumbria, commencing in the Conversion Period.

In 597, a somewhat reluctant Augustine, sent by Pope Gregory the Great, arrived at the court of Æthelberht of Kent.[391] In the same year, St Columba (Columcille),

[373] Chick (2010, Table 6, 188). The heavy penny averaged 1.31g. In comparison, in 768, Charlemagne introduced small *deniers* of *c.* 1.3g. The broader, monogrammed, coin, introduced after the Council of Frankfurt, 794, weighed 1.7g.

[374] Chick (2010, 1–29) for a discussion of the chronology. Only the Offan issues of Beonna's former moneyer Wilred and the implausibly named MANG (surely a contraction of *Mercorium Anglorum*), are deemed to predate this.

[375] Chick (2010, 28).

[376] Imported dirhams and Carolingian *solidi* and *deniers* shown in *Dataset 1* are not given a period number as they are regarded as occasional intrusions despite the comments on the possibility of English imitations of the Louis the Pious *solidus*.

[377] But before *c.* 835 i.e. during Eanbald II's tenure if not before Dore in 829.

[378] A more detailed account of early Northumbrian history to 685 can be found at http://www.anglo-saxon-coinage.co.uk/25.html

[379] Poignantly, 'Can we become strangers to the fatherland?' (From Goethe's *Iphigenia.*)

[380] Blair (2005, 23).

[381] Levison (1946, 3).

[382] Webster and Brown (1997). Wood (1997 and 1998).

[383] Ramm (1978). The square barrows characteristic of the Parisii are almost exclusively confined to East Yorkshire, with Arras near Market Weighton, Wetwang Slack and Garton being notable examples.

[384] Woodman (2012, 9).

[385] Breeze (2009, 73–79) argued for the more imaginative 'land of the piercers of battle-lines, territory of those making gaps between enemy warriors'. Also, Alcock (2003, 44–46).

[386] Marsden (1992, 21–49). Higham (1993, 76–79).

[387] Wood (2008, 11–12).

[388] Orton, Wood and Lees (2007,109).

[389] Hunter-Blair (1948, 99).

[390] Higham (1999, 31–36).

[391] Higham (1997, 53–132).

Irish founder of the abbey on Iona, died, presaging the dominance of the Roman faith over Celtic beliefs.

4.2.3 Kings

Five of the expansionist warrior kings of seventh-century Northumbria died in battle, two were murdered by Cadwallon and two apparently died naturally. This is a contrast with the subsequent century when internecine strife caused the majority of deaths.[392]

Rædwald[393] installed Edwin as king of Northumbria, interrupting the Bernician dominance, and York (now *Eoforwic*, 'place of the boar') became the capital. At the start of his reign in 616, Edwin invaded Elmet, a small British outpost between the Wharfe and Sheaf, distinguished by Brythonic-derived place names and significant defensive earthworks. Elmet was the most northerly territory to be included, at six hundred *hides*, in the *Tribal Hidage*.[394] In 627, it was incorporated into Northumbria.

Edwin, for whom Bede had high regard,[395] waged annual wars to expand his territory as far as Strathclyde, Rheged (Carlisle and Solway), Mersey, Anglesey and Man. His court travelled around his kingdom collecting renders and dispensing justice. His royal palaces included Yeavering, Barwick, Goodmanham and, possibly, Sancton.[396] He received baptism in 627, after conversion by Paulinus at Goodmanham.[397]

At the Battle of Hatfield Chase (*Hœđfeld* near Doncaster) in 633,[398] Edwin was killed by Cadwallon. Revenge, in Bede's eyes, was close at hand,[399] for in 634 at the battle of Heavenfield (*Hefenfelth*, Rowley Burn), Eanfrith's brother Oswald killed Cadwallon.[400] In turn, Oswald was killed by Penda in 642 at the Battle of Maserfield (Oswestry?).[401]

After suffering some years of 'intolerable incursions' and 'godless destruction'[402] in Northumbria, especially around Bamburgh, fighting on British territory in Elmet in 655 Oswy unexpectedly defeated and killed Penda at the Battle of Winwæd (near *Liodis*, Leeds), and temporarily became *bretwalda*.[403] Oswy's second (of possibly three wives), the Irish princess Fin, bore him Aldfrith.

Ecgfrith (645–85), king of Deira from 664, was elevated to king of Northumbria on the death of his father, Oswy, in 670. The following year, he quelled a Pictish uprising in the Battle of Two Rivers and took land between the Firth of Forth and the Tweed.[404] In 674, Ecgfrith defeated Wulfhere of Mercia. Lindsey was seized but lost again in 679 at the Battle of the Trent where Ecgfrith fought Æthelred of Mercia.[405]

The most decisive battle in Northumbrian fortunes took place at Nechtansmere (Dun Nechtain) in 685.[406] Against advice from his counsel, including Cuthbert, Ecgfrith attacked Fortiu but was lured into mountain passes near Forfar by Bridei Mac Bili's feigned retreat. Ecgfrith's force was ambushed and he perished with his army. Influence over Pictish lands north of the Forth was lost, only Carlisle and Whithorn in Rheged were retained. This was a catastrophic watershed in Northumbrian fortunes.[407]

4.2.4 The Episcopacy

Paulinus, sent from Italy by Pope Gregory in 601 to reinforce the Augustinian mission, assisted in the conversion of the Anglo-Saxons and remained in Kent, becoming a bishop in 625. Around that time, he accompanied Æthelburg, King Eadbald's sister, to York, for her marriage to Edwin.[408] Paulinus urged Edwin to convert and he, with many followers, did so in 627 in York, which Paulinus, as bishop, established as England's second metropolitan see. Paulinus also carried out mass conversions at Yeavering, Dewsbury and Lindsey and built many churches including York and Lincoln. He baptised Hild(a) and Eanflæd and consecrated Honorius at Canterbury. A stone replacement of the small wooden minster at York,[409] was initiated in 627 by Edwin and completed by Oswald, who was of Bernician descent.

---

[392] 'For kings, agnatic kinsmen were natural rivals,' Charles-Edwards (1997, 179).

[393] Kind Rædwald of East Anglia is the favoured candidate as occupant of the Sutton Hoo ship burial. Marsden (1992, 77–104).

[394] Higham (1993, 117). Loveluck (2003, 156–57).

[395] *Bede (EH,* II, 16).

[396] The 'Sancton' site, rich in *sceattas*, was revealed to be South Newbald by Booth and Blowers (1997, 15–38).

[397] Earlier in 627, Lilla succumbed to Edwin's would-be assassin's knife and was commemorated at Lilla Howe, an Anglian burial in a Bronze Age tumulus. Spratt and Harrison (1989, 63). Higham (1997, 143–91). Rollason (2003, 46).

[398] Higham (1993, 87–89). Marsden (1992, 100–05). Alcock (2003, 136–39). Rollason (2003, 35, 40).

[399] *Bede (EH,* III, 2).

[400] Higham (1993, 125). Marsden (1992, 105–32). Rollason (2003, 119).

[401] Higham (1993, 129). Marsden (1992, 129–32). Rollason (2003, 59).

[402] *Bede (EH,* III, 24).

[403] Higham (1993, 129–32). Marsden (1992, 133–58). Rollason (2003, 35).

[404] Marsden (1992, 159–86).

[405] Higham (1993, 139).

[406] Higham (1993, 138–39). Marsden (1992, 179–85). Alcock (2003, 131–36). Rollason (2003, 41–42). Woolf (2006, 182–201) relocated the battle from Forfar to Badenoch.

[407] *Bede (EH,* IV, 26). Wood does not accept that it made very much difference to Northumbria's domains (*pers. comm.* Oct 2013).

[408] Bede (II, 9). Mayr-Harting (1991, 66) and Kirby (2000, 33–34) argued that Paulinus brought Æthelburg north earlier than 624. Hunter-Blair (1990, 95), contended that Æthelburg and Edwin were married before 625, but that she did not go to Northumbria until 625. See also Higham (1997, 156–91).

[409] Bede (II, 14). Heywood (1995, *figure* 2 4). Higham (1997, 170–71). Woodman (2012, 26). Plausibly over the Legionary Fortress, the *principia*, but unproven. Sculptured stone may provide evidence. Hall (1988, 126). James (1995, 10). Alcuin, in his poem 'On the Bishops, Kings and Saints of York' referred to *solidis suffulta columnis*, 'strong columns' (line 220, 1509 [Willis, 1848], quoted from Morris (1986, 80)), presumably Roman, supporting Edwin's church, though this may not necessarily imply continuity.

The significance of Paulinus's bishopric in York is explained in the discussion of the York gold shilling below (p. 37). Higham stated '(Edwin) also ensured that his new cult centre reflected his own greatness and wealth as an *imperium*-wielding king: the gold of the great cross and chalice with which Paulinus eventually fled south can only have come from his own hoard.'[410] Clerics in this period were often involved in the minting of coins. Thus, Paulinus was, it seems almost certain, responsible for a variety of gold shilling in York (*Plate* 2, *Figure* 102). However, there are no bishops named on the coinage between Paulinus and Ecgberht. Archiepiscopal history is taken up again in the silver phase.

4.2.5 Coin Production

As shown by *Dataset 1. Periodization*, the northern and southern sequence of phases is similar during the early gold phase. The silver phase exhibits parallel development but the introduction of the broad penny in the mid-eighth century in the south leads to separate patterns of evolution in the ninth century. Viking emissions in the north from the mid-890s mark a reunification of coinage types between north and south.

4.2.5.1 Period 1. The Coinage of Sub-Roman Britain, c. *410–*c. *470*[411]

No native coinage was issued in Roman Britain after 325/6[412] and the supply of coinage from the Continent[413] would have ceased after *c.* 410.[414] The Hoxne hoard, deposited *c.* 407, and the South Ferriby hoard[415] provide evidence for the epidemic of clipping silver siliquae (*Figure* 3).[416] By that time, there would no qualms about such defacement.

The Patching (West Sussex) hoard, unusually, contained gold, silver and hack-silver. The *terminus post quem* is provided by a Visigothic copy of a gold 'Pseudo-Imperial' *Victory solidus* of Severus III, 461–65.[417] The rural economy would soon have subsided into barter and the urban economy more gradually, though the degree of wear on many finds suggests that this process took several decades. The implication is that this de-monetization is an indication of regression—the use of coin would have been perpetuated in a more active, governed economy. The presence of hack-silver in the Patching hoard suggests transition to a bullion economy. The last uses of many Roman coins would have been ornamental then sacrificial (votive, ritual and funerary). It would reasonable to assume that the north followed a similar path.

4.2.5.2 Period 2. Imported Pseudo-Imperial Victory Tremisses c. *470–*c. *587*[418]

From the 370s, pressure from the Central Asian Huns had pushed Germanic tribes westward. The Danube was crossed with Roman acquiescence, a decisive moment for the transition of the Western Roman Empire, as Ostrogoths, Visigoths, Vandals, Burgundians, Lombards and other tribes (such as Saxons and Suevi), were ascendant in the west. People, such as the Franks under Clovis (484–511) and the Visigoths under Alaric II (484–507), far from 'Barbarian', chose to continue the 'Pseudo-Imperial' type, with the *Victory* reverse, in the names of Anastasius, Justin and Justinian (*Figure* 4). Designs conveyed the authority of Rome, the authenticity of a long-established medium, cohesive monetary control and a coherent iconography which communicated not merely imperial authority but also the ethical supremacy of the newly adopted Roman religion.[419]

It is evident that the Continental period of issue of the pseudo-imperial type, *c.* 410–*c.* 587, well preceded its primary (currency) or secondary use (ornamentation, ritual, amuletic or symbolic, *Figure* 6), in England.[420]

Roman coinage exerted enormous influence over early Anglo-Saxon metrology and iconography despite the hundred-year discontinuity in the coin use record, *c.* 470–*c.* 570. The two main streams of influence were first, the imported gold Merovingian coinage of the fifth to seventh centuries, reflecting the continuing influence of the Eastern Roman Empire; and second, *Romanitas*, here taking the form of literary or visual allusions to the Roman past to enhance the authority of the issuer and the authenticity of early Anglo-Saxon emissions (*Figure* 5). 'The English kingdoms were not to regain a circulating currency, so essential to civilized life, until the first gold *tremisses* of dumpy Merovingian module began to be made in Kent a few decades later, around the middle of the seventh century.'[421]

In quantifying the circulation of non-Anglo-Saxon gold, Pol has recorded '48 *solidi* of non-Anglo-Saxon origin and 443 *tremisses* of the same category'.[422]

[410] Bede (II, 20). Higham (1997, 170–71).
[411] *c.* 470 relates to the approximate deposition date of the Patching hoard not to 'The acquisition of the highest office by a Romanised barbarian rather than a Roman patrician' in 476, which, 'hardly signalled the end of the world'. Booth (2014).
[412] Excepting the high-status emissions, celebrating the elevation of Magnus Maximus to Augustus minted in Londinium.
[413] Before 325, most coinage in Britain was supplied, in descending order, by the mints at Trier, London, Lyon and Arles.
[414] But see Moorhead and Walton (2014, 99–116).
[415] O'Neil (1935).
[416] The hoard included 14,212 siliquae, of which 80 per cent were clipped (98.5 per cent clipped or filed according to Sawyer (2013, 40) struck between the reigns of Constantine II (337–340) and Honorius (384–423). Bland and Johns (1993). See also Burnett (1984, 163–68). Guest (1997, 411–23). Abdy (2006, 84–88). Moorhead and Walton (2014, 99–116).
[417] Abdy (2006). The hoard may possibly date from a little later as the *tpq* coin is attributed to the Visigoths, 461–*c.* 470 (? Minted at Toulouse).
[418] Booth (2014) for a discussion of this type in the context 'When did the Roman Empire end?'
[419] 'It was economic necessity that caused the Barbarians to retain the Roman coinage.' Pirenne (2001, 108), *pace* Prou.
[420] Williams (2006, 145–91).
[421] Booth (2014).
[422] *Pers. comm.* 4th April 2015. Abdy and Williams (2006, 11–74).

4.2.5.3 Period 3a. Imported Merovingian Gold Coinage, c. 587–c. 670

In the third quarter of the sixth century, the Pseudo-Imperial *Victory* type was superseded by the gold 'National Coinage',[423] occasionally naming the barbarian ruler, but usually the mint and *monetarius* (moneyer) (*Figure* 7).[424] *MEC* dated this to 587 when Childebert and Guntramn met at Andelot to settle questions of territory and succession.[425]

By the end of the sixth century, in western Europe, bronze and silver had disappeared from circulation and gold was much diminished. Gregory of Tours recorded that the tax system had collapsed because state expenditure—on roads, the civil service, the army and donatives—had ceased and gold had become immobilised in royal hoards, which were often seized with violence and bloodshed.[426] Large gifts and compensations were paid, but again these were hoarded and liable to theft.

When the royal treasuries were exhausted, payment of troops in land replaced gold in the seventh century. Spufford wrote: 'even if gold was losing its fiscal, rental and commercial functions, it was still used. It was, for example, the means of compensation.'[427] He also noted that plague had diminished the population, so reducing economic activity. An adverse balance of payments for luxuries from the Middle and Far East also drained gold reserves. The *solidus* was the unit of account, with the more practical third, the *triens* or *tremissis*, replacing it as the circulating medium. However, the weights and fineness could not be maintained. *Tremisses* had been minted at eight siliquae[428] but after the reign of Dagobert I (629–39) this was reduced to seven siliquae, and only one-third fineness.[429]

The coins found at Sutton Hoo (Suffolk, 1939) were the Merovingian 'national' types naming mint and moneyer on the obverse, with a cruciform reverse, all at the seven siliquae standard. These represented a clear break from Roman prototypes.[430]

[423] Much of the pioneering work on this coinage was carried out by Jean Lafaurie. See the bibliographies in *MEC* (1986) and the major one I have prepared http://www.anglo-saxon-coinage.co.uk/early-medieval-numismatic-bibliography/.

[424] There had been limited, earlier issues of silver in the names of the 'barbarian' rulers.

[425] *MEC* (1986, 93).

[426] Spufford (1988, 15).

[427] Spufford (1988, 17).

[428] A term derived from *ceratonia siliqua*, the locust bean or carob, hence *carat*.

[429] Spufford (1988, 19–20).

[430] Bruce-Mitford (1975, 578–682).

4.2.5.4 Period 3b. Early Anglo-Saxon gold coinage, c. 620s–c. 660s

Southumbria

The Sutton Hoo coins deposited *c.* 630 are exclusively Merovingian[431] whereas the Crondall hoard, deposited perhaps a decade or two later, are predominantly, but not exclusively, native (*Figure* 8).[432] *Thrymsas* (*tremisses* or gold shillings) display a mix of styles: a minority evoking *Romanitas*, emulating Continental prototypes, and more invoking pure Anglo-Saxon spirit.

The Crondall hoard evinces resurgent native activity and gives structure to the arrangement of gold shillings.[433] The best description of the changing artistic syntax from Rome to Anglo-Saxon England is given in Sutherland's *Art in Coinage*. The plastic idiom of Roman coinage is swept aside and replaced by the 'rich gift of all "primitives", the resultant portrait therefore enjoys the simplicity, directness and highly concentrated integrity of all young art.'[434] Dolley was less charitable, but more objective: 'the classical world is a memory and the new idiom one still to be mastered.'[435]

It is evident from descriptions in Sutherland of the Anglo-Saxon gold shillings inspired by Roman prototypes that the earliest of these were not currency items and, indeed, piercings, mounts and loops in later issues indicate that there were non-monetary uses.[436] It is only types known from multiple specimens that can be deemed to be part of a circulating coinage—unique survivors are more likely to be special purpose specimens.[437]

'It is indeed remarkable just how many seventh-century gold coins were accidentally lost...showing that these coins, despite their high value, were regularly being used in trade on these sites.'[438] However, the emphasis here is on 'accidentally lost'; gold Anglo-Saxon coinage did not penetrate beyond the social or mercantile élite. Therefore, it did not fulfil the essential monetary function

[431] The purse contained 37 different Merovingian *tremisses*, 3 gold blanks and 2 ingots. If it be Rædwald's burial, he died *c.* 624. The 24 attributable coins are from different mints. Stahl and Oddy (1992, 129–47) compared the purse to Merovingian material and concluded that 30 of the 37 tremisses with more than 81 per cent gold content, are dated before 622, but the remaining seven, with 70–81 per cent gold, could be before 613, 613–22, or after 622.

[432] Found Hampshire, 1828, deposited 640s (?) 101 gold coins: 1 Byzantine, 24 Merovingian or Frankish, 69 Anglo-Saxon, 7 others. Grierson conjectured that the Sutton Hoo purse was intended to pay a 'grandiose Charon's obol' (1975, 136), and that the Crondall hoard was a king's *Wergeld* (1975, 131).

[433] Stewart (1978) first described the phases of the Crondall, ultra-Crondall and post-Crondall shillings, but with increasing numbers of finds of ultra-Crondall specimens, this hoard is no longer the primary point of reference.

[434] Sutherland (1955, 110–11).

[435] Dolley (1976, 352)

[436] Sutherland (1948).

[437] Including the BM's *solidi*, *SCBI* 1–3: Helena, Valentinian and 'Scanomodu'. Williams (2006, 145–92). This may not be the case in Merovingia.

[438] Blackburn (2007, 78).

Table 3: Proposed Reclassification of the York group

Proposed reclassification		**Obverse**		
Reverse	**Reverse description**	**Vestments**	**Grid—narrow**	**Grid—broad**
Cruciform 1	Symmetrical cruciform 1	*Ai=V/C1*		
Cruciform 2	Symmetrical cruciform 2	*Aii=V/C2*		
Cruciform 3	Hour-glass on each limb of cross	*D=V/C3*		
Legend 1a	SANCTE clockwise	*Bi=V/L1a*		
Legend 1b	SANCTE retrograde		*Bii=GN/L1b*	*Ci=GB/L1b*
Legend 2a	PAULINUS 1			*Cii=GB/L2a*
Legend 2b	PAULINUS 2			*Ciii=GB/L2b*

of satisfying routine, daily transactions. In contrast, the lower denominational value of silver coinage facilitated a substantial broadening of the money economy, so can be regarded as a more successful medium of exchange, attaining a deeper penetration of monetization.

In asking whether there was a money economy in sixth- and seventh-century England, Metcalf concluded: 'In the end, all that we can say is that the English thrymsas seem to have circulated quite freely within their region of issue and, to a limited extent, beyond it, and that continental *tremisses* will not have been handled any differently.'[439]

In England, imported (Merovingian and other) coinage and the quest for *Romanitas* influenced not only the quantitative aspects of early Anglo-Saxon coinage—the metrology, denominations and production—but also the more elusive qualitative features—the iconography and propaganda. For a comprehensive account of Roman influence on early Anglo-Saxon coinage see Abramson (2012a).[440]

Northumbria: The Gold Shilling of York, c. *627–*c. *633*[441]

As more diverse Southumbrian types are found, the centrality of the Crondall hoard to the classification and structure of seventh-century gold coinage diminishes. York's distance of over 230 miles due north of Crondall is the likely explanation of the absence of any representative of the York group from the hoard.

The classification of the York group was evolved by Blackburn, Williams, and Naylor and Allen, with the chronology determined by gold content.[442] Abramson (2019) provides the most comprehensive corpus of this type to date, now including 23 attested specimens, all illustrated, consisting of eight obverse and eight reverse dies (*Plate 1, Map 3*).[443] The evolution of the obverse design from a standard bearer in ecclesiastical garb to a grid-like lower half combined with the transition from cruciform reverses to inscriptions facilitates the reclassification in *Table 3*.

Sutherland stated "the 'legend' seems to be a mere congeries of letter-forms, quite devoid of sense"[444] In April 2016, I transcribed the legend as shown in *Plate 2* (*Figure* 102), which can be very plausibly read as naming Paulinus. This is the most important chronological and historical finding of this study.[445] The obverse iconography may suggest that the issue commemorates Edwin's commitment, on being baptised, to replace the wooden church of York, dedicated to St Peter, to one in stone.[446] This would date the issue to between Edwin's conversion, *c.* 627[447] and his death in battle in 633, and establishes a far earlier date for the York series than previously thought.[448]

[439] Metcalf in Abramson (2014, 67).

[440] Abramson (2012a, 73–104). As regards sources of influence, Blackburn (2011, 592) quoted the example of grave 22 at Brighthampton containing a Roman hoard rediscovered in early Anglo-Saxon times.

[441] *SCBI* 63, 61 suggested the 640s. See Naylor and Allen (2014, 153–58) and Abramson (2019).

[442] Blackburn (1994). Williams (2007b). Naylor and Allen (2014). The latter presented a corpus of 14 specimens following the find of a new variety (D) in 2012 'near Harrogate'.

[443] Abramson (2019). The background to specimens 6–8, Sutherland (1948, nos. 75a–c), Abdy and Williams (2006, hoard 13 nos. 319–21), is detailed in Abramson (2012e, 12–16). I have augmented the classification with two new sub-varieties, Bii and Cii.

[444] Sutherland (1948, 50). Charles Hall illustrated a York shilling of variety B or Ci, fancifully inscribed Eadbald,R,CA, in his 1773 engravings added to Withy and Ryall (1756).

[445] Abramson (2019). A second specimen of this type appeared days after I had disclosed this finding at the Sixth International Symposium in Early Medieval Coinage, Fitzwilliam Museum Cambridge, 28–29 October 2016.

[446] Although the iconograph is likely to be ambiguous.

[447] See *fn.* 408. Conceivably, Paulinus issued the coin as early as 625 with the title bishop, though he was not then Bishop of York.

[448] Blackburn (1994, 208): '...a bracket of *c.* 640–60 is most likely, it is not impossible that these coins could have been minted as late as *c.* 680.' Williams and Hook (2013, 61) favoured Deiran Edwin as prospective issuer over Bernician Oswald, in view of the paucity of coinage in Bernicia.

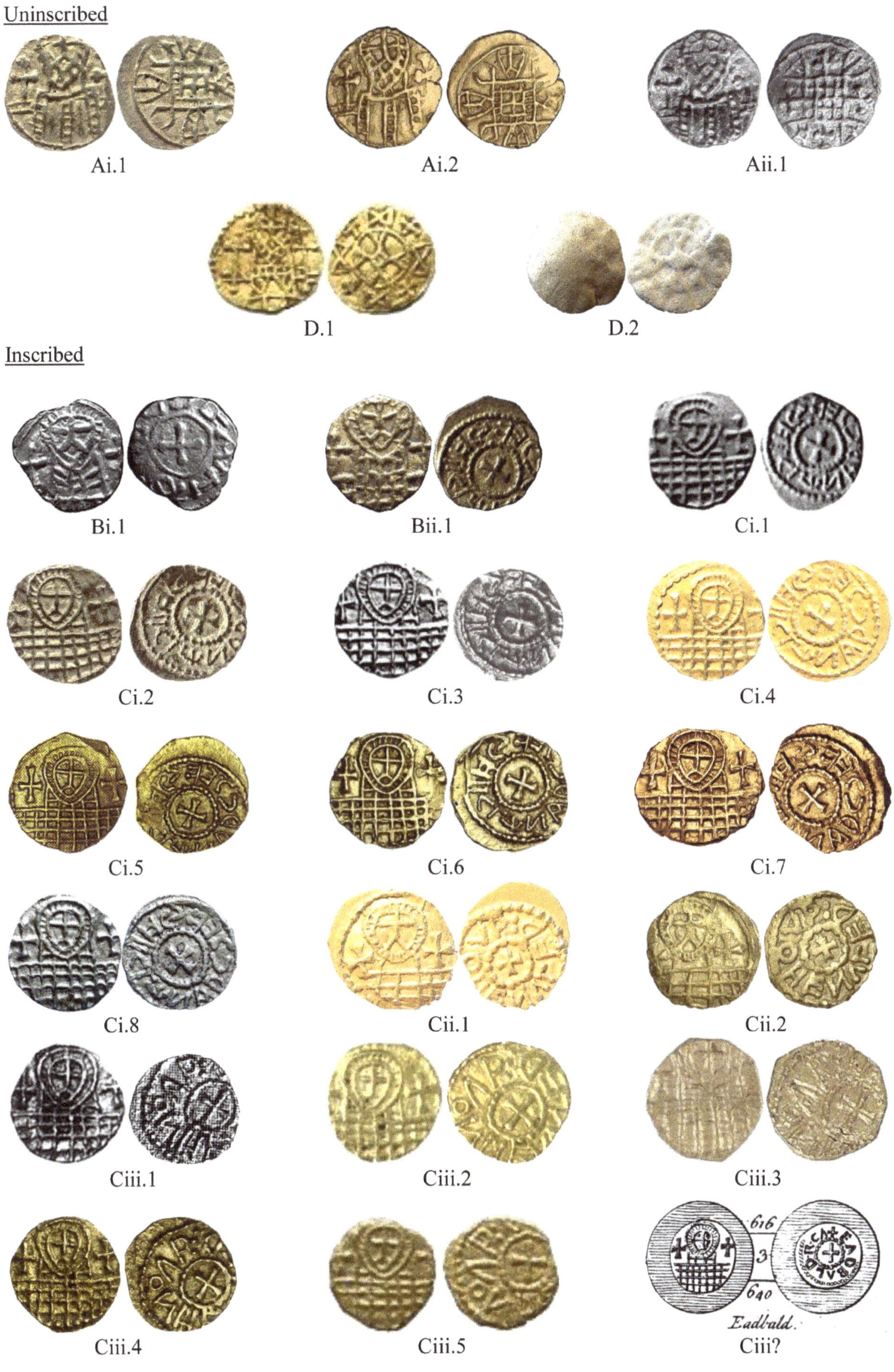

Plate 1: York group of gold shillings.

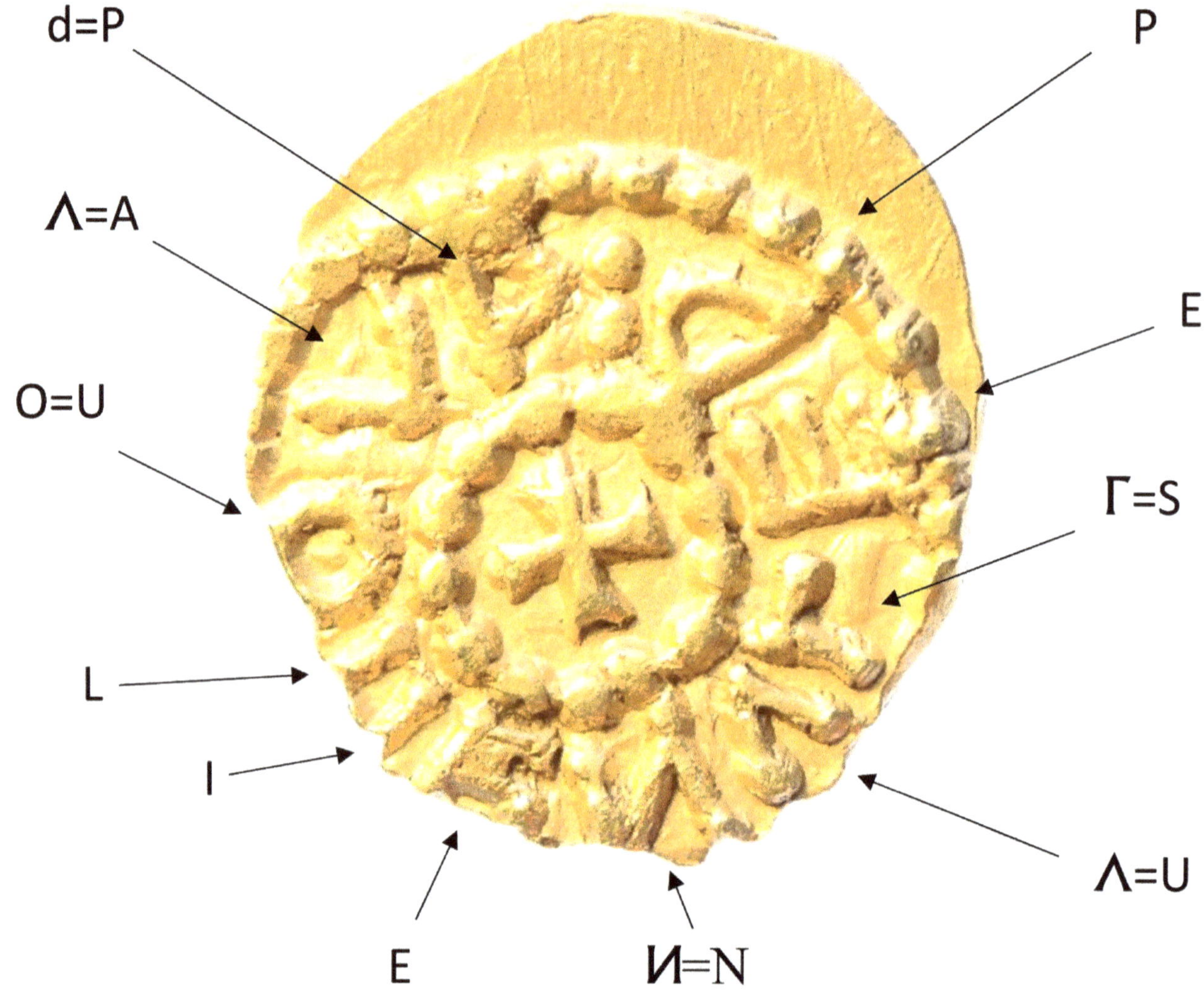

dΛOLIEИΛΓEP = PAOLIENUS EP

Plate 2: York gold shilling (variety Cii.1, EMC 2007.0088). *SCBI*69, 5.

It places York at the forefront of English coinage, though, conceivably, Eadbald's coinage could have commenced, with his conversion, as early as *c.* 617.[449]

The sequence of varieties of the York shilling distinguishes it from other seventh-century gold shillings. The distinction lies in the purposeful regulation of production evident in the York group. Other gold shillings are occasional, possibly commemorative special issues; all the Crondall types are rare and show little continuity until the transitional phase of pale gold shillings, where the anonymous 'two-emperors' type and the named-moneyer emissions of Pada and Vanimundus are better organised. The York group have every appearance of successive productions over at very least the last six years of Edwin's reign. This has significance for the distinct, phased monetization of Northumbria. Again, the variety of Eadbald's reverse inscriptions may show similar intent, but these remain largely undeciphered.

Dataset 15, York Shilling Analysis may give some indication of the mix of (élite) currency and commemorative functions, that is, the more common sub-varieties Ci and Ciii are at the lower end of both the weight and gold content ranges and all the other sub-varieties are extremely rare. The die usage, *Dataset 15, York Shilling Die Comparison*, is also atypical. While the London and Eadbald shillings have, what may be mistaken for, a conventional obverse to reverse die ratio of 1:3,[450] York is 1:1, with eight dies of each side. This is again suggestive of production for commemorative purposes. Admittedly, the corpus is too small to distinguish between commemorative and currency purposes.

The concentration around a locus of York is clear; the outliers, Bawtry and Burton-by-Lincoln, being within the sphere of influence—certainly of Paulinus if not Northumbria. Only the Soest find hints at wider Northumbrian influence and involvement. *Map 3* shows that the uninscribed York shillings are clustered around York in a flat oval with a major axis of 25 miles. Including the shillings of varieties B and the related Ci, inscribed SANCTE, expands the oval north to Thirsk, but significantly, variety Ciii, inscribed for Paulinus, is more widely broadcast, presumably marking his wide-ranging mass-baptismal activity, from Yeavering to Lincoln, and possibly delineating the sphere of Edwin's protection. Though a significant proportion (*c.* 60±5 per cent) of the gold coinage current in England, is imported,[451] it is difficult to assess the degree of local control over the gold coinage from such small numbers. Only the Middleham find is accompanied by other artefacts.[452]

Gannon suggested that the crosses either side of the standing figure are apotropaic.[453] Similar 'standard bearers' are not uncommon in the early-penny iconography.[454] She compared the face on the obverse to that on the haunch of the Sutton Hoo bird mount, though other comparanda suggest themselves.[455]

In discussing the Northumbrian early-penny iconography, she contrasts the lion *courant* of Aldfrith with that shown in the Echternach Gospel but does not remark on the leonine nature of the figure on the gold shilling (*Figure* 9). The resemblance of the design to the later, blocked, door in the west face of the west tower at Middleton-by-Pickering church, North Yorkshire is intriguing but almost certainly accidental.[456] The possible *nomina sacra* interpretations, of the previously undeciphered reverse legend of varieties B and C, and the full spectrum of the iconography, are currently being explored.[457]

I interpret the obverse iconography of variety C as referring to Edwin's stone church. Monarchy and monotheism shared a common interest in monocracy, increasingly commemorated in monumental form, in furtherance of sovereignty. At the Bernician royal *vill* complex of Yeavering, an enclosure, probably a pagan shrine, on the Iron Age hill-fort, was replaced by a roofed ritual structure, probably as an act of syncretism,[458] before Edwin's baptism,[459] and Paulinus's mass-baptisms there. It would have been habit, and possibly curiosity, which brought crowds to a sacred place that was now both royal and Christian. In the second quarter of the seventh century, Paulinus and then Aidan travelled extensively throughout Northumbria selecting significant sites to perform mass-baptisms.

It may have been syncretism, security and land-gifts, which led the Gregorian missionaries to place their minsters within Roman walls, a trend followed by superior minsters after 650.[460] However, the numbers on Roman sites are low compared to those removing Roman materials for use

[449] See *fn.* 53. In the Crondall hoard there are seven die duplicates of the thrymsa with a forward-facing obverse portrait and inscribed for London on the reverse, thought by Baldwin-Brown (1915, 73–74) to be Bishop Mellitus. This was dismissed by Gannon (2003.25) as anachronistic, but again mentioned by her in 'From Gold to Silver in the Seventh Century', Cambridge, 27–28 March 2015. Higham (1997, 137–43).

[450] This would be mistaken because it applies during mass production of medieval pennies when the reverse die, or, more accurately, the stock, is worn more quickly (Abramson 2012e, 19–21); here it is merely coincidental and probably driven, like the York issues, by events to be commemorated, at least for the Eadbald coinage. Gold supplies would not have been sufficient to exhaust the dies.

[451] Abdy and Williams (2006, 11–74).

[452] The inclusion of a York shilling among an assemblage of high-status weapons, evidences the high regard for such a coin.

[453] Gannon (2003, 27).

[454] Abramson (2006, 76–82).

[455] Sutherland (1948, 50) suggested that the inspiration may be the Byzantine follis of Justinian I, 527–65, for Constantinople.

[456] And to an Anglian stele from York Minster, Anglian stele, YM24, see Lang in Carver (1995, 453) where it is described as 'a portrait not far removed from graffiti'.

[457] Garrison (forthcoming).

[458] Pope Gregory instructed Augustine to convert cult sites not destroy them. Blair (2005, 57).

[459] Blair (2005, 52).

[460] Blair (2005, 67).

elsewhere, and even more were built in wood, rendering salvage as of little influence on location.[461]

Unrelated to the York group, but worthy of mention is the remarkable and unique gold *solidus* of Archbishop Wigmund (*c.* 837–54? 4.16g.), in imitation of the *Munus divinum* ('divine gift') issue of Louis the Pious (814–40), thought by Grierson and Blackburn[462] to have been struck at Canterbury, but Blackburn later revised this view[463] as this specimen was of the weight standard of the Carolingian *solidus* not the southern English *mancus*. This coin is pierced in two places and is a presentation or ornamental piece, far removed from the contemporary base *styca* emissions.[464]

4.2.5.5 Period 3c. Southumbrian Pale Gold Shilling, c. 660s

In England, the transition from gold to silver was both gradual and erratic with the gold content declining from *c.* 60 per cent fine for the Crondall and 'ultra-Crondall' issues in the period *c.* 630–*c.* 655, to the 'post-Crondall' gold content of 10–35 per cent (*Figure* 10).

That these were present in Northumbria is evident from a 20 per cent gold shilling, dating to the third quarter of the seventh century, from Bulmer Beck. Blackburn described this unique, floral reverse, find as 'intended to function as a coin and not as an ornament' (*Figure* 11).[465]

Late 'pale gold' shillings contained as little as 4–5 per cent gold.[466] Emissions include those of only two named, Kentish, moneyers, Pada (*Figure* 12) and 'Vanimundus' (*Figure* 13), implying relatively stable control. Both issued in pale gold initially before eliminating gold entirely, presumably better to align with the imported Merovingian *denier* (see Period 4d).[467]

Rigold arranged the well-organised coinage of Pada into a chronological sequence of designs, starting with an obverse bust emulating the helmeted type of Crispus; the later diademed types reflect more the appearance of Constantine, in an attitude of prayer alluding to the alleged dream-vision before the battle of Milvian Bridge in 312.[468] Grierson and Blackburn suggest that the prototype of the rather scarcer Vanimundus shilling is a pale gold *tremissis* of the Austrasian mint Matrico by the moneyer Warimundus. The letters CA, on one variety, copies the mint-mark of Chalon-sur-Saône.[469]

By the 660s the pale gold shillings were superseded by silver emissions.[470]

4.2.6 Illustrations—Gold Periods 1–3

Figure 3: Clipped siliquae, Cattal hoard. (Courtesy York Museums Trust[471])

Figure 4: Merovingian pseudo-imperial Victory *tremissis*. Found Kent.

Figure 5: *Romanitas*: Burgundian *tremissis*, probably Lyon, imitating Justinian. Found Ashford, Kent.

[461] Morris (1989, 102).
[462] *MEC* (1986, 329–30).
[463] Blackburn (2007, 64).
[464] Blunt (1960) reconstructed the pedigree of this unprovenanced coin, once tainted by association with the notorious eighteenth-century forger John White.
[465] Blackburn (2006, 135–40). (CNG 100, 1060).
[466] Williams and Hook (2013, 55–70).
[467] The silver emission inscribed Valdoberhtus may be contemporary with the silver issues of Pada and Vanimundus—see section 4.3.2.2 and Chick (2010, 32).
[468] Wood (2008, 23). Naismith (2012, 58).
[469] Prou (1892, 40–57).
[470] Hines and Bayliss (2013, 509–12).
[471] Cattal, NY, hoard (YORYM 1994.1953.12) http://yorkmuseumstrust.org.uk/. Licence CC BY-SA 4.0

Figure 6: Coin-jewellery: Lombards, gold *tremissis*. In the name of Maurice Tiberius (582–602) perhaps Milan or Pavia. *MEC* 301–04. Found near Driffield.[472]

Figure 7: Merovingian national Series, *tremisses*. L: Paris, found Malton (Courtesy Classical Numismatic Group, Inc., 9500090), R: Sacierge-Saint-Martin (Indre), found Wharram Percy.[473]

Figure 8: Crondall type shillings in native style. L: 'Witmen' type, found N. France. R, 'Wuneeton' type, found near Sleaford, Lincolnshire.

Figure 9: L: Middleton church window. R: York shilling, variety C (Ci.4).

[472] Also illustrated at *Figure* 1.
[473] See *EMC* 2010.0172 for a pseudo-Imperial Merovingian tremissis from this site. These exhibit the decline in gold content suggested by Pol. See *fn.* 561.

Figure 10: Declining gold content in Post-Crondall *gold shillings*. 'Crispus' type, 'Trophy' or 'Oath-taking' type (found King's Lynn) and 'Two emperors' type (found Diss, "near Burgate")

Figure 11: Unique Southumbrian gold shilling *c.* 650–75, *c.* 20 per cent gold, found Bulmer Beck. (Courtesy Classical Numismatic Group, Inc.)

Figure 12: Pale gold shillings: L. runic *Pada*. Type PaIB. R. type PaIA (found near Sherburn, *SL* group 1).

Figure 13: *Vanimundus*. Found NW Norfolk (with two Pada shillings) (*SL* group 2).

4.3 Silver: Periods 4–8

The gradual decline of the precious metal content of the coinage as monetization advanced is chronicled above.[474] Such an advance disguised denominational reduction and it is quite evident that this was, with some qualification, a managed process: it was implemented uniformly across polities and gradually, as indeed such a monetary policy had been executed over time across the Iron Age tribes,[475] though in both cases Gresham's Law drove all to follow the initiator. It is this compulsion which qualifies the degree to which monetary change is managed. Inevitably, an individual polity such as Northumbria must work within pressures (of supply and demand) generated externally and is restricted in its autonomy. This applies to the monetary sphere as much as any other.

Northumbrian history in the long eighth century, with reference to kings and archbishops, and coin production, is related below. Also discussed are the Primary silver *sceattas* of Aldfrith imported Southumbrian and Continental *sceattas* and Merovingian *deniers*. The *sceattas* current during the period of Aldfrith's incompetent successors are then described: the putative northern non-regal emissions (Series J, 51), Secondary Southumbrian

[474] Metcalf (1993–94, 29–84). Williams and Hook (2013, 55–70).
[475] Van Arsdell (1989, 48–50).

and Continental *sceattas*. Finally, the fantastic beast issues of Eadberht's *renovatio*, the contemporary joint issues and the subsequent inscriptional *sceattas* are examined, followed by an evaluation of the periodicity.

4.3.1 Historical Background: Northumbria after the Battle of Nechtansmere, 685

4.3.1.1 Kings

Aldfrith (Flann Fína mac Ossu, *c.* 633–704) the illegitimate scion of Oswy and Fin, became king following the catastrophe at Nechtansmere.[476] He had been educated in the Irish tradition, away from the Mercian threat, at Malmesbury (with Aldhelm) and at Canterbury by Theodore and Hadrian. He visited Ireland in the early 680s, possibly being there at the time of Ecgfrith's vicious attack. Aldfrith gained a reputation as a scholar and sage, he may well have been at Iona in 685 under the tutelage of Adamnan. His elevation to the throne was supported by Cuthbert, possibly a relation. He restored the Northumbrian fortunes in a largely peaceful reign disturbed only by the 'turbulent priest', Wilfrid.[477]

Aldfrith reigned during the Golden Age of Northumbrian insular art and the production of illuminated manuscripts[478] including the Lindisfarne, Durham and Echternach Gospels and the *Codex Amiatinus*. This was the period when the great Northumbrian monasteries were established, each by a prominent figure: Wilfrid at Ripon and Hexham, Cuthbert at Lindisfarne, Benedict Biscop at Jarrow and Monkwearmouth, Hilda at Whitby. Such a propinquity of talent often generates, by collaboration or competition, outstanding achievement. The Hexham, Hoddom and closely-linked Bewcastle and Ruthwell crosses[479] are possibly a little later, but several famous jewels (the Ripon jewel[480] and St. Cuthbert's pectoral cross) date from this time as does the 'Franks' casket.[481] Northumbrian missionaries travelled widely and worked assiduously on the Continent—the main source of acculturation.[482] Significant libraries were assembled at York and Iona. The first silver *sceattas* were introduced bearing Irish uncial lettering.[483] Aldfrith died in 704 at Driffield, assumed to be a royal palace, and is regarded as one of the most learned of all English monarchs.[484]

[476] Higham (1993, 140–41). Hawkes and Mills (eds.) (1999). Woolf (2006, 182–201).

[477] Higham (1993, 120–55). Hawkes (1997, 311–44). Hines (1997, 391).

[478] Possibly facilitated by the move from parchment to vellum in the sixth century. There were two main influences on style—*Romanitas* and Hiberno-Saxon.

[479] Orton, Wood and Lees (2007).

[480] Hall, Paterson and Mortimer (1999, 268–80).

[481] More correctly, the 'Auzon cabinet' but named after the donor (to the BM in 1867), Sir Augustus Wollaston Franks. The iconography bears stylistic similarities, in its syncretic, transitional character, to the *sceat* coinage. The use of runes may convey more than just alphabetical characters. Webster (1999, 227–46). Lang (1999, 247–55). Vegvar (1999, 256–67).

[482] Cramp (1999, 11).

[483] Webster and Backhouse (1991, ch. 4).

[484] Marsden (1992, 187–217).

Aldfrith's one weakness was his succession. His marriage to the ascetic Cuthburg, sister of Ine of Wessex, resulted in the birth of Osred in 696, before Cuthburg entered the monastery of Winburn.

After Aldfrith's death, Berhtfrith, a *patricus* and warrior thane (of the dynasty of Beornhæth and Berhtred) undertook the guardianship of Osred and immediately faced a challenge from a rival thane Eadwulf, who usurped the throne for two months until Wilfrid pronounced in favour of Osred.[485] Eadwulf's usurpation was a decisive watershed in Northumbrian succession for now ostensibly legitimate scions could be challenged by warrior thanes. Future monarchs could not achieve the greatness of their illustrious predecessors and Northumbria would never regain its pre-eminence. Seventh-century Northumbrian monarchs typically died in battle; their eighth-century successors usually perished as the result of internecine strife, though this friction may also have been a driving force under the unifying influence of the archiepiscopacy. Despite this, the Golden Age, at least in some artistic and literary fields, was to continue until the catastrophe of 867.

In 711, Berhtfrith inflicted a defeat on the Picts but unfortunately by 716, Osred proved to be incompetent and dissolute, and was eventually lured by his kinsfolk, Coenred and Osric, to a bloody demise, probably on the Mercian border.[486] Coenred acceded for two years but was little better than Osred. In 718, the obscure Osric succeeded for a period of 11 years. He adopted Ceolwulf, Coenred's brother as his successor, in 729.[487]

Ceolwulf proved an ineffectual, monkish, king. In 731, he was kidnaped by rebellious thanes and forcibly tonsured. Having made substantial endowments to Lindisfarne, he abdicated there in 737 and survived a further 27 years.[488] He nominated his cousin Eadberht as his successor.[489]

Eadberht (reigned[490] 737–58, d. 768), son of Eata, faced internal rivalry and slew Eardwine (son of the usurper Eadwulf and grandfather of King Eardwulf) in 740, and Offa, son of Aldfrith, in 750. He was supported by his brother Archbishop Ecgberht of York and they issued joint coinage, Eadberht having re-introduced the Northumbrian *sceat*. In 740, Eadberht campaigned in the north but this gave an opportunity for Æthelbald of Mercia to attack, possibly in retaliation for Eardwine's murder. Eadberht campaigned more successfully in 750, capturing the plain of Kyle.[491] He retired to a monastic life in York and was buried alongside Ecgberht who predeceased him by two years.

Oswulf (758) succeeded his father Eadberht, but was soon murdered by members of his own household, possibly

[485] Yorke (1990, 92 and 171).

[486] Marsden (1992, 217–22).

[487] Marsden (1992, 223–28). Rollason (2003, 192).

[488] Higham (1993, 153).

[489] Marsden (1992, 229–32).

[490] Regnal dates are quoted hereafter.

[491] Higham (1993, 141).

including his successor.[492] A patrician, Æthelwold Moll (758–65) now seized power though he is not recorded in the genealogies.[493] Æthelwold faced one rebellion, possibly by Oswine, brother (?) of Oswulf, in 761. He married Æthelthryth in 762 and their issue was Æthelred. Æthelwold Moll was deposed (and tonsured) by the *witenagemot* at *Pincanheale* in 765.[494] He issued coins, of the highest rarity, jointly both with his son Æthelred and also with Archbishop Ecgberht.

Alchred (Alhred) (765–74), Eadberht's son-in-law, husband of Osgifu, was next to take the throne. He initiated the mission of Willehad to Bremen and produced coins jointly with Archbishop Ecgberht.[495] He was deposed by Archbishop Æthelbert and exiled to Pictland,[496] whereupon, Æthelred I (first reign, 774–79), son of Æthelwold Moll, was appointed. Again, he was deposed by the Council of Archbishop Æthelbert, to live in exile during the reigns of Ælfwald I (779–88) and Osred II (788–90), but then restored (789–96). In his second reign, he produced coins jointly with Archbishop Eanbald I.[497]

Ælfwald I (779–88) was the son of Oswulf.[498] During this reign the coin design changed from the 'fantastic animal' reverse to the inscriptional type featuring named moneyers. His moneyer Cuthheard also produced coins for Æthelred I, Eardwulf (extremely rare, seven known), and Eanred. Ælfwald was murdered at Chesters (Cilurnum, Hadrian's Wall) and buried at Hexham Abbey. He was succeeded by his first cousin Osred (as Osbald, a violent and despised man, is thought to have killed Ælfwald's son Bearn by conflagration at Selectune (Silton?) in 780).[499]

Osred II (788–90) the son of Alchred by Osgifu, despite uniting competing factions, was soon exiled to the Isle of Man (?) and forcibly tonsured but returned in 792,[500] when he was captured and murdered, probably by Æthelred.

Æthelred I (restored 790–96) served a troubled second reign marking a descent towards anarchy. Æthelred made an early, unsuccessful, attempt to dispose of his rival Eardwulf, who was left for dead outside the monastery at Ripon (*Inhrypum*).[501] In 791, two sons of Ælfwald, Ælf and Ælfwine, were murdered. The following year, Æthelred married Offa's daughter Ælfflæd at Catterick. The year 793 marks the Viking attack on Lindisfarne, for which Alcuin blamed Æthelred's ungodliness.[502] The impact of the Council of Frankfurt, 794, will not have been neutral in Northumbria. The Council, where Charlemagne assembled all the western bishops, ruled against the persecution of witches while regarding witchcraft as superstition. In came down against both iconoclasm and iconodulism, deciding that images may be useful but should not be venerated. It also set certain weights and measures rather than let the market price mechanism operate. It fixed 25 oaten loaves, 12 two-pound wheaten loaves, four *modius* of oats, two of barley, one and a third of rye and one of wheat to be worth one new *denier*.[503] A capitulary of 797 for the Saxon area, set 12 *deniers*, or one *solidus*, as the price of a year-old calf.[504] In 806, the price for a sheep or pig was set at four *deniers*, and two pairs of shoes at seven *deniers*. 'Even the poorest might have a coin or two in their purse.'[505]

Despite support from Charlemagne, Æthelred was murdered in 796 by conspirators (including the earldormen Ealdred and Wada) who then elevated the aging, dissolute and murderous, Osbald, who ignored Alcuin's warnings to reform. In an increasing unstable kingdom, he ruled a mere 27 days before being exiled to Lindisfarne, thence to refuge in Pictland. He died in 799 with an unmarked burial in York Minster.

Eardwulf (796–806) had survived Æthelred's attempt on his life in 790. His second wife was an illegitimate daughter of Charlemagne, an even more ambitious diplomatic manoeuvre than Æthelred's marriage to Offa's daughter. In 798, he killed Wada (who conspired against Æthelred) at the Battle of Billington Moor. In 799, a Moll (possibly descended from Æthelwold Moll) was killed at the 'urgent command' of Eardwulf. In 801, he fought Coenwulf of Mercia who had given asylum to his rivals. He was deposed in 806 (but *possibly* returned in 808, with the support of Charlemagne and Pope Leo III). The date of his death is unknown but he is thought to be the Saint Hardulph to whom Breedon-on-the Hill is jointly dedicated.[506] The first specimen of the exceedingly rare

[492] Marsden (1992, 231–32).

[493] A letter sent by Pope Paul I to Eadberht and Ecgberht ordered the return of monasteries, at Stonegrave, Coxwold, and 'Donaemuthe' taken from Abbot Fothred, to his brother named as "Moll", who may be the same person. Marsden (1992, 232), Blair (2005, 131), Wood (2008b, 17–18), Rollason (2003, 181–82), draws a parallel between the use of the term *Patricus* by Charles Martel in connection with the 'mayors of the palace' and the patrician monarchs of Northumbria, such as Moll.

[494] Kirby (1991, 151).

[495] Higham (1993, 149). Yorke (1990, 94–95).

[496] Holas-Clarke (2006, 228). Rollason on Oswulf in *DNB*. Gift to Bishop Lul (2003, 16–17).

[497] He was also named on the reverse of the rare *sceat* of his father, Æthelwold Moll (see 53).

[498] Kirby (1991, 152–70).

[499] Higham (1993, 149 and 153).

[500] He was tonsured to prevent him trying to regain the throne. The tonsure represented an irreversible spiritual change from laity to clerisy, which in a deeply Christian culture few would have dared to offend God by rejecting, even if it had been imposed by force. But by returning, presumably in an attempt to reclaim the throne, Osred did think he could renounce being a monk. (*Pers. comm.* James Booth).

[501] *EHD* (3, 346).

[502] Higham (1993, 173). *ASC* reported evil portents. Alcuin in his letter to Æthelred, proclaims: 'The satiety of the rich is the hunger of the poor'. In 796, on the deaths of Æthelred I, Offa, his son, and the archbishop of York, Alcuin came to see this as a divine judgment Garrison (2001, 26). Alcuin makes the earliest reference Yorkshire as *Euboracia* (793, Garrison, *pers. comm.* 20 October 2015). *Donemuthan* was attacked the following year (*ASC*, 794) but identification of this (by Simeon of Durham) as Jarrow is unlikely as is the Yorkshire River Don which then drained into the Trent. Perhaps Aberdeen is a candidate.

[503] Naismith (2012, 287), described 794 as a famine-stricken year, which may imply that these prices were ephemeral. The *denier* increased in weight from 1.3g to 1.7g.

[504] Hodges (2012, 43).

[505] Coupland (2007, I, 212–13).

[506] Along with Beonna and Cotta, both of Breedon. See Yorke (1990, 89, 93–98). *Fn.* 620.

sceat of this monarch was unearthed in 1994.[507] His son Eanred eventually succeeded to the throne.

4.3.1.2 The Episcopacy

Ecgberht (tenure 732–66), the son of Eata and brother of king Eadberht (king 737–58), was appointed Bishop by his cousin Ceolwulf.[508] Bede recalls that Pope Gregory III had decreed that there should be 12 bishops in England after the conversion, among whom the bishop of York should 'receive the *pallium* and be metropolitan'.[509] Within months of taking office in 734 he 'laudably recovered the *pallium* which had been neglected by eight bishops since the time of Paulinus the first archbishop of York.' Perhaps the stick-like, standing figure on the joint coinage with his brother Eadberht, shows this recently restored *pallium*.[510]

The diocese was elevated to an Archbishopic in 737. Ecgberht corresponded with Boniface and was an associate (student?) of Bede, whose advice that the diocese be divided was not pursued. He worked with Eadberht in an ultimately unsuccessful attempt to return *bookland* to secular control. He founded the exceptional school and library at York and wrote a law code for the clergy, *Dialogus ecclesiasticae institutionis*, which included *wergeld* for clerics. He issued coins jointly with Eadberht, Æthelwold Moll and Alchred. The joint issues mark a significant diplomatic achievement not just in inferring unity between church and state but in their continuity across rival dynasties. Ecgberht was buried at York cathedral.

Æthelbert (tenure 766–80) ordained at York by his relative Ecgberht, was put in charge of the school and library, which he was instrumental in extending. This involved travelling widely including a visit to Rome. He taught missionaries, including Alcuin, and sent them to northern Europe. He oversaw the reconstruction of the cathedral after the fire of 741. In 773, he received the *pallium* from Pope Adrian I. His council deposed and exiled Alchred to Pictland in 774 and he probably withdrew support from Æthelred I. He built a new church in York during his retirement. That no coins survive showing his name shows that emissions were an episcopal option not a necessity.

Eanbald I (tenure 780–96) and his colleague Alcuin had been put in charge of the rebuilding of the cathedral by his predecessor Æthelbert. Alcuin was sent by Ælfwald I to collect Eanbald's *pallium* from Pope Adrian I. Eanbald presided over several Synods; that of 786 barred illegitimate royal heirs and ordered that tithes be given by all men to the church; that of 786 condemned regicide in a time of growing instability. His archbishopric witnessed the first Danish attacks on Northumbria. He issued coins jointly with Æthelred and consecrated Eardwulf shortly before his own death and burial at York Minster.

***4.3.2 Coin Production: Brief Introduction to* Sceattas**

> 'the value of an object lies not just (or even) in its scarcity or utility but also in the historical, sentimental and cosmological qualities with which it is felt to be imbued.'
>
> John Moreland (2000, 30)

The *sceat* was produced between *c.* 660s and *c.* 760 in the south and up to *c.* 810 in the north. In the periodic scheme set out below, the Southumbrian *sceat* has better continuity and earlier migration to the broad penny, so that in the south Periods 6 and 7 are not fragmented, and Periods 8 and 9 cover the broad penny (this is Period 12 in the north).

The Anglo-Saxon system developed into a hugely varied, single denominational, silver *early-penny* coinage of a value more, but not entirely, aligned to regular economic needs.[511] *Romanitas* remained a strong presence throughout this transition (*Figure* 15).[512]

Sceattas bear witness to a more widespread sophistication than other élite, contemporary artefacts permit. They give an insight to the social, religious, political and economic *milieu* they serviced. A characteristic of early-penny iconography is the syncretic conflation of motifs not conventionally combined. It seems that we may be confronted here with intentional ambiguity, possibly to ensure that the Conversion message had the widest possible appeal among coin users of diverse traditions. For instance, serpents are used in a way conventional to the Christian repertoire to represent evil, sometimes counterpoised with a bird representing the 'holy-spirit' but are also used as protective (some Series J and Q variants see *Figure* 16–*Figure* 18, where pairing related *sceattas* occasionally adds dynamism to proverbs) or apotropaic elements (e.g. an *Uroboros* on either side of primary Series B, *Figure* 19) surrounding Christian symbols.[513]

Perhaps the Anglo-Saxon penchant for riddles and magic, with the added lure of runes, influenced coin design. Dolley commented on: 'a number of designs harking back to pagan motifs with all the confidence of a neophyte Christianity as convinced of its own acceptance as eclectic in its art.'[514] In contrast, the anonymous and crude rendering of the voluminous Rhine-mouths issues of Series D and E (*Figure* 20), may be an attempt by pagan traders to gain currency by deliberately avoiding identity and message.

It is generally assumed, not unreasonably, that the best executed variety of each type is at the head of the series

[507] http://gilliscoins.com/reference/eardwulf/index.htm where A = Abramson, B = Bude.
[508] To whom *EH* is dedicated.
[509] *EHD* (no. 170, 740).
[510] Booth (1984). Bude's die study (2016) reveals three postures for the reverse figure—standing, walking and sitting. In the latter, the hands are in the orans position. Gannon is not convinced.

[511] Op den Velde and Metcalf (2009–10). Abramson (2012d).
[512] Abramson (2012a)
[513] Gannon (2003, 36 and 136).
[514] Dolley (1976, 353).

(*Figure* 21). For example, Series R, emulating primary Series A and C, shows a steady deterioration in execution and alloy over an extended period (*c.* 710–*c.* 750). What started out as a well-designed, if stylised, obverse bust degraded into a few component elements and the reverse votive standard degenerated into geometric symbols (*Figure* 22).

The early-penny coinage is divided chronologically into two phases by the Aston Rowant (Oxfordshire) hoard, deposited *c.* 710. Rigold catalogued the generally well-regulated and conservatively styled Primary series (which had commenced by the 660s) prior to the metal-detecting era, but his work remains relevant. The subsequent explosion of creativity in the Secondary series extended to mid-eighth century and exhibits an erratic decline in style and alloy. The coinage is also divided territorially, by the Humber, with the north literate and conservative[515] and the south rarely either.

Sceattas are found throughout the North Sea trading area including Denmark, Frisia, Francia and England. 'There was a fair amount of North Sea exchange, it is true. By the eighth century there was more of it than could be found on the seaways of at least the western Mediterranean.'[516] Clearly, users were not troubled by the wide variety of designs, presumably handling with confidence motifs not previously seen. Moreover, standards of execution varied enormously—portraits equivalent in artistic merit to the best of early Anglo-Saxon art are found alongside unrecognisable, naïve specimens. While coins from numerous, typically anonymous[517] regal, episcopal[518] and mercantile sources all fall into a recognisable metrology, variations in size, weight, and alloy are not inconsiderable (*Figure* 23). This possibly indicates that recipients were reasonably tolerant of, and confident in, what they could have regarded, to some extent, as a *fiat* currency, or that standards changed over time, or differed between areas.[519] These features are characteristic of monetization.

Erratically variations over time and between emissions in the fineness of the output was presumably determined by the silver supply available to the issuer. It is worth noting that there were domestic sources of silver[520]—not all supply required the export of produce. Salzman mentioned several early northern sources for silver including, Alston Moor in Cumbria; Ashford, Bakewell, Crich, Hope, Matlock, Metesford, Wirksworth, in Derbyshire; and Weardale, in County Durham.[521] Reece listed the Mendips, the Peak District and Flintshire.[522]

Spufford dismissed hoards and political action as viable long-term sources of the additional silver required for the substantial early-penny coinage.[523] As the gold *tremissis* became more debased, more silver was required for that coinage and, subsequently, this may have been a source of supply for the *sceat*, but mining and trade flow must constitute the main sources. *MEC* noted that 'the economic niche filled by the silver must have been quite different from that of the gold'[524] and argued that a major source of silver for minting in Merovingian Francia, was silver plate originally gifted by senatorial families to the Church then secularised by Pepin—there were far more ecclesiastical *deniers* struck than there had been *tremisses*.

England exported slaves and wool, and Frisia bought pottery, brooches and Coptic bronze vessels. Silver made up the balance in England's favour. Frisia exported glass, bronze-work and pottery to Scandinavia and received furs in exchange.[525] Again, Frisia paid the deficit in silver. Until its fall to the Franks in the 730s, Frisia sold on these luxury goods to Francia in exchange for goods. Settlement would have been in silver mined, most likely, from the argentiferous deposits at 'Metullo', Melle (*Figure* 24) and minted initially at nearby Poitiers.[526]

It remains uncertain what the value of a *sceat* may have been. Were it equivalent, for example, to a day's pay, a single denomination of such value is a substantial, indivisible amount not easily exchanged for the daily necessities of life.[527] Page discussed the work loads of different ranks.[528]

Metcalf (1993–94) and Gannon (2003)[529] remain the main sources for study of the classification[530] and iconography, respectively,[531] and Abramson (2006 and 2017) for comprehensive visual guides to the main varieties.[532]

Sceattas of Northumbrian Series Y and East Anglian Series Q share syncretic design elements and styles (*Figure* 25). Series Q is an imaginatively varied, well-executed and comparatively rare, ecclesiastical coinage which complements *Gipeswic's* trading currency of

[515] Conservatism in coin design, even the immobilisation of an *idée fixe*, serves to inspire confidence.
[516] Wickham (2005, 818).
[517] Other than Northumbrian.
[518] Gannon (2003, 17), suggested that those with Christian imagery were the emissions of minsters, though Marion Archibald had raised this in an earlier, unpublished lecture on the *Monita Scorvm* variety (Metcalf, 1993–94, 435).
[519] The Cothen hoard of presumably intentionally selected light-weight *sceattas* may be an exception. Op den Velde and Metcalf (2014b, 27–51).
[520] Which usually occurs with lead.
[521] Salzman (1970, 41–68).
[522] Reece (1991, 62).

[523] Spufford (1988, 30).
[524] *MEC* (1986, 96).
[525] Spufford (1988, 31–32).
[526] Sixty miles from where Charles Martel defeated the Muslims at Tours in 732. Coupland (2010b, 316).
[527] Abramson (2012b). At a gold to silver ration of 12:1 this would value a tremissis or gold shilling at say two week's pay, which would be reasonable in terms of a Roman soldier's pay. An alternative would be to assess buying power—early law would suggest that a sheep is worth perhaps two to four *sceattas*. Walbers (2012, ch. 5, 235–99, esp. 289–92). See section 2.8.
[528] Page (1972, 94–95). He also made the interesting suggestion that blacksmiths made coins (82–83). Also, Hinton (2011, 195). *Table* 1
[529] Gannon (2003).
[530] Metcalf (1994, 1) addressed the questions: "where and when the coins were struck, and in what quantities…how they circulated and…the purposes for which they were used." To these, Gannon (2003, 1) added the art-historical appraisal.
[531] See Abramson 2012b for a critique of Cribb's 'Money as Metaphor', with its particular applicability to the iconography of *sceattas*.
[532] Abramson (2012d).

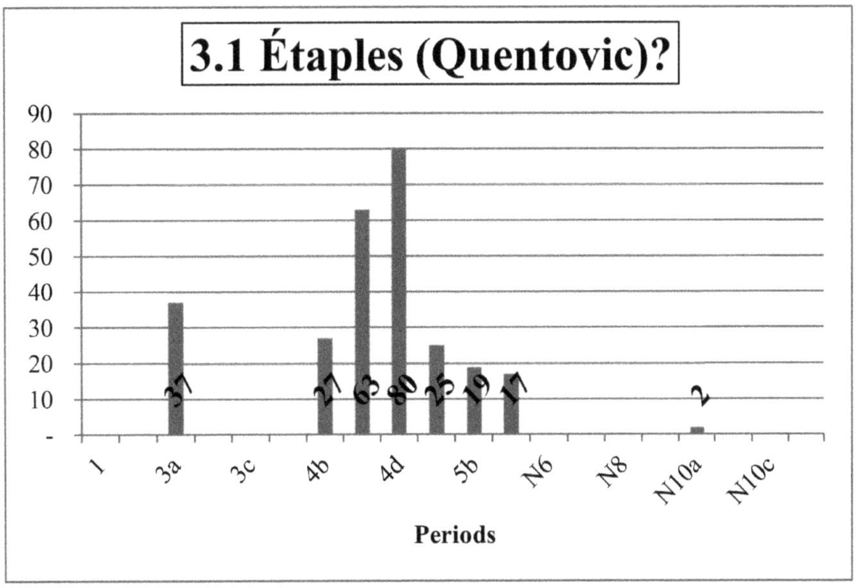

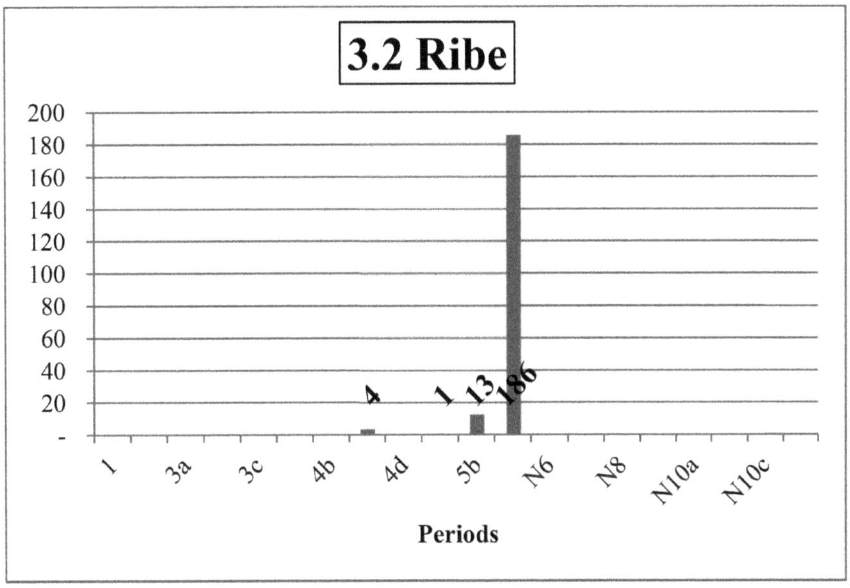

Graphs 3: Site finds by period arranged regionally by weighted average of peak activity, Continental. Sources: *Datasets 1* and *8*. Numerical axis varies.

the long-lived, abundant and conservatively designed Series R. As the number of main varieties now exceeds 680[533] (excluding sub-varieties), only the Northumbrian varieties will be discussed in any detail. The well-executed, epigraphic Northumbrian series allows greater discrimination in typology than is possible elsewhere in the early-penny coinage.

4.3.2.1 Northern Coinages in the Eighth Century

The extent to which the silver *sceat* enabled mercantile monetization is reflected in the mix of regional emissions present in the circulating medium as signified by single finds. During the primary phase, Aldfrith's coinage was supplemented by *sceattas* from both Southumbria and the Continent. In the interval of Aldfrith's successors,[534] before Eadberht's *renovatio monetæ*,[535] these two components were augmented by what may well be non-regal northern currencies—possibly including the trading elements of Series J, types 36, 37 and 85[536] (and, arguably, the exotic species of the 'fledgling' variety.[537])

Therefore, periods of the northern coinage, while the *sceat* was still current in the south, can be represented as:

4. Primary silver *sceattas*:
    a. Aldfrith of Northumbria
    b. Imported Southumbrian *sceattas*

[533] Abramson (2017). Were the Low Countries' emissions (Series D and E) not grouped at a relatively high level, the number of varieties would exceed 1,200.

[534] Osred Coenred, Osric and Ceolwulf.

[535] Here not used in the fiscal sense as in Naismith (2015, 6).

[536] *SL*18–20.

[537] *SL*44.

c. Imported Continental *sceattas*
d. Merovingian *deniers*
5. Imported secondary *sceattas* during the Incompetent Succession:
a. Putative northern non-regal emissions
b. Southumbrian *sceattas*
c. Continental *sceattas*
(d. Merovingian *deniers*[538])
N6. Eadberht's *renovatio* and continuation of the fantastic animal type by his successors.[539]

4.3.2.2 Period 4. Primary Sceattas

Period 4a–c. Primary Silver Sceattas, *c. 660s–c. 710*

Metal-detecting has allowed the view of Dolley that: 'the Northumbrian proto-penny seems never to have become a really viable proposition' to be overturned.[540]

As the northern coinage discontinued during the rule of Aldfrith's successors, it was only during Aldfrith's reign that primary *sceattas* were issued in the north and only after Eadberht's enthronement in 737 that secondary production commenced. However, the Northumbrian coinage can be compartmentalised, without direct reference to the watershed Aston Rowant hoard of *c.* 710, as follows:

Period 4a. Northumbrian Primary Sceattas, *c. 685–c. 704*

A single type (*Figure* 26) covers Aldfrith's reign, 685–704.[541]

Metcalf associated the 'Maltese cross' variety (*Figure* 27) with Aldfrith,[542] although the find-spots do not support a northern connection.

Period 4b. Imported Primary Southumbrian Sceattas, *c. 660s–c. 710*

During Aldfrith's reign there was insufficient monetary control to recycle rapidly all currencies arriving through Northumbria's extensive coastal, estuarine, riverine and inland borders. There are several northern survivors, including issues with presumed moneyers' names—atypical in the southern coinage—such as 'Saroaldo', 'Valdoberhtus' and Æthiliræd (*Figure* 28).

The Series A variety shown here (*Figure* 28, L. i), if genuine, is of the highest rarity and may pre-date Aldfrith, showing that *sceattas* may have circulated in the north before Aldfrith's reign. The illustration at (*Figure* 28, L. ii) is a rare primary *sceat* of pale gold.[543] Blackburn speculates that the Valdoberhtus emission (*Figure* 28, R) may date from the reign of Dagobert II, 676–79.[544] The Series CZ and 'Saroaldo' specimens (*Figure* 29), are late primary and probably post-date Aldfrith.

Though these may not fall within Aldfrith's reign, for the purposes of the current study, the end points of the northern and southern primary *sceattas* are equated.

Period 4c. Imported Primary Continental Sceattas, *c. 685s–c. 710*

> 'the glimmer of a hypothesis comes to mind, involving sheep on chalk uplands.'
>
> Michael Metcalf (2003, 43)

Single losses in Frisia predominantly derive from two densely populated areas: the *terpen* area of western Friesland and the 'Big Rivers' (Rhine mouths) region together with Domburg. Series D, more clearly associated with the former as it is 'relatively more dominant in the north'[545] (*Figure* 30), is contemporary with primary Series E, which, being from the more southerly, commercially vigorous, Rhine mouths area is more prevalent in the trade with England, as evidenced by frequent and widely-scattered finds (*Figure* 31).[546]

The primary coinage of the Low Countries has been interpreted by the author.[547] The association of Series D with Domburg and Series E with Dorestad (Wijk-bij-Duurstede) is no longer supported by finds evidence. Op den Velde and Metcalf controversially consider the production of Series D to exceed 26 million[548] and the mint places to be Friesland, possibly Wijnaldum and the Big Rivers region,[549] Type 2c is thought to be an export currency for trade with England. The extent to which the Franks controlled Frisia seems to have little impact on the free use of Series D *sceattas* north and south of the Rhine—or elsewhere in the Low Countries. It probably did not suit the pragmatic aims of rival political powers to disrupt trade.

Op den Velde and Metcalf compute a total volume of Series E, over its entire duration, of 55 million *sceattas*;[550] again this is not undisputed.[551] The Continental primary phases commence in the mid-690s, perhaps a couple of decades later than the English coinage and closes with the death of Radbod. The secondary phase lasts about

[538] As it is not possible to distinguish these as before or after *c.* 710, in *Dataset 1,* all Merovingian *deniers* are included in Period 4d.
[539] At this point in the period numbering it is necessary to distinguish between northern and southern emissions by the prefix N or S.
[540] Dolley (1976, 352).
[541] Bude has recorded a unique specimen with a different legend.
[542] Abramson (2011, 23–24).
[543] Pale gold specimens of Series F are also known to exist (Naismith 'From Gold to Silver in the Seventh Century' workshop, Cambridge 27–28 March 2015.
[544] Chick (2010, 32).
[545] Op den Velde and Metcalf (2009, VIII).
[546] Despite the predominance of Series D in the Aston Rowant hoard (*SCBI*63, 38).
[547] Abramson (2012b 120–21).
[548] Op den Velde and Metcalf (2003, 74). Based on an estimate of 2,670 dies, this assumed 10,000 *sceattas* per die—even half of this would be a substantial output. The relative paucity of die links was assumed to push the estimate upward when this should have given pause. The relative paucity of die duplicates may imply short-lived dies.
[549] Op den Velde and Metcalf (2003, 96).
[550] Op den Velde and Metcalf (2009–10, 123).
[551] Abramson (2012b, 112).

20 years, *c.* 720–*c.* 740, with the final phase extending possibly to end of the century, almost as late as the final *sceattas* of Northumbria and Jutland (Ribe). Dating is based on hoard evidence, with hoards far more common than in England. The four different primary types suggest four different sources, but these cannot be identified more precisely than the Big Rivers region—with Domburg and Dorestad remaining the most likely mints. Unfortunately, whilst Op den Velde and Metcalf can differentiate emissions according to weight distributions and designs, they are unable to identify the secondary and tertiary mints precisely or be definitive about the source and types of English imitations.

Their volume estimates rely on computed die numbers[552] and assumed outputs per die—factors that are disputed.[553] It may be that the technical skills developed in the large mints in such trading centres (and the 'dumpy' flan) enabled die productivity to approach outputs seen in medieval times (say 10,000 for a reverse die).[554] Metcalf estimates that one-fifth of all *sceattas* in England in the Primary phase are Frisian, suggesting a concentration of these, for commercial reasons, in sheep-rearing areas on chalk upland.[555] This is certainly borne out by Primary D and E finds in the Yorkshire Wolds. Yorke suggested that these types may have been tolerated in circulation rather than recycled as they derive from the Anglo-Saxon homeland.[556]

Period 4d. Imported Merovingian Silver Denier, c. *670–*c. *710*

Silver *deniers*, the third phase of Merovingian coinage, were first struck around 670,[557] and were minted to a uniform metrology but greatly varied design in a decentralised structure (*Figure* 32).[558] There were as many as 600 local mints,[559] employing up to 1,600 *monetarii.*[560] The metrological uniformity implies a high level of control—or an irresistible centripetal force drawing mints to a common standard and witnessing the growth of local trade. A possible overlap between the late debased *tremissis* and the silver *deniers* at this time, may have resulted in an exchange rate of a debased *tremissis* to four *deniers* and, therefore, the *solidus*, as unit of account, would consist of 12 *deniers*. However, Pol has pointed out that, with the exceptions of Quentovic and Dorestad, the Merovingian mints continued to issue gold until coins were 70 per cent debased, whereupon they uniformly and abruptly switched to silver around 670.[561]

A small number of Frankish silver *deniers*, generally scarcer than *tremisses*, have been recovered in Northumbria. Significantly, what is arguably the prototype of the Series J obverse with facing heads, is a *denier* from Reims. (*Figure* 33L).

4.3.2.3 Period 5. Secondary Sceattas

4.3.2.3.1 Incompetent Succession, c. *704–*c. *737 and Later*

> 'for about thirty years, ever since King Aldfrid was removed from this life, our province has been involved in such folly and error'
> Bede's letter to Ecgberht (734, §13).

To the thirty-three-year gap between Aldfrith and Eadberht, 704–37, can be allotted the wide variety of Southumbrian and Continental types found in Northumbria, allowing the possibility that some types (e.g. of Series J[562]) may have been minted locally and that others were imitated contemporaneously.

What may also contribute to the replacement of local issues by imported currency during this period—the Golden Age of Northumbria—is, arguably, a favourable balance of payments. This probably now consisted mainly of sheep or wool as slave trading is more likely to be associated with the expansionism of the seventh century.[563]

Period 5a. Putative Northern Non-regal Emissions, 704–737 or Later

The source of Series J remains uncertain but may be in south Northumbria or north Lincolnshire. Lengthy arguments from both Metcalf and Naylor have identified the main constituent elements of the, as yet inconclusive, debate. Thirty-one of the 231 *sceattas* and *deniers* in the postulated Étaples hoard are Series J, analysed in *Dataset 20, Quentovic*, which may point to a source at Quentovic

552 Using Good's formula (originally for assessing bird migrations).
553 Esty (2006).
554 The upper or punch-die carries the reverse image to be imprinted on the blank. The upper die takes the full strike and Greenhalgh (*pers. comm.* 16th March 2018) estimated that the stock reduced by 6mm per 1,000 strikes, until becoming too short to handle. A well-tempered reverse die will last a minimum of 10,000 strikes whereas an obverse die will last around three times as long.
555 Metcalf (2003, 40. 2014, 244).
556 'From Gold to Silver in the Seventh Century', workshop, Cambridge 27–28 March 2015.
557 *MEC* (1986, 94) made a case for this coinage being initiated by Ebroin, Neustrian Mayor of the Palace (as does Jean Lafaurie in *Revue Numismatique*, 6th series, XI (1969, 120–21)).
558 The precise role of the *monetarius* is uncertain. It could have been as a financier licencing minting for profit rather than an overseer with practical skills such as procurement and preparation of material, die design, engraving, preparation, and striking. Die engraving was less decentralised than minting, related dies being observed at several mints. *MEC* (1986, 101) stated that standards of execution inevitably declined in such a distributed model.
559 Pirenne (2001, 105 and 110) *pace* Prou, regarded this multiplicity of sources not as true mints but as the result of tax farming whereby collected metal was converted into coin locally. Naismith (2012, 245) stated that there were 'never fewer than a dozen' mints operating at any one time, out of 150 in total.
560 Prou (1892), Belfort (1892–95).

561 'From Gold to Silver in the Seventh Century' workshop, Cambridge 27–28 March 2015. Hence, the Frankish transition to silver was not a precedent for England, given the grave-goods chronology of Hines and Bayliss (2013, 509–12).
562 Metcalf (1994) and Naylor (2006). See particularly Bonser (2011, 159–80) for finds from Sledmere.
563 Pelteret (1995, 256).

but Sledmere has been similarly prolific.[564] All that can be concluded from this comparison is that Quentovic is a likely source of the rare type 72 and its intriguing variant.[565]

Another coin which may merit consideration as a non-regal emission of the north in the secondary phase, now dubbed the 'fledgling' type for its reverse gaunt bird with triquetra-knotted, triple tail *Figure* 35).[566] The key element is the fish in the bird's mouth, which may allude to a story in Bede's *Life of Cuthbert.*[567] Northern followers of his cult may not have been literate but would certainly have understood the message. More material evidence is provided by the provenances—at least five the known 13 specimens are northern finds.

Period 5b. Imported Secondary Southumbrian Sceattas, c. *710s–c. 750s*

The extent of inland regional trading links is suggested by the presence and mix of distinctive early-penny types in numbers (*Figure* 36).

As a corollary, the presence of solitary specimens of some scarce, so-called eclectic, varieties indicates the breadth of trading relations (*Figure* 37).

Period 5c. Imported Secondary Continental Sceattas, c. *710s–c. 750s*

The enormous variation in style of the later Series E (*Figure* 38, *Figure* 39), 'the vast trackless wastes of the later porcupines',[568] may indicate that minting became widely dispersed with a consequent reduction in economies of scale, such as high die output.

Here classification of secondary Series E differs from that of Metcalf and Op den Velde, in that the designs displaying cruciform elements are grouped, whereas Metcalf and Op den Velde sub-divide these issues on other criteria.[569]

Finds of Series G (*Figure* 40) are known from several sites in Northumbria including Sledmere (twenty-one specimens[570]), Driffield and a Garton-on-the-Wolds grave find.[571] The origins of this ubiquitous type are uncertain; association of the image, portraying Constantine's dream-vision, with York can probably be discounted given Bede's failure to mention Constantine's elevation by his troops in York in 306.[572] A more plausible candidate is Quentovic as first suggested by Metcalf,[573] though only six of the 231 *sceattas* and *deniers* deemed to constitute the putative Étaples hoard are of this type.[574]

Finally, to this sub-period can be added several exotic Continental species found in Northumbria (*Figure* 41).

The more esoteric *sceattas* of great rarity show a paucity of die duplication, which may imply that smaller (conceivably peripatetic) coin-makers did not develop skills comparable to their peers at trading currencies and the former's dies had little longevity.[575]

Period 5d. Imported Merovingian Silver Denier, c. *710–c. 750*

Merovingian *deniers* probably remained current into period 6, the secondary early-penny phase but are not included in *Dataset 1* due to insufficiency of numbers and difficulty of dating relative to the Aston Rowant hoard.[576]

Imported *dirhams* and Carolingian *solidi* and *deniers* are shown in the *Dataset 1* but are not given a period number as they are regarded as occasional intrusions despite the presence of English imitations of the Louis the Pious *solidus*.

4.3.2.3.2 Periods N6–N8: Eighth-century Northern Sceattas

Period N6, 737–780s: Eadberht and Successors

Returning to Eadberht's reformed coinage, the animal reverse resumed as a livelier, noble beast with features which may reflect a typical early-penny ambiguity (*Figure* 42). It is now a hybrid beast with stag-like attributes which may exhibit Celtic origins.[577] The type extended into the 780s under Eadberht's successors Alchred, Æthelred I (first reign) and Ælfwald I (*SL*70–73) (*Figure* 43).

Eadberht's coinage consists of several successive issues whose differencing marks have been classified by Booth.[578] However, Booth's Class F which displays considerable diversity and a gradual deterioration in execution (the beast has become linear) is at the end of Eadberht's reign, *after* Class G which is more cohesive (*Figure* 44). The deterioration then continues into subsequent reigns with the reverse design reduced to a stylised, emaciated beast and the lettering becoming erratic. There is a recovery

[564] *Graph* 3.1, illustrates the chronological dispersal of finds.
[565] Abramson (2012d, 249). The source of the extremely rare Series J, type 60 (*SL*18–10) remains elusive.
[566] Abramson (2002, 335).
[567] Marner (2000, pl. 15). My thanks to Richard Morris for pointing this out (*pers. comm. c.* 2008?)
[568] Metcalf (1993–94, 222).
[569] But they accept my interpretation of Metcalf's 'Mixed Grill' variety (2009, 47).
[570] Abramson (2011, 167).
[571] The latest of the grave finds, containing eight *sceattas*, a number occurring elsewhere. Rigold (1988 221), Rigold and Metcalf (1984 252), Blackburn (2011, 593).
[572] Mary Garrison (*pers. comm.*) 24th October 2014.
[573] Metcalf (1993–94, 268).
[574] *Dataset 20, Quentovic.*
[575] The earliest surviving English dies are from the smithy at 16–22 Coppergate, York (Ottaway, 1992, 525–27) implying that minting was an occasional part of a metalworker's employment. Blackburn (2011, 595).
[576] Philippe Schiesser, Société d'Études Numismatiques et Archéologiques (*pers. comm.* 12/11/14): 'The dating of *sceattas* is more precise than the *deniers*. We rely on the presence of *sceattas* in the hoards of *denier* for the date.' Moreover, I invoke the 'Reece apologia' (section 6.3.1) in defence of my failure to align the cessation of the northern and southern primary *sceat* phases.
[577] See *fn* 1343.
[578] Booth (1984).

in standard of execution in Ælfwald I's reign, when the varying styles of beast and modes of lettering must reflect different engravers. A comparable dip in Mercian coinage may indicate a prolonged English recession.[579] The productivity shown in *Dataset 3, Sceat Frequencies* frames this recession between Eadberht and Æthelred I.

As at August 2013, Bude's die study indicates 209 reverse dies for Eadberht alone and 57 for his joint issue with Ecgberht. Assuming *c.* 5–10,000 coins per die (by no means a safe assumption either side) this approximates to 1.33–2.66 million coins, a reasonable working hypothesis for the entire reign.

Period N7, Joint Issues, 737–796

The joint regal/episcopal issues (*SL*74–78), which, after the 'standing bishop' issue of the brothers Eadberht and Ecgberht, are inscriptional, may have been the precedent for Ælfwald I replacing the fantastic beast on the reverse of his coinage with the moneyer's name.[580] The abandonment of the reverse portrayal may have been for theological reasons,[581] though naming the moneyer has the distinct advantage of shifting responsibility for the integrity of the coinage from issuer to moneyer.

Joint issues imply a high level of political organisation. While it was imperative for the king to issue coinage, it was voluntary for the Archbishop, so any concession here is made by the monarch to a conceivably more powerful cleric. This may not have been difficult between the siblings Eadberht and Ecgberht,[582] but after the retirement of the former, the latter shows considerable diplomacy in continuing joint issues with aggressively competitive, rival Bernician and Deiran dynasts. While the bishop sits comfortably in York (*Figure* 45), the king is peripatetic, constantly on the move to collect renders, dispense justice and assert his authority. This imbalance is also apparent in the early Anglo-Saxon laws, *Table 1*, and is not redressed until the late ninth-century Alfredian law codes.

Period N8, 780s–800s: Inscriptional Reverse Sceattas[583]

Given the similarity of the obverse inscriptions of the two *sceattas* illustrated below (*Figure* 46), seemingly engraved by the same hand, there can be little doubt that the change of type, from portrayal to epigraphic, took place during the reign of Ælfwald I, despite the conventional wisdom that the latter is an emission of Ælfwald II.[584] This change may be related to the 786 legatine mission.[585]

The reverse inscriptions of these issues name the moneyers of Ælfwald I, Æthelred I (second reign) and Eardwulf to 806. No coinage is here ascribed to the reign of Ælfwald II or any putative second reign of Eardwulf.[586] The five named moneyers (*Figure* 47) are the long-lived Cuthheard (sole moneyer for Eardwulf, *Figure* 48), the prolific Ceolbald,[587] the scarce Tidwulf, the extremely rare Hnifula and the enigmatic 'Cudcils' (Cuthgils). The volume of production must fall well short of that estimated for Eadberht, given the far fewer die variations. This phase displays generally competent execution, except in the case of 'Cudcils' which is poorly engraved and struck in baser metal.[588] Two specimens struck by Cuthgils for Ælfwald I have been found (*Figure* 49).

4.3.3 Conclusion

These chronological divisions help to distinguish Northumbrian *sceattas* from the rest of the early-penny coinage (*Plate 3, Figures* 1–10). The distinct features are:

1. Named Issuers

Throughout the production of Northumbrian silver *sceattas* and base-metal *stycas*, the issuing authority are named.[589] The inscriptional types name five moneyers, two of whom, Cuthheard and Cuthgils, serve more than one monarch. Occasionally, Southumbrian *sceattas* name what are taken to be moneyers[590] but it is not until Beonna of East Anglia issued his *sceat*-like coinage in the 750s that a known issuer's name appears (*Plate 3, Figure* 1).[591]

The period of activity in Northumbrian *sceat* production is framed by the twin disasters of Nechtansmere in 685 and Lindisfarne in 793. It can be assumed that Æthelred's active phase of named moneyers predated this and Eardwulf's corpus is negligible.

579 Booth (2011). A possible cause is disrupted trade across the North Sea due to Frankish intervention in Frisia.

580 This division disguises the change from the 'fantastic animal' type to the inscriptional type. This occurred during the reign of Ælfwald I, but the two earlier joint issues of Æthelwald Moll are inscriptional (*SL*76–7). The issue with his son Æthelred has the 'initial' cross within the legend on both obverse and reverse.

581 Influences may have included Byzantine iconoclasm and the Islamic view of portrayal as blasphemous.

582 Significantly, it is the bishop who is portrayed. Woodman (2012, 33–35).

583 Here meaning with obverse and reverse inscriptions around central motifs, but no portraiture.

584 Pirie (1995, 24–27). Her argument, partly based on letter forms, has been discredited with further finds of the *sceattas* of King Eardwulf.

585 *Story (2003, 55–78). Woodman (2012, 4–5).*

586 Booth (1987, 64–65).

587 The moneyer of this name who coined at London for Ceonwulf of Mercia (North, 1994, 361) could be the same, but lettering styles differ.

588 Yet, strangely, the most highly prized, possibly due to the 'shrine' motif and false attributions to St. Cuthbert (Lord Grantley, *NC* Series 3 no. 17 134–44 and *BNJ* 8 (1911, 49–53). The 'fledgling' *sceat* is much more likely to allude to Cuthbert. Lyon ((2016, 12) convincingly postulated that the Cuthgils issue post-dated the Viking attack on Lindisfarne.

589 Seven monarchs (one restored, Æthelred I) and two archbishops on the *sceattas* and three monarchs (one restored, Æthelred II) and three archbishops on the *stycas*.

590 Pada, Vanimundus, Valdobertus, Epa, Vernus, Saroaldo, Æthiliræd, Tilberht, Wigræd and Tiluwald. There are other inscriptions which plausibly may be moneyer's names—LEL, TANUM (Gannon suggests this is probably MONETA—*pers. comm.)* derivatives of Epa, and VILL… Many are runic or partly so. Dolley (1976, 353) referred to 'this tiresome pseudo-epigraphy'.

591 His moneyers are Efe, Wilred (who later minted for Offa) and Werferth.

2–6. Joint Issues

A characteristic of the Northumbrian coinage, rarely seen elsewhere,[592] are the joint issues where monarchs and arch/bishops are clearly named (*Plate 3*, *Figures* 2–6).

The continuing internecine strife,[593] was to some extent reflected in deteriorating execution and volume of coinage. However, the joint issues disguise the regicide—or underline the political acuity of the Archbishops.

There is one further case of a joint issue, but this time it is the dynastic plea by Æthelwald Moll for the succession of his son Æthelred (*Plate 3*, *Figure* 6, *SL*77).

1. Named issuers

Beonna's named moneyer's Efe
(One of three from Freckenham, Suffolk) and Werferth (Thetford, Norfolk), (*SL*113).

2-6. Joint issues

Ecgberht with Eadberht
(also see illustration above), (*SL*74)
Found: Seamer (rare two crozier variety)

Ecgberht with Alchred, (*SL*75)
Found South Newbald.

Ecgberht with Æthelwald Moll, (*SL*76)[1]
Found Driffield (?)

Eanbald I with Æthelred I, (*SL*78)
Found Thorpe-le-Street

Plate 3i: Evaluating periodicity. Stewart (1991), Booth (1984), Alchred/Ecgberht 6. Pirie (1992a, Appendix. Source: Abramson collection except no. 10.

[592] Archbishops of Canterbury minted under Offa.

[593] Higham (1993, 145). Yorke (1990, 87).

Æthelwald Moll
L: with Æthelred (*SL*77), found Kilham. R: Æthelred I 'Double obverse' (*SL*81-10), found South Newbald

7. Literacy and inscriptions

Epigraphic southern sceats (*SL*24, 92 and 93 respectively):
Top row with 'porcupine' reverses, l-r: *DE LUNDONIA/SCORUM*, Runic Æthiliræd sceat, rare *SEDE* type.
Second row: SAROALDO type (*SL*7), found Wetwang, near Driffield, East Yorkshire

8. Consistency of type and extended duration

The 'Wodan/monster' sceat of Danish Series X
Ribe type (found Sheffield) and Insular variety (Warminster, Wiltshire), (*SL*103-4)

9. Mint place

Typical sceat of Hamwic
(*SL*48, unmatched obverse and reverse)

10. Successor coinage

Carolingian denier of Pepin III (751-68),
Dorestad, 0.92g, MEC 1,719. Found Melbourne, Cambridgeshire, Spink lot 0219 26-06-2013, ©Spink.

Plate 3ii: Evaluating periodicity.

The plea was eventually fulfilled after the intervening reign of Alchred. This is the only instance of overt political propaganda on a *sceat*. Also illustrated here is a rare and enigmatic 'double obverse' *sceat* of Æthelred (*SL*81–10).

7. Literacy and Inscriptions

Again, the standard of literacy, clarity and consistency of inscriptions and skilled execution of lettering is unparalleled, though the current die study of the coinage of Eadberht by Bude has revealed that one engraver, his 'Retrograde Man', was likely to have been dyslexic.[594]

Admittedly, some of the southern eclectic groups such as DE LUNDONIA/SCORUM and Æthiliræd,[595] are epigraphic and literate, but these are rare and did not constitute major trading issues (*Plate 3*, *Figure* 7).

8. Consistency of Type and Extended Duration

There are instances of long-lived trading currencies, Frisian Series D and E, East Anglian R, and especially Danish X, where (essential elements of) a specific design has become an *idée fixe* to enhance and prolong the currency of the type. D and E are held together as cohesive groups only because of the presence of specific design elements (the 'porcupine' and degenerated votive standard) whereas, R and X deteriorate steadily over 40 years in the case of the former, and over 70 the latter, which is possibly the only early-penny variety outside Northumbria which extends well beyond 750 (archaeology at Ribe suggests that Series X was still current in *c.* 800 (*Plate 3*, *Figure* 8).[596] The fantastic animal and inscribed types of Northumbrian *sceat* extend from 685 to, arguably, 829, even if production is sporadic.

Political Image

Joint issues, consistent motifs and skilled execution continued despite the fissiparous tendency. Even in the heat of intense rivalry, there must have been a common desire to maintain governance, protect the mint and project a unified image. It was arguably the authority of the Archbishops which overcame factional dynastic strife.

Consistency of Metrology

The silver content of the Northumbrian *sceat* remains in the 50–70 per cent range.

9. Mint Place

Only in the cases of Ribe (X), Domburg (D), Dorestad (E), Hamwic (H, *Plate 3*, *Figure* 9) Ipswich (R) and York (Y), can we be confident of the mint place of different types of *sceat*.

In these instances, the authorities exercised a degree of control over production and usage not matched elsewhere. These are the anchor points for what otherwise would be a worryingly anonymous coinage.

10. Successor Coinage

The coinage reform of the Carolingian Pepin the Short[597] ushered in the broad penny (*Plate 3*, *Figure* 10),[598] which was then adopted by Offa of Mercia. A recent find of a Pippinid coin at Melbourne near Cambridge is suggestive of a close link as is the find of a denier of Charlemagne at South Newbald as recorded by Booth and Blowers.[599]

Beonna issued coins of early-penny module[600] and Offa's earliest, light emissions are of the small flan variety.[601] However, very soon all Southumbrian monarchs were issuing broad pennies. The variation in issues reduced as the political hierarchy crystalized; before long it was only occasional issues (e.g. of Offa, Alfred and Edward the Elder) which broke away from the immobilised bust/cross pattern. However, the Northumbrian coinage continued essentially unchanged to *c.* 806 and then, after an undefined interval, in the same module, but initially in silver-enhanced base-metal then in brass. This silver-alloy emission is here assumed to be Eanred's attempt to continue the early-penny coinage. This was in Period N9, which can be regarded as a transitional phase before the base *styca*.

***

Despite the cultural achievements of eighth-century Northumbria, a long-term economic decline following the disaster of Nechtansmere seems to have set in. This was exacerbated by dynastic feuding and the diminution in the 'tax net' by the introduction of *bookland* in perpetuity, not just for life, after the Synod of Whitby.[602] Wilfrid pressed for greater endowments when he saw the wealth of churches abroad. This was intensified when the Pope defeated the attempt of Eadberht and Ecgberht to return lands to secular ownership, but then the secular nobility came to expect to be rewarded by land grants too. At least, well-endowed religious houses were able to perpetuate the Golden Age of

594 Bude (2016).

595 Three specimens found at Sledmere, Abramson (2011, 170).

596 Feveile (2008, 53–67).

597 Pepin III, Mayor of the Palace, 741–51, King of the Franks, 751–68.

598 Probably as a response to the reduction in weight of the *denier* resulting from the chaos following the Arab invasion of Francia.

599 Booth and Blowers (1983, 139–45).

600 Archibald (1985) and Archibald, M. M., V. Fenwick, and M. R. Cowell (1995); C13 in the latter is the 1984 Whithorn find of a Beonna sceat by Efe. Beonna's rare interlaced type show an increase in diameter to *c.* 14mm and the light coinage of Offa and his contemporaries were 17–18mm.

601 Chick (2010, 57–142).

602 *Folkland* is defined as land held under ancient, unwritten custom and it could not normally be removed from the relatives of the holder. The legal concept of *bookland*, land subject to charter, arose in the seventh century in respect of land that could be 'alienated' (i.e., disposed of) at will. It ultimately developed into ownership in the modern sense. Wormald (2006, 153–58). Charles-Edwards (1997, 192–99) described four associated strands: i) perpetual/hereditary rights, conflicting with ii) the right to freely grant the land, iii) freedom from secular dues and iv) these rights were ecclesiastical. Multiple-estates could now be broken up (Pelteret, 1995, 251).

Northumbrian literature, though the discontinuation of the Northumbrian chronicle after the start of the ninth century, deprives us of more certain knowledge of the later kings. No complete Northumbrian charters survived the Viking invasion.

4.3.4 Illustrations—Silver Periods 4–8

Figure 14: Evidence of Northumbrian missionaries in Frisia. Primary Frisian *sceattas*, possibly inscribed *Willi(brodr)*, Bishop of Utrecht.[603] Central crozier on reverse (see also *Figure* 31).

Figure 15: Romanitas in secondary phase early-penny portraiture of Series K and T[604] (coin right, found south Humberside).

Figure 16: Rare Series J variant: the defeat of evil in two acts.[605]

Figure 17: Rare Series J variant: the defeat of evil in three acts.[606]

We now move to a consideration of whether the base *styca* coinage of the ninth century was symptomatic of long-term decline or of healthy economic and fiscal activity.

Figure 18: Series QII: the defeat of evil in two acts (*SL* group 64).

[603] Abramson (2012b, 121–22).
[604] Abramson (2012a, 73–104), SL 249.
[605] Finds evidence from a probable hoard, offered at auction by cgb.fr in June 2013, suggests that the variety on the right was possibly minted in Quentovic.
[606] Abramson (2012d, 249) for an explanation of the iconography.

Figure 19: Series B: syncretic imagery—apotropaic *Uroboros*. Found Castle Acre, Norfolk (*SL* group 16).

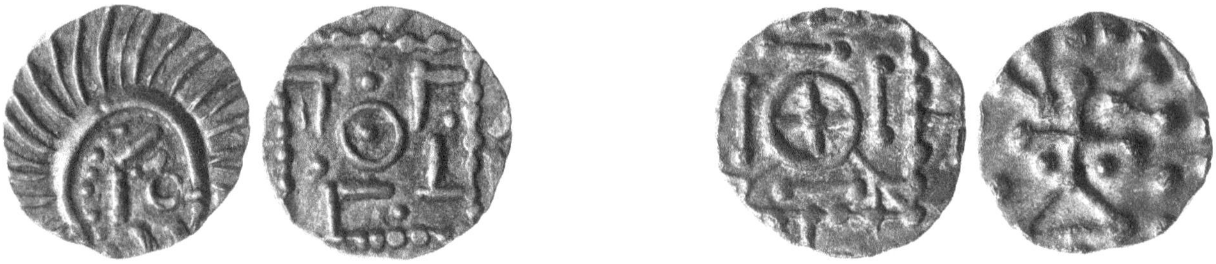

Figure 20: Series E (left) and D (right): intentional anonymity.

Figure 21: Progression through Series A. L–R: rare Valdobertus variety, found at Thwing;[607] Series C (inscribed ᛖᛈᚫ); early Series R (found Sledmere).

Figure 22: Deterioration in late Series R. L–R: Tilberht; saltire cross reverse (found Rotherham); type 70 exhibiting geometric loss of identity (found Adwick-upon-Dearne, Doncaster).

Figure 23: Metrological variations in circulating coinage, Series E and U.[608]

[607] Mark Blackburn supported an early date for this exotic species (Chick, 2010, 32).
[608] Abramson (2012b, 110). Millimetre scale shown.

Figure 24: ***Denier*** **of Melle. Monograms of Metalus and Nemfidius of Marseilles, found Ashford, Kent.**

Figure 25: Early-penny reverses compared. a–d: Northumbrian Series Y (a and c, 737–58) and East Anglian Series Q (b, 740s and d, 725–45). Find-spots a–d: '4 miles east of York', Norfolk/Cambridgeshire, South Newbald and Harwell.

Figure 26: Aldfrith ***sceat*****. Found Kilham, East Yorkshire (*****SL*****69).**

Figure 27: 'Maltese cross' variety. Found Norfolk, north-west Norfolk.[609]

Figure 28: L: Series A (***SL*****3). R: 'Valdoberhtus'. L: i) var. A1, found 'Yorkshire', ii) var. A2, pale gold. R: 'Valdoberhtus', found Alne, North Yorkshire (*****SL*****3–50).**[610]

[609] Another was found at Pangbourne, Berkshire (*SL*102–80).

[610] Op den Velde and Metcalf (2009–10, nos. 3466–8+, 377, plate 92), shows five die-linked specimens of this very rare type, including this coin.

Figure 29: L: Runic Series CZ. Found 'Yorkshire' (*SL*5). R: 'Saroaldo'. Found Wetwang, near Driffield, East Yorkshire (*SL*7).

Figure 30: *Sceattas* of primary Frisian Series D. L: variety 2c (found Sledmere), the English version of 2c (Driffield) (*SL*8). R: variety 8 (Sheffield) (*SL*10).

Figure 31: *Sceattas* of the four primary Series E varieties (*SL*87–90). First row: 'plumed bird' (found Pocklington), *VICO* mule (Upper Poppleton). Second row: variety D (Driffield), and a rare variety G variant inscribed VVILLI... with central crozier[611] (Aylesbury).

Figure 32: Merovingian silver *deniers* of the named mint/moneyer type: L: Rouen (Civitas Rotomagensium)/ERMOBERTO. R: *Ecclesia racio* type, attributed to Limoges, found Market Rasen, Lincolnshire.

[611] Plausibly referring to Willibrord. See Wood (e.g. 2000, 149–66).

Figure 33: Mint-monogrammed *deniers*. L: Reims, found near Bridlington (the prototype of Series J). R: Marseilles? Found Durham area?

Figure 34: Typical of Northumbrian finds dating to *c.* 710–*c.* 725, Series J (l. Malton, type 85 and r. Pocklington, type 37) (*SL*18–19).

Figure 35: The rare 'fledgling' *sceat* with its possible allusion to Cuthbert.[612] Found by Ian Postlethwaite, June '97 at Binnington (*SL*44).

Figure 36: L: Series U, Thames Valley, *c.* 710–*c.* 735. R: Series O, *c.* 720–*c.* 735. L: found Kilham—others at Whitby, Wetwang and near Driffield, *SL*45. R: found Upper Poppleton—others at Boynton, Sledmere and Wetwang, *SL*58.

Figure 37: Exotic species. L–R: rosette type (found Sledmere), rare variety of the 'Wodan'/monster type (Boynton) and the 'animal mask' type (Wetwang) (*SL*32, 105 and 112 respectively).

[612] First recognised by Richard Morris.

Figure 38: Secondary Series E (*SL*95–7). Finds from Driffield.

Figure 39: Secondary Series E (*SL*95–7). Finds from near Scarborough, East of York and Malton.

Figure 40: Series G: left, with rotated reverse, Kilham, right, Fimber (*SL*21).

Figure 41: Eclectic Continental varieties, both were imitated in England. L: 'Interlace' type found Rudston (*SL*60) and R: 'Hexagram' type,[613] found Wetwang (*SL*109).

Figure 42: A selection of *sceattas* of Eadberht. L–R: Class *Ai* (*SL*70–10, find-spot unknown) (*SL*70–60) Rillington and *Biv* (*SL*70–90) Fimber.

Figure 43: Scarcer fantastic animal types. Alchred (*SL*71–10), Æthelred I (*SL*72–10, first reign) and Ælfwald I (*SL*73–20). Found: east of York, Market Weighton and 2 miles west of Thirsk.

[613] Op den Velde and Metcalf (2014a, 122–40).

Figure 44: Eadberht: Booth class G (L: *SL*70–310) precedes the decline of class F (R: *SL*70–180). Found: L. Thwing, R. Sancton.

Figure 45: Eadberht and Ecgberht joint issue *sceat* (*SL*74). Find-spot unknown.

Figure 46: Ælfwald I. L: fantastic animal type (*SL*73–20) and R: inscriptional type by Cuthheard (*SL*79–10).

Figure 47: The named moneyer types of Æthelred I (second reign) (*SL*80–85). Find-spots: N. Yorkshire, North Elmsall, Sledmere, near Wetwang, Weaverthorpe.

4.4 Copper Alloy: Periods N9–10: Ninth-century Northumbria

> 'I look upon these which our ancestors called stycas, two whereof made a farthing;
> like the widow's mite in the Gospel, where we meet this word.'
>
> William Nicolson, Archdeacon of Carlisle, to Ralph Thoresby of Leeds, 25th November 1695.[614]

The transition from precious to base metal suffered political and economic discontinuities, *Table 2*, and the process unfolded erratically over two centuries. However, Northumbria's management of its independent monetary strategy, long past the point of departure from southern coinage, can be deemed successful, and is discussed below.

Northumbrian history in the ninth century, again with reference to kings and archbishops, is described below. The silver-alloy emissions of Eanred are distinguish from the subsequent base *stycas*. The taxonomy departs significantly from Pirie's classification presenting a far simpler approach. The interpretative opportunities provided by hoards are distinguished from single finds Finally, monetary affairs between the fall of York and the first Viking pennies of York are briefly considered.

4.4.1 Historical Background

4.4.1.1 Kings[615]

In the ninth century, the dynasty of Eardwulf brought some stability, particular in the long reign of Eanred and the resumption of coin production: 'The styca could be seen as evidence of efficient royal control of the economy and a sensitive response to changing circumstances rather than as evidence of decline.'[616] In contrast to this now accepted view, Dolley held to the earlier convention that: 'Northumbria, victim of Scandinavian plundering, still held aloof, but her poverty is mirrored in the substitution of copper for silver as the metal of her coinage. The coins remain essentially proto-pennies...but their purpose can only have been fiscal, a reminder of the neglected tax function of the whole of later Anglo-Saxon coinage.'[617]

Little is known of Eardwulf's successor Ælfwald II (806–08). Later records (Roger of Wendover's *Flores Historiarum)* are probably unreliable.[618] On stylistic grounds, coins in this name are here attributed to Ælfwald I.

The reign of Eanred (808?–840?),[619] son of Eardwulf, may have started after Ælfwald II or a temporarily restored Eardwulf.[620] The Anglo-Saxon Chronicle records that in 829, Ecgberht of Wessex 'conquered Mercia and all that was south of the Humber', so becoming the eighth *bretwalda.*[621] Eanred 'offered him submission and peace' at Dore, near Sheffield.

During the tenure of Eanbald II, i.e. by 835, Eanred initiated what may be deemed to be a continuation of the early-penny coinage, albeit in poor silver, issued by named moneyers. A second emission, during Wigmund's tenure, introduced base *stycas* in substantial numbers.[622] The recorded northern regnal dates in the ninth century are possibly quite unreliable. The reign of Eanred's son Æthelred II (first reign conventionally given as 841–43/4) was briefly interrupted, perhaps in 843/4, by the little-known usurper Redwulf. *Styca* production continued. Æthelred II was restored and served until his assassination in 849/50. The moneyer Eardwulf was prolific during the restoration, issuing *stycas* in brass.

Osberht (849–62) possibly a kinsman of Redwulf, was overthrown by Ælla (862–67), recorded to be a 'tyrant'. Subsequently Ælla and Osberht united against the *micel here*, the Great Army of the Danes lead by Halfdan. Both were killed in the Viking attack on York in March 867,[623] vividly recounted in the saga of *Ragnar's Sons*.[624] Osberht's early emissions restored tin to the coin alloy resulting in a bronze *styca* but the coinage became chaotic as his reign progressed.

4.4.1.2 The Episcopacy

Eanbald II (tenure 796–*c.* 835?) was a student of Alcuin who gave him much support—often in tangible, practical form as with the gift of metal for the roof of the York Minster bell tower. He assisted Æthelhard, Archbishop of Canterbury after Offa's despoliation and denounced Eardwulf's adultery. Eanbald's coin emissions parallel those of Eanred in alloy, with Æthelweard and Cynewulf issuing silver-alloy coins and subsequently Eadwulf the only certain episcopal moneyer for the base *stycas*. Numismatic evidence suggests a long tenure, possibly into the mid-830s but Eanbald's terminal date is uncertain and little is known of his successor, Wulfsige (*c.* 835?–837), who issued no coinage.[625]

---

[614] Later Bishop of Carlisle. Pirie (1982, 85). The letter discussed the Ripon hoard.

[615] Based on Abramson (2012d).

[616] Yorke (1990, 97). Davies (1994, 123): 'the economist welcomes them as evidence of the degree of penetration of coinage among the population and as clear proof of the increase of the coinage habit.'

[617] Dolley (1976, 355). He cited Lyon (1957) and Pagan (1969).

[618] The Annals of the Frankish Kingdom record however, that in 808 Eardwulf visited his father-in-law, Charles the Great, at Nijmegen, on his way to Rome, in search of help from the Pope. The Pope sent his envoys with Eardwulf back to Northumbria.

[619] See *fn* 663

[620] Might Eardwulf have retired to Breedon-on-the-Hill where he is buried and venerated as St. Hardulph? Pirie (1995, 24). (*Pace* Rollasson and Dornier).

[621] After Ælle of Sussex, Ceawlin of Wessex, Æthelbert of Kent, Rædwald of East Anglia, Edwin, Oswald and Oswy of Northumbria, though it is uncertain what real authority this title conferred.

[622] '*Styca*' is probably derived from the German for small piece, *Stűck*, but now pronounced "sty-ka" or "sticker".

[623] Higham (1993, 167).

[624] http://www.germanicmythology.com/FORNALDARSAGAS/ThattrRagnarsSonar.html

[625] And is not to be mistaken for the moneyer of similar name (variously Wulfsic, Wulfsixt, Wulfsige) who issued coins for Æthelred II and Osberht.

Rollason argued that in York, the ninth-century archbishops were more powerful that the monarchs.[626] Joint issues (and southern law codes)[627] support this view though Blackburn confined this to a wider secular rôle, which may explain the issue of the gold mancus of Archbishop Wigmund (tenure 837–54).[628] Rollason's view is favoured here.

Letters of Lupus, abbot of Ferrières,[629] refer to the peace between the English monarchs in May 851 and with the Bretons in August 851. Were this the case, it may have facilitated Osberht's return to a bronze coinage. Wulfhere (tenure 854–92 or *c.* 900) made peace with the Danish invaders after the attack on York in 866/7 but took refuge with Burgred of Mercia after the 872 rebellion against the Danes, before being recalled from Addingham in 875 by Guthred.[630]

Dataset 3, Summary, lists the ninth-century Northumbrian issuers.

4.4.2 Coin Production: Northumbrian **Sceattas** *or* **Stycas***? The Silver-alloy Emissions of Eanred*

Why did the Northumbrians retain the *sceat*, then the *styca*, instead of following the south in adopting the broad penny? Offa's light coinage may have appeared experimental to the authorities in the north,[631] whose numismatic habits were rather conservative. Besides, the contrast between the light penny and the *sceat* was not that great. The earliest date to emulate the broad penny would have been after Eadberht's retirement but Archbishop Ecgberht may well have influenced continuation of the familiar as the Archbishop of York was more powerful than the new monarch at this time.

In any event, both the northern and southern coinages seem to be in retreat in the third quarter of the eighth century, whether the problem was disruption to North Sea trade or further afield. Perhaps Offa's move to the heavy penny (a clearer contrast to the *sceat*) was a gesture of Mercian confidence or defiance in the face of Viking incursions—it must have been around the time of the attack on Lindisfarne. After this, there seems to have been a collapse of confidence in the north evinced by the paucity of Eardwulf's coins and the absence of coins of the illusive Ælfwald II.[632] There was no incentive to issue any coin, let alone risk adopting the penny.[633]

Presumably it is the same *monetarius*, Cuthheard, who had been employed in the mint since, at the very latest, the introduction of the inscriptional reverse by Ælfwald I,[634] who became one of Eanred's Period N9 moneyers of the early silver-alloy coins.[635] The chronology is uncertain; it could be argued that these came near the start of Eanred's reign otherwise Cuthheard is endowed with remarkable tenure for those precarious times.[636] Moreover, one would expect an economic recovery to have occurred by two decades after the 793–94 attacks. It is plausible that Eanred was attempting to resume the early-penny coinage and it is considerably later in his reign that he issued further, base coins. Only one of the 'Group A' moneyers, Æthelweard, convincingly has the longevity (or acuity) to be re-engaged in minting the brass coinage,[637] indicating another lengthy cessation.

Eanred replaced silver with zinc, perhaps realising that this was a constructive step economically.[638] Hence, the currency of the Northumbrian *sceat* is here extended to include these silver-alloy emissions and the *styca* is regarded as starting only when the copper alloy included zinc not silver. Indeed, any distinction seems increasingly contrived, as what we are seeing here is precisely the gradual, albeit fragmented, process of monetization.

Belief that it would simplify matters to abandon both the terms '*sceat*' and '*styca*' and merely refer to early (or proto-) pennies on the plausible grounds that this is historically more accurate, is misguided.[639] Conflating these two distinct denominations as pennies and then differentiating the early- from the broad-penny does not add clarity. Moreover, common parlance, general comprehension and routine use in numismatic and historic literature render this unfeasible.

Northumbrian *stycas* are amongst the most unpretentious of currencies. They state the name of the issuer, monarch or archbishop, on the obverse and the moneyer's name on the reverse. Out of the entire corpus, only a tiny number of coins, struck by the moneyer Leofthegn, portray an animal (*Figure* 50).[640]

The initial silver-alloy emissions of Eanred (*Figure* 51) are chronologically skewed towards earlier *sceattas* by the presence of the moneyer Cuthheard and are distanced from

[626] Tweddle and others (1999, 131–34).
[627] *Table* 1.
[628] Blackburn (2007, 64).
[629] A monastery given to Alcuin implying a bond with York (*EHD* 807).
[630] Blackburn (2004, 329–30) advocated the view that Wulfhere influenced the choice of liturgical phrases on the York regal coinage *c.* 895–905. (Woodman 2012, 49).
[631] It is worth noting that Ceolbald also struck for Offa.
[632] As correctly stated by Keary (1887–93, vol. 1, 143), despite repeated denials commencing with Heywood (1887).
[633] Pirie (1995, 25), recognised this argument but dismissed it as 'a mere canard'.
[634] Cuthheard probably minted the fantastic animal types given the identical obverse rendering of 'Ælfwald'.
[635] See Pirie (1995 *fn.* 44) and the appendix on ESM analysis by M. R. Cowell which shows that the first found King Eardwulf sceat was only 44 per cent silver, comparable to Eanred's early emissions.
[636] Or, conceivably, a succession, say, of father and son?
[637] Pirie (1996, 36): 'Edilueard was the only official from the earlier phase who continued to work, with new colleagues, for the new archbishop, Uigmund.'
[638] Plausibly, in straitened circumstances, the requisite quantum of silver, to continue a silver-alloy coinage, was unavailable, but see *fn.* 643, Naismith (2012, 247).
[639] See Naismith (2017, 67–68).
[640] In his 1957 BNJ article Lyon identified this as a reversion to the "fantastic animal" design found on the Northumbrian sceattas; he notes: "even the triquetra is included".

the later base issues by the absence of 10 of the 11 earlier 'Group A' moneyers of Eanred.[641] From around 830 to 866/7, *stycas* were issued, usually in base metal (*Figure* 52),[642] for four monarchs (one restored) and three archbishops by a total of 26 moneyers.[643] The only elaboration is the repertoire of around 50 different central motifs.

Towards the end of Eanred's reign there is a substantial increase in the number of moneyers presumably in an effort to augment the volume of silver-free coins produced, in response to several factors: economic growth, increased penetration of coinage into lower levels of society occasioned by the fall in intrinsic value and the attraction of the fiscal pull of the 'widow's mite'.

Increased production is accompanied by a decline in mint discipline. Dies are matched promiscuously and combinations proliferate.[644] The die-linking is extensive, but illusory as regards sequencing though it may demonstrate the likelihood of a single mint. The output seems to be random—the product of a system which sets no store by the matching of moneyer with a particular device. Central motifs are used in various combinations adding further permutations to the typology. Standards of literacy vary and both legends and individual characters appear in various scripts, languages and aspects. In the first edition of the *BNJ,* Creeke lists hundreds of variations in issuers' and moneyers' names.[645] Thoresby blamed the decline on 'the intolerable Bunglers of the Age'.[646]

4.4.3 Hoard Evidence

In the case of *sceattas*, distribution evidence from single finds has been paramount, since there are relatively few hoards. However, the Northumbrian source of *stycas* is not in dispute[647] and it is the voluminous evidence of several very substantial hoards that has facilitated recording of the different types, their chronology, die-linking and frequency. Pirie lists these meticulously in *CKN*.[648]

Adamson published the Hexham (Northumberland) hoard of *stycas* in *Archaeologia*[649] supported by excellent line drawings by Basire on 23 plates in 1834 and a further seven plates two years later, totalling 944 specimens from a total of around eight thousand *stycas* discovered in 1833 (with additions in 1841) (*Figure* 53). These are helpfully reproduced by Pirie.[650]

A further five thousand *stycas* were discovered at St Leonard's Place, York, in 1842 and there have been two finds at Bolton Percy (Ulleskelf), North Yorkshire—several thousand coins in 1847 (*BP*1) and 1,775 in 1967 (*BP*2).[651] Informal sources report a further 430, apparently low-grade, specimens found there by metal-detection, *c.* 2010–12.[652] *Dataset 3, Styca Hoard Comparison,* includes St. Leonard's Place, 'Stonyhurst' and Bolton Percy. See *Graph* 4.4.

There are no *stycas* of Wulfhere in the St. Leonard's Place hoard, four in the 'Stonyhurst' parcel and 13 in the Bolton Percy hoards. All three hoards rank highly in the representation of moneyers. Care must be exercised in interpreting recorded hoard issuer proportions as can be seen from a comparison of the Hexham hoard as noted in *CKN* and *EMC* (156 coins, 3.85 per cent episcopal) and what is shown in the Adamson plates (937 coins, 7.12 per cent episcopal), which themselves are a fraction of the *c.* 8,000-piece hoard. There have been many other hoards: Ripon 1695, Kirkoswald 1808,[653] York Micklegate 1827, York Railway 1840, York Exhibition Buildings, 1879.[654] The putative Walmgate hoard (deposited *c.* 865, found *c.* 1856) of 'many hundreds of *stycas*...corroded into one mass' is tantalisingly close to the site of the Walmgate Viking hoard (deposited *c.* 915, found 1856) both found by workmen laying a sewer.[655]

As regards the 1831 parcel located at the Jesuit Stonyhurst College in the Ribble Valley, Pirie extracted a manuscript entry from the archives (*Figure* 54), which gives provenance to this assemblage:

> ...found by some work men who were digging near St Mary's Abbey in York...in the year 1831', attached to an invoice for £2-0-0 from Henry Chapman who, though a Petergate Museum employee, sold the coins privately through his antiquarian business.[656] Pirie suggests the coins may have been found when water pipes were connected to King's Manor.[657]

This hoard is particularly strong in period N10a, brass, a significant element of which is episcopal (i.e. Wigmund). Possibly, this is diagnostic of the find-spot, an ecclesiastical site but it seems counter-intuitive that the silver and tin alloy coins were filtered out for use and the brass kept.

Whilst it may be self-evident, it bears stating that these large hoards are exclusively composed of the northern

[641] See *Dataset 3. 'Group A' Moneyers* and footnote.
[642] Interestingly, silver continued to be used for ornamentation, suggesting that debasement was an intentional monetary policy, Naismith (2012, 247).
[643] I list 36 in Abramson (2012d) of which 11 are 'Period N9' and only one, Æthelweard, convincingly belongs to both groups. Lyon (1957, 234), on stylistic grounds, suggested that the interval between his omissions was 'a fairly short time'.
[644] Booth (1997b, 26).
[645] Creeke (1905, 65–96).
[646] Pirie (1982, 85).
[647] Although Pirie continued to question whether York was the sole mint.
[648] Also see Pirie 1994 and 2000.
[649] Vols 25 and 26
[650] *BAR 180* (1987, 257–327). There are 156 Hexham coins in the Yorkshire Museum, which are far from a random selection, and 800 *stycas* neglected in the BM with those from Hexham in disarray (Pagan, 1997, 281). *Graph* 5.2.
[651] In connection with which Richards deduced that northern England had a 'money economy, where coins despite variations in weight and purity, had an agreed face value.' (2010, 30).
[652] *Fn.* 356.
[653] *Graph* 6.3.
[654] This list is not exhaustive—more information is available from Pirie's *CKN* (1996, 16–19) and Pagan, *BAR* 180 (1987, 147–58).
[655] Pirie (1975, xxxii–xxxiii, nos. 8 and 10). Tweddle and others (1999, #137, 277).
[656] Pirie archive, Stonyhurst College file and Pirie (1994, 25).
[657] Pirie (1994, 28).

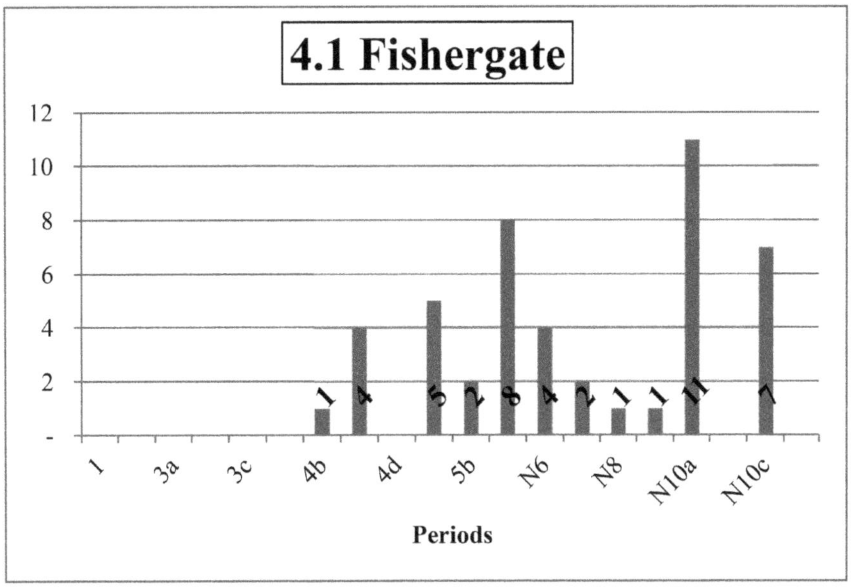
4.1 Fishergate
12
10
8
6
4
2
-
1
3a
3c
4b
4d
5b
N6
N8
N10a
N10c
Periods
1
4
5
2
8
4
2
1
1
11
7

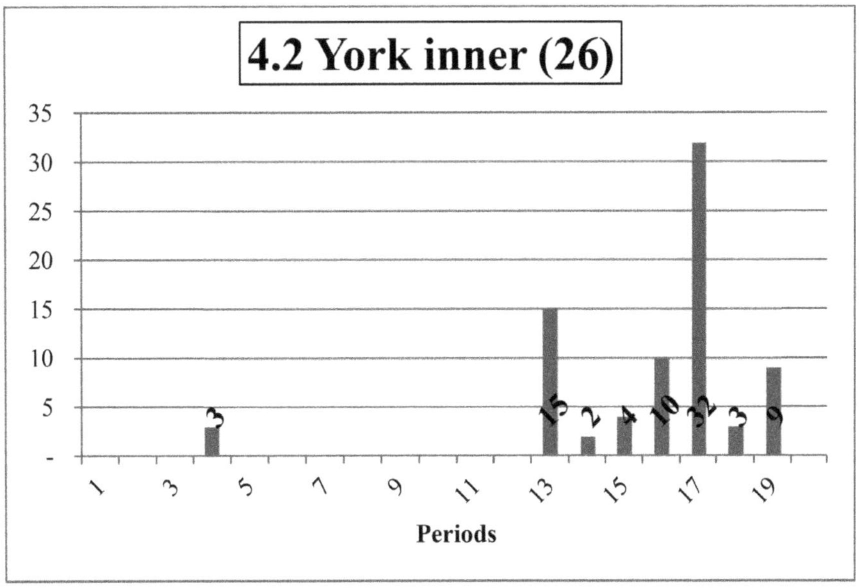
4.2 York inner (26)
35
30
25
20
15
10
5
-
1
3
5
7
9
11
13
15
17
19
Periods
3
15
2
4
10
32
3
9

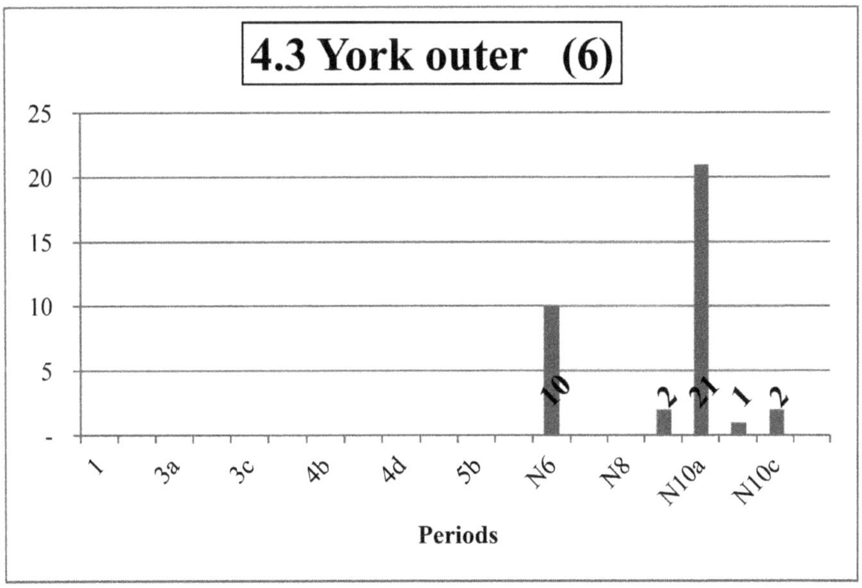
4.3 York outer (6)
25
20
15
10
5
-
1
3a
3c
4b
4d
5b
N6
N8
N10a
N10c
Periods
10
2
21
1
2

Graphs 4

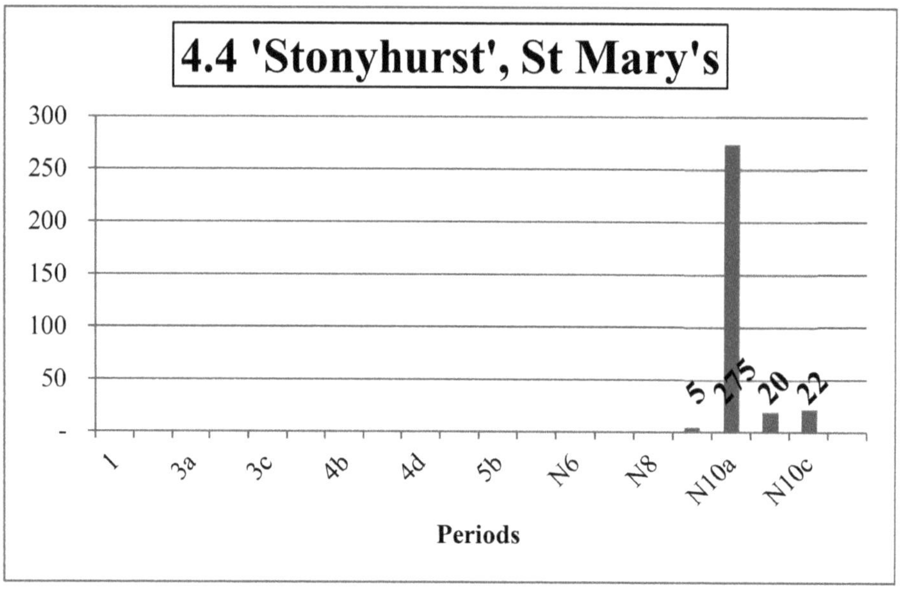

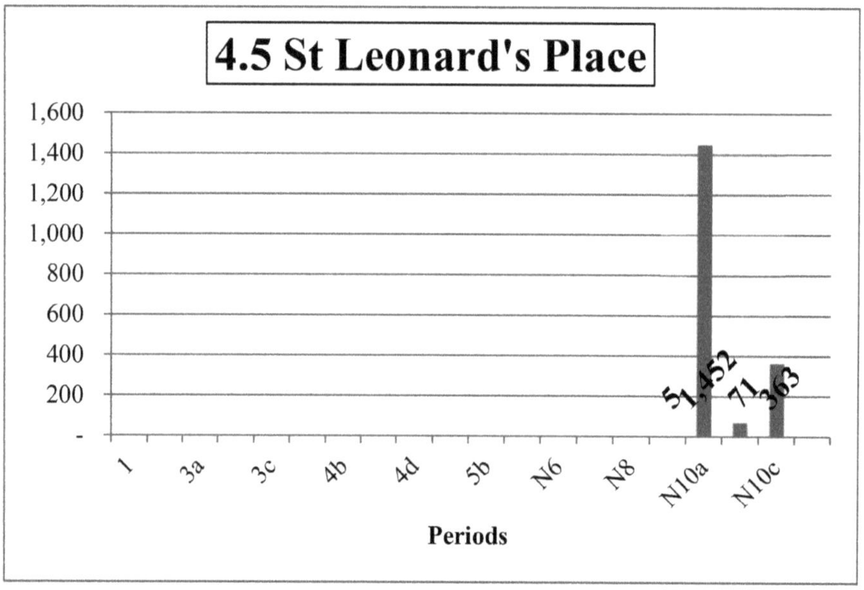

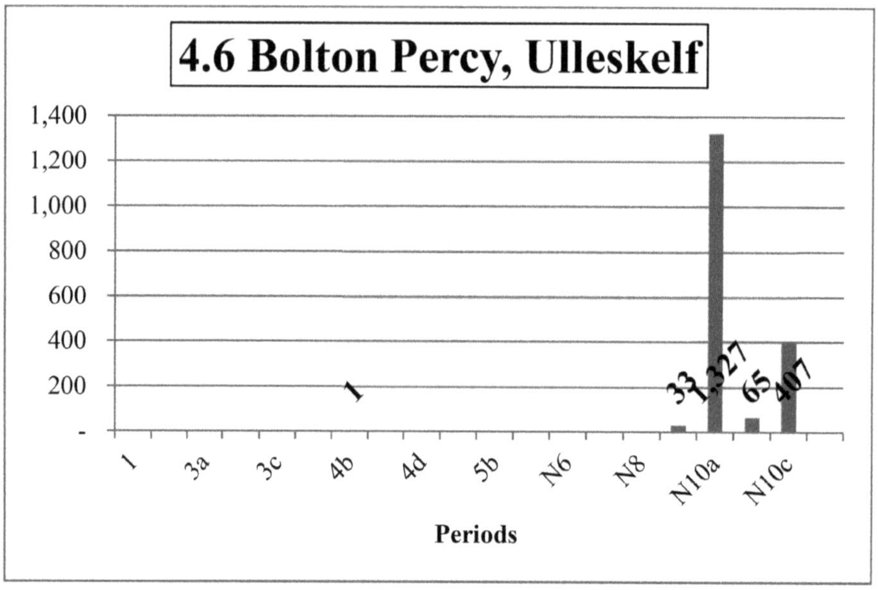

Graphs 4: Site finds by period arranged regionally by weighted average of peak activity, York and environs. Sources: *Datasets 1* and *8*. Numerical axis varies.

widow's mites. A plausible explanation is that this reflects tight monetary control and no other species were in circulation. The sheer volume of the hoards, resonant of the Roman *antoniniani*, deposited in the tens of thousands, demonstrates both the low value of the denomination and the substantial volume of circulating medium.

4.4.4 Single Finds

'Randomness is all.'

Michael Metcalf (1998, 171).

It is fortunate that much hoard material, supported by a wealth of local finds, has been assembled at the Yorkshire Museum and other local museums and universities.[658] Single finds are so widespread that they often go unreported—rumour in the detecting community is that less than one tenth of finds (of all artefacts, not merely *stycas*) are reported. The *stycas* were omitted from Pirie's Sylloge volume of *Coins in the Yorkshire Museums*[659] as she intended to dedicate a separate Sylloge to this coinage.

4.4.5 A Simpler Approach

Fortunately, I have now digitized Pirie's corpus to form the foundations of the numismatic database.

If one divorces the obverse and reverse and considers issuers and moneyers separately rather than in combination,[660] and largely ignores the proliferation of central motifs, the entire corpus falls satisfyingly into a neat, accessible arrangement facilitating both identification and, to some extent, sequencing.[661] My periodization recognises the broad shifts in metallurgy,[662] constituting Periods N9–10, ninth-century issues, which sub-divide into:

Period N9, *sceattas*: silver-alloy emissions, before 835 (if not 829),

Period N10, *stycas*:
a. Brass, *c.* 837–*c.* 850,
b. Bronze, *c.* earlier 850s, and
c. Base and blundered *c.* mid–late 850s?–867

This structure is not intended to ignore the continuing problems of uncertainty of metallurgy, coinage or regnal chronology. In the latter regard, the silver penny found in the Trewhiddle, Cornwall, hoard in 1774, could be crucial. It is now thought to belonging to Eanred of Northumbria, but in the style of mid-ninth century pence.[663]

Should this cause regnal dates to be deferred a decade, it reduces Osberht's reign to a more convincing duration and increases his annual productivity nearer to expectations.

Period N10a covers all of the base emissions of Eanred, Æthelred II (both reigns),[664] Redwulf as well as the base emissions of Archbishops Eanbald II (by Eadwulf)[665] and Wigmund. Period N10b is occupied solely by Osberht and Wulfhere whose issues are confined to this period and are in bronze.[666] The commencement date of the final chaotic Period 10c is uncertain. Lyon also identified an earlier phase of blundered specimens at the end of Æthelred II's restoration, well before the chaos in Osberht's reign.[667] Blundered *stycas* strictly from Period N10a may be mis-consigned, in the database, to Period N10c, such that the chronology is slightly disrupted, though they are relatively few in number (twenty-one in my database, though Pirie mentions 50 from Hexham at the BM[668]).

However, as Gilmore remarked in arguing for a brass rather than silver standard, we are 'faced with consistent inconsistency'.[669] He did make two observations: that the silver available from recycled coinage would become more diluted over time, and that the ninth century perception of brass may differ from ours—zinc may have been more desirable than tin.[670] This is a significant proposition and perhaps could be restated as tin being more available, and therefore less valuable, than zinc. This would overcome the paradox of an improvement in alloy when the standard of execution under Osberht shows a deterioration compared with that of Æthelred II's restoration moneyer Eardwulf and even Osberht's contemporary Wulfhere.[671]

However, Peter Northover in challenging Gilmore's proposition suggested that Osberht's bronze *stycas* would have a more attractive colour and better wear resistance (at the expense of being much harder).[672]

Pirie suggested that the situation after Æthelred's assassination would have been 'far from settled'.[673] The state of Osberht's coinages shows that matters remained troubled. In terms of monetization, growing confidence in the circulating medium facilitates the introduction of an increasing proportion of unofficial emissions—the

[658] Booth (1997a).
[659] *SCBI* 21 (1975)
[660] *Dataset 1, Analysis.*
[661] Abramson (2012d, supplement), which assumed the quality of execution decays over time.
[662] Subject to the important caveats at *fn.* 666 and at section 6.4.1.2.
[663] Pirie (1997, 65–68). It may mark Eanred's submission to Ecgberht of Wessex at Dore in 829. Booth (*pers. comm.* Oct. 2013) stated: 'It was bizarrely, in the Trewhiddle Hoard, which was full of much earlier material (Offa particularly)'. Lyon (2016, 14) concluded that the conventional dates of accession from Eanred onwards should be delayed by a decade.
[664] I treat Eardwulf as Æthelred's sole restoration moneyer (Metcalf and Northover 1987, 212) and invoke Reece's *apologia* (section 6.3.1).
[665] The veracity of these and Æthelweard's credentials as an N9 moneyer need to be established.
[666] Metcalf and Northover (1987, 212), but note that their conclusion that Osberht's *stycas* are tin-rich is based on a sample of only three coins, insufficient to determine this apparent change as being policy, source or chance. The sub-division between N10a and b still stands on the grounds that the monarchy and episcopacy were simultaneously renewed.
[667] Lyon (1957, 231).
[668] Pirie archive, Carlisle, 22nd July 1981.
[669] Gilmore (1987, 167).
[670] Gilmore (1987, 169).
[671] The execution of Wulfhere's obverses is superior to the reverse by Wulfred.
[672] *Pers. comm.* 8th January 2015.
[673] Pirie (1991).

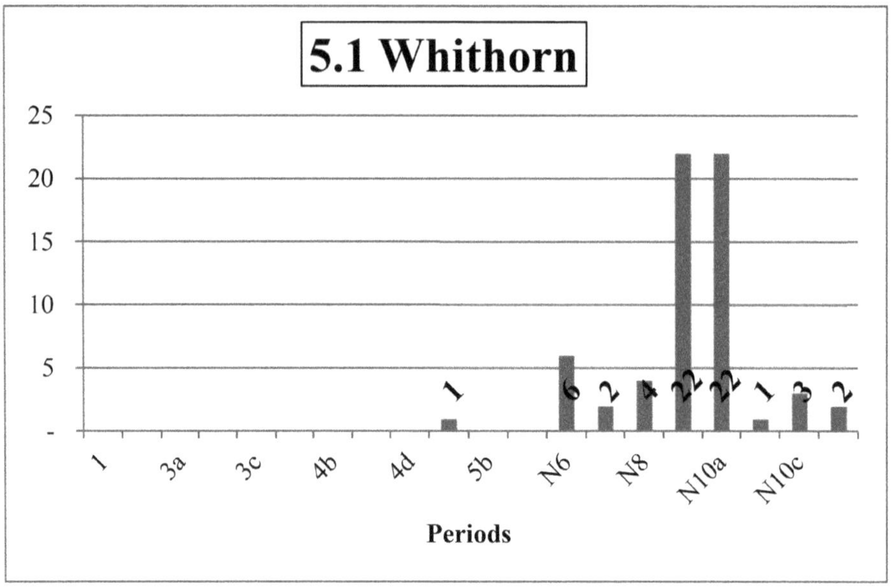
5.1 Whithorn
25
20
15
10
5
-
1
6
2
4
22
22
1
3
2
1
3a
3c
4b
4d
5b
N6
N8
N10a
N10c
Periods

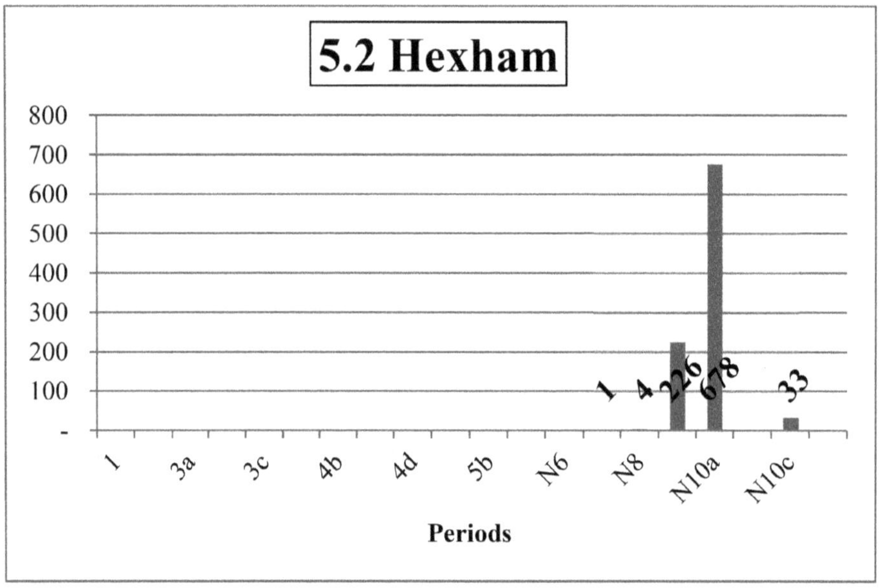
5.2 Hexham
800
700
600
500
400
300
200
100
-
1
4
226
678
33
1
3a
3c
4b
4d
5b
N6
N8
N10a
N10c
Periods

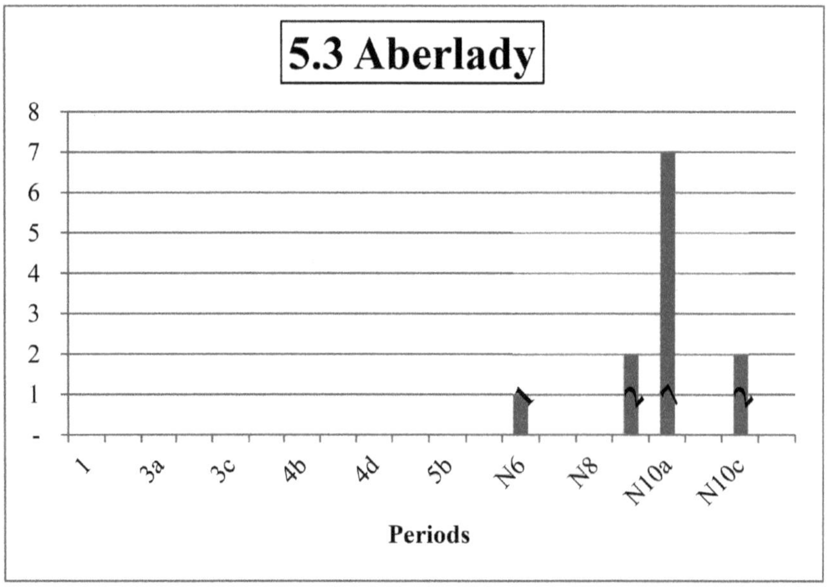
5.3 Aberlady
8
7
6
5
4
3
2
1
-
1
2
7
2
1
3a
3c
4b
4d
5b
N6
N8
N10a
N10c
Periods

Graphs 5

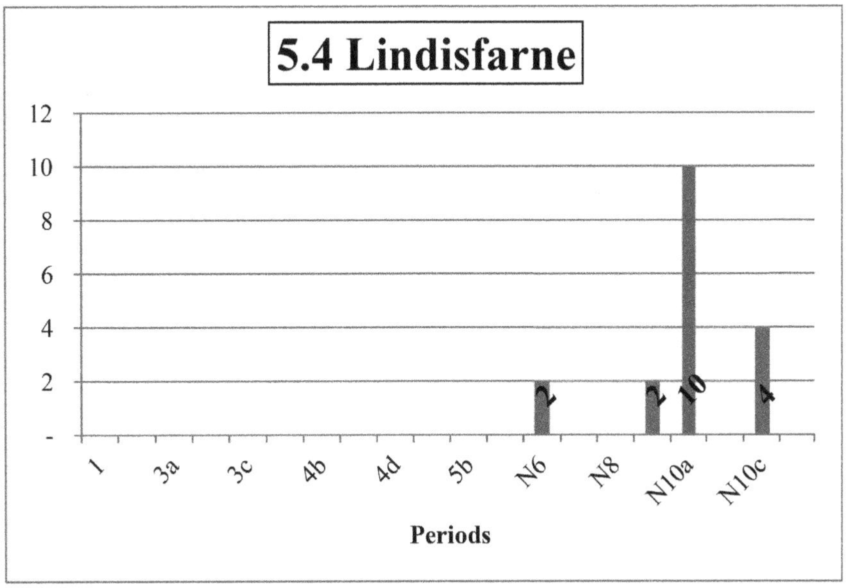

Graphs 5: Site finds by period arranged regionally by weighted average of peak activity, Bernicia i. Sources: *Datasets 1* and *8*. Numerical axis varies.

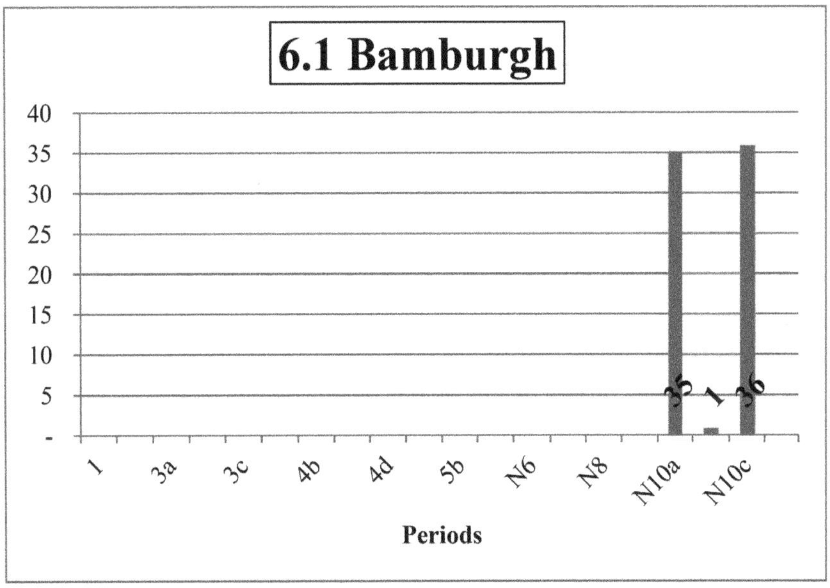

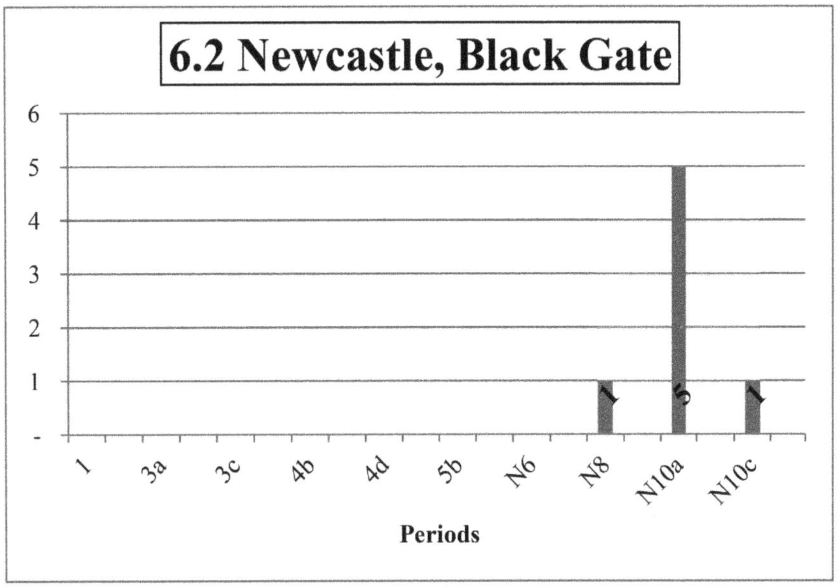

Graphs 6

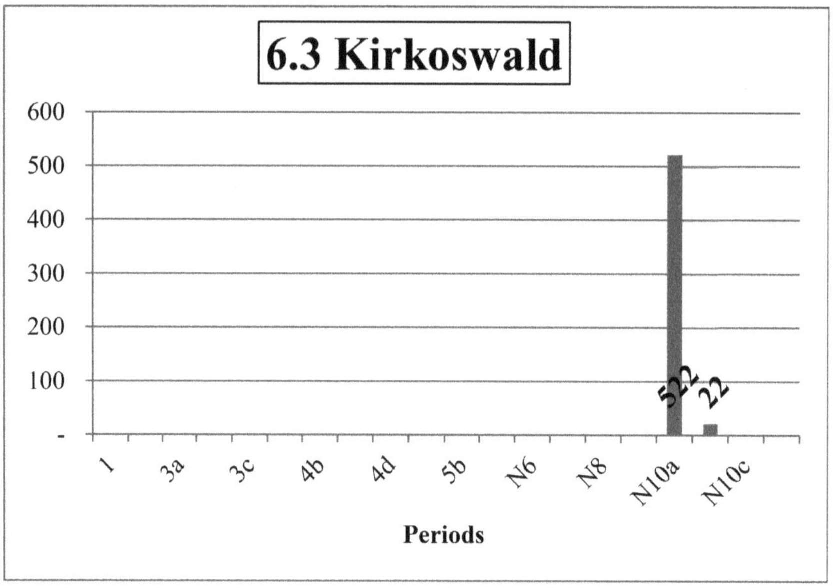

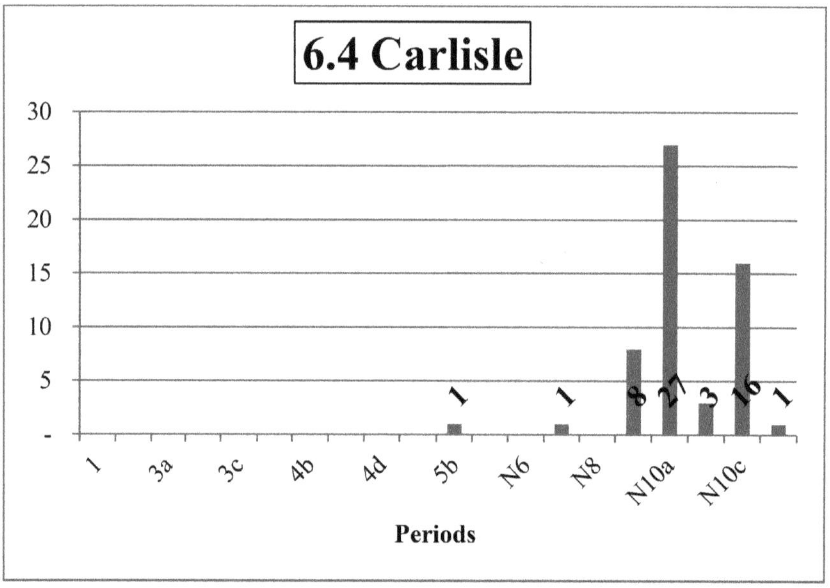

Graphs 6: Site finds by period arranged regionally by weighted average of peak activity, Bernicia ii. Sources: *Datasets 1* and *8*. Numerical axis varies.

presence of counterfeits is a marker for monetization—and this is undeniably the case in the latter days of the *styca* coinage.

4.4.6 Sphere of Influence

In connection with the Blackfriars, Carlisle, excavation (1977–79), Hugh Pagan remarked, in 1990, on subsequent finds of *stycas* from Carlisle as well as finds from the Scottish Solway coast, Paisley, the island of Colonsay and the Kirkoswald, Cumbria, hoard of 1808: 'the coinage of Northumbria penetrated north and west of Northumbria proper.'[674] Again, it was Pirie who recorded and published finds of northern and western *sceattas* and *stycas*.[675]

My study is more extensive but the least that can be gained from Pirie's list of sites is a recognition of the widespread distribution of coin-rich locations even though, as a list of find-spots, it is far from complete. A more comprehensive picture, particularly of southern finds which may not have been Pirie's main concern, emerges from mapping the database, *Map 1*.[676] The database also facilitates periodizing the recorded finds. The results of these exercises are described in Geographical Analysis below.

[674] Pagan (1990, 181).

[675] Her two-dozen hoard and site studies, some unpublished, are in the Pirie archive, private papers, July 1981, City of Leeds Museum Depository.

[676] And, of course, from Pirie's *Inventory* (2000).

4.4.7 The Interval before Period N11, the Viking Penny of York

The Viking coinage of York, which started around 894, will not be described, but a few comments on monetary activity and northern finds of coins relating to the period between the fall of York and the Viking coinage may be instructive.

Dolley referred to 'the very different importance that can attach to geographical provenance in different centuries.'[677] In Northumbria, a degree of control was exercised over the circulating medium in the periods it was being produced. Incoming *intrusions* are less frequent when the Northumbrian *sceat* is in production. Outgoing intrusions are infrequent and were probably candidates for immediate recycling,[678] certainly when the broad penny circulated in Southumbria. The situation with the base *styca* is more clear-cut—for the best part of the ninth century England suffered, *prima facie*, immiscible currencies.[679] Most intrusions went straight into the melting pot. One may infer that the *styca* was a *fiat* currency, outside the realm of the king's guarantee. If *stycas* circulated in the south, it would have been at intrinsic value—raw material for recycling.[680] That they are found widely, such as in the mixed hoard at Talnotry, may show that they were used as small change or may have compensated for the paucity of early Offan coinage.

As Pirie recorded,[681] finds of *stycas* in Carolingian territories are outnumbered by finds of Carolingian *deniers* in the north of England. For Charlemagne and Louis the Pious (768–840) she listed 10 British finds of which half have northern find-spots, and for Charles the Bald and Pepin II of Aquitaine (840–77), she listed twelve, five of which are northern finds. These numbers may be too small for statistical validity, but they intimate a trading balance in favour of the north.

In evaluating what was the most successful of the *wics*, Coupland wrote: 'In sum, the evidence of the coinage, especially the superb range of finds from Wijk-bij-Duurstede, reveals very clearly Dorestad's economic boom and bust. Under Charlemagne the port enjoyed a dramatic rise in its fortunes around the turn of the ninth century, a rise which continued through the reign of Louis the Pious, into the 830s. Around 840 that situation changed dramatically, as Viking chieftains seized control of the port, believing no doubt that they had got their hands on the proverbial goose that lays the golden eggs.'[682] Silting and the disruption of the Frankish civil war, during the reign of Louis the Pious, were also contributory factors in Dorestad's reversal.[683] It may be that Quentovic was the beneficiary of Dorestad's decline. Coupland demonstrated that as Quentovic languished until the 850s when, particularly after Charles the Bald's coinage reforms of 864 and the opening of new mints nearby, it started to thrive.[684] These two *wics* 'did indeed trade places.'[685]

It may be that this concept can be taken back in time in that Dorestad's rise dates from Northumbria's decline following the 793 Viking raid on Lindisfarne, The consequential loss of commercial confidence led to a steep decline in trade and, therefore, in coin production. The Council of Frankfurt (May 794) may have stimulated Dorestad to seek alternative outlets for its trade and increase commercial intercourse with Scandinavia. Viking incursions and Scandinavian monetization is discussed at section 2.10.

Models of monetization and markets in theory and practice, have now been reviewed, an hypothesis of monetization postulated, the historical background described, the picture has been imbued with detail from one of the most prolific and diagnostic of material sources—the numismatic evidence, whether re-constructed from the archaeological record or unearthed by metal detection, and a chronological framework constructed. In Part Two, tools are developed for application in the case studies, to assess the rôle of coinage in the emerging economic pattern of regional settlement.

[677] Dolley (1976, 349).

[678] Wiechmann (1998, Abb. 1). Simon Coupland (*pers. comm.* 30 March 2014) reported a Northumbrian *sceat* of Series Y, Eadberht, Booth class B (*SL* 70–50), found at Valais, Switzerland.

[679] *Stycas* and broad pennies are rarely found in the same hoard (Pirie, 2000 21), though the Talnotrie (now Talnotry) hoard contains both—together with a fragment of a *denier* of Louis the Pious and a *dirham* of al-Muttawakkil. Archibald in Webster and Backhouse (1991, 273) and (Pirie, 2002, 211). The Hoddom hoard also contains a fragmentary *denier* of Louis the Pious (Pirie, 2002, 212). That both are fragments hints at fragility rather than a bullion economy.

[680] Higham (1986, 303).

[681] Pirie (2000, 21–24).

[682] Coupland (2010a 105–11).

[683] Spufford (1988, 53) records the closure of the mint as 875.

[684] Coupland (2003, 209–32). Pirie noted the find in October 1991, of a *denier* of Charles the Bald at Pontefract: 'it emphasises that, during the years between the cessation of Northumbria's own coin-production (*c.* 855) and the introduction of the Viking coinage (*c.* 895), continental money was reaching this northern kingdom and may have been acceptable here as currency.' (Pirie archive, Offprints, Recent Finds).

[685] Coupland (2007, XIII, 227).

4.4.8 Illustrations—Copper-Alloy Periods N9–10

Figure 48: The named moneyer types of Eardwulf by Cuthheard (*SL*86–10). Found 'Newbald side of Sancton'

Figure 49: Inscriptional issues of Ælfwald I by Cuthgils (*SL*79–20). Courtesy L: Mike Vosper (WS6425) and R: Patrick Finn (11/50).

Figure 50: The only *styca* with portrayal. The 'hound' type of Leofthegn with triquetra in field.

Figure 51: (L) Eanred's initial silver-alloy early-penny coinage: Eadwine for Eanred.

Figure 52: (R) the subsequent base issues: Wendelberht for Æthelred II. Found Driffield.

Figure 53: The Hexham bucket. (Courtesy Pirie archive)

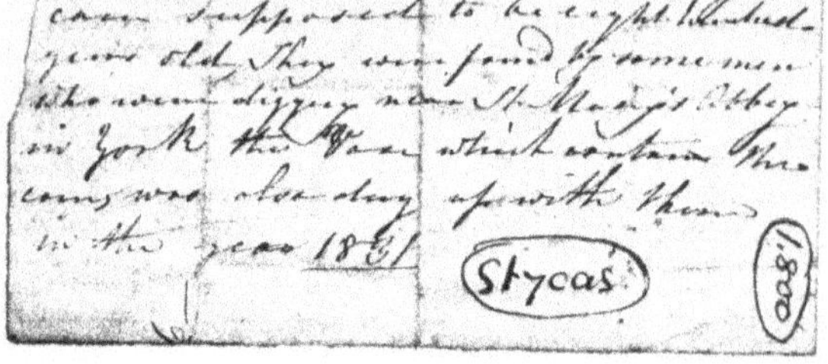

Three hundred and sixty coins supposed to be eight hundred years old. They were found by some men who were digging near St. Mary's Abbey in York the Vase which contain the coins was also dug up with them in the year 18[illegible]1

Stycas.

Figure 54: 'Three hundred and sixty coins…'

PART TWO

ANALYSIS AND INTERPRETATION

> 'Computers have the added advantage of forcing us to order our data in such a way that its hierarchical relationships are explicitly acknowledged and, if necessary, reorganised.'
>
> Steve Roskams, Excavation 21.

Having discussed, in Part One, the historic, economic and numismatic background to this study, the biases in the data are now discussed. The quantitative methodology, involving the construction of numismatic and artefactual datasets and the qualitative approach, wherein case studies are based on interrogation of the datasets by location, period and type, are then described. Temporal and spatial analytical tools are developed and deployed, augmented by early-penny source analyses to assess regional monetization and trading patterns, based on coin use through time.

Integral to the quantitative and qualitative methodologies discussed below is the periodization established above. Inevitably, the structure proposed appears more definitive than can be justified by the often-erratic transitions between the periods specified. Evolution is not linear as it responds to exogenous developments. The structure enables us to distinguish the exercise of Northumbrian monetary control, its lapses, vulnerabilities and points of departure from Southumbrian policy, which is more influenced by Continental precedent. The milestones of Northumbrian coinage at each phase include Paulinus's shilling at the forefront of English coinage, Aldfrith as the first named monarch on the silver early penny, the literacy of that coinage in the north, Eadberht's *renovatio* and Eanred's transition away from precious metal. Each period is delineated, differentiated and justified in *Dataset 1*. Lesser numismatic findings including conventional numismatic metrics, which are more concerned with coin production, are briefly summarized at the end of chapter 6.

The periodization and, indeed, association of coins with artefacts both build on precedents set by Naylor as described in chapter 2. When used in combination with the artefactual database some of the granularity of these numismatic periods is lost as the dating of artefacts is, inevitably, generally less precise. This does not prevent broad judgements about site continuity, the density and variety of artefacts, settlement and trade patterns, the level of economic activity, extraction of surplus or the balance and exercise of power.

5

The Quantitative and Qualitative Methodologies

This chapter commences with a discussion of the constraints on the interpretation of finds and the extent to which metal-detector finds are reliable and representative or biased. The relative significance of hoards and single finds is also discussed.

5.1 Evidential Constraints

In assessing the extent to which the PAS database is truly representative, several limitations on the integrity of the data must be explored.[686] In listing 69 site-based analyses the authors of *VASLE*[687] commented: 'It is recognized that the real culprit is modern agricultural practice and that most finds are recovered from the plough-soil in which they are being abraded with each new ploughing and would eventually be destroyed without record if it were not for the activities of detector users.'[688] The advent of metal-detecting since the 1960s has led to a step-change in the recovery of materials and sites. However, there are a number of factors constraining and influencing archaeological discovery and enquiry:[689] Instances of how these affect Northumbria are quoted. This is best summarized in Richards and Naylor[690] and is discussed at section 5.1.7.

5.1.1 Access Factors

1. Urbanisation:[691] with reference to northern England, the large industrial conurbations, many of which lie along the M62 corridor, have obscured or obliterated pre-existing settlements. This does not mean an absence of artefacts (e.g. the Paulinus Cross at Dewsbury) but inhibits site reconstruction, interpretation and access unless demolition provides temporary admittance for 'rescue' archaeology.
2. Natural features: woods, lakes, coasts, alluvium and wind-blown deposition may prevent investigation either by denial of access or physical disguise. Coastal erosion has certainly removed evidence along Yorkshire's east coast.
3. Denial of access: military and industrial 'danger zones' (e.g. ranges, mines, slag heaps, chemical and nuclear sites), SSSIs, 'agri-business' farms and much private land (especially in Northumbria and, for example, Sledmere)[692] are not made available for investigation.

5.1.2 Search Patterns

4. Granting of landowner permission to search is a major factor in the distribution of finds.
5. Ease of vehicular access influences search patterns (e.g. A64 and A170 in the Vale of Pickering).
6. Group searching (rallies) tend to bias finds distribution.

5.1.3 Soil Factors

7. Plough-zones: the limit of plough-zone farming is around 300 metres elevation. Above this level, the soil is not routinely churned, and artefacts are less likely to surface to within metal-detecting or field-search range (e.g. the North York Moors). Infrequent ploughing, for example on pastoral as opposed to arable land, may also inhibit the rate of detection.
8. The type of soil in which artefacts are lost will have a significant bearing on the extent of chemical attack and survival.
9. The composition of the artefact is a major determinant of survival, especially in combination with points 8 and 10. Metal-detecting detects metal.

5.1.4 Detecting Factors

10. Detecting neglect: non-ferrous and fragmentary ferrous artefacts, particularly if common, may be discarded by the detectorist, even though these may provide clues to the archaeologist. Even small value metallic finds may be trivialised. Selective recovery falls short of best practice. The problem of discard, particularly of ceramic sherds, is compounded by loss of identity when artefacts are relegated to a spoil bucket.[693]
11. Detecting bias: artefacts are found only where they are sought. Moreover, once a find has excited interest, there will be a focus of attention on the target area, which may imbue it with disproportionate significance (e.g. Monument Field, Sledmere), Additionally, detectorists vary significantly in diligence, patience, availability and equipment (e.g. Ryther and Cottam). Such find densities can skew outcomes unduly.

[686] Robbins (2012).
[687] Richards, Naylor and Holas-Clark (2008). http://intarch.ac.uk/journal/issue25/2/4.4.html
[688] Richards and Naylor (2009, 132).
[689] This list is not ranked by any specific criterion but moves roughly from the general to the specific.
[690] Richards and Naylor (2011, 135–47).
[691] Richards, Naylor and Holas-Clark (2009) 2.6.2 Modern constraints on data recovery
[692] Baron Redesdale, Lord Anthony Hill (Yeavering), Lord Middleton (Wharram Percy) and Sir Tatton Sykes IV (Sledmere) are significant landowners in this context.
[693] The Heritage Journal: https://heritageaction.wordpress.com/2009/12/22/metal-detecting-a-letter-to-english-heritage/ which states: 'most detected, recordable material is NOT being recorded and the bulk of the damage is being caused by ordinary, non-nighthawking, non-lawbreaking non-reporting metal detectorists.'

Blackburn encouraged detectorists to report all finds irrespective of 'rarity, legibility or condition'.[694]

12. Detecting selectivity: the operator can tune the instrument to detect specific metallurgical signatures. In particular, base metals can be 'tuned-out' so that the proportion of such metals may be significantly underestimated which could lead to a misrepresentation of site use.
13. Loss of context: as soon as an artefact is removed from the soil the archaeological context is jeopardised, even though much else can be discerned from the find. Items in plough-soil are unstratified in any event.
14. Detecting disinformation: provenances may be unreliable where a finder is seeking to disguise the location of a site (e.g. the two 'near Malton' sites), even though confidentiality can be provided by the finds recording regime.

5.1.5 Post-extraction Factors

15. Misidentification of significant artefacts. Errors occur through ignorance, incompetence and fallibility. A cursory examination of the major online databases reveals the PAS finds database to lack uniformity of description and accuracy of identification, compared to *EMC*, even though the former will often be far richer in detail. It is detrimental to further research that the major cleansing of early medieval finds data, carried out over 18 months in 2005–07 by Naylor as part of the *VASLE* project, has not been adopted by PAS.
16. PAS resourcing, especially in the calibre of FLO's recruited, influences the recording of finds. Moreover, England north of York and Liverpool were not served by FLO's until 2003. Night-hawking was prolific on many north-eastern sites (e.g. Yeavering Bell).[695]
17. Reporting bias: In 1997, de Jersey reported that finds local to Oxford were more likely to be reported to the Celtic Coin Index.[696] The dispersed FLO network may have overcome this.
18. Collecting neurosis: collectors can be secretive and careless. Surprisingly few recognise the importance of provenance.[697] Dealers and collectors, when buying from finders, often find it convenient to neglect their responsibility for due diligence under the treasure regime. An artefact can pass through many hands with accuracy jeopardised at each stage.

5.1.6 Legal Factors

19. Illicit activity: site-plunder (West Heslerton), night-hawking (Butterwick) and non-disclosure are corrosive.[698] In the year to September 2000, 1,788 finders reported to PAS compared to an estimate of 13–30,000 enthusiasts.[699]
20. Internet 'fencing': anonymized internet auction disposal aided by uncooperative site supervision, and an under-resourced or incompetent regulatory regime, facilitates loss of heritage. Conventional auction houses are generally more compliant following the 1998 Washington conference on Nazi loot.[700]
21. Perceived exploitation of the treasure regime by its management creates resentment and dissuades finders from future disclosure.
22. Legal non-disclosure: the following are excluded from the 1997 Treasure Act:
    a. Single coin finds, even if of precious metal.
    b. Nine or fewer coins from the same find if they contain less than 10 per cent gold or silver
    c. Single finds of metallic, prehistoric objects (e.g. the Crosby Garrett helmet).

There are other constraints which may impair the quality and quantity of data available for research. Adding to the *EMC* is voluntary, the main sources being coins included in the *BNJ*'s Coin Register and the *SCBI*.[701] Since 2011, greater selectivity has been exercised over inclusion of specimens in the Coin Register.[702] Unprovenanced coins and more common types are excluded. As explained above, *CKN* was not an *SCBI* and is therefore not currently included in *EMC*.[703]

5.1.7 Discussion

Bevan summarized much of this bias as: 'a) variation in post-depositional preservation and modern recording, b) a spatially-varying density of past users, as well as c) those culturally-mediated processes responsible for finally trapping artefacts in the ground.'[704] In recognising the shift in the electronic era from data gathering to analysis and in reviewing the challenges of cleansing and enhancing data extracted from the PAS and *EMC* databases, Naylor and Richards concluded: 'the value of these data sets, and the quality of the research undertaken from them, can only be as good as the underlying data.'[705] *EMC* is a specialist data-set controlled by standardized rules whereas PAS is more diffuse in its scope and operation; there are far greater inconsistencies in description and classification. This is exacerbated by the limited output formats available. It would not be an exaggeration to conclude that both reliance on PAS and expenditure of research time on interpreting its data, are compromised.

694 Blackburn (2003, 26).
695 Walton and Broughton (2009, 148).
696 de Jersey (1997, 1–13).
697 The de Wit collection of sceattas (now in the Fitzwilliam Museum) recorded provenance for only 11 per cent of the coins (*cf.* Abramson *c.* 72 per cent). The majority were creamed from two highly respectable sources—Spink and Patrick Finn—but, for whatever reason, finds data was not retained, nor was the collection ticketed.

698 Oxford Archaeology (2009).
699 *P&U* (2003, 3 *fn.*). Richards and Naylor (2009, 168).
700 https://en.wikipedia.org/wiki/Nazi_plunder
701 But only *SCBI* vols 1–50 at the time of writing.
702 Due to resource constraints.
703 However, *CKN* and *EMC* are not mutually exclusive. *EMC* takes data from many sources and some specimens appear in both listings. My recovered *CKN* in digital format (see 73) has been shared with YMT in view of their intention to re-image the *stycas* at York.
704 Bevan (2012, 500).
705 Naylor and Richards (2005, 83–91).

While one empathises with the view that destructive extraction must be avoided,[706] especially for mercenary motivations, one cannot assume that better techniques will be developed before the archaeological record is degraded or even destroyed by other forms of exploitation i.e. industrial, agricultural, developmental or environmental. However, once the damage has been done, or the context lost, there remains merit in mitigating the loss to the heritage by curating, preserving and studying finds. Moreover, Bevan (2012) pointed the way to a broader perspective.

How do these constraints affect Northumbrian finds? According to Naylor and Richards,[707] topography and the 300m limit for ploughing are the major influences. The Roman and A-roads are magnets for detectorists (*Map 4*) but access north of Newcastle (*fn.* 692) and in the urban areas inhibit detection. The settlement pattern in the south-east of the region is densest and cultural cores are a focus of activity. These are the formal constraints but what is not stressed here are two distortions. First, non-reporting, whether illicit or through neglect or disenchantment with the regime, is substantial in the region and probably correlated with high unemployment in the primary economic sector. Second, clustering skews the regional picture.

The concentration of detecting resources occurs either when specific sites acquire a reputation as prolific or when a particularly diligent detectorist reports finds in minute detail.

The effect of this distortion can be seen in the case studies, which by considering coins and artefacts attempt to overcome Metcalf's warning that: 'The relative isolation of the numismatic evidence has the disadvantage that its conclusions can rarely be independently verified.' He cautions against partial interpretation of the data to fit theory,[708] counsel heeded in the following chapters. Moreover, the substantial volume of the databases and the broad-brush approach based on parishes rather than specific sites help to overcome the limitations described above. Biases are further countered as both *co-occurrence* and the Roman comparisons measure proportions which are subject to the same distortions, rather than absolute numbers, so they are valid whatever the detecting complications.

5.2 The Quantitative Methodology: *Database 1*: Coins

Numismatic data sources relevant to this study are shown in *Database 1, Sources*, each with its own principles, protocols and problems.[709] A data manipulation exercise was undertaken in April 2014 to combine these sources into a single, searchable, sortable format.

In the context of a global rather than forensic study, the inevitable omissions, duplications and mis-descriptions, are of secondary concern and subsequent researchers should be able to follow, and where necessary repair, the audit trail.[710]

Pirie's *CKN* corpus as prepared for publication was forwarded to me by Galata Print Limited in a Microsoft Word® document and saved as an Excel® spreadsheet under 32 column headings. Careful data realignment was required to assemble like information into designated columns. Pirie's granularity of details is not matched by *EMC*.

Data from *EMC* was exported directly into an Excel® spreadsheet and, once re-aligned, organised to replicate the *CKN* format. These two spreadsheets were collated resulting in a database of around 370 *sceattas* and 7,000 *stycas*. A relatively small number of specimens (1.8 per cent) were added from PAS.

Numerous, but perhaps not all, inconsistencies were resolved, and duplicates eliminated, to the level at which any residual errors were unlikely to influence outcomes.[711] Adding further accumulations to this data-set,[712] is thought unlikely to have any significant effect on the statistical distribution.

My intention in creating *Database 1* was to capture data from formal sources at a fixed point in time. Each formal source has its limitations and my narrative and tabulations are much informed by data and images from other channels, including, but certainly not restricted to, information from detectorists, rescued curatorial archives predating the Treasure regime,[713] and my own collection.[714] These data are not compiled into *Database 1* but are separately identified in *Dataset 1*

5.2.1 Data-Sets and Summaries

Notwithstanding the constraints described previously, the numismatic database created from the various mainstream sources is considered to meet the necessary and sufficient conditions for valid statistical analysis. It is fully representative of the coinage, it is of sufficient volume to minimise the impact of anomalies and to give a high level of confidence to computations. The two databases can be structured and analysed in a variety of arrangements as described below. Various pivot tables (i.e., cross-tabulations) were used automatically to sort

[706] http://paul-barford.blogspot.co.uk/2009/06/goldilocks-and-finders-of-roman-coins.html, 09/06/09.
[707] Richards and Naylor (2011, 138–39 and 141–42)
[708] Metcalf (1997, 301).
[709] See Evidential Constraints above.

[710] See Reece *apologia*, section 6.3.1.
[711] A subjective assessment but Reece's *apologia* applies (section 6.3.1).
[712] E.g. the Lorin Kay collection, of 688 (not particularly selective) *stycas*. Abramson (2012c, 305–09).
[713] *Viz* Pirie and Bonser.
[714] Which is not random but selective on variety, provenance and condition.

Table 4: Dataset Sources

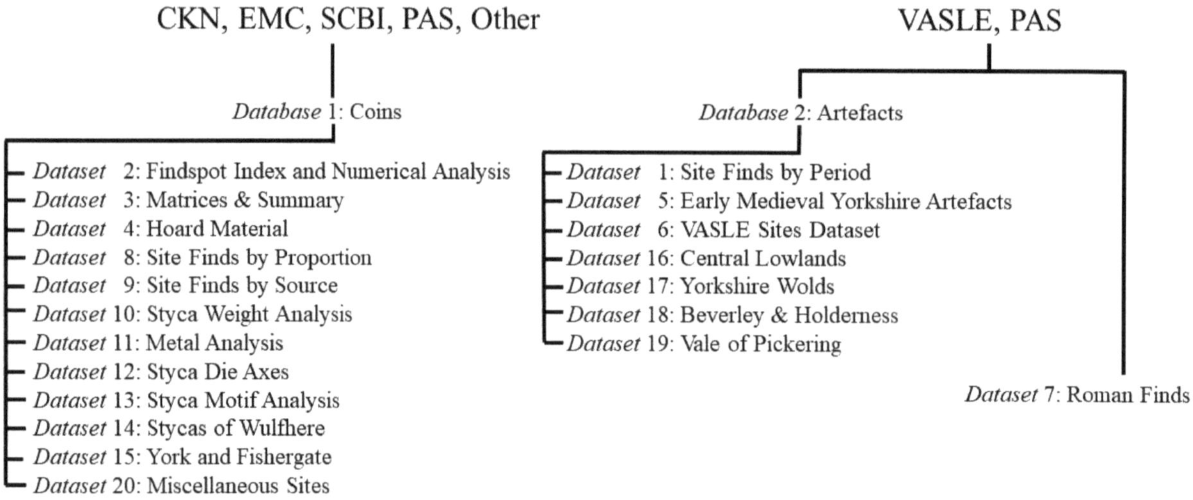

The databases and datasets supporting this study are available to download from www.barpublishing.com/additional-downloads.html

and count the data stored in the master databases and present the results in a series of datasets as described below and at *Table 4*. Of these, *Dataset 5* is the most productive source for analysis. High-level data is abstracted in the first tabs of each dataset, supported by detailed workings.

5.2.1.1 Dataset 1*: Site Finds by Period*

While acknowledging the conventional micro-analyses, Blackburn and Metcalf have shifted the emphasis to distribution analysis. Of these outcomes, particular attention will be paid to temporal, geographical and source analyses below.

The dataset opens with a resumé of the periodization. *Dataset 1, Summary* starts with a high-level summation of the entire database giving totals for different data levels: all finds, provenanced finds, hoards, and singletons. It then takes the granular distribution of site finds in each period for each region to a summary level. Sites with less than four finds are excluded. The chronological patterns of higher or lower loss within a region can be seen to be broadly representative of changing patterns of circulation, with greater numbers of finds indicative of more monetary activity. Where comparison across these regions was conducted, care was taken to ensure that the relative proportion for different periods are compared rather than the absolute numbers, as the latter will be subject to greater variation with regard to recovery bias.

Tabs within the dataset show regional correlations to the global norm, regional distributions analysed by coin type, volume ranking of sites and stability of settlements.

5.2.1.2 Dataset 2*: Findspot Index and Numerical Analysis*

Dataset 2 groups parishes by the volume of coin finds to show the inverse correlation of find size and frequency.

5.2.1.3 Dataset 3*: The Matrices*

Data was abstracted from *Database 1* to *Dataset 3* for gold, silver and base coinages by source and reign. The opening summary tab of *Dataset 3* analyses the chronological data by metal and source. For the *styca* coinage, matrices of issuers and moneyers, for each source, were extracted from *Database 1* into *Dataset 3, Matrices*. These are shown including and excluding hoard material and are then combined into summary matrices, again with and without hoards. For the base coinage, the source to be included can be selected and hoard material excluded.

The summary matrix of issuers and moneyers, excluding hoard coins, constitutes the base data-set—the normal distribution of finds in and of Northumbria—to which newly discovered hoards can be compared in future. This approach facilitates the computation of array correlations, *Dataset 3, Hoards*.[715] By creating a matrix of issuers and moneyers, a normal distribution can be computed for comparison with similar matrices. The matrices are in spreadsheet format and a single number representing the array correlation for a matrix when measured against the normal matrix signifies how closely matched or disparate these matrices are. *Dataset 3, Hoard Matrices,* compares and summarises each hoard against the base data-set.[716]

In separate tabs, the Hexham material is compared to the normal distribution and the 'Group A' moneyers listed. The *sceat* and *styca* frequencies by issuer are given to assess productivity.

[715] Excel CORREL function uses the Pearson Product-Moment Correlation Coefficient which is a statistical measurement of the correlation (linear association) between two sets of values, x and y, the sample means of the two arrays, given by the formula:

$$r = \frac{\Sigma(x-\bar{x})(y-\bar{y})}{\sqrt{\Sigma(x-\bar{x})^2\,\Sigma(y-\bar{y})^2}}$$

[716] But not the small 'Railway' hoard. Pirie (1987, 260–67). NB: the selection of Hexham hoard material in the Yorkshire Museum is not random but highly selective.

5.2.1.4 Dataset 4*: Hoard Material*

Specimens from the major hoards are extracted from the *EMC* checklist.

5.2.2 Hoards and Single Finds

It is important not to treat all finds as similar in character. Singletons and accumulations convey different signals and these must be distinguished.

There are many reasons for hoarding coins.[717] These can be characterized as defensive, ritual and socio-economic. The former includes circumstances of fright, flight and fight, where the depositor has failed, through loss of life, liberty, opportunity or memory, to recover the property, but instead has unintentionally bequeathed us a valuable inheritance. Ritual reasons comprise votive and burial deposits; an excellent example of the former are the offerings cast into the river where Dere Street crosses the Tees at Piercebridge where, for example, the bending of coins prohibits other than sacrificial use. Grave goods are a potent diagnostic tool, among which coins can give vital clues on wealth, belief and chronology.[718] Socio-economic deposits are those where the motive is carefully pre-mediated, rather than a reaction of fear. These include personal banking of surplus,[719] official treasuries, accumulating with a view to gift exchange, fulfilling the obligations of reciprocity, and accumulating in order to exchange.[720]

Essentially, a hoard gives a picture of the circulating medium over a period of time, whereas a single loss is a random event. The reasons for the loss of individual coins can be characterized as defensive and negligence. Again, fright, flight and fight constitute the panic responses leading to unrecovered loss, but probably a more prevalent cause is carelessness—clumsy or arthritic fingers, insecure storage, difficult terrain, crowded places and haste rendering the loser unaware or the loss inaccessible.

For the period under review, singletons dominate until the threat of the *micel here* when hoards become prevalent.[721]

In summary, hoards facilitate interpretation of chronology and the longevity of emissions. However, their composition can be selective. This contrasts with single finds (excluding those with a secondary use[722]) which, being fundamentally random, are more representative of the mix of the circulating medium. In reality, a significant proportion of finds fall between these two descriptions and are from the contentiously named 'productive sites',[723] being the numismatic term for a scatter of related detector finds within a closely-defined area. These could be from a scattered hoard or from a high level of activity, typically economic or ritual, within a specific zone. The constraints on the interpretation of such finds are described above.[724] However, we can conclude that the body of numismatic evidence accumulated in the database is now sufficient to provide confidence for extrapolation. New finds fine-tune the picture but the chances of overturning the fundamental building blocks of early Anglo-Saxon, or any other English coinage, is diminishing.

Dataset 2 shows that the vast majority of locations produce single or very few coins whereas a minute number disclose large hoards. As would be expected, the dominance of single finds is more marked in the south, with only Torksey, Littleborough and Norwich attaining double figures. Pirie's claim of a cluster of purse-hoards, of 20 to 30 *stycas* is not distinct.[725]

5.2.3 Conventional Numismatic Production Metrics

Numismatic micro-analyses proceed along conventional lines predicated by metrology (*Dataset 10, Styca Weight Analysis*), metallurgy (*Dataset 11, Styca Metal Analysis*), inscriptions, design elements and provenance with a view to determining temporal and geographic identities. In *styca* studies, orthography and epigraphy are important. Other attributes such as die axes (*Dataset 12, Styca Die Axes*) and central motifs (*Dataset 13, Styca Motif Analysis)* are also worthy of study. My digitization of Pirie's corpus expedites such analyses. However, while the outcomes of these methodologies are briefly summarized in the final chapter, they are not further pursued in the core of this study.

The methodology favoured here assesses and interprets the proximity and density of numismatic and artefactual finds, referred to as distribution analysis, *Dataset 5, Density*.

5.3 The Qualitative Methodology: *Database 2*: Artefacts

The association of coins with other artefacts is central to establishing the extent of monetization. As noted in chapter one, *co-occurrence* provides a measure of the relative proportion of coins to other artefacts, and hence an approximate measure of the level of monetary activity on any given location. *Database* 2 extracts, in detail, the relevant material from *VASLE* and adds subsequent finds from PAS *(Map 5*). Information about other archaeological evidence for the sites producing coins or other portable artefacts was checked by searching the ADS online

[717] Booth (1997b, 15–38). Blackburn (2006, 47–53). Graham-Campbell (2011, 151–58).

[718] Hines and Bayliss (eds.) (2013). Scull and Naylor (2016), though this related to south and east England.

[719] Over 51,000 Anglo-Saxon coins paid in Danegeld have been found in Scandinavia, which greatly enhances the reconstruction of the coinage of the period. Sawyer (2013, 6).

[720] This last motive is illustrated by my review, for *JMP* of Metcalf and Op den Velde's article on the Cothen hoard. *JMP*101 (2014, 27–51). The relevance of this hoard of underweight sceattas is that die duplicates are known from Heckington and Fishergate.

[721] Blackburn (2003, 23 and *figure* 3.2). *Dataset 2, Summary* shows the inverse correlation of find size and frequency (by parish).

[722] Blackburn (2003, 23–24).

[723] Richards (1999b, 71–80). See section 2.7.

[724] See also Richards (1999b).

[725] Pirie (2004, 67).

catalogue, incorporating Historic England's Pastscape database and other digital resources.

5.3.1 Dataset 5: *Early Medieval Yorkshire Artefacts*

Dataset 5, Artefacts extracts artefactual data by location and type (and, in more contracted form, by functional categories) from *Database 2*. Numismatic data by location, extracted from *Dataset 2*,[726] is imported to *Dataset 5, Artefacts* to facilitate qualitative analyse. *Dataset 5, Summary* gives the regional overview and analysis, including *co-occurrence*. Other tabs also show significant indicators: artefactual variety, density of finds, coin mix by metal and age, and settlement stability. This combination of numismatic and artefactual data is used extensively in assessing regional monetization below.

While it would be desirable for there to be a close physical proximity, it is sufficient to show that coins, and the objects for which they were exchanged, co-existed in the same community.[727] For this purpose, settlements will stand as surrogate for precise find-spots. In interrogating the PAS database for artefacts, York, East and North Yorkshire, together with 33 northern Unitary Authorities,[728] stand proxy for Northumbria.

However, not only must the constraints described earlier be borne in mind in assessing these finds and whether they are representative,[729] but also one must be wary of the conflation of dissimilar artefacts, both qualitatively and quantitatively. Moreover, significant caveats circumscribe the use of PAS data, even when cleansed. Only 1.8 per cent of the numismatic database was sourced from PAS, with all its vagaries, whereas the majority of the artefactual dataset is sourced here,[730] therefore, far greater caution must be exercised. For example, 95 of the objects extracted at Rudston (*c.* 9 per cent of the PAS, East Yorkshire dataset), are tiny fragments of burnt copper alloy and lead from just six cremations,[731] and 88 beads from Newby (*c.* 25 per cent of the PAS, North Yorkshire dataset), have been consolidated into two necklaces, as conjectured in the finds report. To 'smooth out' misclassification and avoid dealing with a proliferation of artefact types, often almost identical in nature and use, a higher-level functional categorization has been applied as summarized by region in *Dataset 5, Artefacts*. Occasionally, this fails to overcome the problem of an artefact having more than one prospective use. Note that craft and industrial materials and artefacts are combined as 'work-related' or 'tools', but the end-product of those activities may be dress accessories, toilet implements etc. There are countless alternative classifications—the more populous classes could be subdivided and the least popular consolidated. There are only second-best solutions.[732]

To further mitigate the deficiencies of PAS, a comparison has been made with the dataset embedded in *VASLE*. This was cleansed by Naylor, 2005–07,[733] but had not been updated since April 2009. It groups several artefacts in the 'other' category. *VASLE* also mined data from excavation reports on some formally investigated sites, *Dataset 6*.

Database 2 gives a matrix of sites and functional categories with a reallocation of 'other' items[734] and additional sources listed. There are 19 northern sites in *VASLE* included in this study. For these sites, *VASLE* data has here been adopted and adapted by augmenting that data with PAS finds up to the end of April 2015.[735] Other than the foregoing, this data has not been cleansed and it will be taken, in this study, very largely, at face value.

A further qualification emanates from difficulties over periodization in the 'Anglo-Scandinavian' and Viking period. Fifty-one artefacts of the former have been retained as they may pre-date the fall of York, but the latter have been eliminated.

A final caveat is that the singly-detected objects in this dataset have been revealed only during the current PAS treasure regime. Objects from earlier formal investigations, such as those captured through *VASLE*, may be discussed in the separate case studies, though not included in the dataset. The methodology of compiling data from widespread metal-detection is the essence of this study, and while the net is not, and can never be, comprehensive, what has been captured here suffices for current purposes.

This chapter explained the limitations of the archaeological evidence, the sources, construction and content of the numismatic and artefactual databases and the method of abstracting datasets from these. Chapter six describes the analytical techniques to be applied to these datasets in the subsequent case studies.

[726] Originally from *Database 1*.

[727] *VASLE* and Walton (2011) took a similar approach. Lucy (1999, 24–43) provided a useful gazetteer of Anglo-Saxon cemeteries. Entries are cross-referenced in *Dataset 5*.

[728] Of which, 25 gave a nil return.

[729] Not to mention the additional difficulty of the same findspot residing under two local authorities.

[730] VASLE mined additional data (*Dataset 6*) and I will refer to other artefactual finds, such as the garnet cloisonné panel from 'Site B' near Pocklington (*Figure* 96).

[731] This data has been consolidated. There is a small number of other such groupings including beads, sherds, weights and metal working debris (34 of 35 pieces again from cremations at Rudston, the 35th is a piece of jewellery from Aldbrough). These are insufficient of these to have any significant bearing on the interpretation of finds.

[732] Lipsey and Lancaster (1956, 11–32).

[733] But, regrettably for all subsequent researchers, was never adopted by PAS.

[734] *Database 2, VASLE Reallocation of "Other"*.

[735] Twenty-three numismatic additions to PAS between April 2014 and April 2015 included four new coin locations, now shown in *Dataset 5, Artefacts*.

6

Data Analysis

'The question of monetisation is, of course, one that forces sweeping generalisations about a topic that is, indeed, of a very heterogeneous character.'

Svein Gullbekk, Monetisation in Medieval Scandinavia[736]

The quantitative aspect of this chapter explains and applies analytical techniques to the numismatic database described above. This concentrates on establishing norms against which individual sites or regional profiles can be measured. The qualitative approach adds further analytical tools so that the numismatic material can be assessed in its archaeological setting. The cases studies which follow are given greater dimension by this integrated approach.

6.1 Quantitative Analysis

6.1.1 Analytical Tools

The combination of data from both numismatic and artefactual databases facilitates the use of several simple but effective analytical tools. *Maps 5 and 6* shows locations of both artefacts and coin recovery.

*6.1.2 The Normal Distribution of Coins (*Dataset 1*)*

Database 1, excluding hoards, is summarized at the head of *Dataset 1, Summary*, according to various criteria:

A. All specimens in *Database 1* whether hoard material or single finds, whether provenanced or not (7,575 specimens)
B. All specimens with provenance (i.e. find-spot) including hoard material (5,452)
C. All hoard material (4,114)
D. All (ostensibly) single finds, whether provenanced or not (3,365)
E. Items not from hoards and without provenance (2,123)
F. Items not from hoards and with provenance (1,242)

It is helpful to nominate one of these bases as the most appropriate for comparisons and correlations. The first three can be eliminated on the grounds of the bias potentially introduced by hoard material, albeit the St Leonard's Place and Bolton Percy hoards were probably deposited at the end of the era, during the Viking attack on York,[737] and that only 160 of the chronologically skewed Hexham coins are included in *Database 1* (67). How these were infiltrated into the private and institutional market for coins is unknown but there is a greater residual risk that unprovenanced specimens[738] originate from hoards compared to ostensibly 'provenanced' coins. On this basis, Selection D is discounted. Selection E has over 99.5 per cent correlation with the hoard material and on these grounds, let alone the absence of *sceattas*, is rejected. The guiding principle in selecting between the non-hoard constructs, is Metcalf's *dictum* 'randomness is all'. Therefore, though the smallest selection, F is deemed a sufficiently large corpus to minimise statistical distortion and is preferred for comparative purposes.

An important anomaly is thrown up by the first comparison, Fishergate, against *Database 1*, namely that the composite totals from the find sites is far more than the provenanced total in *Database 1*, showing the extent to which finds, even from responsible sources, have failed to be captured. The constituent elements of this shortfall include i) the main feeder to *EMC*, Coin Register, no longer capturing all specimens but only those thought noteworthy through rarity or condition, ii) difficulties in cleansing data from PAS, iii) *CKN* only cataloguing specified holdings in York and Leeds and iv) additional material from Pirie and the author. Nevertheless, statistical confidence in the periodic proportions in the *styca* corpus is high, based on Pirie's diligence.

The clearest anomaly in *Dataset 1, Correlations* is the poor correlation to the norm of *sceattas* in the Central Lowlands. *Dataset 1, Analysis* is more complex. Assessing sites with four or more finds, the Central Lowlands, Vale of Pickering and Bernicia have an age profile favouring the ninth century, whereas the Wolds and Beverley are earlier, peaking in the eighth century. When all sites are brought into consideration, the evidence is less polarised,[739] suggesting that small scale transactions occurred in most places at most times.

6.1.3 Dataset 7*: Roman Finds Distribution*

In the Roman period, coinage permeated daily life,[740] and therefore provides a suitable control dataset. As at December 2015, *c.* 228,000 single Roman coins and 377 hoards, were registered on PAS[741] for all-England, typically, clustered around the Roman roads and fortifications (*Map*

[736] https://www.academia.edu/1300696/Monetisation_in_Medieval_Scandinavia
[737] See *Graph* 4.5 and 4.6.
[738] Such as was the 'Manchester parcel' of *stycas* from the Hexham hoard. (Sugden and Warhurst, 1979).
[739] Except for Beverley where the ninth-century gains false emphasis due to the anomaly of only one site being prolific.
[740] Cloke and Toone (2015). *Map 4*.
[741] Walton (2011, 44) augmented her PAS dataset with earlier data largely derived from Reece (1991). It is assumed here that the PAS dataset is representative of Roman finds generally.

4, Dataset 7, Finds Comparison). This compares to a total of 1,558 single early Anglo-Saxon entries consisting of 18 gold shillings, 1,132 southern *sceattas*, 61 northern *sceattas* and 348 *stycas*. However, the Roman material would suggest that much of the geographical distribution of early medieval coin finds is conditioned by detecting and reporting, meaning that comparison between different areas is difficult in absolute terms and requires comparison to be made in proportional terms.

Where detection of Roman coins is unrestrained, constraints (e.g. of access) can be dismissed for later periods. The metallurgy, age mix, distribution and frequency of Roman coinage in the region may be fertile ground for future research. In the meantime, in respect of the constraints listed above, caution must be exercised, specifically for data extracted from PAS. On the input side, problems of bias, context, curation,[742] accuracy and residuality,[743] present formidable obstacles. As regards output, selection of search results by Unitary Authority has little relation to historical political geography and does not facilitate easy comparison.

However, some broad observations may be made. There is a paucity of Roman coinage finds in Bernicia other than at strategic locations such as the Great North Road and Hadrian's Wall. In the Central Lowlands, there is also a heavy concentration along the Great North Road. The PAS records 459 Roman coins for the York Unitary Authority.[744] Their distribution is widespread with several prolific 'hot-spots': in the East Riding, the greatest concentrations are around Rudston, Langtoft, Pocklington, Welton and Hedon and in North Yorkshire, Catterick, Boroughbridge, Cawton, Spofforth and Tadcaster.

The entries for these two substantial counties have been re-allocated to the regions used in this study. *Dataset 7* shows correlation of 91 per cent between Roman and early Anglo-Saxon coin finds, at the regional level, which is not sustained for other portable antiquities (29 per cent).[745] The distribution of Roman finds does not correlate closely between coins and artefacts (65 per cent) but is very close for the early Anglo-Saxon period (98 per cent). The implication is that the Roman artefactual distribution is anomalous,[746] so that here comparisons, in the individual case studies, are largely confined to the numismatic databases.

6.2 Qualitative Analysis

The combination of data from both numismatic and artefactual databases facilitates the use of some simple but effective analytical tools. *Maps 5 and 6* show locations of artefacts and coin recovery.

6.2.1 Co-occurrence

In this study, the propinquity of coins and portable artefacts is taken to determine the extent of monetization. This is here justified on the basis that if coins were functioning as money, they will be found routinely with the types of items for which they may have been exchanged. This relationship will vary from place to place and through time. Moreover, the range of goods which may be purchased by the current denomination will vary with the face value of the coinage and the scarcity of the goods. The symbiosis of the medium and the goods for exchange is anchored at the extremes: an absence of coinage, while not conclusive, suggests little or no penetration of a formal medium whereas an abundance is indicative of full, or at least fuller, monetization. Were a gold shilling found in the same location as a high-status artefact,[747] this probably implies little, numismatically, beyond the use of coinage by the élite. On the other hand, were base coins to be found regularly with everyday objects such as dress accessories, this speaks of a more widespread acceptance of the medium. Were coins held for other, for example decorative or ritual, purposes, co-occurrence with other artefacts may be occasional rather than routine.

Some measure of synchronicity is required to assess the regularity of coins found with portable artefacts. As stated in chapter one, 'An expedient indicator, *co-occurrence* is the ratio of the number of locations with both artefacts and coins to those with just artefacts'.

$$\text{co-occurrence} = \frac{\text{no. locations with artefacts and coins}}{\text{no. locations with artefacts}}$$

Aside from the peripheral groupings in *Datasets 1* and *5*, there is a clear demonstration of monetization, which can be compared between regions, all subject to the same caveats. The Venn diagram below shows that monetization, on this basis, is substantial (*Figure* 55).

Though clearly a device, *co-occurrence* does have some merit. For the entire dataset of coins and artefacts,[748] this ratio works out to 44 per cent. These data are from formally recorded sources though the proportion could vary depending on the extent of non-disclosure. Excluding the eclectic mix of peripheral sites at the end of *Dataset 5,* for which numismatic data is partial, improves the *co-occurrence* to over 48 per cent. The proportions for the Wolds is 70 per cent, Vale of Pickering 53 per cent and Central Lowlands 39 per cent. Albeit an artifice, this quotient is useful in demonstrating relative levels of monied activity. To demonstrate monetization as here defined, it would be desirable that coins surfaced at all

[742] Continued use of artefacts.
[743] The survival of disused objects in later layers. Vince (1994b, 9–14)/
[744] *Dataset 7.* As at 19th December 2015. Roman coin finds are recorded for 48 northern 'counties', but half have 10 coins or less.
[745] After redistribution of North Yorkshire and East Riding entries to Central Lowlands, Vale of Pickering and Holderness.
[746] See Future Research (185).

[747] Such as the York shilling found in the Middleham weapons assemblage.
[748] Even if only a single item has been found.

sites producing artefacts, i.e. *co-occurrence* of 100 per cent, as may be the case for the Roman period (despite the apparent anomalous distributions shown in *Dataset 7, Finds Comparison*). It is not necessary beyond this threshold to demonstrate greater volume of coinage or velocity of circulation; monetization has been achieved.

While not part of the definition, there is some complementary evidence which helps identify monetization. First, the appearance of 'unofficial' issues and counterfeits is an indication that the volume and acceptability of coin is sufficient cover for mercenary individuals to forge simulacrums. Plated copies of gold shillings were contemporary emissions; the more anonymous southern early-penny coinage was infused with imitations; the corpus of *stycas* not only suffered innumerable facsimiles but lapsed into a pervasive and substantial late blundered phase.[749] Second, as user confidence in coinage increased, the issuing authority struggled to resist the temptation, particularly in straitened circumstances, to adulterate the intrinsic worth. Generally, Gresham's Law applied and prices inflated accordingly. However, during the secondary (particularly southern) early-penny period and the northern *styca* phase, inconsistent metrology and metallurgical uniformity seems to have been overlooked such that the circulating medium was to variable extent *fiat*—accepted above its intrinsic value. It would have been too tedious to weigh each 'widow's mite'. Such toleration is a sign of confidence in the coinage and, in the present context, is an attribute of monetization.

6.2.2 Additional Analytical Tools

Dataset 5 provides a matrix of artefact types by location, grouped and summarized regionally.[750] The implications are discussed at the end of each case study. The statistical distribution of artefacts may be summarized as follows:

***Dataset 5* (extract): Statistical distributions of objects on PAS by location and type[751]**

	Of 217 locations the top 5/10/20 locations account for:	Of 127 types the top 5/10/20 types account for:
Top 5	47.7 per cent of finds	55.9 per cent of finds
Top 10	63.6 per cent of finds	68.7 per cent of finds
Top 20	76.8 per cent of finds	81.5 per cent of finds

This table encapsulates the extent to which specific locations such as Cottam, South Newbald, and Wharram Percy are rich in objects, have been more exhaustively searched or assiduously reported, and also how specific types of objects (pins, brooches and strap-ends) dominate quantitatively.

Dataset 5, Summary quantifies the regional picture by a variety of criteria. York and the Central Lowlands together with the Yorkshire Wolds and the Vale of Pickering give a clear yet diverse picture of regional economic intensity—the extent to which the dataset is skewed both spatially and typologically is considerable. This will be explored in the relevant case studies.

Dataset 5, Summary gives the matrix of artefacts in functional categories by region. That over two-thirds of all finds should be personal dress accessories and below one-eighth work related (or, including tools, below a fifth), presents a rather unbalanced view of social and economic activity in the period. Undoubtedly, dress accessories were more than merely functional, and this may have contributed to better survival. Either work-related artefacts failed to survive or have been selectively discarded or ignored. The case studies demonstrate the extent to which the Central Lowlands were metro-centric and the Yorkshire Wolds autonomous.

Supplementary analyses of usage patterns facilitated by the datasets include:

i) *Dataset 5, Density*, the geographical density of coin and artefact finds and sites, showing, in summary, the spatial dominance of the Wolds over the lowland regions studied.
ii) *Dataset 5, Coin Metal Mix*, the regional mix of coins found with artefacts by metal, showing, in summary, that the dominance of copper-alloy coinage over silver is less marked in the Wolds.
iii) *Dataset 5, Coin Age Mix*, a similar analysis by age, showing, in summary, the sites in the Wolds to have greater longevity than those in the lowlands.
iv) *Dataset 1, Stability—Coin Sites*, showing the degree of stability for individual sites with coins and the increasing use of coinage, and
v) *Dataset 5, Stability*, showing the degree of stability for individual sites with both coins and artefacts and, again, increasing monetization.

These provide a comparative assessment of the intensity, period and longevity of occupation and the mobility or security of sites, and they are discussed in the case studies.

Although the focus here is on usage, some production analysis is included in the following tables, and briefly mentioned in the text as indicated:

i) *Dataset 3, Sceat Frequencies*: Early-penny frequencies and productivity,
ii) *Dataset 3, Styca Frequencies*: *Styca*: frequencies and productivity,
iii) *Dataset 3, Summary, Eighth Century: Sceattas*
iv) *Dataset 3, Matrices: Analysis of Styca Issuers and Moneyers*

[749] Abramson (2012e, 30–72).
[750] Generally listed in a southbound arrangement.
[751] By way of explanation of this table, of the 217 locations included in *Dataset 5*, the top five most productive sites have 47.7 per cent of the artefacts found, representing 55.9 per cent of the variety of artefacts classified.

6.3 Application of Analytical Tools

Having constructed a framework for the evaluation of numismatic and artefactual finds, regional studies have been undertaken to test the hypotheses presented above. In cases covered adequately by previous authors, only a synopsis of the site characteristics is given. For the purposes of this study, Northumbria is taken to be territorially stable after the Battle of Nechtansmere, 685.

The first study undertaken, York and its Environs, includes the Anglian settlement at 46–54 Fishergate, York. The second region, described as the Central Lowlands, is the entire plain from Darlington to Doncaster, framed between the Pennines to the west and North York Moors, Howardian Hills and Yorkshire Wolds to the east. Treatment of this substantial area as one region is justified on the bases that both the geomorphology and the characteristics arising from the data are uniform, which further implies that the estate management of the region, whether in regal or episcopal ownership, was subject to similar regulation.

The other regions are conventional: the Yorkshire Wolds, Beverley and Holderness, the Vale of Pickering, Bernicia and the north. The western periphery of the Wolds is deemed to include the descent into the Central Lowlands.

6.3.1 Temporal Analysis

A mix of early coinage may be expected from any Northumbrian 'productive site' or coin-rich excavation which saw activity throughout the period of coin use from *c.* 570 to the fall of York. However, it would be quite exceptional to find Continental or English gold [3a–c], and Merovingian silver [4d] is scarcer than gold. In a normal distribution, this early period material is very unlikely to occur. The matrix only provides information on the frequency of *sceattas* and *stycas* [4–10]. Of the 374 eighth-century Northumbrian *sceattas* analysed [4a and 5a], 51.3 per cent are from the reign of Eadberht (including the joint issue [N6–7] and 24.3 per cent are from the two reigns of Æthelred I [N6 and N8], 17.9 per cent being by the named moneyers of the restoration [N8]. Aldfrith [4a], Alchred and Ælfwald [N6 and N8] are respectively responsible for 7.0 per cent, 7.0 per cent and 8.6 per cent, while Æthelwald Moll and Eardwulf [N8] are amongst the rarest of all English coins. This pattern changes little if annualised, *Dataset 3. Sceatta Frequencies*. Æthelred I is most productive, followed closely by Eadberht but with Aldfrith, Alchred and Ælfwald all similarly unproductive. With precious little to show for Eardwulf's lengthy reign, one infers an uncharacteristically feeble production effort.[752]

However, it is evident that selectivity in the sources used—or partiality in the selection—has skewed the, albeit incomplete, data recorded here for *sceattas*. While the proportions appear reasonable for Northumbrian material only 34 non-Northumbrian *sceattas* are included. Representation of Series D, E, G and J is weak. Even the Coin Register no longer records finds deemed unexceptional. At any northern site hosting frequent exchange, one would expect to see a *sceat* of Aldfrith admixed with primary Series E and D, the *lacuna* before Eadberht populated by Series J and G, probably with the former more prominent, a scattering of secondary Southumbrian issues, probably with some later E. Once Eadberht has established controlled minting, his emissions will be matched by the more common Southumbrian material (e.g. Series R) and there may be a one or two 'exotic' species, with a specimen of Series Q often present. South Newbald may represent a different sort of site—probably a regal site, a *vicus regius*, where controls could be exercised more conscientiously. To a limited extent, the informal finds data incorporated into the site studies help compensate for any perceived or real imbalance in the database.

One can be more confident of the ninth century material presented in *Database 1*. There is no doubt that this is a representative body of data, indeed the most comprehensive, searchable, sortable corpus yet assembled. For the non-hoard material, which must be more representative than the potentially biased hoard accumulations, Eanred accounts for 22.3 per cent of finds and Æthelred II (both reigns), 42.9 per cent. However, in terms of annual production, the latter is very significantly more assiduous, and this momentum carries through the usurpation of Redwulf but diminishes under Æthelred II's sole restoration moneyer, Eardwulf, to output levels not dissimilar to Eanred's.

Anomalously, Eanred had 27 moneyers compared to Æthelred II's twenty-one. While only Æthelweard of Eanred's 11 'Group A' moneyers convincingly continued under Æthelred II, 11 of Eanred subsequent 16 Period N10a moneyers do so. This pattern may suggest a lapse after the initial silver-alloy emissions of Period N9, before minting momentum grew towards the end of Eanred's reign, continuing to a peak under Æthelred II. One can assume that the restored Æthelred II felt that his former moneyers who continued (voluntarily or otherwise) under Redwulf's usurpation (nine of Redwulf's eleven) were treacherous, when production of the coinage demanded integrity,[753] *Dataset 3. Styca Frequencies*.

When annualized, the moneyer-productivity of Osberht and the three archbishops appears paltry. As all four enjoyed longevity, averaging their moneyers' output according to tenure may not be meaningful. One can assume that the attributable production took place reasonably efficiently over a relatively short period or was sporadic. Osberht employed six moneyers but none of the archbishops more than four. In Osberht's case, the emphasis here is on

[752] Plausibly just for his investiture.

[753] Charles-Edwards (1997, 172). Metcalf and Northover (1987, 213).

'attributable production' as most of the blundered *stycas* were probably minted during his reign, so the picture is distorted. One may be drawn to question how reliable is the date of Osberht's accession and how disruptive was Ælle.

In contrast to the gradual debasement, according to Metcalf and Northover,[754] it was during Osberht's reign (and presumably Wulfhere's tenure) that the proportion of tin increased in relation to zinc resulting in a bronze *styca* replacing the previous brass coin.[755] Though not wishing to resurrect Pirie's 'groups and phases', a simple periodization has been created: silver-alloy issues, Period N9 (5.3 per cent, including hoards and blundered specimens), brass N10a (69.0 per cent), bronze N10b (4.1 per cent) and blundered N10c (21.6 per cent, reverting to brass). The predominance of brass includes the work of three prolific moneyers, Monne (17.6 per cent), Eardwulf (13.2 per cent) and Forthred (12.3 per cent), accounting for 43.1 per cent of the ninth century database (and half of the brass), *Dataset 3. Matrices*. Three factors—the dominance of just three moneyers, the special motif *stycas* of Leothegn for Æthelred II and the improvement in alloy to bronze—signify a high potential for control, in production and design, in Periods N9 to N10b.

Dataset 3, Hoards and *Hoard Matrices* confirm earlier studies;[756] the Bolton Percy hoard(s) and St Leonard's Place parcel (no. 2) show high correlations with the base data-set and with each other (and *Dataset 3, Styca Frequencies*). They respectively include the emissions of 32 and 29 of the 36 moneyers. This strongly suggests that they were laid down as a result of the Viking attack on York.[757] However, the Hexham hoard[758] includes only 23 moneyers, and correlates highly with the base data-set only until the restoration of Æthelred II in 843/4, as shown by *Dataset 3, Hexham Analysis,* around which time this hoard can reasonably be assumed to have been deposited.[759] This comparison also shows that the silver-alloy 'Group A' moneyers of Eanred and archiepiscopal material are over-represented in the Hexham hoard, signifying selectivity.

Analysis of site finds by period, *Dataset 1*, facilitates graphical representations of finds as in *Graphs 1 to 11*, ranked chronologically by region for many of the sites studied. *Dataset 8, Site Finds by Proportion*, shows this data by proportion for sites and periods. The weighted average of peak activity shows which sites were active early. This exercise has been carried out for coin-rich sites both under Northumbrian influence and beyond, for comparative purposes.[760]

Having set the precedent in dividing the Romano-British coinage into periods, Reece analysed the finds from 140 sites by period. He gives a persuasive *apologia* 'If anyone attempted to check my work the result would be chaos because there are so many occasions on which I made a snap decision to include or exclude.'[761] Here the passage from database to dataset, and abstraction into tables, gives an audit trail but, inevitably, reliance has been placed, to a significant extent, on identifications by other parties.

This exercise has helped reveal the strengths and weaknesses of the periods devised. On the positive side, it has not been difficult to allocate many thousands of specimens to their appropriate period. There are a similar number of periods to Reece's division of the Roman era of coin-use, spanning a comparable time-frame. On the negative side, there are areas where greater certainty needs to be acquired through research. Further metallurgical testing of the ninth-century material would be helpful to validate the partition of the coinage into its constituents.[762] Assaying the composition of the emissions of Æthelweard for both Eanred and particularly Eanbald II, would be instructive.[763]

6.3.2 Dataset 8*: Geographic Analysis*

Following the case study structure of this study, the numismatic material for over 60 locations has been analysed in *Dataset 1*. An analysis by metal is also given together with proportions of imported coinage for both the Primary and Secondary early-penny phases. This data is also organised to show proportions by site and period, *Dataset 8, tabs 1* and *2*.[764] The methodology proposed by Naylor,[765] is applied in *Datasets 8* and *9,* extracted from *Dataset 1*. Site finds listings in *Datasets 15* to *19,* give a more granular analysis for each region, including sites with one or more coin finds in the study period. Results are discussed in the case studies and explored at section 8.1.3. Summarising this data by century provides a window on the progression of monetization within and between regions.

Dataset 8, Site Finds by Proportion, also enables data to be arranged by region, *Graphs 5 to 10*, to demonstrate that the uniformity of coin mix in the Wolds is the result of active circulation whereas Bernician sites are sparse and late. *Dataset 8, Site Finds by Proportion* ranks all sites from the earliest.[766]

---

[754] Metcalf and Northover (1987, 187–233).
[755] But see *fn.* 666.
[756] Lyon (1957).
[757] Lyon (1957, 231), found that Osberht and Wulfhere are under-represented and concluded that a much earlier date is indicated. This is refuted by my analysis.
[758] As illustrated by Adamson—see Pirie (1987, *BAR* 180, 369–28). *Dataset 3, Hexham Analysis*.
[759] Lyon (1957, 231).

[760] All locations in the database with five or more finds have been analysed by period.
[761] Reece (1991, 9).
[762] Probably testing to destruction in view of the surface enrichment problems associated with XRF.
[763] See Future Research.
[764] *Dataset 8, Worksheet* imports the raw data from *Dataset 1, Summary.*
[765] Naylor (2007, 44–46)
[766] Abstracted from *Dataset 8*.

DMAP software has been used to plot data extracted from *Database 1* to demonstrate usage and broad trends.[767] My observations on these maps are:

1. Gold, *Database 1* does not adequately represent known imported gold and York shillings.[768]
2. Northumbrian *sceattas*, *Map 7*. Again, *Database 1* does not fully represent the corpus of extant specimens. However, it suffices to demonstrate the circulation of Northumbrian types, especially in the Central Lowlands, Vale of Pickering, the Wolds and coastal sites from the Firth of Forth to Hamwic. Lincolnshire is well represented but more southerly finds are few.
3. Southumbrian *sceattas* found north of the Humber, *Map 8*. These form a similar distribution to local issues as would be expected—economic activity continued in similar locales using a well-mixed coinage.
4. *Styca*s, *Map 1*. Coverage is much more widespread than expected implying that *styca*s may plausibly have been used as small change despite the absence of mixed hoards. However, other than Viking sites and small multiple finds in the Lincolnshire Wolds, all Southumbrian *styca* finds are singletons.

Bude's distribution of *sceattas* of Eadberht,[769] is much narrower than may have been expected, possibly indicating Southumbrian recycling of Northumbrian specimens that may have been used in payment of imports to the north. The focal point is well to the east of York, possibly biased by the constrained access to discovery in urban areas.

Map 9 shows all find-spots in *Database 1*.

6.3.3 Dataset 9*: Source Analysis*

As a potential signifier of the reach of domestic and Continental trading relationships, it is helpful to identify the assumed source of coins recovered. Metcalf pioneered distribution analysis in this field and numismatics is indebted to his perceptive and diligent interpretation of finds. While some of his work remains speculative, it is secure enough to use as the basis for allotting finds to original sources with the caveat that a worn coin will not have made a direct journey from origin to loss, *Datasets 8* and *9*. It is the mix of varieties in the locally circulating medium which indicates the reach and vibrancy of commerce—this is clear at Sledmere and Hamwic whereas both volume and mix are less convincing at, for example, Fishergate and the Vale of Pickering.

Dirhams and Carolingian gold and silver coins are here treated as occasional intrusions rather than as an intrinsic part of the currency. *Dirhams*, being easily fragmented were part of the bullion economy rather than being used for small change—they are fragmented far too irregularly for this. However, the picture on imitative *solidi* of Louis the Pious,[770] should be revised in view of the lead test piece found at Torksey (*Figure* 56, *Figure* 57). There must be a strong suspicion that these were local imitations and there is a case for allocating them a distinct place in the periodic table, *Dataset 1*. Moreover, were it the case that they were intentionally made for exchange purposes, then they form part of the process of monetization.

Dataset 9, Summary analyses the proportions from each external source, particularly Continental *sceattas*. While the absolute number in some categories is modest, the outcome is consistent with expectations:

- There are as many Merovingian gold *tremisses* as silver *deniers*, both rare but found in similar numbers.
- Gold shillings are rare.
- Metcalf has noted that the proportion of *sceattas* from the Rhine-mouth area, Series D and E, especially in the primary period, is significant (typically 20 per cent but 30 per cent in Humberside) and skewed to sheep-rearing areas, mainly chalk uplands such as the Yorkshire Wolds.[771] In this dataset, these form an even higher proportion of the circulating medium and inclusion of informal data from just one site, Hayton, increases the proportion of such finds in the Wolds from 9.7 per cent to 19.0 per cent of *all* finds in the study period (two-thirds of primary *sceattas*). *Dataset 9, Summary* demonstrates the dominance of Continental *sceattas* in their Primary phase and their subsequent decline.
- Ribe's Series X occurs infrequently.
- Series G, probably from Quentovic,[772] is plentiful.
- Series J is common north and south of the Humber, but its constituent types need not be from a common source.
- There is a broad selection of Southumbrian *sceattas*, both primary and secondary, though the prolific finds at Sledmere skew the overall prevalence and mix.
- East Anglian Series R and Q are present at many sites, albeit it as single representatives.
- There is a sprinkling of 'exotic species',[773] rare varieties typically rich in religious iconography, possibly signifying peregrination.

6.4 Numismatic Findings

While a watertight compartmentalization of coin production and use is not possible, and the emphasis in this study has been on the latter, several significant numismatic findings on both production and use, derived from the periodization and data analysis, are stated here chronologically. Some lesser findings are given at section 6.4.3.

[767] http://www.dmap.co.uk/

[768] *Dataset 15, York Shilling* (3 tabs). Abramson (2019).

[769] Bude (2016)

[770] Blackburn (2007, 80–82).

[771] Metcalf (2003, 43, 2011 and 2014, 244). See section 2.9.

[772] Metcalf (1993–94, 270).

[773] Especially from Sledmere.

6.4.1 Production

During in the evolution of the coinage, as Southumbria typically[774] emulated Continental precedent, Northumbria was innovative: Paulinus's shilling, Aldfrith's *sceat*, Eadberht's *renovatio*, joint coinage and Eanred's *styca*.

Regarding seventh-century gold, the York shilling is differenced from contemporary shillings by its longevity and variety, *Dataset 15, York Shilling* (3 tabs), *Map 3, Plate 1*. Previously dismissed as blundered, the two inscriptions are now understood. For varieties B and Ci, the formulaic legend is a *nomina sacra* commencing SANCTE,[775] and, as a result of my recent work, the legend on varieties Cii and Ciii is now widely accepted as reading *PAULINUS EP*, not only enhancing the standing of these well-executed coins but placing this coinage at the forefront of Anglo-Saxon issues. Precise dating of the emissions of gold shillings by an historically documented figure, in this case Paulinus, is unprecedented.

The typology has been extended to create sub-varieties now that the corpus has grown to 22 attested specimens. This shows both a high level of organisation behind the coinage and a perceptive grasp of theological iconography. Furthermore, the growing list of specimens has diluted the initial focus on finds in urban York. The distribution is widespread, witnessing, for the inscribed varieties, Paulinus's mass-baptismal activity and further finds can be anticipated. The less rare varieties of the group may be élite currency and the rare and unique specimens are, more likely, commemorative special issues rather than a medium of exchange.

The association of Aldfrith's first Northumbrian silver coinage with the primary phase of *sceattas* is little challenged by the recent discussion on the dating of grave finds. Archaeological evidence advances the transition from gold to silver by one or two decades, which is accepted in this study, though my identification and dating of the Paulinus shilling implies the duration of the gold coinage is not truncated. The southern primary early-penny phase is earlier and of longer duration, than the northern primary *sceattas*.

While functionally identical, the secondary early-penny phases of north and south are also dissociated, with the former starting and ending later. This disconnect is not merely temporal and spatial but political and religious. The southern *sceattas* are typically anonymous, rich in Conversion Period iconography and intentionally ambiguous often with apotropaic elements. The northern *sceattas* are conservative and uniform and, from commencement, carry the issuer's (or -s') *imprimatur*.

Bede noted that Wulfhere approved Bishop Wilfrid's appointment of four priests, including a Padda and an Eappa, to baptize the West Saxons.[776] Solely on the grounds of propinquity, Padda could be associated with the *thrymsa* moneyer PADA (rendered in runes) i.e. he is in the right place, time and relationship.[777] Bede described how a young boy's death by disease on the anniversary of Oswald's demise was regarded as preventing an epidemic from spreading throughout Eappa's monastery at Selsey.[778] This event was celebrated widely each year. On the basis that Eappa's unusual name on the coinage would be excellent propaganda for the Church, as well as acting as an amuletic 'touch-piece' perceived as preventing plague, and so enhancing the currency of the coinage, Eappa could be equated with the moneyer EPA as inscribed on the widespread, long-lived and prolific 'runic bust' *sceattas* of Series C, D and R, despite the slight delay. Admittedly, Bede may have drawn our attention to this; perhaps he was discouraged by the use of runes.[779]

The proposal by Pirie, Booth and Lyon (*fn.* 663) that Eanred's accession date need be put back by several years is here supported by reference to annualized productivity.

Database 1 lends itself to conventional numismatic interpretation as follows:

6.4.1.1 The Normal Distribution, Stycas

As described above a normal distribution for large assemblies of *stycas* is a useful tool e.g. for dating hoards, *Dataset 3, Styca Frequencies*, shows frequencies and productivity. However, a more granular analysis of moneyers, particular as regards die links, is essential for chronological purposes.

6.4.1.2 Dataset 10*: Average Weights,* Stycas

Average *styca* weights (1.06g) and standard deviations (0.13g) have been computed from *Database 1* by issuer and moneyer and may be useful in identifying trends, *Dataset 10*. Weights are available for 4,715 specimens, sufficient to give a high level of confidence in the statistics. Wulfhere has high weight and low deviation. Blundered specimens are the lightest (0.98g) and counterfeits the heaviest (1.41g), both with high standard deviations.

6.4.1.3 Dataset 11*: Metal Analysis:* Stycas *CKN*

CKN records composition analysis by two methods, neutron activation (NA), 49 specimens, and X-ray fluorescence (XRF), 188 specimens, *Dataset 11*.[780] Neutron activation measures one element only and NA results have been accepted in the present study only for

[774] Transition to silver may have been a southern English initiative.
[775] Abramson (2019).

[776] Bede (IV, 13).
[777] Although on the various coin types of Pada, the name is rendered in runes, which may have been anathema to one of Christian persuasion.
[778] *Bede (EH,* IV, 14). Alcock (2003, 36–37).
[779] Oswald may have been a better candidate to be named on a touch-piece. Higham (1993, 106).
[780] The major problem with XRF is its very limited depth of penetration.

the 22 specimens—those by the 'Group A' moneyers in phase I, i.e. two silver-alloy coins issued by Eanbald II and 20 by Eanred. Only 164 of the XRF measurements are sufficiently comprehensive[781] to include. Certain fields in *CKN*, i.e. those with no entry and those marked 'Not Recorded' and 'Not Detected', have been given a null value. The results are summarized by issuer for each major element. Metallurgical studies of *stycas*[782] remain deficient and this is certainly an area for future research. In the meantime, the silver-alloy/brass boundary is secure but the brass/bronze/brass boundaries though unproven are accepted for the purposes of this study.

6.4.1.4 Dataset 12*: Die Links*

Die links are recorded in *CKN* as an alphabetic suffix to the catalogue number. Such links demonstrate the sequence of usage of successive dies and hence determine the chronology of variations within the species. An underlying assumption is that exhausted/obsolete dies are retired when their productive life is deemed to be at an end. This could be through, for example, wear and tear or organisational and political change. Die duplication is very much the exception in the early-penny coinage but is a frequent occurrence for *stycas*. Die links may be indicative of chronology during the better organised periods of *styca* production,[783] but not otherwise.

6.4.1.5 Die Axes

CKN gives obverse/reverse orientations for 4,605 specimens, *Dataset 12.* These are divided between regular orientations—those at 90°, 180° and 270°—and others. This assumes that square mounted dies can only be rotated in right angles. Dies mounted in square-cut piles enable the moneyer to align the obverse and reverse, otherwise the rotation between obverse and reverse is random. Such indications could be significant as the coinage descends into chaos. The results are analysed by moneyer and show that six of the 11 'Group A' moneyers are above two-thirds regular and amongst the 11 most regular producers. As Lyon remarked, 'when the *styca* coinage was in a flourishing state—i.e. from *c.* 837 to *c.* 847—regularity of die-axis is the rule rather than the exception, thus suggesting that square-cut dies were used.'[784]

6.4.1.6 Die Longevity

The production durability of dies is contentious. Greenhalgh demonstrated practically that 50,000 strikes is attainable,[785] Metcalf assumed a 'conservative' 10,000,[786] Esty allowed for variations in die manufacture relating to carbon content to harden the dies.[787] I endorse the latter, and would distinguish between the major trading Series of *sceattas* (D, E and R) where the mint workers probably developed sufficient skills to become proficient (i.e. possibly exceeding Metcalf's estimate) and the numerous 'exotic' issues of *sceattas*, where possibly peripatetic moneyers may not have had adequate skills, materials or equipment to make robust dies.

6.4.1.7 Dataset 13*: Motifs*

CKN records the obverse and reverse central *styca* motifs numerically.[788] Pirie vested the motifs with great significance,[789] dividing them between cruciform and secular types: where these are uniformly cruciform or secular on both obverse and reverse, this is a type-specimen, or if mixed, a variety. She alone regarded this as a major element in her die study.

6.4.2 Coin Use

6.4.2.1 Gold

Abdy and Williams listed finds of gold coins, in England, *c.* 410–675. Very few are known from Northumbria, *Figure* 116.[790] The immediate implication is that this modest volume of finds of imported gold coin may indicate commercial or social intercourse with the Continent at these find-spots, but the level of activity is low as gold usage was restricted to élite transactions. Pirie suggested that these coins originally came to southern *wics* and were subsequently traded northward.[791] It should be noted that imported gold and silver seem to have been found in similar quantities generally[792] perhaps indicating a better level of control over the imported silver.

Blackburn continued the corpus for the eighth to eleventh centuries,[793] listing the 29 British finds of gold coins for the period 700–1200, including two Islamic coins of the eighth century, and two Anglo-Saxon coins[794] plus 16 Carolingian coins and their derivatives for the ninth

[781] I.e. where the sum of measured components approaches 100 per cent.
[782] *BAR* 180 (1987) included metallurgical studies by Gilmore and Pirie (175–86), Metcalf and Northover (187–234). See *fn.* 666.
[783] E.g. for the sole/dominant moneyers of Æthelred II's restoration and Wulfhere.
[784] Lyon (1957, 237).
[785] Abramson (2012e, 19). Greenhalgh has demonstrated that the reverse stock is reduced by 6mm for every 1,000 strikes.
[786] Op den Velde and Metcalf (2003, 44–45 and 74–75).
[787] *Pers. comm.* 21st February 2016. See 105.
[788] Figs 3–6, but also see Abramson (2012d, Catalogue of Motifs 33–34).
[789] Pirie (1996, 31).
[790] A small number of Byzantine copper *nummi* are known from Meols and were found with imported artefacts part of the early sixth-century trade between western Britain and the Mediterranean. The volume of such finds, discounting modern losses, is not high but the coastal and inland distribution is widespread. Sawyer (2013, 45–46). Griffiths (2003, 65–68). Over 3,000 artefacts are recorded from this beach entrepôt, including Iron Age, Carthaginian and Northumbrian coins. The Byzantine coins are from the hinterland of the site and may indicate trade in wine and oil required for liturgical purposes. Also note the low-denomination Byzantine coins at the Rendlesham *vicus regius* (Christopher Scull, 'Rendlesham Re-Discovered' lecture 07/10/14).
[791] Pirie (1992b, 11–15).
[792] Based on the 26 imported gold specimens and 27 silver *deniers* in the author's collection as at February 2016, though collecting bias may be present.
[793] Blackburn (2007, discussion 67–73 and corpus 81–82, Appendix A).
[794] Also included in Blackburn (2007, Appendix B).

century. That these are mainly imitative *solidi* of Louis the Pious (*Figure* 56) becomes more significant in the light of a lead trial piece of this type from Torksey (*Figure* 57), probably dating from the mid-ninth century. Even were such imitations to have been produced domestically, the variation in authenticity, weight and purity, judging from the known specimens, made for an unreliable medium, more likely to have been treated as bullion.[795]

Byzantine Emperor Leo III, *c.* 720, overstruck Arab dirhams with *IhSYS XRISTYS NICA*, 'Jesus Christ conquers', to efface the *Kalima*, the Moslem credo.[796] By the same reasoning, Offa's gold mancus copying a gold dirham of Al Mansur dated AH 157 (= AD 774) but inverted, is an intentional mark of disrespect (*Figure* 58).[797]

To Blackburn's list is now added the *solidus* of Arichis II of Beneventum from Alnwick (*Figure* 60).[798] This is of significance, especially in the context of putative links between York's *Alma Sophia* and Beneventum. Blackburn's inventory of (legible) English gold coin finds, *c.* 675–1250, includes only eight specimens.[799] Historical sources record the rôle of gold coin in the payment of tribute and purchase of land,[800] but this may have been for recording purposes rather than actual exchange.

There is a scattering of imitative *solidi* of Louis the Pious, fragmentary *dirhams* and southern broad pennies on northern sites, though rarely more than one. The former may have been offered for high-value transactions in preference to an unwieldy cache of *stycas*, the latter two presumed to be lost from hack-silver by the passing *micel here*, a fairly common valediction, as noted in many of the site studies.

6.4.2.2 Silver

The turbulence of the era is reflected in the coinage. A clear example are the brackets of the twin disasters of Nechtansmere and Lindisfarne, which frame the northern *sceattas*. *Table 2* shows the intermittent minting activity. Clearly, Nechtansmere did not disrupt coin use—it may indeed have stimulated Aldfrith's introduction of the silver coinage—it heralded a loss of influence and prestige rather than core territory, albeit militarily costly. In contrast, the attack on Lindisfarne was a major blow to the confidence required to underwrite North Sea trade and caused a disruption to both coin production and use. These twin disasters are not, as yet, marked by hoards; the former, self-evidently, as it was a doomed act of Northumbrian aggression beyond its northern frontier and before *sceattas* circulated, but explanations for the latter are more complicated. In 793, the *sceat*, of which there are few hoards in any event, was a high denomination and the circulating medium probably modest in volume, so there may have been little to hide. There had been relative political stability and possibly little opportunity for a panic response to the attack. The areas and people at risk may have made little use of coinage and those who were making use of coinage, commercial traders, were probably more mobile.

Of significant interest historically, is the presence of imported primary *sceattas*, *Dataset 9*, especially from the Low Countries, and the composition of the Southumbrian and Continental secondary coinage between the emissions of Aldfrith and Eadberht. These are indicative of wide insular and Continental trading relationships, as exemplified by the near Hayton finds, but over-interpretation is a constant concern, hence the focus not only on random finds but, with caveats, on the condition of those coins.

Conversion Period iconography is abundant in the southern secondary *sceattas* and while the richest endowed varieties are not the high-volume trading currencies, the reach of coin use would have been extended by evangelical activity. The frequency of single occurrences of exotic species and Series Q *sceattas* suggests a steady peregrination of pilgrims, especially from East Anglia.

6.4.2.3 Copper Alloy

The weakness of the monetary system in England was exacerbated by a unitary denomination—certainly there was no small change for gold shilling or silver *sceattas*—and these successive denominations had a significant, though largely unascertainable, value.[801] *Stycas* were the first Anglo-Saxon emission than can be regarded as small change. Low-value coinage is comparatively uneconomical to produce, which is perhaps why the *styca* descended into chaos.

While Booth's model of promiscuous use of dies is unequivocally preferred over Pirie's complex die links, the decline into production chaos is chronologically uncertain, but what is quite evident from the *styca* distribution, *Dataset 2, Map 1,* is the widespread, if numerically slight, use of *stycas* in Southumbria. The presence of *stycas* at Flixborough suggests that The Lincolnshire Wolds were not commercially separated from the Yorkshire Wolds by the Humber.

[795] Grierson (1951, 11), first proposed that imitative Louis the Pious *solidi* were struck in England. The list included a find at Stamford Bridge in early 1940s, Christie auction 17/11/70, lot 46a, Stewart (1978, 162), Andrews (1988, 72). The Spink and Son Limited catalogue for auction 199, 25th June 2009 87, lists the then-known nine English finds of imitative *solidi* of Louis the Pious.
[796] Spufford (1988, 39).
[797] Spufford (1988, 50).
[798] See the case study on York and its environs (96).
[799] Blackburn (2007, Appendix B)
[800] Blackburn (2007, 55).

[801] An equivalence between a *sceat* or broad penny and a day's pay for a labourer (Abramson 2012b, 117), is an expedient proposition. The distribution of finds of *stycas* may be more widespread than previously thought, but the absence of mixed *styca*/penny hoards argues against their use as small change. Occasional emissions of halfpence are known from the late ninth century onwards but it is only in the era of short- and long-cross pennies (respectively 1180–1247 and 1247–1489) that halving and quartering pence provided change in any significant volume.

Stycas are present in numbers at the Viking camps at Torksey, 'the riverine site North of York',[802] Littleborough and Thetford presumably brought by the *micel here*, though whether these are for exchange (as coin or bullion), recycling, gaming or as singular curiosities, cannot be determined. The intriguing possibility that the later blundered *stycas* were Viking imitations remains, given that Vikings imitated local coinages elsewhere.[803]

While Talnotry and Lochar Moss are the only mixed hoards, could there have been a convenient exchange rate between brass *stycas* and broad pennies? Alas, the metrics are variable for both—composition, weight and the relative value of copper to silver. For the purposes of illustration only, applying an exchange rate of eight *stycas* to the penny.[804] against the new silver *denier* of 1.7g, fixed in 794 by the Council of Frankfurt, as worth 25 oaten loaves,[805] the *styca* was worth three loaves. Admittedly conjectural, possibly anachronistic,[806] this intriguing exchange, in the absence of mixed hoards, remains theoretical but does underline, despite the wide parameters, use of the *styca* for everyday transactions. For the purposes of discussion, a gold shilling may be envisaged as worth a fortnight's pay[807] and a *sceat*, a day's pay.

Styca hoards, mainly from seats of ecclesiastical power, and, plausibly, treasuries, demonstrate the fiscal efficacy of the 'widow's mite' for mass settlement of obligations to the church. The disadvantage of *stycas* was that for higher level transaction an unwieldy quantity was needed. Hoard evidence shows that large accumulations of these base coins were assembled but that does not prevent other media—such as the *solidi* of Louis the Pious—being used in satisfaction of indebtedness.

During the quiescent periods is there any sign of substitution? The dataset was interrogated for the alternate use of coins and artefacts (pins and strap-ends). The proportions hint at the possibility but, with the absence of clear chronology for fastenings,[808] periodic substitution may be suspected but cannot be identified.

Based on current numismatic understanding of both identity and chronology, the mix of types has been interpreted, or the original reported findings re-interpreted, in virtually all the sites studied. Among many examples of significant findings are the articulation of contributory factors to the decline of Whithorn and Whitby and recognition that metallic debris at Ryther and 'Site B' near Pocklington is of more significance than merely a nuisance to detectorists.

6.4.3 Lesser Numismatic Findings

At a detailed level, some new interpretations of specific early-penny varieties are postulated, including, for example, regarding the reverse of Series Z as portraying a wild boar, held in high esteem by both Celts and Romans, rather than the conventionally-understood hound.[809] The northern source of the trading varieties of Series J (types 37 and 85) is endorsed. The more exotic varieties (types 36 and 72), together with the ubiquitous Series G, are likely to come from Quentovic.

The order of Booth Classes F and G is reversed, in what has now been dubbed Eadberht's *renovatio* coinage. The poorer quality coins of Cuthgils (section 4.3.2.3.2) are distinguished from those of the other named moneyers of Æthelred I.

Based on arguments of both iconographic fashion and monetary integrity, the initiation of the change from animal reverses to named-moneyer early-penny issues under the auspices of Ælfwald I is favoured over the shadowy Ælfwald II. No emissions are ascribed to Ælfwald II, though there are rare, later, blundered *stycas* ostensibly in this name. The emissions of the moneyer Cuthheard are identified as crucial to this argument (section 4.4.2).

The point of departure (section 2.9) between the northern and southern coinages is highlighted, explaining why the Offan adoption of the precedent of the broad *denier* on a small flan may not have swayed the north to follow suit; by the time of Offa's heavy coinage, the north was reeling from the loss of prestige and commercial confidence consequent upon the attack on Lindisfarne.

The silver-alloy emission of Eanred was an attempt to restore the *sceat* and it is temporally isolated from the base *styca* by the near-comprehensive discontinuity of moneyers in Eanred's second, brass, *styca* issue.

Eardwulf (section 4.4.5) is regarded as Æthelred II's sole restoration moneyer, as those coining for Redwulf sacrificed their integrity.

Of the regal *stycas*, Osberht's are somewhat enigmatic. There are very few coins with a literate inscription and productivity figures are used to question his longevity, *Dataset 3, Styca Frequencies*, unless output was fitful. In similar vein, the abandonment date given by archaeologists for both Beverley minster and *Lundenwic* is questioned; 851 is almost inconceivable numismatically[810] and dates

[802] Provisionally 'Ainsbrook' after the finders, but widely known to be Aldwark. Finds are not included in the Database.

[803] 'This debate is in its infancy.' *pers. comm.* Andrew Woods, Leeds IMC, 9th July 2015.

[804] As implied by William Nicolson to Ralph Thoresby (65), though this cannot be relied upon.

[805] Durliat (1980, 138–54).

[806] At a time when silver and copper circulated together and were abundant, say late Roman Republican times, 16 copper *asses* of 12g each constituted a silver *denarius* of 4g, a Cu:Ar ratio of 48:1. Applying this to the period of study, one silver *denier* of 1.7g would be worth 77 copper *stycas* of 1.06g, valuing a loaf of bread at 3 *stycas*.

[807] Based loosely on a private soldier's pay and allowances in Late Antiquity (Spufford, 1988, 8).

[808] The proposed allocation of pins at Cottam between eighth and ninth century is too broad a period. Haldenby and Richards (2016).

[809] See Driffield.

[810] Blundered *stycas* and that of Osberht are unlikely to be so worn this early.

of 866–67 and 871–72 respectively, consistent with the activities of the *micel here*, are preferred.

The significance of the paucity of Vale of Pickering finds is discussed below. Likely locations of the two 'near Malton' attributions (section 7.6.1.1) are proposed: Binnington and West Heslerton.

6.4.3.1 Dataset 14*: Archbishop Wulfhere*

The archbishops continue to exercise minting rights into the ninth century though there is a paucity of *stycas* of Eanbald II and Wulfhere. *Dataset 14* shows where Wulfhere's coins are found. That twice as many *stycas* of Wulfhere occur in hoards, compared to the thinly spread, provenanced, single finds *may* demonstrate that hoarders preferred tin to zinc, such that this issuer's coins were secreted from the circulating medium. However, over a third of the total are unprovenanced, so that this conjecture is not wholly secure. As an aside, it is quite plausible that a cruciform late seventh-century stele from the minster was inscribed for Wulfhere a century after it was first engraved.

Chapter six described the limitations, sources and composition of the datasets. Chapter seven applies this analysis in evaluating the case studies and also makes significant numismatic findings derived from the periodization and data analysis.

6.5 Illustration—Chapter 6

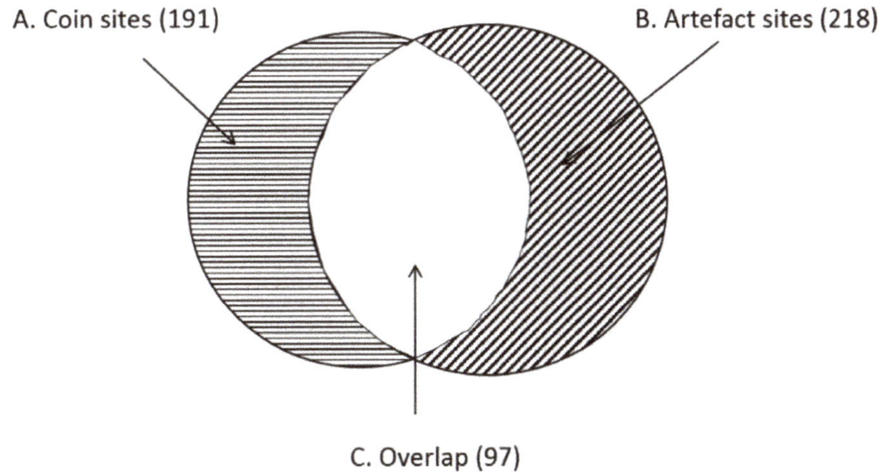

Figure 55: Venn diagram of the number of locations producing artefacts, coins and both.

Figure 56: Imitative *solidus* of Louis the Pious found West Lindsey, Lincolnshire, 4.38g. (Courtesy Spink & Son Limited)[811]

Figure 57: English/Frisian trial strike of an imitative gold *solidus* of Louis the Pious (814–40). Found Torksey, 22.64g.[812] *EMC* 2001.0290.

[811] Auction 227, lot 484, 17–18 December 2014, PAS LANCUM-9E265D.

[812] Blackburn (2007, 71–72).

Figure 58: Offa's gold mancus, Chick, 2010, type 1a 55 (with kind permission of the Sylloge of Coins of the British Isles project)

7

Case Studies

> 'they give money to the kings, and under pretence of erecting monasteries they acquire possessions, wherein the more freely to indulge their licentiousness; and procuring these by a royal edict to be assigned over to them in inheritance, they get the deed by which these privileges are confirmed...having gained possession of farms and villages, they free themselves from every bond, both human and Divine.'
>
> Bede's letter to Ecgberht (734, §12).

Having set the theoretical background, expounded a hypothesis of monetization, developed quantitative and qualitative methodologies, and developed analytical tools, these can now be applied to specific regions and locations. The Northumbrian finds are now organised in temporal and spatial frameworks, populated by analysis of the dataset. Constantly heedful of the caveats set out above, the finds are assessed by period and location, and conclusions are drawn on the penetration of coinage into the economy, its distribution and chronology. An underlying assumption is that condition is indicative of longevity, distancing loss from production both temporarily and spatially.

Northumbria's warrior society, rich in livestock, was economically active in the geographical regions identified above, which for the purposes of this study are distinguished as: York and its environs, the Central Lowlands, the Yorkshire Wolds, Beverley, Holderness, the Vale of Pickering and Bernicia and the North, *Map 2*. Within each region, the analysis is parish-based.[813]

When the location of detected finds is disclosed, the find site tends to be characterized by attributes which attract metal detectorists, namely, crop marks and earthworks. This holds true for the sites cited below but when archaeological reports of other relevant evidence have been lodged[814] these are briefly described.

7.1 York and Its Environs (*Dataset 15*)

> 'Roman power first founded this great city with its walls and towers...
> In order to make York an emporium for trade by land and sea alike.'
>
> Alcuin[815]

Following an introduction to York's Anglian period, coin and artefact finds in the general area are investigated focussing on the major sites in York, specifically the Minster and especially 46–54 Fishergate, before consideration of sites in 'inner' and 'outer' York . The major hoards have been discussed in detail above and will be mentioned only in passing.

The confluence of the Ouse and Foss is tidal and provides a strategic site breaching the east-west glacial ridge, which was an important prehistoric land route. The Magnesian limestone ridge is a narrow belt running north-south on the east flank of the Pennines overlooking the Vale of York and has been preferred as a route since Neolithic times.[816] The Roman *Legio IX Hispana* took advantage of the topography with the construction of a wooden fort above the flood plain, which developed into a legionary fortress and major colonia.[817] Septimius Severus proclaimed York capital of *Britannia Inferior*.[818]

7.1.1 Archaeology: The Anglian Period

Nuttgens surmised that with the Anglian invasion along the Humber, the old wooden bridge was destroyed and the British sought refuge in Elmet: 'The Anglian kingdom of Deira was centred in the wolds of the East Riding, so that York itself was effectively on its edge. It was a kingdom of many villages and few towns.'[819]

Given that the Roman garrison constituted a substantial proportion of the urban population, an economic deterioration followed the withdrawal of troops. As central authority declined, many urban dwellers will have returned to the countryside. Farmers will have been unable to dispose of surplus produce unless they sought new markets; arable land will have been left fallow or turned over to grazing. Inability to profit from surplus may have been of little concern. According to the foundation mythology of *Eoforwic*, the decline of York was reversed when Edwin installed flood prevention and reclamation measures, however there is no evidence of inundation where it would be expected.[820] Nor is plague given much credence as a cause of decline.[821]

Up to half a metre of 'black earth', attributable to biological action accumulated over Roman structures, although survival of some architectural features is

[813] Manby and others (eds.) (2003, *figure 7*). See also Loveluck (2003, 151–70).
[814] With, for example, ADS or Pastscape.
[815] Poem translated by Mary Garrison, June 2015. Also see Hill and Cowie (2001, 113).
[816] Gaunt and Buckland (2003, 20).
[817] Hall (1988, 125).
[818] Heywood (1995, 7).
[819] Nuttgens (1976, 17).
[820] Hall (1988, 125–26) and (1996, 32–34). Muir (1987, 79). James (1995, 9 *fn.* 104, in Carver)
[821] James (1995, 9).

attested historically.[822] Unfortunately, these unstratified, undiagnostic 'Anglian greys' obscure the chronology in many York sites.[823] According to Mainman: 'The suggestion that areas within and outside the walls were used for agriculture and gardening[824] was given some tangible support by a regular undulating surface perhaps representing furrows observed below the earliest Viking-Age occupation at Hungate.'[825]

York Minster[826]

> 'And this beautiful salubrious place, with its noble setting,
> Would have many settlers because of its fruitfulness.'
>
> Alcuin[827]

Evidence for the Anglian occupation of York remains slender. Stratification at the *basilica*, particularly in the layers between the mortar floor and the collapsed walls and roof, could have been diagnostic of the extent of Anglian activity. Regrettably, the picture is unclear and open to multiple interpretations. A small number of York ware sherds could well be intrusions: 'The post-Roman events beneath the collapsed *basilica* roof become more coherent the more closely they are placed in time to the abandoned 4th century cultural assemblage which mainly characterizes them.'[828] This is endorsed by radiocarbon dating of the unusual and substantial so-called 'small pig horizon', presumed to be the specialism of a community rearing animals within the fortress and slaughtering in the *basilica*.[829] A further change of use is seen in the presence of metalworking in the area of the *contubernia*.[830] The *basilica* may have been used as a market hall at this time.[831] Further degradation can be envisaged before the late seventh- or early eighth-century phase of grave cutting and inscribed stele. From these, and Anglo-Scandinavian robber-trenches, it can be presumed that the ground had been levelled.[832]

Contemporary with the hypothesised use of the *basilica* as a market hall, the centurion's quarter of Barrack 2, where eastern Mediterranean *amphoræ* were found, may have been a villa. However, the stratification is unclear and 'chronological stepping-stones are as few as ever'.[833] There is the bezel of a Merovingian finger ring, and a concentration of Anglian material, in the dark soil above the collapsed structures, but some of this may have been transported.[834]

The animal bone assemblage in the *basilica* has more sheep and older cattle than might be expected, leading Rackham to conclude that this is a modest subsistence farm supplying a small community with essentials, not a market operation with large holdings.[835] The Anglian period shows an abundance of pigs in the ultimate phase of the *principia* building, which, according to Rackham, signals a subsistence strategy rather than husbandry.[836] O'Connor used the near absence of pig phalanges and metapodials at Fishergate to propose that there was no backyard rearing there and prepared carcasses were brought in,[837] which infers that the activity at the *principia* could be seen as specialisation not subsistence.

Replacement of the small wooden minster in stone,[838] was initiated in 627 by Edwin (for which sculptured stone may provide evidence)[839] and completed by Oswald. But as early as *c.* 670, Wilfrid and Chad needed to carry out repairs, possibly as Aidan and Colmán brought Lindisfarne to prominence, causing some diversion of resources, until Ecgberht's acceptance of the *pallium*, in 735, restored York's pre-eminence.[840]

The Anglian material at the Minster is probably the most important of that period found locally, demonstrating flourishing activity, despite the paucity of literary evidence.[841] The carved stone finds match the number found elsewhere in York and have advanced understanding significantly. Though the majority are uninscribed Anglo-Scandinavian pieces, the Anglian stonework is of a form not known elsewhere in Northumbria—stele—incised crosses rather than free-standing cross-shafts. The crispness of these shows that they were erected internally. They are carved on pale Magnesian Limestone, have usually been re-used, and are, therefore, fragmentary and unstratified.

Lang claims 'the names engraved on the Anglian pieces cannot be identified in the literary sources with known personages',[842] even though stele fragment, YM22,[843] is clearly inscribed (*Figure* 59). Were this memorial stone to commemorate Archbishop Wulfhere, it would be of significance. Given the possibility of a subsequent

822 *Ibid.*, and see footnote on Alcuin (*fn.* 839).
823 O'Conner (1994, 136).
824 Tweddle and others (1999, 211–12).
825 Mainman and Hall (2015a).
826 Woodman (2012, 25–67).
827 *Fn.* 815.
828 Carver (1995, 189).
829 O'Connor (1994, 137). Mainman and Hall (2015a).
830 A *contubernium* is a squad of eight legionaries, the smallest military unit.
831 Carver (1995, 190).
832 Carver (1995, 191).
833 Carver (1995, 190).
834 Carver (1995, ch. 5, 12/6).
835 Rackham (1995, ch. 6.9, 554).
836 *Ibid.*
837 O'Conner (1994, 139).
838 *Bede* (*EH, II.*14). Heywood (1995, *figure* 2 4). Woodman (2012, 26). Plausibly over the Legionary Fortress, the *principia*, but unproven.
839 Hall (1988, 126). James (1995, 10). Alcuin, in his poem 'On the Bishops, Kings and Saints of York' referred to *solidis suffulta columnis*, 'strong columns' (line 220, 1509 [Willis, 1848], quoted from Morris (1986, 80)), presumably Roman, supporting Edwin's church, though this may not necessarily imply continuity.
840 James (1995, 10).
841 Lang (1995, 434).
842 Lang (1995, 433 and 453, plate 121).
843 The fragment, in five pieces, is 21cms high, 25cms wide and 13.3cms thick, with narrow modelled moulding.

inscriptional superimposition, this prospect must remain unproven but tantalising.

Stocker's work on *spolia*, demonstrated extensive medieval re-use of dressed stone from the Minster, both casual and functional.[844] This occurred in other ecclesiastical premises under episcopal control.[845] Even were the authorities distributing *spolia* freely, there would still have been consequences for employment and transportation, let alone the investment in building with its economic leverage.[846]

Close parallels with ecclesiastical stonework found elsewhere in Northumbria, led Lang to conclude that the *atelier* of the 'York Metropolitan School' exported their output widely in the north,[847] which undoubtedly would have made a considerable contribution to economic activity. Lang remarked on the profusion of later funerary sculpture in Ryedale compared to its near absence in the Wolds (apart from Sherburn),[848] a contrast to the numismatic material.

Certainly, the variety of post-Roman pottery sherds found during the Minster excavations implies a wide communications network.[849] There is a small number of hand-thrown pots dated between the fifth and eighth centuries and 171 sherds of the local, friable, York ware of the eighth to ninth centuries. These York ware fragments are exclusively from medium-sized globular jars, which Holdsworth suggested may indicate a local commodity.[850] Holdsworth associated the first rough wheel-thrown York ware with Mayen wares, inferring a Rhenish connection from the latter part of the eighth century—a seventy-five-year advance on previous estimates of the introduction of large-scale thrown-ware production. Rhenish pots were widely traded and occur in significant numbers, for example, at Dorestad.[851] How specie flow supported trade in pots is not yet evident. Among the Anglo-Scandinavian pottery finds are 65 sherds of Torksey ware, which post-date the *micel here's* overwintering in Torksey, 872/3.

Carver argued both for an Anglian cemetery below that of the Anglo-Scandinavian phase and the placing of the Anglian church adjacent to this, which would be at the junction of *via principalis* and *via praetoria*. He set out three models of activity from minimal to maximal, but it would be difficult to sustain any interpretation other than 'fitful rather than continuous activity.'[852]

[844] Stocker (1999, 211 and 356).
[845] Morris and Stocker (1987).
[846] Alcock (2003, 51).
[847] Lang in Carver (1995, 440). Lang (*CASSS*, vol. 3, ch. 7) stated: 'Examples also occur elsewhere in York at St Mary's Abbey (no. 1), St Denys (no. 1), and St Mary Bishophill Junior (no. 6), with a surprising outlier at Gainford (no. 20) in co. Durham (Cramp 1984, i, 86–87).'
[848] *CASSS*, vol. 3, ch. 7.
[849] Holdsworth (1995, ch. 6.2, 471).
[850] Holdsworth (1995, ch. 6.2, 469).
[851] Holdsworth (1995, ch. 6.2, 471).
[852] Carver (1995, 191).

Over a hundred Anglo-Saxon graves have been excavated from below the Norman cathedral, of which 13 have stone covers, 13 are charcoal burials, five have elaborate coffin fittings and one probably uses a section of Viking boat as a bier. These are high status burials from the late ninth and tenth century.[853]

Based on a careful reading of Alcuin, and the topography of royal and episcopal sites in contemporary centres, Morris has argued for the cathedral being separate from a *monasterium*, which he believed to have been situated in the *Colonia*, on the west bank of the Ouse, in the Bishophill area, viewing York as a multifocal centre.[854] Morris noted, in connection with York's supposedly thirty-altar *Alma Sophia*, that the similarly-named churches at both Benevento[855] and Constantinople[856] stood adjacent to royal palaces. 'The sense of the dedication was in direct imitation of the prototype in Constantinople.'[857] Certainly, Alcuin and his mentor Ælberht had travelled in Italy but Garrison felt that Morris is wrong to elide the church dedications.[858] St. Willibald of Wessex (d. 787) spent several years in Beneventum.[859] Naismith augmented this putative link: Arichis II was one of very few western European rulers to have evaded Charlesmagne's conquests,[860] so it is not surprising that he may have tried to forge contacts with other independent kingdoms as suggested by the loss of a test-marked *solidus* of his at Alnwick (*Figure* 60).

Other possible seventh- and eighth-century churches include St Peter the Little, All Saints Pavement, St Mary Castlegate, St Michael, St Stephen, St Gregory, St Mary Bishophill Senior and Junior, where there are grave monuments, and St Martin which has a sculptural frieze. This impressive rate of construction indicates a prolific expansion unachievable without a substantial and reliable flow of *materiel* and finance.

The Anglian Settlement at Fishergate

> 'To York, gathered from many kingdoms they come,
> With hope of gain, seeking for themselves the riches
> of the rich land:
> Fortune, home and hearth'
>
> Alcuin[861]

[853] Kjølbye-Biddle (1995, 517).
[854] Morris (1986, 80–89). An early medieval text showed that St. Cuthbert was granted land in central York in the pivotal year of 685. (Rollason and others (1998, 50–51, 140–41). Mainman and Hall (2015a) which may support the claim of Norton (1998, 14–15), for the site of *Alma Sophia* to be the Minster Chapter House.
[855] *Sancta Sophia*, completed by Arichis II.
[856] *Hagia Sophia.*
[857] Morris (1986, 83–84). See Woodman (2012, 37 and *fn.* 76) for discussion.
[858] Garrison, *pers. comm.* 10th February 2015.
[859] (*NC*, CXIX, 1, March 2011, *fn.* 16: Hugeburc's *Hodoepricon*). See Hodges (2012, ch. 4), for a discussion of the significance of Beneventan San Vincenzo al Volturna.
[860] Naismith (2012, 13 and 2015, 11).
[861] *Fn.* 815.

During 1985–86, YAT examined the site at 46–54 Fishergate, formerly occupied by Redfearn National Glass Factory. Fishergate lies on a Roman road outside the main area of activity, south-east of the fortress, on elevated ground east of the confluence of the Ouse and Foss.[862] The excavation produced over 9,700 finds including domestic and personal items (*Figure* 61) and evidence of craft and industrial workings, though no *foci* for these activities were identified.[863] Total excavation of a site of around 2,500m^2 (0.25ha) took place using recovery techniques of coarse-, site- and bulk-sieving to secure artefacts of 1mm. There is no mention of metal detection.

The site revealed a 'period 3' (Anglian, late seventh to mid-ninth century) settlement consisting of an early, planned, phase 3a, of large properties, followed by a more limited settlement, 3b, extending into the late ninth century. The two phases are separated by a distinct charcoal-laden layer, including unburnt animal bones, across the site.[864]

Looking first at the non-numismatic evidence, the nearby inhumation cemetery for this early medieval population dates from the early eighth century, possibly earlier.[865] Burials have been revealed including four intact cremations at Fishergate House, and a fifth on Blue Bridge Lane. Architectural features included post- and stake-holes, ditches and pits evidencing domestic occupation and craft-working. Southumbrian and Continental artefacts demonstrated long-distance exchange. Pits for the disposal of craft and pottery waste and animal bones seem to be aligned, possibly to partition the settlement. Metallic waste—lead, copper alloy and iron slag—indicate the level of technology. Animal waste products may be from the manufacture of pins and combs. Wool working is evidenced by finds of needles and shears, clay loom-weights and spindle whorls.[866] Tweddle believed an animal-engraved bone knife-handle fragment to date from around 700 (*Figure* 62).[867]

Regarding glassware, Hunter and Jackson concluded that 'Evidence of quality craftsmanship...places York within the mainstream of north-west Europe'.[868] The Mayen lava quern-stone is thought to have been shipped down the Rhine to be finished at Dorestad for export.[869] It appears that a colony of Frisian merchants left York in 773,[870] although Hall over-interpreted the presence of a Frisian *sceat* at Coppergate as 'confirming contact between the two areas.'[871]

The conventional interpretation of the excavation is that the seat of royal and ecclesiastical power, if these coexisted in close proximity, were probably based in the Roman Legionary fortress.[872] The Fishergate community may have been geographically distinct from this centre, but served it economically, as a *wic*.[873] According to Mainman: 'The range and proportion of continental pottery found with the local and regional wares at Fishergate places the site in the same class as the large contemporary trading sites of Hamwic, Ipswich and London.'[874] In re-assessing the Hamwic pottery, the best documented and most prolific of these three *wics*, Andrews indicated that previous analyses gave undue emphasis to imported ware, which constituted 18 per cent of the assemblage.[875] Even though the range of foreign sources is wide, including Tating-, Badorf- and Mayen-ware, '(t)he number of imported fabrics that can positively be identified is extremely limited, and the occurrence of good associated groups rare.'[876] There is also a paucity of both repeating imported types and local imitation so the chronology is largely numismatically determined. Mainman claimed that in the eighth and ninth centuries, the imported element at Fishergate falls from around 40 per cent in periods 3a–b to about 20 per cent in 3c.[877] However, the catalogue conflates foreign imports with vessels of unknown provenance.[878] Furthermore given that the region is largely aceramic in this period, apart from imported wares, the importance of the imported wares may have been overstated. In sum, using the ceramic assemblage as the basis for claiming Fishergate as a *wic* is unsound.

Biological analysis shows a specific and restricted food supply indicating that the putative *wic* was provisioned by the centre from food rents lacking diversity.[879] While pigs seem to have been prepared elsewhere, other livestock arrived on the hoof, and other sources of meat are few.[880] Dobney and others, also report that the site 'gave disappointingly little evidence for invertebrates, despite extensive sampling...there were rare occurrences here of a limited fauna associated with human occupation.' They also found that 'plant remains were sparse...the rarity of [weeds] is remarkable for an occupation site.' Unless waste failed to be preserved, was thrown into the river or hauled to nearby farms, they concluded that the density of occupation was low.[881] A restricted range of species,

862 Kemp (1996, 77–82).
863 Kemp (1996, 15–63). Rogers (1993, 1217 and 1439–44).
864 Kemp (1996, 56–59).
865 Rollason and others (1998).
866 Kemp (1996, 71–74). http://www.archaeologicalplanningconsultancy.co.uk/mono/001/
867 Rogers (1993, 1309–11).
868 Rogers (1993, 1343).
869 Rogers (1993, 1329).
870 Whitelock (1979, *EHD* vol. 1 500–1042), Altfrid's *Life of St Liudger* 725. Sawyer (2013, 67).
871 Hall (1988, 128). Hill and Cowie (2001, 113). Rollason (2003, 178–79), where he attempted to difference Fishergate from royally planned emporia (Hamwic, Ipswich, Dorestad, Birka) in that there was no protection for the Frisian merchants (who, he speculated, were resident there) after one of them killed the son of a local noble in the course of a disturbance, precipitating the departure of the Frisians.
872 O'Connor (1994). Carver and others.
873 Rogers (1993, 1441). O'Conner (1994, 141).
874 Mainman (1993, 649).
875 Andrews (1988, 73).
876 Andrews (1988, 111).
877 Mainman (1993, 582).
878 Mainman (1993, 655–56).
879 Kemp (1996, 95–105). Mainman and Hall (2015a) mention the 'unusual emphasis on cattle' as evidence of outside control.
880 O'Conner (1994, 139).
881 Dobney and others (2000, 133–34). Hall (1996, 84–85). O'Conner (1994, 141–42), who suggested that waste could have been treated selectively.

low density occupation, and lack of neonates may be indicative of a controlled *wic* assemblage. However, other environmental evidence may support the argument that Fishergate was not an emporium, and Smith concluded that 'it may be unsafe to use the absence of neo-natal bones to characterize the Fishergate site as a 'consumer' settlement.[882] On balance, the environmental evidence may be inconclusive, but the fact that many nearby settlements, albeit with the aid of metal-detecting, have far larger assemblages of numismatic material, must cast doubt on the status of Fishergate as a *wic*.

Dixon Lane and George Street[883]

This site, only 300 metres from 46–54 Fishergate, may be of significance in establishing the status of Fishergate. A gold ring of the late fourth or fifth century may indicate activity around the time of the Roman withdrawal, though, like other local sites, the stratigraphic evidence for sub-Roman continuity is virtually absent.

Topographic evidence of the occupation of the site in the late seventh century, common between here and Fishergate, includes a boundary ditch, timber buildings, one (maybe two) sunken-featured building (*Grübenhaus*) and rubbish pits. Artefacts in common include copper-alloy dress pins, glass beads and fragments. Shared crafts are indicated by antler and bone comb components and loom-weights used in textile manufacture.[884] These topographic, artefactual and craft-working similarities with Fishergate led the excavators to conclude that these may have been part of the same *wic*.

Significantly, unlike Fishergate, personal items from the Anglo-Scandinavian period were also found comprising bone dress pins, a twisted wire ring, an arm ring and more comb-making debris. Such spatial continuity 'is of significance for our understanding of how that political and economic transition affected the topography of York.'[885]

York's other archaeological sites have been described, in summary, by Tweddle, and others, 1999 and Naylor, 2002.

Modifications to the topography, especially roads and rivers with their fundamental rôle in transport and trade, could be diagnostic in interpreting post-Roman York. Re-alignment, via Monk Bar and Goodramgate, of the Roman *porta decumana*, as early as mid-eighth century, could have been initiated by ecclesiastical authority. In this connection, Aldwark, bears the only street name of Old English derivation.[886] Evidence for various water-management schemes protecting some areas and inundating others,[887] is starting to accumulate.[888]

The Roman cemeteries at Heworth, half a mile north-east of the fortress, continued in use into the fifth and sixth centuries.[889] Decorated cremation urns have been found here (*Figure* 63) and at The Mount.[890] Burials at 1–9 Micklegate, 7–17 Spurriergate, 16–22 Coppergate and near St Helen's church provide further evidence of Anglian activity (*Figure* 64, *Figure* 65).[891]

Two kilometres south-east of the centre, the cemetery at Lamel Hill, on the moraine from Heslington Hill towards Fishergate, revealed seventy, probably Christian, burials, although no associated church was identified. At nearby Bellevue House on Heslington Road, YAT excavations exposed a further 50 burials carbon-dated to the late seventh or eighth centuries.[892]

Hall argued that the several hundred hand-made fragments of pottery at Coppergate evince a 'tradition of ceramic production' pre-dating the Viking period.[893] This logic, that the relative sophistication of Coppergate did not spring fully-fledged from nowhere, implies pre-existing activity awaiting discovery. Though the Minster and St. Mary Bishophill demonstrate that the degree of continuity from sub-Roman times is speculative, it is more certain that York's growing ecclesiastical wealth was built on commercial success: 'Alcuin (adopting Bede's description of London) called York an emporium—"a general seat of commerce by land and sea alike." '[894]

In a recent study, Spall and Toop have described 2001–02 excavations at Heslington Hill and Fishergate with reference to 'the elusive transition between the Roman and Viking city.'[895] Both local and non-local ceramics at these two sites, dating to *c.* 550–650, are similar in character, leading the authors to conclude that the abandonment of the former is coincident with the expansion of the latter, less than 2km along the same gravel terrace, as part of a contemporary pattern of movement from upland settlements to more productive, lower-lying land (*Dataset 1, Stability—Coin Sites*).[896] 'The shift closer to the fortress

[882] Smith (2006, 100). Also, we may be judging the lack of dietary diversity with modern eyes 181.
[883] http://www.iadb.co.uk/i3/item.php?ID=IADB:1307:U71
[884] Though Fishergate also had evidence of spinning and fibre preparation, *AY* 17/9 1441.
[885] http://www.iadb.co.uk/i3/item.php?ID=IADB:1307:U71, 5. Conclusion. Iron clench bolts found here are associated with burials and are comparable with similar items found at the Minster as part of a boat re-used as a bier, Kjølbye-Biddle (1995, 500).
[886] Tweddle and others (1999, 160). This name is shared with the prolific Viking site five miles south-east of Boroughbridge, where numerous *stycas* have been found. Seventy-two artefacts found by Mark Ainsley and Geoff Bambrook (hence the codename 'Ainsbrook' for Aldwark) are recorded at PAS 2007 T186 ref. ARSNY.
[887] E.g. King's Pool on the Foss. The Ouse was wider and tidal with several fish species now extinct (*pers. comm.* Andrew 'Bone' Jones, 8th April 2015).
[888] Mainman and Hall (2015a).
[889] Hall (1996, 54–55). Possible fifth-century burials include an inhumation at Hungate and an un-urned cremation at Driffield Terrace.
[890] Hall (1996, 33–34).
[891] Mainman and Hall (2015a).
[892] *Ibid.* Tweddle (1986, 176).
[893] Hall (1988, 128).
[894] James (1995, 10). Alcuin (*fn.* 839).
[895] *Med Arch* (52, 2008, 1).
[896] *Med Arch* (52, 2008, 18–19). See *Dataset 1, Stability—Coin Sites* for my suggestions of possible settlement shifts.

reflects the general increase in investment and economic activity concomitant with the establishment of the major ecclesiastical centre.'[897]

The spring-line to the east of York would have had significance for dwellers in the dry chalk Wolds. At Heslington East, in the second half of the fourth century, the monumentalisation of the Roman well, re-using masonry to access a subterranean source, signifies its importance for both functional and ritualistic purposes. Infill included ceramics, a discarded bucket, fauna and flora, *spolia* (e.g. a finial) but mainly silt and stones.[898] Intentional contamination of a potable and revered water supply by butchered sacrifices (fill 2093), can be discounted early in the well's life, unless a collapse of masonry had occurred and the well failed quickly.[899]

York's Roman buildings were not 'robbed out' until the twelfth century, so that the topography of Anglian York may well have appeared as Roman York, but in disrepair. The Roman infrastructure encompassed defences, civic and communal buildings, dwellings, bridges, streets, sewers, wharves and cemeteries. All were neglected. 'On the north-west side of the fortress, however, investigations have revealed a sequence of late/post-Roman and early medieval repair and rebuilding. After an initial renovation with a dry-stone wall and cobbled sentry walk, successive earthen ramparts topped with a timber palisade enveloped and oversailed the Roman wall.'[900] Residues of structural timber dating after *c.* 375–400 have been found in remains of buildings on the south-west bank of the River Ouse.[901] The corner tower at Feasegate and wall excavations between Stonegate and Coney Street suggest surviving Roman topography into the ninth century and later.[902]

7.1.2 Coinage

Graph 4 illustrates the chronological dispersal of site finds and hoards, showing that apart from Fishergate where the finds span the silver and base phases, *stycas* predominate.

York Minster

Of the sites in *Dataset 15, Inner York—Single Finds*, Coppergate and York Minster both contribute 13 specimens of the study period and a denier. While the former is predominantly a Viking site, excavations at the Minster produced Roman, Anglian, Anglo-Scandinavian and later finds. The *sceat* and *styca* finds from the Minster are unexceptional and few; conceivably, commerce was discouraged on sacred grounds, irrespective of coin issuance by ecclesiastical authorities. Of the three *sceattas* the earliest is a Series J coin in poor condition and possibly imitative. The Eadberht *sceat* has an unusual central device (triskeles); the Æthelred I *sceat* is by Ceolbald. The earliest of the 10 ninth-century coins is a silver-alloy coin of Eanred of the moneyer Eadwine. There are also brass *stycas* of Eanred, Æthelred II (both reigns) and Osberht but none of Redwulf or, counter-intuitively for the site of the Minster, of the ninth century Archbishops.[903] Archibald estimated the date of deposition of a corroded, fragmentary, broad penny of Egbert of Wessex (802–39) minted at Canterbury by Tidbearht, to be *c.* 830–60, speculating that it denoted an ecclesiastical relationship.[904] However, in discussing a find of a *denier* of Charles the Bald, from Quentovic, issued in large numbers from 864 after the Edict of Pîtres, she revised this, in view of the absence of peck marks, suggesting that coins were deposited together in Barrack Two of the centurion's quarter, in 864–67, prior to the Viking victory, though pecking is not necessarily associated with Viking incursions this early.[905]

Fishergate

> 'The World is run…not from castle walls but from counting houses'
>
> Hilary Mantel, *Wolf Hall* (2010, 378).

It is now possible to describe and interpret the coin finds in greater detail than achieved by Kemp,[906] *Plates 4–7* and *Dataset 15*, which is now reconciled to earlier, somewhat inaccurate, listings.

The earliest coins are the primary phase emissions from the Low Countries: two Series D *sceattas* and what may be a Series E, variety G *sceat.*,[907] All are worn and corroded. One of the Series D coins has a laterally reversed bust, thought by Metcalf and Op den Velde to indicate a contemporary English imitation.[908] Clearly, all three have remained in circulation for a long period and cannot be taken as evidence of either economic activity on the site prior to *c.* 710 or direct trade with the Continent. Nor can two heavily worn Series G *sceattas*, transitional from primary to secondary phases, be taken as evidence of anything but the longevity and ubiquity of Quentovic's currency. Of greater significance is the coin of late Series B (BIIIC)[909] and five of Series J. The former shows few signs of wear and three of the Series J specimens are close

[897] *Med Arch* (52, 2008, 20). O'Connor (1994, 146), decried emphasis on diachronic change in environmental archaeology.
[898] Roskams and others (2013).
[899] See Hines (1997, 379).
[900] Mainman and Hall (2015a).
[901] Ottaway (2004, 146–49).
[902] *Ibid.*

[903] YAT's *Northern Archaeology Today* magazine issue 3 (2013) reports the find of a coin of Eanbald II.
[904] Pirie (1995, Carver ch. 6.7, 527–30).
[905] It is absent from Torksey. Archibald (2007, 49–53).
[906] Kemp, presumably, did not have the benefit of Metcalf's *T&S* published the same year. I include the coins (but not the illustrations) from excavations at Fishergate House and Blue Bridge Lane, held by APC, the Archaeological Planning Consultancy.
[907] According to Blackburn's chronology (posthumous revision in Abramson, 2012d).
[908] Metcalf and Op den Velde (2003 10 and 87, type 2c, sub-varieties 3c, 3h and perhaps 4c). A 'contemporary imitation' implies an unofficial reproduction which circulated alongside the original, rather than a fake.
[909] Metcalf (2011, 25) referred to this specimen, arguing for an East Midlands source for BIIIC and the Maltese cross derivative of the Aldfrith type (2011, 23–25, *SL*102–80). He suggested that the Aston Rowant variety of Series Z (*SL*102–70) may also be Aldfrith-derived.

to pristine. The other two have an imitative appearance. Series J, popular during the native Northumbrian coinage *lacuna* between Aldfrith and Eadberht, is regarded, especially with the iconography of the facing heads, as a putative northern emission. The relatively unblemished appearance of these three coins supports that view and provides evidence of the use of coinage at Fishergate by the 720s (*Figure* 66).

A *sceat* of early Series R, whose finds focus favours Ipswich, is again heavily worn and corroded. Although trade between *Eoforwic* and *Gipeswic* is evidenced by pottery,[910] this specimen is likely to have been in heavy use and does not corroborate direct trade.

With the exception of a very rare 'triquetras' type (*Figure* 67) late in the coinage,[911] the remaining coins fall into two groups: seven specimens each of secondary Series E and the local Series Y. While only one of the Series E *sceattas* is sufficiently well preserved to support a direct trading link,[912] the fact that these have not been recycled into local coinage may be an indication that, together with Series J and G, they were tolerated locally, as evidenced by the composition of finds at other northern 'productive sites',[913] possibly indicative of weak local control.

The Series Y *sceattas* include four fantastic animal types of Eadberht, and three inscriptional types. One of the fantastic animal types is in a condition which may suggest it has not travelled far from its minting place, the other is so worn that it could be imagined to be an East Anglian coin of Series Q,[914] a Series with affinities to Series Y.[915] Two of the inscriptional types are joint regal/archiepiscopal issues, for Eadberht with Archbishop Ecgberht, and Alchred also with Ecgberht. The third inscriptional type, mistaken by Pirie for a *styca*, is for Æthelred I by the long-serving moneyer Cuthheart, which extends the use of *sceattas* at this site into the 790s (*Figure* 68).

Seven of the 19 ninth-century finds are rendered of limited use as they are worn, corroded or blundered. The others, as in *Dataset 15, Fishergate Catalogue (Figure* 69), include a silver-alloy coin of Eanred and *stycas* of Eanred, Æthelred II (both reigns) and Archbishop Wigmund. The presence of the silver-alloy coin shows re-adoption of coinage after the post-Lindisfarne depression but the absence of coins by Osberht and Archbishop Wulfhere[916] shows a potential decline before the fall of York to the Vikings.

It is curious that a penny of Æthelberht of Wessex (858–865/6, *Figure* 70) should also have been found in the pit at Cottam 'B' near the jaw-less female skull—could they both have been brought by the *micel here*?[917] Certainly, this is an historical marker as the Fishergate site seems to have been abandoned around this time as indicated by the absence of Torksey, York and 'York d' ware and Anglo-Scandinavian shelly pottery.[918] The penny of Æthelberht may have accompanied the Vikings as small numbers of similar pennies are thinly but widely distributed in the north.

To recapitulate the main features of the coinage at Fishergate, atypically, *sceattas* outnumber *stycas* 3:2, and among the 27 *sceattas*, imported Continental coins (twelve) dominate with only seven indisputably Northumbrian coins, from *c.* 737 to the 790s, though the source of the five Series J specimens is assumed northern. The primary phase *sceattas* are worn so cannot be used to argue for an early transactional date. There are only two Southumbrian *sceattas*, one East Anglian the other an exotic species.

Among the ninth century coins, there is only one silver-alloy emission of Eanred, none for Eanbald II, 11 brass *stycas* and seven blundered. There are no coins of Osberht or Wulfhere indicating decline before the fall of York.

7.1.3 Comparison with Normal Distribution

Database 1 gives data for periods 4a to N10c covering only *sceattas* and *stycas*. Tempering Metcalf's *dictum* 'randomness is all' with sample size, *Dataset 1, Summary*, selection F, 'Provenanced, not hoard' (1,242 coins), was deemed the most appropriate base for extrapolation.[919] In *Dataset 15, Actual Vs Expected*, the distribution of this selection is compared to the number of finds at Fishergate (48 coins) and to all York (164 coins). The correlations[920] for *sceattas* at all York and *stycas* at both all York and Fishergate are strong but there is no correlation to norm for *sceattas* at Fishergate, which remains anomalous, displaying a counterintuitive preference for Continental *sceattas* over local issues. See *Graph* 4.1.

[910] Mainman (1993, 568) though Ipswich/type wares 'were never a significant part of the assemblage' and York forms the northern limit of its distribution (581).

[911] Metcalf (1993–94, 422–25), *SL* 110–60. The imagery of this type is typical of Conversion Period iconography.

[912] Though it is underweight (0.70g) and under-size (7mm) as are the Cothen hoard coins (Metcalf and Op den Velde (2014)).

[913] Bonser (2011, 159–80).

[914] *SL* 64–40 obverse or 65–30 reverse.

[915] In arguing for Ely as the mint for Series Q, Newman (2008, 18) mentioned the Northumbrian connection: 'it may be significant that Æthelthryth had an admittedly unconsummated marriage to Ecgfrith of Northumbria and a period at the monastery at Coldingham in the north before founding her house at Ely in AD 673.' It is noteworthy how many of the sites studied below produce a singleton of the diverse Series Q. Hutcheson favoured Bawsey as the source of Series Q. Hope-Taylor (1977, 321) alluded to cultural affiliations noted at Yeavering.

[916] Though this absence is not significantly different from norm. The absence of coins of Redwulf is inconsequential as *stycas* of the first and second reigns of Æthelred II are represented.

[917] Kemp (1996, 83). Haldenby and Richards (2016). This is only the third known specimen of Æthelberht's inscriptional type (N 620) for this moneyer, Winiberht (Naismith 2011, C210a–c). Note that the moneyers of both Æthelberht pennies found in Northumbria (at Fishergate and Cottam 'B'), Winiberht and Wulfheard, share, coincidentally, the names of moneyers in the late *styca* series.

[918] Mainman (1993, 651). There was a limited re-occupation in C11–12th with the construction of St Andrew's church and the later Gilbertine Priory (1195, dissolved 1538).

[919] See discussion on the suitability of this base, section 6.1.2.

[920] Using the Pearson Product-Moment Correlation Coefficient. See *fn*.715.

Plate 4: Fishergate *sceattas* (1). Source: York Archaeological Trust. Key: References (e.g. 8-10) are to *Sceatta List* (Abramson, 2012).

Plate 5: Fishergate *sceattas* (2). Source: York Archaeological Trust. Key: References (e.g. 75-10) are to *Sceatta List* (Abramson, 2012).

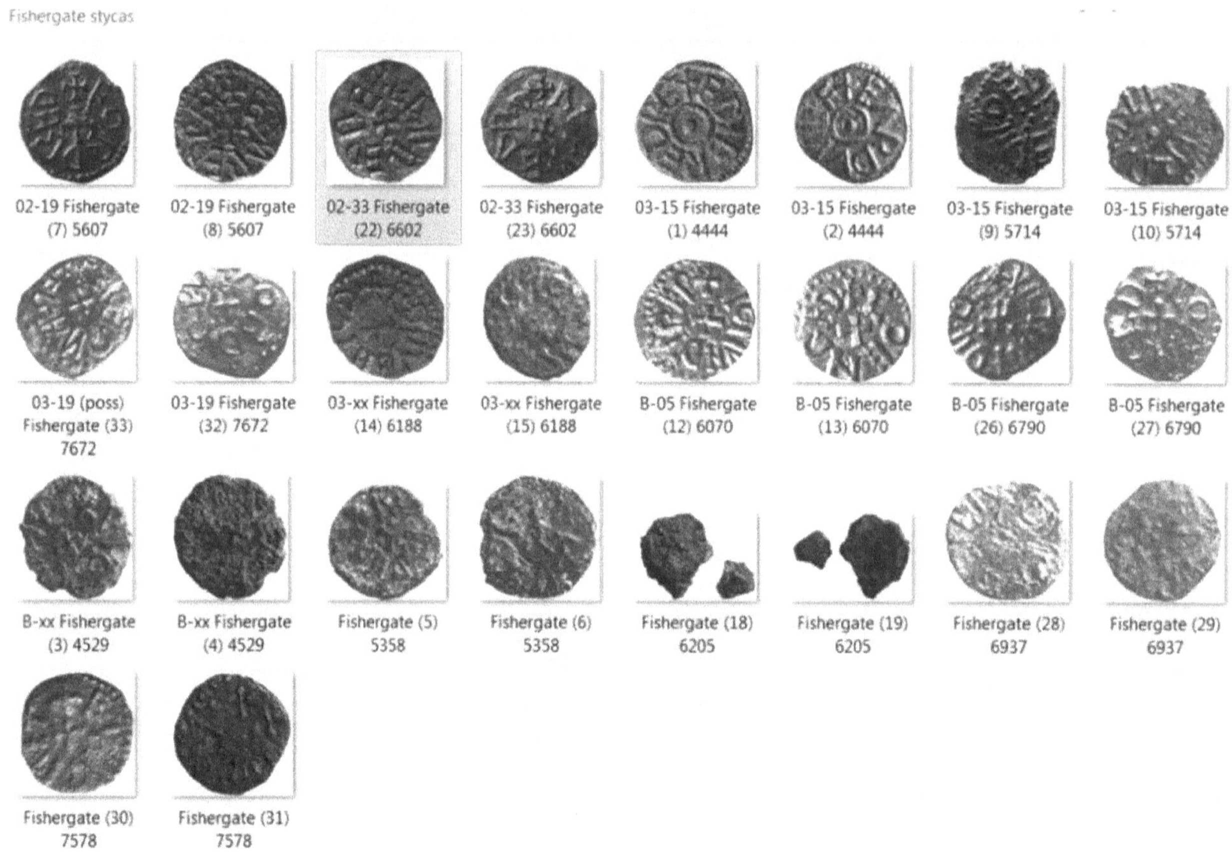

Plate 6: Fishergate *stycas*. Source: York Archaeological Trust. Key: References (e.g. 03-19) are to *Sceatta List* (Abramson, 2012).

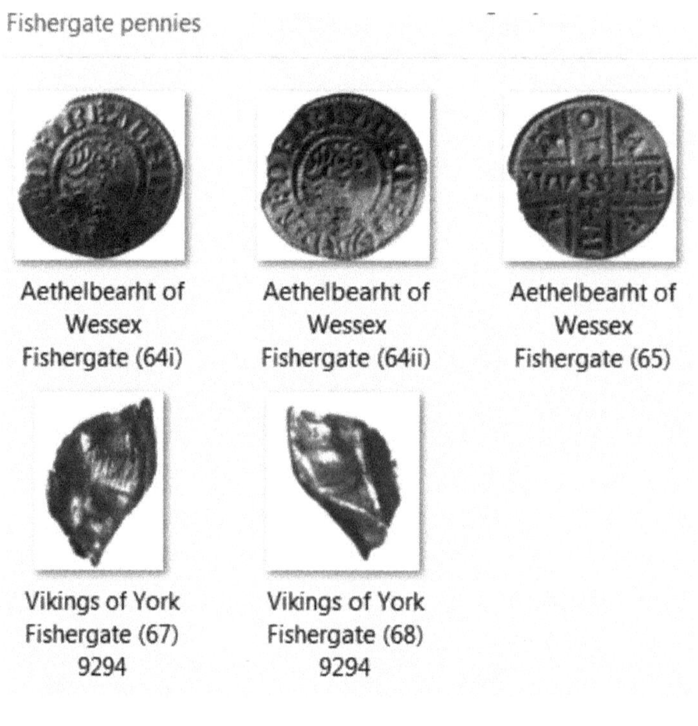

Plate 7: Fishergate pennies. Source: York Archaeological Trust.

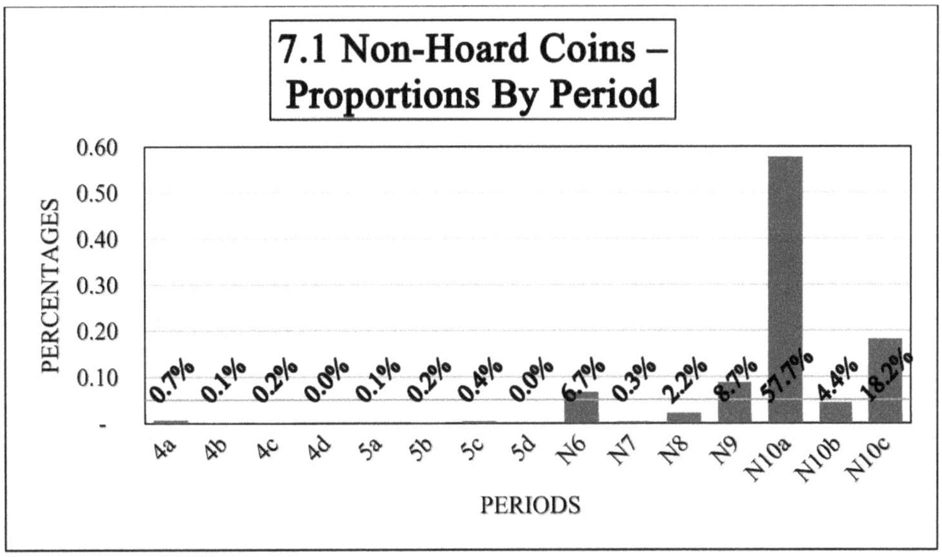

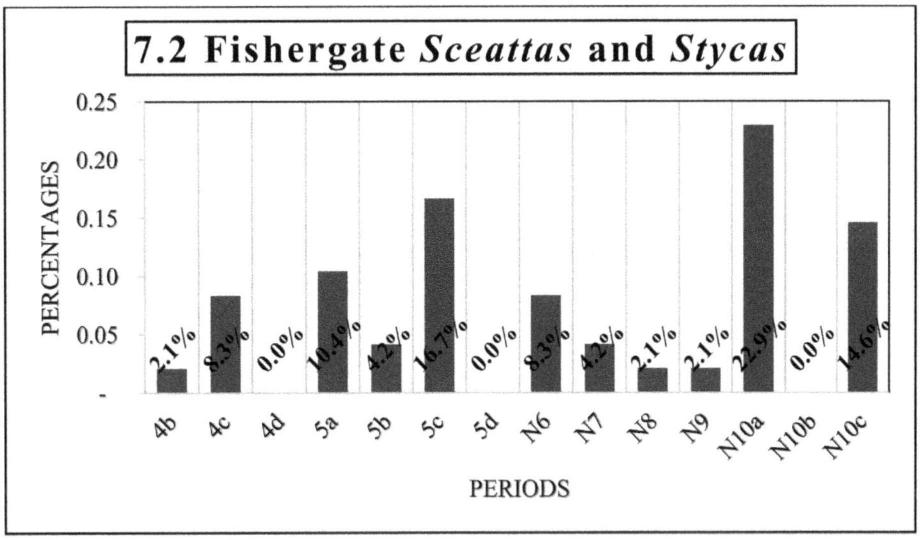

Graphs 7: Histograms of a) the Base Data Set (excluding hoards) and b) Fishergate *sceattas* and *stycas* by period. Source: *Dataset 1* and *8*. Numerical axis varies. Purpose: To compare the Fishergate corpus to the normal distribution.

The sample at Fishergate may be unrepresentative. However, it may be concluded, subject to future finds at adjacent sites that Fishergate is, relative to the norm, strong in imported Continental *sceattas* and deficient in *stycas*.

With due concern for statistical validity, it may be surmised that Fishergate was engaged in international trade in the eighth century but domestic transactions were deficient in the ninth. Given the size of the sample, one may speculate, only with great caution (and specific caveats on indirect specie flow and recovery patterns), that the site seems to be showing a healthy balance of trade in both the primary and secondary early-penny periods.

Graph 7 shows the Fishergate assemblage to provide a marked contrast to *Database 1* excluding hoards in the early-penny Periods 4a–5d which are overly represented at Fishergate. Given the small sample of *stycas* at Fishergate, the ninth-century distribution is a close fit to the norm.

7.1.4 Comparison with Roman Finds

For both coins and artefacts, York appears to be more significant in the Anglian period relative to other regions in the study: *Dataset 7, Finds Comparison* shows Anglian coins to constitute 4.5 per cent of the total and 9.0 per cent of the artefacts (2.6 per cent and 1.6 per cent respectively in the Roman period). Compared with the Roman period, there is a similar proportion of artefacts but Roman coins are a magnitude more plentiful, demonstrating far stronger monetization and a higher level of economic activity in the Roman period.

7.1.5 Fishergate Comparisons

Through a collaboration of excavation and metal detection, a small number of highly significant, coin-rich, early Anglo-Saxon sites have been explored. Consequently, understanding of the chronology, metallurgy, metrology, distribution and iconography of this numismatic material has evolved rapidly. Indeed, coinage of this period is now able to fulfil the same diagnostic rôle conventionally reserved for numismatic material in other periods.

Comparisons can be drawn between Fishergate and the volume and mix of finds at other prolific local sites, such as South Newbald and Sledmere,[921] and at several *wic* sites, *Dataset 15, Wic Comparisons 1 and 2*,[922] and *Dataset 20*. The assemblages here exclude earlier and later stray finds and include only the finds of the period *c.* 685–866/7. Ribe and South Newbald show a significant concentration of the local coinage type(s); this is far less marked at Fishergate, Sledmere and Hamwic.

For a site in the heartland of economic activity in Northumbria, given how extensively Fishergate has been excavated, it is surprising how few coins have been discovered. Comparisons can be drawn with numismatically better endowed *wics*, which have been similarly characterized as probably the mints of specific early-penny types where the degree of control is determined by the extent of recycling of incoming types,[923] for example, at Hamwic (Series H) and Ribe (Series X). As a template for assessing other *wics*, Hamwic merits further consideration.

The carefully recorded excavation of the Hamwic site,[924] rich in coins, pottery and other artefacts, provides a yardstick against which other prospective *wics* can be assessed. A clear choice of contender as the *wic* of York, *Eoforwic*, is Fishergate.[925] The methodology of the excavation and recording of this site was comparable to Hamwic, and the artefacts, except for the coins, have been published.[926]

The entire Hamwic site extends to around 49ha,[927] and though only a modest proportion has been excavated,[928] this still represents an expanse between six and 10 times that of Fishergate, except that the excavators at Hamwic employed a conservative extraction policy, possibly due to resource constraints. Most of the material was taken from rubbish pits but these were divided vertically and only half the content removed, as a deliberate sampling policy, and the rest left for posterity.[929]

As regards methodology, riddling techniques similar to Fishergate were used and again metal detecting was absent. In the mid-nineteenth century, Saxon deposits were removed from the central area by brickwork diggers and few stratified deposits remained. Pagan has forensically reconstructed the corpus of older finds from the site, including eight reports of individual, or groups of, *sceattas*.[930] It is difficult to be precise, but these may total around 33 specimens, though one may presume that there were also an unascertainable number of undisclosed finds. Other recovery factors come into play such as the likelihood that further excavation adjacent to Fishergate would be productive. Nevertheless, one may conclude, taking these earlier finds into account, that the Hamwic site is, proportionately, somewhat more productive of *sceattas* than Fishergate. However, as argued below, it is mix not volume which is crucial.

Referring only to those of which we have certain knowledge, Metcalf was able to state: 'Since we must assume that many coins changed hands safely for every one that was accidentally lost, the finds offer evidence of a very large number of transactions...The number of transactions rather than the number of coins is therefore the key statistic which measures how active the urban monetary system was.'[931] Of the 129 *sceattas* found at Hamwic, 61 (47 per cent) were of the local Series H type (*Figure* 71).[932] What may be gleaned from this near equivalence is that trade in the *wic* was, roughly, balanced. Hamwic bought from its hinterland paying in coin and, from the mix of other early-penny types found, sold to most early-penny producing areas with the strongest presence being *sceattas* of the Low Countries (nineteen of the 129 *sceattas* are Series E[933]) and Ribe (eleven are Series X, though four of these are imitative, now considered 'insular'—i.e. English—emissions.).[934]

Metcalf noted only five occurrences of die duplication of Series H at Hamwic from the estimated 170–260 obverse dies and around 400 reverse dies,[935] from which he projected production of five million *sceattas*, 'the implications for the social structure of the town deserve careful thought.'[936] This can be compared with Bude's estimate of *c.* 367 reverse dies for Eadberht, a substantial corpus.[937] Mapping Bude's distribution, gives a find-spot

[921] Finds of the period at these two sites have been collated over several years.

[922] Though probably sites of dissimilar nature, Heckington and Royston are also shown.

[923] Sceat emissions at *wics* may be comparable to Greek city-states who initially issued coins as much as a badge of identity as a currency.

[924] Andrews (1988) with the coins described and catalogued by Metcalf. Metcalf (2011) investigated the monetisation of the East Midlands using a methodology of comparing proportions of English and imported coins between *wics* and 'the countryside at large' but arriving at no secure conclusions.

[925] As argued by Kemp (1996, 109), and assumed by Blackburn (2003, 34) and others.

[926] Andrews (1998).

[927] Birbeck and others (2005).

[928] Stated to be 3 per cent by Andrews (1988, 15) and 5 per cent by Metcalf (in Andrews, 1988, 17).

[929] Andrews (1988, 17) and *pers. comm.* Michael Metcalf, 4th September 2014. Most of the coin finds were from these rubbish pits and can safely be regarded as stray losses. See also Blackburn (2003, 25).

[930] Andrews (1988, 60–70).

[931] Andrews (1988, 17).

[932] Andrews (1988, catalogue 22–91.5). Of the 125 Series H sceattas on *EMC*, 55 have a findspot of Hamwic and 53 elsewhere, but predominantly in the Wessex area, and 17 are uncertain. (Extracted 17th August 2014.) *EMC* shows 48 (45 per cent) of the 107 finds at Hamwic are Series H.

[933] Andrews (1988, catalogue 4–20).

[934] Andrews (1988, catalogue 115–24). There are only two Merovingian coins, 126–27.

[935] Andrews (1988, 18).

[936] Metcalf assumed 10,000 strikes per die (19), which is neither unreasonable for a trading currency nor uncontested. Bude's study (2016) shows 50 per cent of Eadberht's dies to have one surviving specimen only, which possibly argues against longevity. 'It may not be that all dies were created equal' Warren Esty (*pers. comm.* 21st February 2016).

[937] Bude (2016).

locus well east of York, reflecting usage not production. Other than the 23 Series H *sceattas* constituting the Kingsland (Southampton) hoard, all eighth- and ninth-century coins unearthed at both Hamwic and Fishergate are stray losses or single finds.[938]

The earliest specimens at Hamwic are two Merovingian coins[939] and the earliest *sceat* a coin of Aldfrith.[940] In common with Fishergate, among the earliest *sceattas*, coins of primary Series E and Series D are worn and corroded.[941] The Ribe types could date from the 710s. A primary Series C *sceat*, of the rare CZ variety appears imitative.[942] An *Æthilirœd sceat*, in fresh condition may also be early in the coinage.[943] However, there is currently insufficient evidence of monetization in the primary early-penny phase. The relative chronology of the various Hamwic varieties is tabulated in *SL*.[944] The ubiquitous Series J, G and R, are common to Hamwic and Fishergate,[945] otherwise, crucially, Hamwic displays a *far* greater variety of secondary types—L, M, N, O, U, V and W, demonstrating Hamwic's full participation in the network of urban monetization in the secondary phase and, as a likely consequence, permeation into the hinterland.

As remarked earlier, the occurrence of imitative *solidi* may be indicative of an attempt at a bi-metallic domestic currency or part of a bullion system. At Hamwic there are three Carolingian coins including a gold imitative *solidus* of Louis the Pious (Andrews no.148).

Specific contrasts can be drawn between major emporia and Fishergate from *Dataset 15, Wic Comparison 1* and *2* and *Dataset 20*. The presence of an Aldfrith *sceat* at Hamwic but not at Fishergate is contrary to expectations. In the Primary phase, at both sites, there is a paucity of domestic coinage outweighed by primary Continental *sceattas*. In the secondary phase, the proportion of local coinage at Hamwic is high, but surprisingly low at Fishergate;[946] growth of local currency is greater than imported coinage, perhaps demonstrating at Hamwic that more produce was being sold into the local economy even if Frisia and Ribe are well represented. At Fishergate, the numbers are too small to support speculative interpretations but the absence of *sceattas* from Ribe, when they occur in numbers at Hamwic, again indicates that Fishergate is not functioning freely as a *wic*. This implies that Fishergate is distanced, organisationally more than geographically, from the economic hub of York.

Andrews discussed the chronology of the pottery finds at Hamwic.[947] However, the absolute chronology is indistinct due to difficulties of dating discard and conservatism in design, even in imported wares. As regards distribution,[948] there is a hint that earlier deposits contain a higher number of imported vessels—perhaps foreign traders brought these to the waterfront. This type of economic activity is likely to accelerate growth. The imported pottery occurred mainly in periods 3a and 3b, which correlates with finds of *sceattas*. Analysis of black burnished wares at York and Ipswich indicates that they received the same material as was passing through Quentovic.[949]

Given that the Hamwic excavations were many times larger than those at Fishergate, the volume of finds is not grossly disproportionate, but of more significance is the rich mix of coins at Hamwic, including several exotic species, in contrast to the limited number and diversity at Fishergate.[950] Indeed, the lack of variety at the latter contrasts with the abundant array of both the hinterland produce and incoming trade.[951] Perhaps the causal factor is the motivation of the controlling authority. Fishergate may be oppressed by an austere, presumably ecclesiastical, authority with little interest in exploiting economic resources; there is no evidence of such restrictive behaviour at Hamwic,[952] on the contrary, it is likely that a regal power wished to enhance its wealth by participating in broadly based domestic and Continental trade, though this should not be interpreted in terms of a substantivist York and formalist Hamwic—York's cultural strength grew from territorial affluence as much as transcendental conviction.

Of the other prolific sites included in *Dataset 15, Wic Comparison 1* and *2*, the array at Rendlesham with its distinctly early start for Anglo-Saxon activity, resembles that at Coddenham, and the conclusion, that this is an area far richer and more long-lived economically than Northumbria, is reinforced. Heckington[953] is active in local and overseas trade throughout the gold and silver phases, and the mix is similar to Rendlesham except that Heckington does not have its own local coinage and lacks those of Hamwic, Ipswich[954] and York. Heckington

[938] Andrews (1988, 16). *MEC* (1986, 171).

[939] Andrews (1988, catalogue 126–27). There is also a fragment of an Iberian Ummayad dirham, possibly dating to around 700CE and hinting at commercial links. There were no sceattas of Aldfrith at Fishergate.

[940] *Ibid.* 125. The archaeological context of this specific specimen determined that this type was an emission of Northumbria not Lincolnshire.

[941] Except for secondary issue no. 12 (*SL* 94) which is virtually as minted and tertiary issue no. 11 (*SL* 100). Note that the three Series E phases do not correspond exactly with the two general phases.

[942] Andrews (1988, catalogue 2).

[943] Type 105, *SL* 92, date uncertain, but thought by the author to be primary.

[944] Abramson (2012d, Groups 46–49, 133–37 and Appendix 4, 239–41).

[945] Andrews (1988, catalogue 1, which is misidentified as Series C—it is Series R).

[946] In the secondary phase, Series J, the putative northern emission, is proportionately stronger in the northern *wic*.

[947] Andrews (1988, 111–16).

[948] Andrews (1988, 116–20).

[949] Mainman (1993, 574).

[950] Mainman (1993, 582) also indicated that the variety of pottery types found at Hamwic is greater than at Fishergate though the proportion of imported wares is smaller.

[951] Wickham (2005, 352).

[952] Though the variety of meat consumption is limited. Saunders (2011, 12).

[953] Situated two miles east of Heckington, at Garwick, and formerly referred to as the South Lincolnshire 'productive site'. Metcalf (forthcoming).

[954] See *Dataset 20, Ipswich*.

is more diverse than Fishergate throughout; and in the Primary phase more diverse than Hamwic, but less so later. Royston had wide domestic and overseas trading relationships but an absence of local control, i.e. there is little recycling, probably because there is no specific emission associated with this area. There is no clear export product at Fishergate comparable with the pottery export of Ipswich. Each of these prolific southern sites can be assumed to have had an economic purpose and the contrast with Fishergate is stark.

Fishergate's relationship with the other Anglian sites in York, at Bootham Bar, Clifford Street, Tanner Row and Skeldergate, is uncertain. Economically, Fishergate compares unfavourably with other prolific northern sites such as South Newbald, Sledmere and even Hayton, as well as the Lincolnshire sites at Flixborough (Riby and Heckington),[955] within reach of the northern sphere of influence.

Fishergate may not be the *wic* of York, *Eoforwic*,[956] but, based on the artefactual fingerprint, a subsidiary site of restricted use, for example, for processing, manufacturing or bonding goods, or, as suggested by the comparison of early-penny volumes and mixes with other sites, a point of departure for exports.

The eighth-century patterns for *Hamwic* and *Lundenwic* are similar but the former has almost lapsed by the time that Lincoln is active, towards the end of the period of study. *Lundenwic* remains active throughout but well below the peak of the first half of the eighth century.[957]

The purpose of reviewing these southern emporia was to provide a comparison for the Fishergate accumulation. These sites present a cohesive and consistent picture distinct from the narrower context of Fishergate. The results endorse the conclusion that Fishergate is not convincing as a *wic*.[958]

7.1.6 Inner York

At Dixon Lane and George Street, craft-working implies trade with Southumbria and the Continent though the coin evidence is slender—just one 'shrine' type *sceat* of Æthelred I and a *styca* of Æthelred II's moneyer Monne.[959]

A putative hoard, consequent on landscaping in Parliament Street, of at least three York gold shillings, from the same dies, and possibly as many as six specimens, was deposited before 1846. These are recorded by Sutherland (*ASGC* 75a–c) but may include specimens associated with Hall and Clarkson (*Figure* 72).[960]

Dataset 15, Inner York—Single Finds has been compiled from two sources of single finds of *sceattas* and *stycas* in York with specific site details: specimens listed in Pirie's inventory,[961] but not elsewhere, have been augmented by items in the study database. The hoards are excluded. See *Graph* 4.2.[962]

In respect of the Coppergate finds, Hall remarked on the irregular context in the second half of the ninth century *above* the fired surfaces and associated human remains archaeo-magnetically dated to around the time of the fall of York, 860. The inference is that the 'coins were deposited in contexts that apparently accumulated appreciably later than their striking…This difficulty in interpretation at the 16–22 Coppergate site represents in microcosm the problem of discussing generally whether *stycas* continued in circulation in the later 9th century (91).'[963]

However, of greater importance is the relative frequency of single finds; they may not be imposing in volume but this is more than compensated for by the widespread distribution,[964] demonstrated by 26 individual find-spots in *Dataset 15, Inner York—Single Finds*. Pottery sherds of the period are distributed over at least three dozen inner-York sites. Crucially, these scattered finds are mere pinpricks in the archaeological fabric giving a highly-restricted view into the densely developed Anglian urban landscape. That these single coin finds, augmented by the nine larger hoards in Pirie's 2000 inventory, give an abundant volume of circulating *stycas* in York, is uncontested. We therefore now have a solid basis to argue that *stycas* were ubiquitous in the economic environs of York and monetization, as here defined is an irresistible conclusion. However, it is important to establish that this was not merely an urban phenomenon as has been claimed for monetization in Roman Britain.[965] That volumes of Roman coinage were very substantially higher does not detract from Anglian monetization, as a threshold has been crossed when routine transactions depend on the use of coin.

[955] Flixborough is 60 miles north of Heckington and 30 miles west of Riby Cross Roads.

[956] Hall (2003, 173).

[957] Blackburn (2002, *figure* 30.2). The MOLAS report (Cowie, 1987–2000) stated that the purse hoard deposited within the dark earth 'was probably buried in 851', a known date of a Viking incursion. This seems unduly precise and it is unlikely that the extent of blundering evident in the hoard occurred this early in Osberht's reign. Besides, a *styca* of Osberht (*c.* 850–67, *CKN* 1260) is considerably worn, consistent with circulation over several years. It is far more probable that the hoard was secreted in 871–72, when the *micel here* over-wintered. See *Dataset 20, London.*

[958] Scull (1997, 280), 'interpretation of the Fishergate site…remains hypothetical.'

[959] Kjølbye-Biddle (1995, 4.4.7 Coin catalogue, C. Barclay).

[960] Hall (1774), Sutherland (1948), Grierson (1962), Grierson and Blackburn (*MEC*, 1986), Pirie (1992b), Tweddle and Morten (1992), Abdy and Williams (2006, hoard 13, nos. 319–22) and Abramson (2012e, 12–16). For my reclassification and interpretation of this important gold coinage see Abramson (2019).

[961] Pirie (2000, 1, 12–21 and 84–105).

[962] See O'Connor (2003, *figure* 15).

[963] Pirie (1986b, 17).

[964] As is the case with recoveries of Byzantine *nummi*.

[965] Walton (2011, 289–94). According to Patrick Ottaway's keynote speech 'Economy and society in Roman York: a review of the evidence', at *Connecting through Coinage*, King's Manor, York, Friday 13th July 2014. This view is contested and was challenged by Adrian Marsden's paper on counterfeiting, 'Britain before barbarous radiates: irregular coinage in early Roman Britain' at the same conference.

7.1.7 Outer York

The small number of finds on the periphery of York, summarized by issuer in *Dataset 15, Outer York—Single Finds*, are of limited value as the sites, and probably a large number of other finds, are undisclosed. See *Graph* 4.3. Pirie lists three such sites,[966] the largest, referred to as the 'near York productive site' and explored in 1987–88, produced a *sceat* of Eadberht and nine brass *stycas*. A silver-alloy coin of Eanred by Cynewulf was found at Dunnington church in 1991 and Dunnington has also yielded a variety Ai York gold shilling (*Figure* 73) a *sceat* of Aldfrith, a secondary Series E *sceat* and a *styca* of Osberht. Another Aldfrith *sceat* was found at Osbaldwick. Entries in *EMC* described as 'near York' include eight *sceattas* of Eadberht, one of Alchred and eight brass *stycas*. Two extremely rare *styca* moneyers in my own collection, Badigils and Fulcnoth, described as found 'near York' support York as the main, if not sole, *styca* mint.

Reported finds for 'outer' York can be assumed not to have come from a single site and to be a gross underreporting. Given that the perimeter of York is less urbanised but becoming more intensively developed, there have been greater opportunities than in the centre for metal-detection and new building sites should have been productive. Therefore, this slight accumulation is paradoxical. The mitigation of a wide, if thin, distribution cannot be demonstrated, and the likely explanation is the inadequacy of formal reporting channels.

A further gold shilling, of York variety Aii, now in the British Museum, is known from "near York" (*Figure* 74).

The paucity of these finds suggests that some adverse recovery phenomenon, either access or reporting, could be at work. As revealed below, finds in the Central Lowlands and Vale of Pickering are sparse, though the wide spread supports the case for extensive monetization. The Wolds present a stronger case in terms of frequency, distribution and mix.

7.1.8 Artefact Dataset

Unfortunately, other than the finds for Fishergate imported from *VASLE*, the artefactual dataset for Anglian York is virtually absent. PAS (EY) includes a Borre style disc brooch, but this is Viking. The search on York produced only nine objects from seven locations, mostly treated as Central Lowlands rather than outer York. *Prima facie*, this paucity is a flaw in interrogation or recording, though conceivably no Anglian finds have occurred during the PAS regime.

The artefactual fingerprint for Fishergate, extracted from *VASLE*, is at *Dataset 15, Fishergate Artefacts*. Further analyses for Fishergate and York sites, combined with the Central Lowlands, are at *Dataset 16*. As would be expected for an excavated site, where more care is exercised over discard, in comparison to the other regional functional fingerprints, Fishergate appears different in character with the proportions reversed: tools and work-related items constitute 66.7 per cent, compared to a norm of 17.9 per cent, whereas dress accessories compose only 21.3 per cent (*cf.* 67.3 per cent). There are no burial or clerical artefacts and no weapons; but perhaps more significant is the presence of only one artefact classified as mercantile, as defined in *Dataset 5. Artefacts*. This supports my view that Fishergate was not itself an emporium but perhaps subsidiary to the emporium of York providing industrial and craft activities.

7.1.9 Conclusion

Our understanding of the organisation and topography of early Anglian York is hampered by the limited artefactual evidence. While, in the south, the Patching hoard provides evidence of the urban transition from coinage to bullion as late as the 470s,[967] the nature of post Roman authority at York, the balance between political and ecclesiastical power and the extent of urban development, all remain unclear until the rise of the Idings. To their dynasty, territorial expansionism, underpinned, if not driven, by adoption of a new faith, was foremost, as recorded historically from the perspectives of Bede and Alcuin. 'It has long been suggested that Anglian York was a polyfocal settlement, with separate areas for royal, religious, secular and trading/industrial use. York is recorded as both *Eoforwicceastre* and *Eoforwic*.'[968] Economic history demonstrates that military aggression can be a driver of growth and, even in adversity, Northumbria was sufficiently resourceful to recover, albeit gradually, from serious setbacks of 685 and 793, dates which bracket the success of the *sceat*.

The iconography of the gold coinage and joint emissions of silver, despite the internecine strife of the eighth century, allow us to address some of these questions with more conviction. Cohesion was provided by the church which, a generous interpretation may suggest, re-directed political friction into economic and cultural wealth. While the Archbishops may have remained in their stronghold, possibly still in the fortress, delegating spiritual matters—such as pastoral care, conversion and reinforcement of their theology—to their peripatetic priests, the monarchs had more worldly concerns and needed to travel the kingdom constantly to secure their terrestrial and fiscal wellbeing. Numismatic finds not only help to identify royal palaces but reflect this balance of power favouring the ecclesiastical authorities who kept warring dynasts in check. Assessing the pace of economic, particularly urban, development remains

966 Pirie (2000, nos. 106 and 116–17).

967 Abdy (2006, 75–98).

968 http://www.iadb.co.uk/i3/item.php?ID=IADB:1307:U71, 3.4 Phase 5 Anglian (8th to mid-9th century), AY 7/1 3; AY 7/2 298.

a matter of conjecture except to the extent that the number of coin-revealing sites, rather than the number of coins revealed, gives a clear impression of eighth-century monetization under Eadberht, even if other issuers were less energetic. Furthermore, at times in the ninth century, there was an almost frenetic tempo to minting with the resultant deterioration in production standards reflecting the miniscule *seigniorage* on such a base denomination available as profit to the minting authority.

In assessing the balance of royal and aristocratic power and the status of the church in York, Rollason[969] contrasted 'the sparsity of evidence for York as a royal centre' with 'a clear picture of it as an ecclesiastical centre' illustrating his argument by reference to the inscription on the Coppergate helmet (*Figure* 75).[970] The successive joint coinage emissions were a clear statement of episcopal power. The issue of siblings Eadberht and Ecgberht may denote an equivalence of authority. However, it is the archiepiscopal sibling, who came to office first and is portrayed.[971] Bude's die study demonstrates that there are no die-links between the regal and ecclesiastical *sceattas* at this time;[972] separate, episodic, production could imply independent minting and one would expect the ecclesiastical mint to be in York. Continuation of joint issues to successive rival monarchs seems to be an astute archiepiscopal initiative—and a regal concession to an equal or superior power. While it was a royal imperative to mint it was not an episcopal necessity. Hence, regal issues predominate numerically[973] but the joint *sceattas* indicate that real power lay with the church.[974]

That the king led an itinerant lifestyle attempting to collect renders, but the archbishop's revenues were submitted, presumably without need for him to travel, may further demonstrate the balance of power. The view is supported by the consideration of early law described at section 2.8.[975]

The Golden Age of Northumbria encompassed the rich culture and powerful influence of Benedict Biscop, Cuthbert, Bede, Alcuin, Wilfrid, Willibrord, and Hild the illuminated manuscripts of Lindisfarne and Durham, the Echternach Gospels, the Codex Amiatinus and the Bewcastle, Ruthwell and Hexham crosses. The Coppergate helmet (*Figure* 75) and Ormside bowl (*Figure* 64) are representative of substantial Anglian wealth. This was the period when the great Northumbrian monasteries and numerous minsters were established in the richly diverse countryside. Northumbrian missionaries made deep inroads on the Continent. It is inconceivable that this profusion of artistic culture could blossom without the economic foundations of a truly international emporium, the rival of any Continental trade centre. It would be difficult to argue that, with its appearance of impoverishment, Fishergate fulfils this crucial rôle. That only 15 *sceattas* and 39 non-hoard *stycas* are listed does not auger well for Fishergate as the economic hub supporting York's glorious Anglian credentials. Until a numismatically more productive emporium is located in York, the initial phase of monetization in Northumbria should not be regarded as an urban phenomenon, but more as characteristic of royal sites.

Looking more broadly at the territory under York's influence there can be little doubt that the economic growth was inversely related to the monetary denomination. While *sceattas* signify domestic and Continental mercantile penetration into the wealth-producing hinterland, witnessed by a thin but widespread distribution of finds, it is the base *stycas*, in their millions, which facilitated economic exploitation of resources through greater specialisation, market organisation and surplus extraction.

Having explored the relatively meagre coinage of the city of York, which provides tantalising glimpses into the urban heart of Northumbria, the above claim of monetization can now be substantiated in the interconnected, rural settlements stretching across the Central Lowlands and the dry-chalk Yorkshire Wolds. The coin and artefactual recoveries attest to the wealth of these strategically sited communities and the extent of their trading relationships, though in the Central Lowlands, the accumulated evidence is thinly dispersed with comparatively few archaeological anchors.

---

969 Rollason (2003, 202–08).

970 The inscription is translated as: 'In the name of our Lord Jesus Christ and the spirit of God, let us offer up Oshere to All Saints. Amen.' See Garrison (forthcoming).

971 Probably enthroned rather than genuflecting. Bude (2016).

972 Bude (2016). The separation is supported by differing inscriptional error rates and use of the final character 'Γ' as a centring device.

973 Approximately 10:3 according to Bude's die-study (2016).

974 Hall (1996, col. pl. 5).

975 Ch. 9. Southumbrian Monetary Evolution, specifically in laws 2, 3 and 10 of Æthelberht's code (19 and *Table* 1).

7.1.10 Illustrations—York and Its Environs

Figure 59: Headstone of Archbishop Wulfhere, 849/50–900. L: York Minster, Anglian stele,[976] +HIC//CESPITE VVLFHER/... ERA/QVIESCVNT. R: Bronze *styca*, Period N10b, VVLFHERE AREP, Thirsk.

Figure 60: *Solidus* of Arichis II (758–87), Beneventum, *c.* 774. Found Alnwick. Test marks imply use in trade.

Figure 61: The Fishergate Ring[977] *cf.* facing bust on Series Z *sceat*. From Driffield (*SL*102–40). (L: Courtesy York Museums Trust)

Figure 62: Bone knife handle fragment, 36.5mm. Rogers, Figure 633 (item 5528) 1309. (Courtesy York Archaeological Trust)

[976] ©The Corpus of Anglo-Saxon Stone Sculpture, photographer T. Middlemass'. YM22 http://www.ascorpus.ac.uk/catvol_search_results.php?id=908
[977] PAS YORYM 1951.58, in the Yorkshire Museum. Image http://ecx.images-amazon.com/images/I/61QdOzRd6dL._UL1500_.jpg manipulated in Adobe Photoshop.

Figure 63: The Heworth Urn. (Courtesy York Museums Trust)[978]

Figure 64: The Ormside bowl found in 1823 near a Viking warrior grave and presumed to have been looted from York. (Courtesy York Museums Trust)

Figure 65: C5th–6th glass bowl, The Mount. (Courtesy York Museums Trust, 1992.203)

Figure 66: Fishergate specimens, *sceattas*: Series BIIIc (*SL*16–80) Series J, type 85 (*SL*18–20) Series J, type 85 (*SL*18–25). (Courtesy York Archaeological Trust)

Figure 67: Exotic species from Fishergate. Triquetras type *sceat* (*SL*110–60). (Courtesy York Archaeological Trust)

[978] Image courtesy of York Museums Trust: http://yorkmuseumstrust.org.uk — CC BY-SA 4.

Figure 68: Fishergate specimens, Series Y *sceattas*: Eadberht Booth class B (*SL*70–50) Alchred with Ecgberht (*SL*75–10) Æthelred I, Cuthheart (*SL*83–20). (Courtesy York Archaeological Trust)

Figure 69: Fishergate *stycas*. Eanred, by Forthred (*SL*02–19); Æthelred II, by Eardwulf (*SL*02–33). (Courtesy York Archaeological Trust)

Figure 70: Fishergate penny: Æthelberht of Wessex, moneyer Winiberht. (Courtesy York Archaeological Trust)

Figure 71: The three main types of Series H: Peacock/Celtic cross (type 39, *SL*46–10). Serpents/Celtic cross (type 48, *SL*47–20). Face/Peacock (type 49, *SL*48).

Figure 72: York gold shillings associated with Parliament Street landscaping before 1846. Sutherland 75a–c. Museum locations (L to R): Yorkshire (stolen), Ashmolean and British.[979]

Figure 73: Dunnington: variety A York gold shilling (Ai.1). (Courtesy *EMC* and William MacKay)[980]

Figure 74: York gold shilling, var. Found by Stuart Hodgson, near York (Aii.1). (Courtesy *SCBI*, *SCBI*63 18. *EMC* 2009.0268)

[979] Images courtesy of York Museums Trust (75a), Michael Metcalf (75b) and SCBI (75c, SCBI63, 16).

[980] 2010.0154.

7.2 The Central Lowlands (*Dataset 16*)

'...your diocese is too extensive',
Bede's letter to Ecgberht (734, §5)

The Central Lowlands are here defined as a broader lowland area than the Vale of York. They consist of a widening north-south area of glacial and alluvial deposits thickly overlying Triassic sandstone and Jurassic mudstone, known as *gleys*. The lowland area is framed by the higher ground of the Pennines to the west and the North York Moors and Wolds to the east. The tributaries of the Ouse from the Yorkshire Dales and North York Moors—the Aire, Don, Wharfe, Rother, Nidd, Swale and Ure and Derwent respectively—combine the waters of much of upland north-east England before joining the Trent to flow into the Humber Estuary.

Arable land favouring settlement encompasses the ancient polities of western Deira and Elmet, providing the channel for the communications spine of the Great North Road forming an area 80 miles north to south, from Darlington to Doncaster, and widening southward from 20 to 50 miles—over 2,800 square miles. Though to modern eyes, the Central Lowlands consist of rich agricultural land, the predominant soil type, *gleys*, are naturally poor in fertility and porosity, especially when compacted by settlement.

Possibly of greater interest than the sparse 'outer' York sites is the dispersal of finds in the Central Lowlands. *Dataset 16* analyses, from the northernmost, 217 silver and copper Northumbrian finds and 51 other coins from 80 sites, including 72 coins from Ryther. The majority of sites have one or two Northumbrian finds, only Ripon (ten coins), Stamford Bridge (seven), Wetherby (seven), Carthorpe (five) and 'Site C' near Wetherby (four) have more. A few of the coins in *Dataset 16* are of numismatic interest, including a singleton of Series Q from Lotherton (*Figure* 76):

However, this sample is somewhat distorted as much of the data, other than Ryther, has been extracted from my own, selective collection. Had other sites been as scrupulously researched as Ryther, one could reasonably extrapolate a far higher penetration of coinage generally. Again, it is the widespread and even distribution over a substantial area—characterized as a distributed network of settlements—which is more indicative of monetization than the volume of finds or the reported number of find sites. Several sites, arranged by volume of recorded finds, are described below.

7.2.1 Site Studies

Ryther cum Ossendyke

Ryther lies south of a bend in the Wharfe, one mile west of Cawood. There is a variety of undated crop mark enclosures and a later Saxon church[981] but no Anglian evidence other than the detected finds. There are three productive zones in Ryther: the village, the Church and the 'castle', though at the latter the soil was heavily contaminated with iron, of which seven thousand pieces were removed,[982] presumably the result of metal-working.

Three primary *sceattas* were detected in the mid-90s; all the others are ninth-century Northumbrian coins registered in 2001, clearly the result of some diligent detection and reporting.[983] Private correspondence in the Pirie archive, from detectorist Stephen Pickles, show this to be the case, even though he was active two decades prior to the reporting date.[984]

'Site C' near Wetherby

Undated artefacts and crop marks are known from the Neolithic period onwards.[985] The site of an unfurnished inhumation has produced an Æthelred I *sceat* found close to the new variety of the York Gold shilling (*Figure* 77).

In April 2015, I identified a second specimen of variety D, probably from the same dies (*Figure* 78).

That a second specimen should have been detected within a quarter mile of the first is quite remarkable and might suggest local minting except that the second is worn to the point of being very nearly unrecognisable. It is almost inconceivable that this degree of wear was caused by circulation. A more likely interpretation would be secondary use as jewellery held in an unattached mount which has not survived, although were this worn by a local person, then the possibility of a local minting is not ruled out.

Tadcaster

Evidence of Iron Age and Roman occupation is recorded,[986] but is deficient for the Anglian period though Hieu, Hilda's predecessor at Hartlepool, retired here in 649. Limestone was quarried locally.

A hexagram *sceat* has recently surfaced at Tadcaster (*Figure* 79). This crude *denier*-like coin, currently thought to be from the lower Meuse,[987] is not pristine, so may not have travelled directly from source, but is a significant loss on a busy route.

[981] http://pastscape.org.uk/hob.aspx?hob_id=56270
[982] Per the detectorist's correspondence in the Pirie archive.
[983] *Graph* 12.5.
[984] Pickles also found individual pennies of Edgar (*c.* 973–75), Henry III and VII. On 4th April 1992, he discovered an intact jug containing 813 pennies, half-groats and groats from the reigns of Edward IV and Henry VI at this site, but probably reported as Cawood.
[985] http://pastscape.org.uk/hob.aspx?hob_id=1086024
[986] http://pastscape.org.uk/hob.aspx?hob_id=1199738
[987] Op den Velde (2014, 122–40).

Ripon[988]

Ripon is on the Magnesian Limestone ridge near the confluence of the Ure and Skell. After the Synod of Whitby, *Inhyrpum* was abandoned by Eata of Melrose and reallocated to Wilfrid who constructed a church of dressed stone similar to that at Hexham.[989] A cluster of associated early ecclesiastical sites has been excavated, notably Ailcy Hill cemetery, 200 metres from Wilfrid's church. Radiocarbon dating has established that burials in the century before the transfer to Wilfrid are largely unfurnished and of mixed gender and age; thereafter they are predominantly adult males in iron-bound wooden chests, taken to mark a shift from communal to monastic use.[990]

Though only two *sceattas* are known from Ripon, one is the extremely rare Eardwulf issue. However, from the river bank at Ripon, a mile from the St Wilfrid's church, comes a lead impress of the East Anglian king Beonna with the rare interlace reverse (*Figure* 80), a most unexpected and intriguing find in this northerly location when a trial piece of dies would normally be found at the originating mint. The outer flan is roughly holed possibly for cancellation or for tying as a customs receipt for goods from East Anglia, taxed on arrival at the riverside. Piercing for suspension for ornamentation is considered unlikely.

The reverse design has a similar interlace to the engraving on the base of the hanging bowl from Castle Yard, York (*Figure* 81).[991]

Around 150 *stycas* from the Ripon hoard of 1695, found at Ailcy Hill cemetery according to Thoresby, were divided between him and Archbishop Sharp.[992] Apart from two *stycas* of Wigmund and one of Wulfhere, all are regal, mostly Æthelred II with Osberht well represented.[993] Pirie reasonably postulated both concealment at the time of the *micel here* and the likelihood that the hoard may have been larger: 'Thoresby's own parcel was small.'[994] Certainly, the hoard indicates broad monetization in the mid-ninth century.

Sheriff Hutton

Undated earthworks and crop marks on aerial photographs and extensive field systems are recorded but, again, little definite evidence of activity in the Anglian period.[995] Sheriff Hutton has produced a Frisian *sceat*, considered primary, with an undeciphered reverse legend, only the third known of this variety (*Figure* 82).

There is also a typically imitative annulet type, similar to that found at Garton-on-the Wolds (*Figure* 83).[996]

Single *sceattas* of the Low Countries also occur at Stamford Bridge, Wilberfoss, Upper Poppleton and Ryther

Upper Poppleton

Archaeological records describe enclosures, linear boundaries and associated trackways possibly indicating settlement but of uncertain date.[997] Non-Northumbrian *sceattas* at Upper Poppleton, include the primary Frisian type inscribed *VICO*, a secondary Southumbrian *sceat* of Series O and a Northumbria *sceat* of Ælfwald I (*Figure* 84).

Bolton Percy

Rectilinear ditch-defined enclosures and associated trackways may be late Roman or early medieval.[998] The only recorded early-penny find from this site is a Series F *sceat*, now attributed to Canterbury (*Figure* 85).[999] In stark contrast to Ryther, the Bolton Percy *styca* in *Dataset 16*, again found by Pickles, is likely to be the only one reported of hundreds found at the site in recent years.[1000]

As regards the two major hoards of *stycas*, the portion that were recorded are tabulated in *Dataset 3, Hoard Matrices*.[1001] The 1847 hoard, of around 6,000 *stycas*, was ploughed up by an employee of Colonel Thompson, William Foster, in a field at Woodhill Close. Fennell was instrumental in securing around 450 specimens.[1002] The 1967 hoard, of around 1,500 *stycas*, was professionally excavated after Malcolm Mills of Tilehouse, Bolton Percy, made some stray finds.[1003] Less than 2 per cent of the recorded finds are of silver-alloy coins of Period N9, 21.2 per cent from Eanred's base issue and 65.7 per cent

[988] Woodman (2012, 229–48).
[989] Hall and Whyman (1996, 63).
[990] Hall and Whyman (1996, 117–24).
[991] The author is aware of two *styca*-inset weights in private US collections, which display similar obverse and reverse designs. Metallurgical analysis is awaited.
[992] Pirie (1982, 84–103). Pagan (1993, 114–22) noting that both Thoresby and Sharp lent *stycas* to Sir Andrew Fountaine for illustration in his *Numismata*. Sharp lists *stycas* as one of 'Chief Remarkables' in Fountaine's collection. Thoresby's diary, 17th June 1695, noted the abundance of 'Humane Bones' at Ailcy Hill. The collection of Sharp and his descendants was auctioned by Morton and Eden, sale 91, 7–8 December 2017, including *stycas* (lots 10–21) thought to be from the Ripon hoard.
[993] A scatter of further finds from Ailcy Hill is noted at Pirie (2000, entry 157 also 163–65). *Graph* 12.3.
[994] Pirie (1982, 85).
[995] http://pastscape.org.uk/hob.aspx?hob_id=1183545
[996] Rigold (1960, 49), hoard VIII and pl. 4. Rigold and Metcalf (1984, 252). This was part of a hoard of eight *sceattas*.
[997] http://pastscape.org.uk/hob.aspx?hob_id=1198194
[998] http://pastscape.org.uk/hob.aspx?hob_id=1211121
[999] Metcalf (2014b, 52–71).
[1000] 430 undeclared, low-quality, *stycas* were sold around 2013. These were said to be recent finds (*fn.* 356). It is likely that the report in the Bonser archive from Bryan Snowball dated 10 November 1996 (#146), of a further hoard from Bolton Percy of 227 coins (23 of which Bonser lists) are additional to the 430.
[1001] *CKN* records 643 specimens from the 1847 hoard and 350 from 1967.
[1002] Fennell (1849, 127–32). Pirie (1996, 17–18). http://pastscape.org.uk/hob.aspx?hob_id=56528.
[1003] Pirie (1996, 18–19). http://pastscape.org.uk/hob.aspx?hob_id=56531#

from Aethelred II's reigns, with the tail stretching to the fall of York.

The presence of substantial hoards,[1004] at Bolton Percy show that there was no commercial separation of Elmet during monetization, and this polity may have been subsumed into greater Northumbria.

Middleham

Middleham, on the River Ure in Wensleydale, rises into the Dales two miles south of Leyburn. In 2011, a high-status furnished burial was revealed by metal detection,[1005] with finds scattered over a relatively confined area. Together with a gold shilling of York (*Figure* 86) there are the accoutrements of a warrior including a decorated sword pommel, sword (Figure 87), spearhead, knife, and remnants of a hanging bowl. There are several contemporary, comparable weapon-burials elsewhere.

While this may be the remains of a powerful individual there is insufficient evidence to class this strategic site as a *vicus regius.*[1006] It does demonstrate that Middleham lay on an important route from York to the North-West and that this gold shilling, inscribed Bishop Paulinus, was held in high regard.

7.2.2 Comparison to Normal Distribution

The correlation to norm, *Dataset 1*, based on the more detailed *Dataset 16*, is high. Given the thin but wide-spread veneer of single finds across the substantial area of the Central Lowlands, this is not surprising. For the more significant individual sites, Ryther, with three primary *sceattas* and mainly Period N10 *stycas*, shows a poor correlation of 70 per cent and Ripon, with a narrow spread, no correlation at all, which perhaps shows that intense activity may not reflect broader patterns. Further analyses are detailed below.

7.2.3 Comparison to Roman Finds

The region accounts for over 25 per cent of Roman coin finds and 45 per cent of artefacts, *Dataset 7, Finds Comparison*. For the Anglian period, the proportions are 15 per cent and 11 per cent, reflecting a lower level of economic activity relative to other regions in the north. However, while the table shows a close correlation (91 per cent) between regional losses of Roman and early Anglo-Saxon coins, the same cannot be said for artefacts (29 per cent).[1007] While further research is required to explain this anomaly, what can be concluded from the relatively more prolific Roman finds relates to the different nature of land use. In Roman times the Great North Road provided a major communication channel to Hadrian's Wall with links to strategically placed forts. In Anglo-Saxon times, the Central Lowlands consisted largely of managed estates and economic activity in Bernicia appears subdued. The veneer of Anglian finds may well reflect the controlled management of agriculture in the Central Lowlands during the Anglian period.

7.2.4 The Artefactual Dataset

Dataset 16, Site Finds by Issuer summarizes finds for the region. The ratio of coined to artefactual sites for the Central Lowlands is a rather low 39 per cent, compared to 70 per cent for the Wolds (*Dataset 17. Artefacts—Summary*) and needs to be viewed in the context of the sheer number of locations involved, for either coins or artefacts. Clearly, coins are in widespread use but the formally recorded association with artefact sites is a little weaker than expected.

While *Dataset 16, Artefacts—Details* gives the artefactual distribution in detail, for sites with both coins and artefacts, *Dataset 16, Coin Metal Mix* shows the mix of coin metal on artefact sites. Lest this regional summation, showing healthy coin use in both the eighth and ninth centuries, disguises site variations, the age mixes of coin at sites with artefacts, *prima facie*, favours site migration over continuity, *Dataset 16, Coin Age Mix*. This may be attributable to the underlying *gleys*, though recoveries at individual site are too low for reliable statistical extrapolation. Potential settlement shifts between the eighth and ninth centuries are conjectured in *Dataset 1, Stability—Coin Sites*.[1008]

The picture presented for Fishergate contrasts sharply with that for the Central Lowlands, self-evidently the former is economically convergent, with occupations focussed on a single urban site whereas the latter is economically divergent, with activity spread evenly over a very large rural territory. The contrast is further revealed by comparing functional activity with the norm in *Dataset 16, Artefacts Categories*, with the Lowlands disproportionately favouring dress accessories, and Fishergate work-related artefacts and tools. Clearly, this is affected by the latter having been formally excavated.

Again, the usual caveats apply to PAS data, which is neither a comprehensive, nor indeed an entirely reliable, record. Two hanging bowls from Finningley predate the database.[1009] Nevertheless, were one to give credence to the record, the Central Lowlands assemblage, as shown in *Dataset 16, Artefacts Categories*, is dominated by items of personal dress (*Figure* 89): fastenings and other accessories make up 81 per cent. Admittedly the composition, as detailed in *Dataset 16, Accessories*, differs somewhat from

[1004] Scattered in the case of the more recent finds.
[1005] PAS BM-7C4457: https://finds.org.uk/database/artefacts/record/id/643932.
[1006] The undisclosed find (pre-Treasure regime) of a 'bag of Arabic coins' (*pers. comm.* Adam Swift, Oct. 2015) remains an intriguing prospect.
[1007] Moreover, while the regional pattern of loss of early Anglo-Saxon coins and artefacts is similar (97 per cent correlation) the correlation between Roman coins and artefacts is weak (65 per cent).

[1008] See *fn.* 1302.
[1009] Van de Noort and Davies (1993, 80).

the overall picture—more sleeve clasps, hooked tags and brooches locally, but half the number of pins and virtually no strap-ends—but this may be the result of communal fashion, allowing for the extent that these fastenings are substitutable.

Tools and work-related accessories constitute only 5 per cent of the total, and on closer inspection this includes: ingots (four), nails (three), rings (three), die stamps (two), spindle whorl (two) and a trial piece—direct evidence of processing (e.g. slag) is unrecorded. The majority of occupations were agrarian leaving little evidence of work practices in the archaeological record. There are no styli.

What may be regarded as non-personal items make up a small proportion of finds and many of these are bells and weights. The only hint of commercial activity is that five of the seven weights are from Wilberfoss.[1010] Only 38 of the 127 artefact types are present in the Central Lowlands,[1011] a lack of variety possibly indicating a controlling regime.

Eight locations just south of the Humber, *Dataset 5, Artefacts (Humberside)*, producing 13 artefacts, are excluded from this analysis. None has produced coins.

7.2.5 Conclusion

The overall picture presented by the dispersal of coins and artefacts in the Central Lowlands is a settled, bucolic scene with low levels of technology but sufficiently widespread and routine use of coin, often in association with artefacts, to regard this as a monetized region from the time of Aldfrith to the fall of York. In essence, the picture of single finds is similar in York and the Central Lowlands—a veneer of monetization—though the density of finds spots is greater in the town, reflecting the higher level of recovery. The relatively low number of both coins and artefacts per location and the lack of diversity of artefact types, in contrast to the picture from the Wolds, supports the view that the Central Lowlands continued as a managed estate,[1012] assuming that management varied little whether the owner was regal or monastic. Regrettably, the historical evidence is slender; Woodman lamented the paucity of surviving, contemporary, northern documentation, a mere 21 pre-Norman charters covering York (eleven), Beverley (three), Ripon (two), Durham (four) and Lowther Castle (one),[1013] only one of which falls in the study period.[1014]

[1010] Home of one of the most diligent of detectorists.
[1011] There is no reason to believe that detecting discard practices differ in the Vale.
[1012] Barrow (1969). Naylor (2004, 42). Woodman (2012, 275). Grocock and Wood (2013).
[1013] Woodman (2012, 1–6).
[1014] Durham—grant of land by Ecgfrith to Cuthbert, 685, Woodman (2012, 20 and 229 where Woodman credited Wilfrid with being influential in developing diplomatic practice being interested in recording his possessions).

Recovery factors bear directly on the finds density especially regarding objects with the slender profile of a *sceat* or *styca*. Roman coin losses, with their larger flans, have proportionately fared better in the Central Lowlands[1015] than early Anglo-Saxon coins, the former producing 25 per cent of northern finds compared to 15 per cent for the latter, *Dataset 7, Finds Comparison.* Generally, the soil type in the Vale, predominantly *gleys*,[1016] is less conducive to revealing finds than the dry chalk of the Wolds. Gleys are restricted in fertility and drainage. *Dataset 1, Stability—Coin Sites* and *Dataset 5, Stability* analyse sites active in *either* the eighth or ninth century to suggest prospective shifts.

The above finds demonstrate not only widespread use of coinage from all three phases of monetization but also long-distance trading contacts throughout the region.

7.2.6 Illustrations—The Central Lowlands

Figure 75: Coppergate helmet *c.* 750–75. (Courtesy York Archaeological Trust)

[1015] Especially along the Great North Road, *Map 4.*
[1016] Bautier (1971, 15). Spufford (1988, 9). Fossier (1989, 26). Collins (1991, 162–66). Higham (1993, 90). Van de Noort (1999, 10). Dark (2000, 35). Abdy (2006, 84–90). Higham and Ryan (2013, 41–56).

Figure 76: Lotherton: Series Q1H.[1017] (Courtesy Portable Antiquities Scheme)

Figure 77: 'Site C' near Wetherby: new variety D of York gold shilling (D1). (Courtesy Ricky Brelsford)

Figure 78: 'Site C' near Wetherby: second known variety D of York gold shilling (D2). (Courtesy Ian Briggs)[1018]

Figure 79: Hexagram *sceat*. Found Tadcaster. (Courtesy Craig Best, February 2015)

Figure 80: Ripon: Beonna lead trial piece.

Figure 81: Interlace decoration, hanging bowl base, Castle Yard, York. (Courtesy York Museums Trust)[1019]

Figure 82: Sherriff Hutton, Series E, variety G, one of three known (*EMC* 2013.0236).

Figure 83: Annulet type.[1020] (Courtesy Portable Antiquities Scheme)

Figure 84: Upper Poppleton: Primary Series E, Series O and Ælfwald *sceat*.

[1017] PAS SWYOR-3B48D5
[1018] Now claimed by the BM.

[1019] YAT 7/2, Fig. 64.
[1020] PAS YORYM-9A8ED1

Figure 85: Bolton Percy: Series F.

Figure 86: Middleham: York gold shilling (Ciii.2). (Courtesy York Museums Trust)

Figure 87: Sword pommel with filigree and rope-twist. (Courtesy Portable Antiquities Scheme)

Figure 88: Escrick ring. Found by Michael Greenhorn, 2009. (Courtesy of York Museums Trust (Yorkshire Museum)

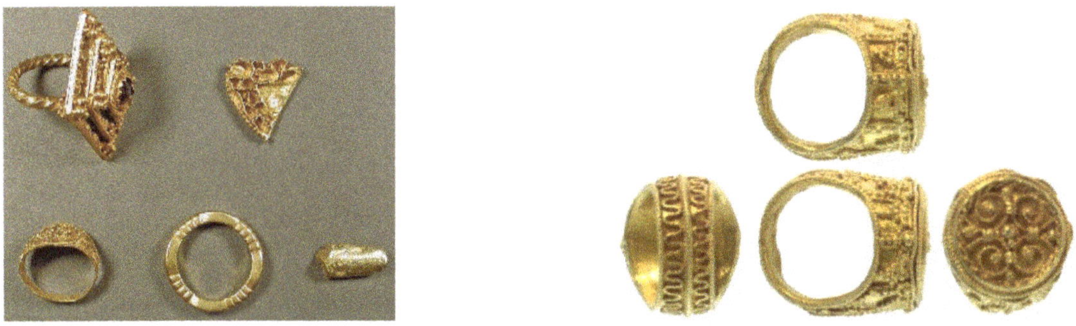

Figure 89: Two views of the 'Leeds' ring hoard, *c.* 700–1100. Found Aberford.[1021] (Courtesy Portable Antiquities Scheme)

7.3 The Yorkshire Wolds (*Dataset 17*)

> 'The answer lies in the soil!'
> Arthur Fallowfield, *Beyond Our Ken* (1958–64), BBC Radio, Home Service.

The Yorkshire Wolds constitute the northerly section of the Cretaceous chalk plateau running north-south through Lincolnshire, reaching the coast between Scarborough and Bridlington. The plateau undulates with glaciated, often dry, valleys, with the Great Wold Valley running from Wharram-le-Street east to Bridlington intermittently carrying the Gypsey Race. The Wolds provide rich upland grazing, punctuated by woodland areas.

It is difficult to discern patterns of abandonment or continuity at the end of the Roman occupation.[1022] The system of villas and towns fell into disrepair, possibly replaced by locally organised rural estates, sometimes referred to as 'multiple estates' at the edges of the Wolds. Satellite dependencies were subsequently, perhaps anachronistically, described as *sokeland* or *berewick*, and extensive tracts on higher or marginal land served as common pastures.[1023] The conventional wisdom among detectorists is that all coin producing Anglian sites also reveal Roman coins.

Attention may now be turned to the characterisation and explanation of the coin-rich sites in the Yorkshire Wolds.

[1021] PAS 2008 T553 and 2009 T221.

[1022] Loveluck (2003 154–55), suggested that a collapse of demand for mass-produced commodities, such as Yorkshire Crambeck ware pottery, would have led to absence of diagnostic material. Want of imported goods in the early decades of the fifth century would have encouraged self-sufficiency 'possibly focussed on former military commands and tribal or kin-linked groups, which formed the basis for subsequent social and political developments, alongside influences from across the North Sea'.

[1023] Fenton-Thomas (2005, 83–87). (Banham and Faith, 2014, 285). By Doomsday, the central Wolds was a landscape of open fields and nucleated villages. Wrathmell (2003, 363) argued that the Wolds and Holderness have more in common with similar landscapes in Lincolnshire and elsewhere than with each other.

These are tabulated by period and issuer in *Dataset 17* and are significantly higher in number than in the Central Lowlands due to the human and geographical recovery factors at play. The soil of the Wolds is more amenable to detection and access is less inhibited due to land use. While it is difficult to quantify this influence, find volumes at major Wolds locations such as South Newbald and Sledmere compare favourably to Fishergate. In both the Roman and early Anglo-Saxon period the Wolds contribute around half of northern coin finds, *Dataset 7, Finds Comparison*, leading to the conclusion that the Wolds remained economically more active than the Central Lowlands.

Three spheres of activity, largely determined by the clustering of reported finds, have been identified:[1024]

Wolds, west:[1025] deemed to include locations on the western periphery of the wolds, descending into the Central Lowlands and running south from Buttercrambe to North Ferriby and linked by ancient trackways. Given that Flixborough is on the Lincolnshire continuation of the Wolds, a brief description of that site is also included for comparative purposes.

Wolds, central: locations on and north of the A166 and west of the B1249, this central area encompasses a roughly triangular zone, though the active centre is defined by Weaverthorpe, Fridaythorpe and Great Driffield.

1. Wolds, east: east of the B1249. Routes crossing this north-south road, from Hull to Scarborough, converge on Bridlington.
2. This division is inevitably somewhat arbitrary and does not imply these were restricted zones. Indeed, there are clear trackways throughout the Wolds connecting settlements to each other and to the larger centres, though this is a non-nucleated region. Significant sites, ranked by volume are discussed below. Beverley and Holderness are considered separately at sections 7.4-7.5.
3. *Dataset 17, Artefacts—Details* shows all artefacts. *Dataset 17, Coin Metal Mix* gives coin metallurgy showing that the Wolds saw similar levels of activity in the eighth and ninth centuries, and *Dataset 17, Coin Age Mix*, demonstrates relative stability rather than mobility.

7.3.1 Wolds West

7.3.1.1 Wolds West

Significant numbers of early Anglo-Saxon coins are clustered around Pocklington, north of Market Weighton, and at several southerly sites, notably South Newbald.

South Newbald[1026]

South Newbald nestles to the west of the Wolds and was well served by the Roman roads running from Brough to York and to Malton. The finds area, on an inhumation site south of Hotham Beck,[1027] is on unstratified sandy soil over Jurassic limestone north-west of a Romano-British villa. Not only is the area rich in Roman artefacts, but a major Anglo-Saxon pagan cemetery is close by at Sancton. Indeed, numismatic finds were initially attributed to Sancton. Leahy discussed the causes and complexities of the irregular parish boundaries.[1028]

Leahy reported 240 finds from South Newbald including 25 strap-ends and 81 pins, many shaftless. In comparing this to other local 'productive sites', he concluded 'the analysis of pins failed to give any useful results'[1029] and differences in the ratio of pin to strap-end losses 'might be attributable to different forms of attire'.[1030] Despite this significant number of metal finds, there are few of high quality and domestic artefacts are surprisingly scarce. Such austerity may suggest a monastery were it not for the absence of stone, stele and styli. The considerable coin assemblage better supports site interpretation as a market or fair,[1031] but given the skeletal remains and royal status of Newbald by 963,[1032] perhaps a minster site where a reeve oversaw transactions, and justice was dispensed, is a better interpretation.[1033]

Coin finds from South Newbald have been covered in two articles,[1034] which present a total of 124 Northumbrian equally divided between *sceattas* and *stycas*, *Dataset 17, South Newbald, Graph* 8.4. (*Figure* 90, *Figure* 91). My database augments this by 56 specimens adding two further issuers. Quite exceptionally, there are only two Continental coins: a *sceat* of Series E and a single *denier* of Charlemagne (768–814). There is a single Southumbrian specimen, a penny of Wulfred, Archbishop of Canterbury (805–32).[1035] All the finds are apparently singletons, condition is variable and the regnal distribution for the northern types is representative of the coinage from *c.* 740 to the fall of York, *Dataset 17*. This clearly indicates

[1024] The Wolds are divided north-south and east-west by lines meeting at Great Driffield, *Map 2*.

[1025] South of the A166, other than Buttercrambe.

[1026] James Booth, *pers comm.* 19 August 2014: There were Roman coins at Newbald (including a beautiful coin of Geta, a surface find by Dave Haldenby) but there were no Southern *sceattas*. The historical record recommences abruptly with *sceattas* of Eadberht, and there are only Series Y *sceattas* and *stycas* thereafter. Nor are there any later Saxon pennies—only late medieval coins, 'a remarkably distinctive distribution'. The site seems to have been occupied and deserted abruptly.

[1027] Eighteen skeletons were reported in the mid-nineteenth century.

[1028] Leahy (2000, 54–55).

[1029] Leahy (2000, 74–75).

[1030] Leahy (2000, 77).

[1031] Leahy (2000, 78).

[1032] Sawyer (1981, 153).

[1033] Leahy (2000, 78–79).

[1034] Booth and Blowers (*NC*143, 1983) collating finds of four detectorists working between October 1979 and September 1982, referring to the site as 'Sancton', and Booth (1997, 15–38, also published in Early Deira), assembling finds reported in Booth, 1984 and 1997a). Blackburn and Bonser (*BNJ*56, 1986, 64–101). Pirie (1996, 67–90).

[1035] One of the *stycas* is sunk into a lead weight (no. 64, *NC*143, 145). Booth (1997, 27) described this as a 'characteristic Scandinavian practice' possibly relating to the final days of occupation.

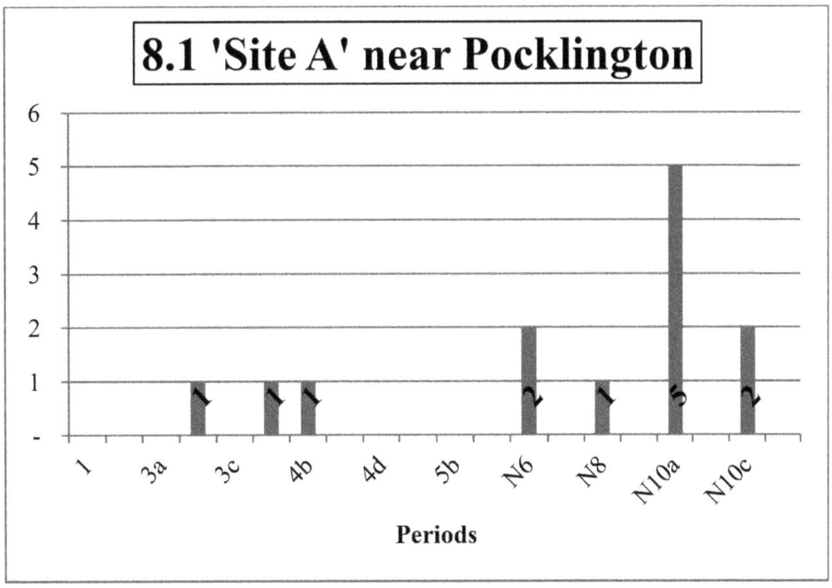
8.1 'Site A' near Pocklington
6
5
4
3
2
1
-
1
3a
3c
4b
4d
5b
N6
N8
N10a
N10c
Periods

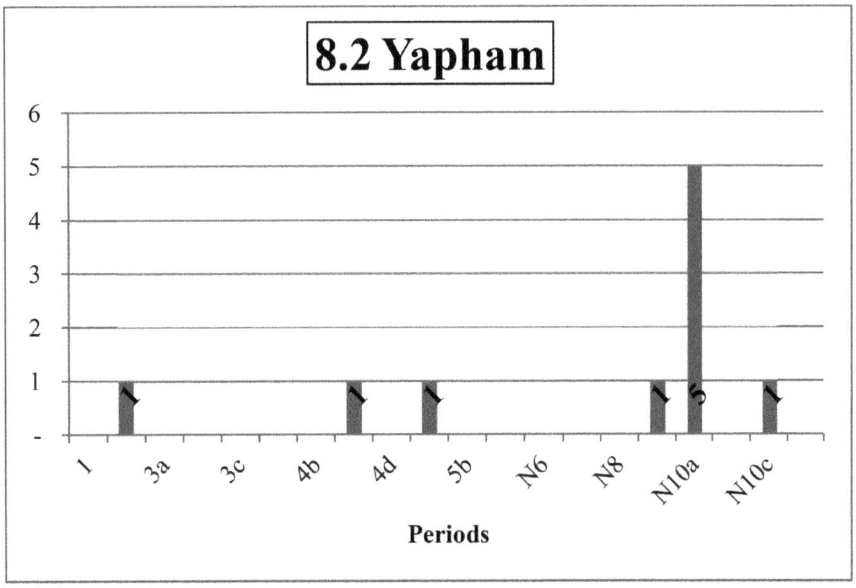
8.2 Yapham
6
5
4
3
2
1
-
1
3a
3c
4b
4d
5b
N6
N8
N10a
N10c
Periods

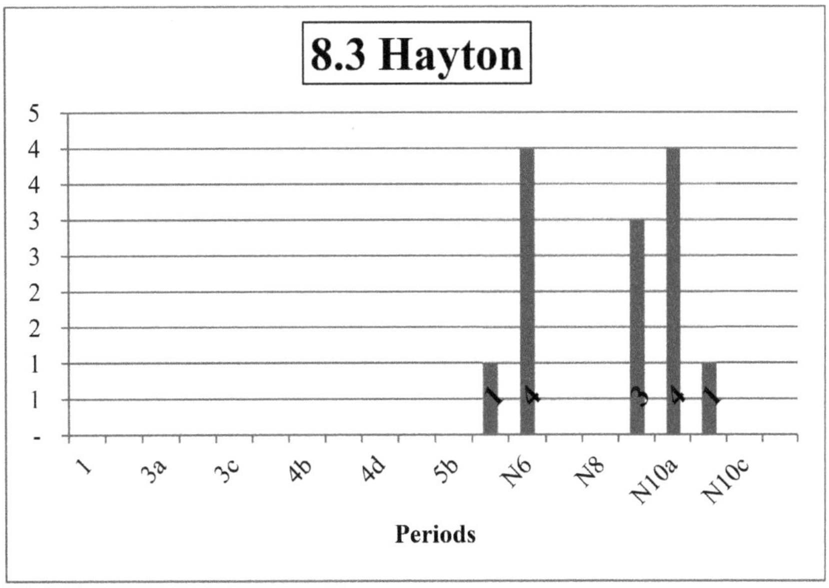
8.3 Hayton
5
4
4
3
3
2
2
1
1
-
1
3a
3c
4b
4d
5b
N6
N8
N10a
N10c
Periods

Graphs 8

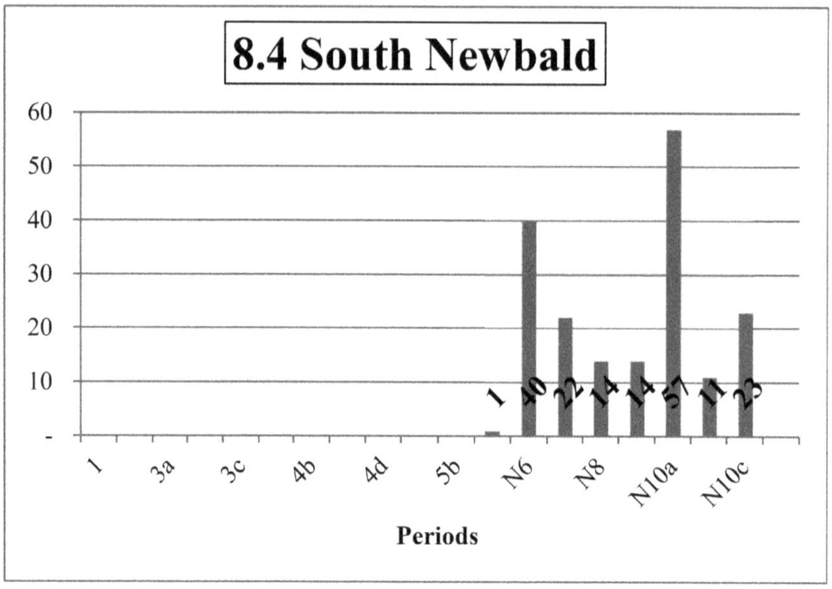
8.4 South Newbald
60
50
40
30
20
10
-
1
40
22
14
14
57
11
23
1
3a
3c
4b
4d
5b
N6
N8
N10a
N10c
Periods

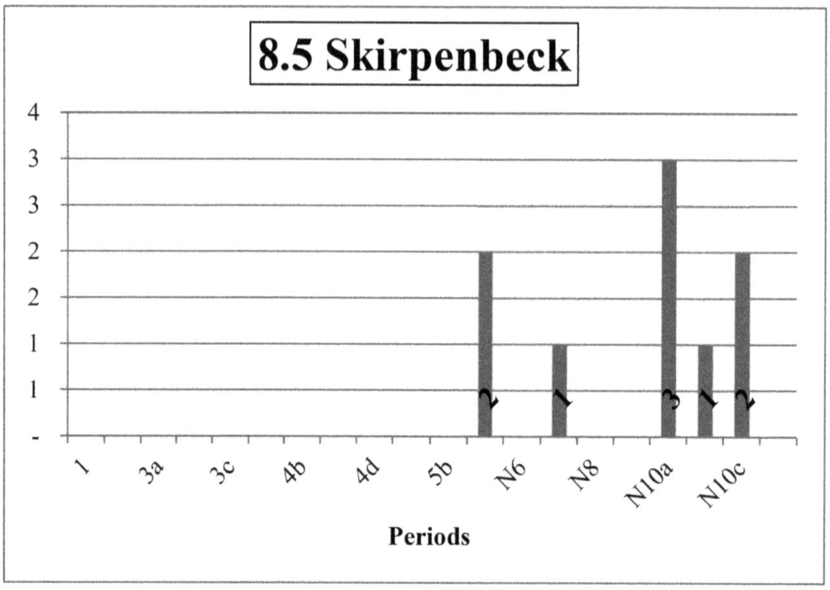
8.5 Skirpenbeck
4
3
3
2
2
1
1
-
2
1
3
1
2
1
3a
3c
4b
4d
5b
N6
N8
N10a
N10c
Periods

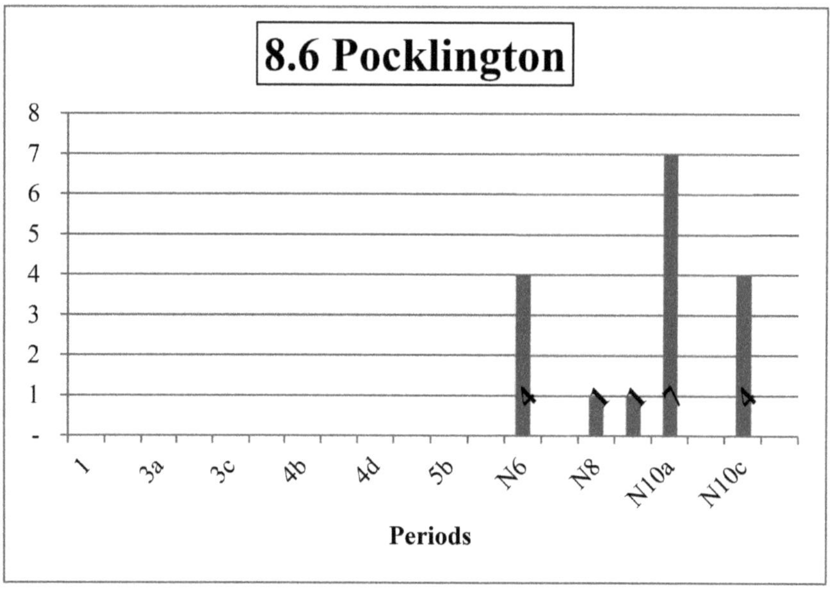
8.6 Pocklington
8
7
6
5
4
3
2
1
-
4
1
1
7
4
1
3a
3c
4b
4d
5b
N6
N8
N10a
N10c
Periods

Graphs 8

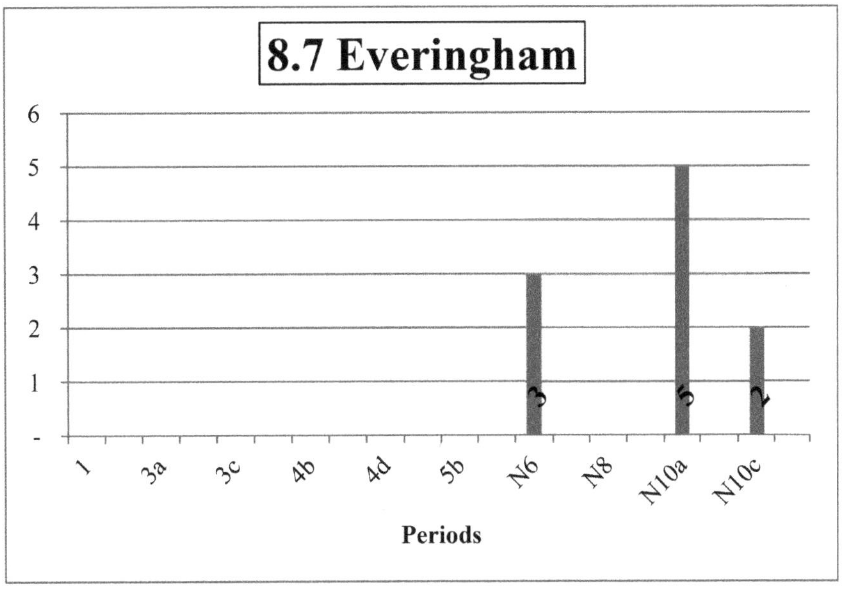

Graphs 8: Site finds by period arranged regionally by weighted average of peak activity, Wolds West. Sources: *Datasets 1* and *8*. Numerical axis varies.

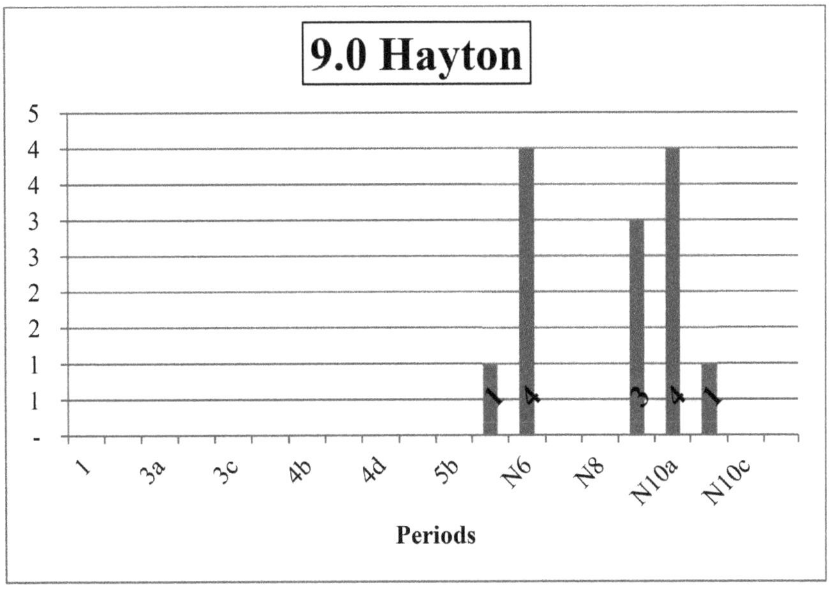

Graph 9: Hayton with additional informal data. Sources: *Datasets 1* and *8*. Numerical axis varies. Purpose: To demonstrate peak activity at Hayton.

a steady rate of accidental loss sustained over the period of occupation. Moreover, the *sceattas* listed by Booth are represented by 89 different dies. This remarkable paucity of die duplications implies both a low survival rate and a substantial coinage when compared to mid-ninth century emissions of pennies. Alternatively, die longevity may have been restricted with consequences for estimates of volume.

The early-penny conspectus, *Dataset 17*, excludes only the great rarities of Æthelwald Moll and Eardwulf. The *stycas* include only one Wulfhere and exclude Eanbald II and Redwulf. Only a fifth of the *stycas* are blundered or illegible.

Can anything be gleaned by comparing South Newbald with Fishergate? Redolent of the probable settlement shift, from Heslington Hill to Fishergate, mentioned above, Booth asked: 'Is it too wildly speculative to suggest that the North Ferriby site was abandoned at the beginning of Eadberht's reign, and its activities moved to the safer inland location of Newbald?' The find of a Southumbrian penny replicates the same phenomenon at Cottam and Fishergate but it is safe to assume that this is coincidental in its singularity though possibly evidences a fleeting Viking presence.

Certainly, the highly distinctive near absence of non-local coins at South Newbald differentiates the two sites and implies that there was more long-distance traffic at Fishergate but more control at South Newbald. The simultaneous abandonment is part of a pattern indicating widespread dislocation at the passage of the *micel here.*

Hayton

Hayton, a ladder settlement at the site of a Roman fort,[1036] straddles the Roman road at Hayton Beck two miles to the south-east of Pocklington. Save a single secondary Series E from the Low Countries, the recorded coin finds are Northumbrian: four fantastic animal *sceattas*, being two of Eadberht and one each of Alchred and Ælfwald I, and seven ninth-century coins including two of Eanred's silver-alloy coinage, one by a rare moneyer Æthelheah, and brass *stycas* of Eanred, Æthelred II (both reigns) and Osberht but no episcopal coins. This presents a diverse but unexceptional cross-section, lost between the 730s and 860s at a likely watering hole for travellers.[1037] Additionally, Pirie has recorded a *sceat*-like object, possibly contemporary, with a radiate bust on one side and what looks like a writhing serpent on the other (*Figure* 92).

However, informal sources suggest something far more significant. A 'productive site' in the vicinity (*Dataset 17, Hayton, Plates 8–9*) has produced at least 86 fully attested *sceattas* with a predominance of secondary Series E, though there are three worn English and 11 Continental primary *sceattas*.[1038] A series G-like coin has a reverse inscription related to *Monita Scorvm sceat* (*Figure* 93). There are no local Series Y coins.

The skewed assemblage illustrated by *Graph 9*, implies either a scattered hoard or a temporary market engaged in direct trade with the Low Countries, plausibly in fleeces from the Wolds. The relatively fresh appearance of some of the primary Series E *sceattas* and lack of copper carbonate deposits associated with hoarded material,[1039] argues against the hoard hypothesis suggesting activity between *c.* 700 and *c.* 750. No artefacts have been reported in connection with these coins.

Buttercrambe with Bossall

Cropmarks and earthworks indicate medieval settlement of uncertain date.[1040] A hoard of 17 Primary *sceattas* is attributed to this settlement, where the Derwent flows into the Central Lowlands (*Figure* 94).

[1036] Loveluck (2003, 154 and 163–64) mentioned a *Grübenhaus.* Halkon (2003, 272–74). http://www.southampton.ac.uk/archaeology/research/projects/landscape_archaeology_of_hayton.page; http://www2.hull.ac.uk/student/archaeology/research/hayton.aspx; http://pastscape.org.uk/hob.aspx?hob_id=61387

[1037] See *Graph* 8.3.

[1038] Other informal sources state the total of *sceat* finds to be *c.* 220, predominantly Series E.

[1039] The predominant component of hard green verdigris.

[1040] http://pastscape.org.uk/hob.aspx?hob_id=1141586

Naylor's report included one Series B, two Series E and he described 10 of the 14 Series D *sceattas* as die linked.[1041] He concluded that, on the balance of probability, this is a scattered hoard.[1042] Accepting this die-linking, one may surmise that they are from the same Frisian source presenting direct evidence of either an incoming Frisian trader or a returning local merchant in the period *c.* 670–*c.* 710. A rare joint issue *sceat* of Alchred with Archbishop Ecgberht,[1043] shows activity into the mid-760s.

'Site B' near Pocklington

Diligent detectorists working at what is here referred to as 'Site B' near Pocklington, have found *sceattas* and *stycas* (*Plate 10, Figure* 95) in a field strewn with pieces of lead—ingots, weights and waste—and sharpening stones of continental (Northern) micas, suggesting metalworking.

The site, which merits archaeological investigation, has also produced a cloisonné panel (*Figure* 96),[1044] among other élite artefacts, and shows continuity as demonstrated by a fragmentary dirham and the Raven type penny (*Figure* 97), although there is site migration between Roman,[1045] Anglian, Viking and medieval occupations.

The broad mix of early-penny types among the 57 finds includes primary phase southern coins of Series A, B (two) and F (two), and Continental D (five), E (four), X and G (two). There are six Series J coins (types 85 and 37) one in near pristine condition, possibly indicating proximity to source. Represented among the secondary phase *sceattas* are Continental Series E (five) and Southumbrian N (two), N/W[1046], R (three), K/R and S, Two of these exotic species, both typically poor, are at *Figure* 98. The 21 Northumbrian *sceattas* include Eadberht (nine), Eadberht and Ecgberht (one) and Æthelred II (eleven).

This volume and wide mix of varieties shows that this settlement enjoyed active and wide trading relationships. This is a site of no obvious strategic advantage other than being where the ford crosses the trackway. That it should have produced such a rich variety of finds is instructive. Curiously only 16 *stycas* have been found, probably all dating to before 850,[1047] but continuity of use is also apparent as finds include late Anglo-Saxon, Viking and Norman periods to the twelfth century.

Pocklington

Pocklington lies on the western edge of the Wolds, north of the Roman Road from York to Beverley. Finds date from Neolithic times onwards and crop marks indicate

[1041] These were found between 2007 and 2012. Six single Series D sceat have since surfaced.

[1042] PAS LVPL-E80948, August 2014.

[1043] *EMC* 2014.0360. *SL* 75–10.

[1044] PAS NLM-1A8B56.

[1045] 226 Roman coins have been recorded.

[1046] Mackay (2004, 112).

[1047] Tony Laverack (*pers. comm.* 24th March 2015).

Romano-British settlement.[1048] Productive fields nearby have produced significant numbers of *sceattas* and *stycas*, not all of which have yet permeated the formal recording system. Two entries to PAS of a primary Series D and a secondary Southumbrian Series O *sceat* are confused and have been discounted. This leaves four fantastic animal *sceattas* (Eadberht three, Ælfwald I, one) and an Æthelred I *sceat* by Tidwulf as the only specimens in the formal record. One of the Eadberht's *sceattas* was the first known of the variety with *AR* on the reverse (*Figure* 99),[1049] the only other specimen is from Rillington.

A Series Q is thought to be from this site. Finds also include silver rich emissions of Eanred and brass *stycas* of Eanred, Æthelred II and Redwulf but none of Osberht and no legible episcopal issues.

Non-local finds in March 2015 include Series E (primary, variety G1) X and R all in fine condition (*Figure* 100), a unique mule (*Figure* 101) and several silver-alloy and brass *stycas*.[1050]

'Site A' near Pocklington

'Site A' near Pocklington is a hamlet west of Pocklington on the western track to the Roman Road. Cropmarks indicate Roman presence—a villa, kiln, coins and four inhumations.[1051]

A York shilling (*Figure* 102) of the Paulinus variety,[1052] five *sceattas* and seven brass *stycas* are recorded, the earliest *sceattas* being of Aldfrith and a primary Series Z coin,[1053] which hint at a busy thoroughfare. Fantastic animal *sceattas* of Eadberht and Alchred, and an Æthelred I *sceat* by Tidwulf, accompany *stycas* of Eanred, Æthelred II and Wigmund. See *Graph* 8.1.

That a York gold shilling in excellent condition and rumours of a second,[1054] should be uncovered at such a small settlement is again indicative of both the thriving seventh-century economy of the area and the widespread use of coin, despite being of evident high value.

Yapham

Yapham is yet another Wolds edge hamlet where Roman and medieval crop marks are evident.[1055] It has yielded a scattering of commonplace *sceattas* and *stycas*[1056]—but with one significant difference. A gilded copper-core imitation Pseudo-Imperial *Victory* type *tremisses* in the name of Justinian I (527–65) was uncovered in 2006 (*Figure* 103).[1057] This counterfeit would have been slipped into the circulating medium in the late sixth century but is enigmatic in its lack of context. The find location is neither a focal nor a transit point. The coin has a test mark and may well have been discarded as worthless when revealed, though perhaps one would expect a greater degree of destruction. Both the perpetration and rejection suggest advancing monetization.

It probably originates from Francia though there is no means of attributing the original or forgery to a particular region. The obverse legend can be reconstructed as DNVSTINIANV...PPI... which, according to Pol, probably dates the original to the third quarter of the sixth century, though it could have been produced later. There are very few Pseudo-Imperial coins that show the emperor's name without the initial 'I' and among the other such coins recorded by Pol (three *tremisses* and one *solidus*) there is no close parallel for this copy.[1058] The presence of an imitative coin implies wide acceptance of the original.

Forgeries are usually seen as a vehicle of deception, but, in common with numerous obsolete Roman *nummi*, they are often found in Merovingian graves, so one may also postulate a funerary purpose.

North Cave

Humberside Archaeological Unit excavated at Dryham Quarry in 1986–87 and demonstrated activity in Neolithic, Iron Age and Roman periods.[1059] A seventh-century female inhumation with grave goods, was found at Everthorpe Hall in 1958.[1060]

A *tremissis*-like gold coin (*Figure* 104) of uncertain origin and struck from dies substantially larger than the flan, was found at North Cave, which is on the ancient western track from Ferriby, a trade route inland from the Humber crossing. This was referred to Pol, a leading expert on this material, but he was unable to give any specific identification other than hinting that it may well have been struck unofficially. *Sceattas* of Series J and secondary E, have also been recorded.

Small Finds

North Ferriby undoubtedly formed the ancient north terminal of the Humber crossing in the Anglo-Saxon period. Finds Anglo-Saxon finds include 11 *sceattas*, mainly of the primary phase, of which three are Aldfrith, two Kentish and five Continental types (from Ribe and the Low Countries), reflecting the flows of a busy coastal site (*Figure* 105).

[1048] http://www.pastscape.org.uk/hob.aspx?hob_id=61392
[1049] Bonser archive 5th June 1994 and *EMC* 1996.0130. *SL* 70–60.
[1050] See *Graph* 8.6.
[1051] http://www.pastscape.org.uk/hob.aspx?hob_id=59481 to 59491.
[1052] Naylor and Allen (2014, 157), C9, "near Pocklington'. A die duplicate of this coin *EMC* 2016.0318 was auctioned in December 2016.
[1053] Duplicated on PAS.
[1054] *Dataset 15, York Shilling Corpus, no. Unseen 3.* Unseen metal detector find Sunday 26th October 2008, 'Site A' near Pocklington, and sold unrecorded to a US collector.
[1055] http://www.pastscape.org.uk/hob.aspx?hob_id=1163459
[1056] See *Graph* 8.2.
[1057] PAS YORYM-761506.
[1058] *Pers. comm.* 5th February 2015.
[1059] http://www.pastscape.org.uk/hob.aspx?hob_id=1063092
[1060] Geake (1997, 158).

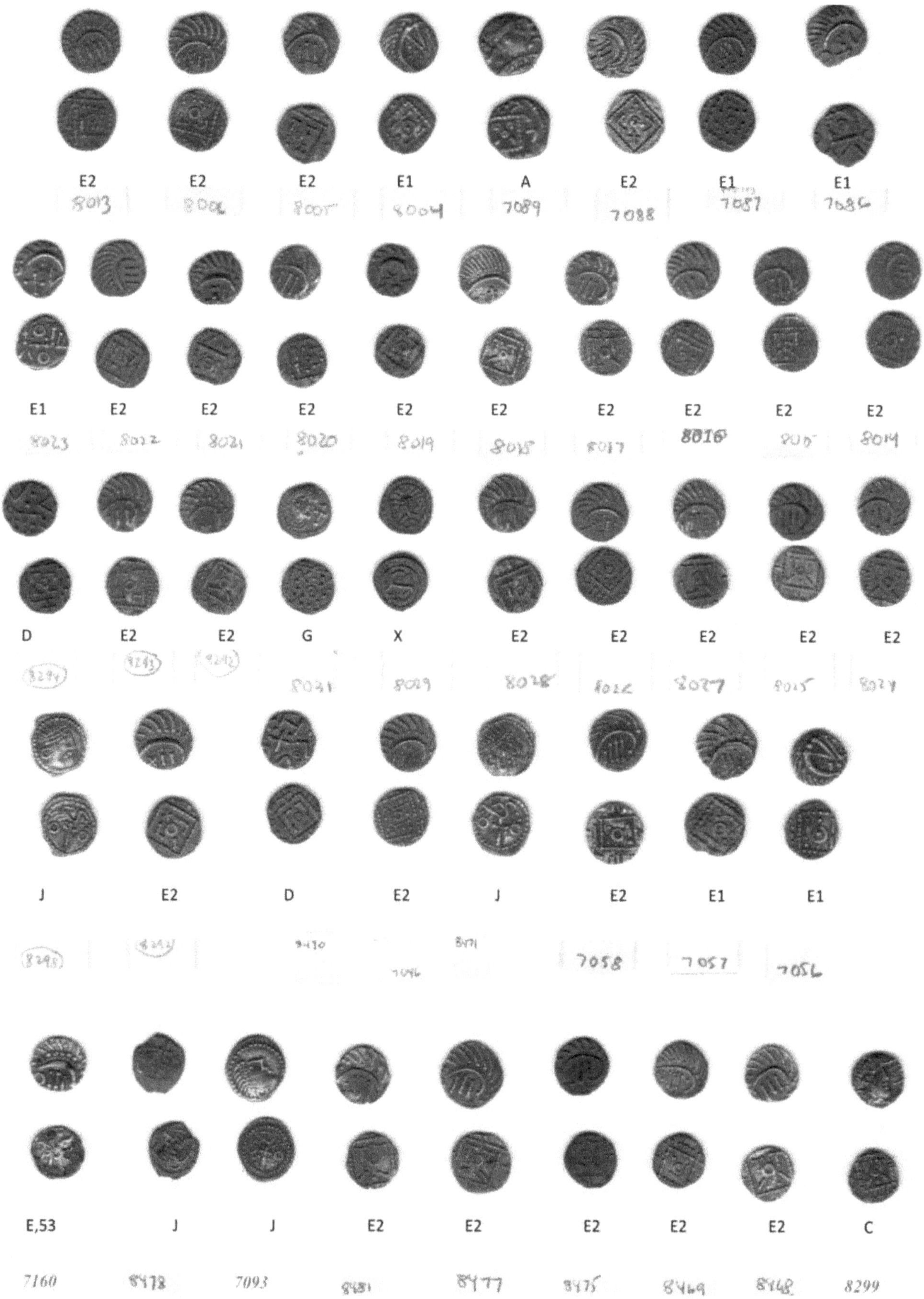

Plate 8: Near Hayton productive site (1) (unsorted). Source: R. Bude, *pers comm*, Dec 2015. Key: typed references are *sceat* series.

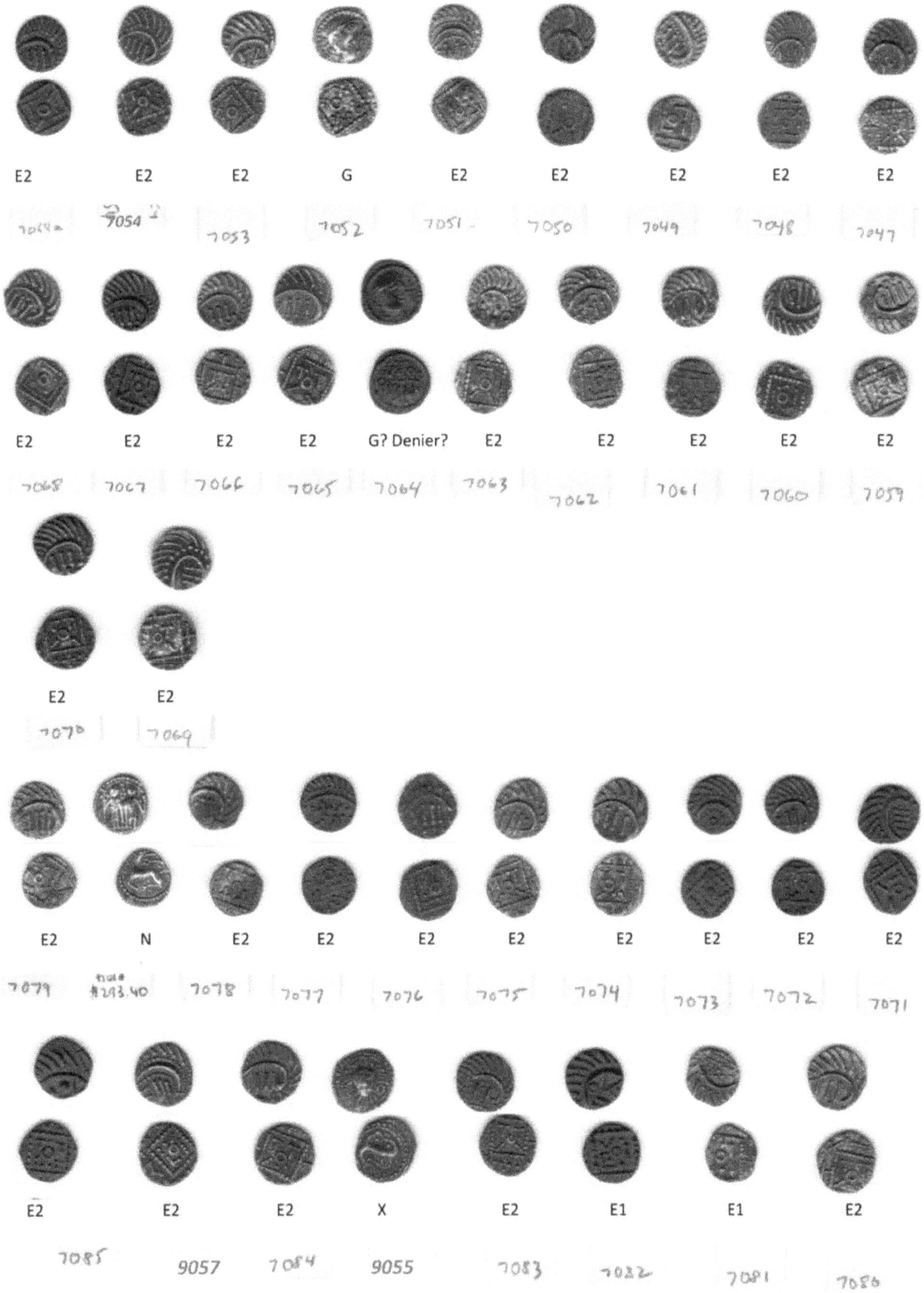

Plate 9: Near Hayton productive site (2) (unsorted). Source: R. Bude, *pers comm*, Dec 2015. Key: typed references are *sceat* series.

Plate 10: ***Sceatta*** **finds from 'Site B' near Pocklington. Source: Martin Moore and Tony Laverack, March 2015.**

Of comparable scale are finds from the parishes of Skipenbeck, Everingham, Thorpe-le-Street, Harswell and Market Weighton (including a *sceat* of Eardwulf) in the vicinity of which, continuation of sub-Roman industrial activity, is little in evidence.[1061]

Finds from 10 other sites demonstrate the widespread use of both silver and base coin in this area, albeit in modest numbers, *Dataset 17, Small Finds i) west*. This is merely the detectable tip of the iceberg, for instance, *styca* finds from Middleton-on-the-Wolds, a site rich in Roman and Iron Age coins, are reported informally.[1062]

Flixborough

A comparison with the excavation finds from Flixborough may be helpful, especially as the site is located on the Lincolnshire continuation of the Wolds on a north-south axis across the Humber Gap, only eight miles south of the Humber. Anglo-Scandinavian influence is apparent and there are many medieval deserted villages. At Flixborough, the material culture is demonstrated by the rich variety of finds including an intact carpenter's tool kit, a ring inscribed with the first half of the alphabet and many styli.[1063]

At least 56 *sceattas* and *stycas* have been unearthed at Flixborough.[1064] The six primary *sceattas* are all from the Low Countries,[1065] while the 23 secondary *sceattas* are more mixed: there are four Series J varieties,[1066] and two *sceattas* of Eadberht, but Continental varieties, from Domburg, Dorestad and Quentovic, still constitute more than half the total.[1067] While this is not proof of direct trade, as none is pristine, exports of wool from the Wolds could be implied.[1068] Archibald surmises that imported *sceattas* may not have been recycled as there was no mint nearby.[1069] The evidence from the Series J specimens is insufficient to sway the debate on the source of this Series.[1070] Again, Series Q has a sole representative, in common with other northern 'productive sites' such as Carlisle and Whitby. This and two Series R *sceattas* may show contact with East Anglia.[1071] From this relatively small accumulation of coins it is difficult to be confident of the health of domestic trade at this site. Furthermore, what is evident is that coin finds are from a restricted time span of about half a century, commencing in the late seventh or early eighth century, well after this high-status site had been established, and ceasing before the decline in alloy of secondary *sceattas*.[1072] The delay in commencement may be attributable to gradually commercial evolution at the site. The early cessation may be illusory as early-penny usage possibly continued until, even beyond, the appearance of the Offan penny dated to the 760s.

Of the 27 ninth-century Northumbrian coins, only nine have an identifiable issuer or moneyer, one of which is a silver-alloy coin of Eanred. The others are irregular brass *stycas*, a disproportionately high number, with several dies unseen elsewhere. Archibald speculates that there are some stylistic similarities with the purse hoard from Beverley, hinting at an *atelier* north of the Humber, resting her case on the absence of types from the great *styca* hoards.[1073] The lack of bronze *stycas* of Osberht or Wulfhere as occurs in some other northern sites, leads her to venture that the irregular *stycas* here are a result of the disruption following Redwulf's usurpation (i.e. they are from the first group of blundered *stycas*).

All the *stycas* are more worn than the *sceattas*, suggesting a higher velocity of circulation or greater longevity. Nearly all were extracted from disturbed strata, such that the numismatic contribution to precise site chronology is limited. What is significant, at this southerly location, is that *stycas* are present in similar numbers to the *sceattas*. The *stycas* must be assessed in the context of finds of post-early-penny silver coins, namely, two eighth-century specimens and eight ninth-century pennies. These include a broad *denier* of Pepin the Short (751–68),[1074] a light penny of Offa (one of the earliest known[1075]) and pennies of Archbishop Ceolnoth of Canterbury (833–77), Berhtwulf of Mercia (840–52), and for Wessex: Æthelwulf (*c.* 855-8), Æthelberht (2) (858–65) and Alfred (3) (871–75).[1076]

Archibald notes that these pennies were substantially higher in intrinsic value than the late, typically debased, *sceattas* and may indicate an increased sophistication in commodity production—perhaps a shift from export of

[1061] Halkon and Millett (1999). Halkon (2003, 273–74). See *Graph* 8.5 and 8.7.

[1062] *Pers. comm.* Tony Laverack, 19th March 2015.

[1063] Evans and Loveluck (2009, esp. 123–42). Blair (2005, 208). Webster and Backhouse (1991, 69a–w), stated that 16 styli were found.

[1064] There are differences in the finds listings between *EMC* (based on Blackburn 1993 (Lindsey 87)), Pirie (2000) and Archibald (Evans and Loveluck, 2009, ch. 13). I have relied on the latter.

[1065] Series D (2c and 8) and E (3 VICO and 1 variety G2).

[1066] I.e. types 36, 37 (2), 85 and 72. I attribute the latter to Quentovic (see putative Etaples hoard, *Dataset 20, Quentovic*).

[1067] Respectively, Series E (9), G (2, one fragmentary, one imitative, both poor) and J, type 72 (1).

[1068] Metcalf (2011 and 2014, 244). A caveat on condition as an indicator of immediate source should be applied.

[1069] Archibald (2009, 404).

[1070] Naylor (2006, 159–70). Note that four of the Series J types illustrated by Archibald at plates 13.2 and 13.4 are in a good state of preservation.

[1071] The only other Series included are N and U both of which have distributions from the Thames Valley north to beyond The Wash.

[1072] The latest is probably the Series R8 sceat.

[1073] Archibald and others (2009, 417–18). Pirie (1987, 127 and 1991). Detectorists in the Beverley-'Site B' near Pocklington area report the occurrence of contemporary *styca* counterfeits. (Martin Moore, *pers. comm.* 7th January 2015)

[1074] Minted at Quentovic, perhaps indicating continued contact. Archibald and others (2009, 405). Specimens are known from elsewhere, such as Kilham. This new type was the precedent for Offa's broad penny.

[1075] Chick, 7a 57. Moneyer Odd.n?

[1076] These show a dominance of Canterbury issues—five of the eight ninth-century pennies. Similar proportions obtain at Riby Cross Roads (Steedman 1994, 212), where a local detectorist (*pers. comm.* 4th February 2016) reports 13 of 21 ninth-century pennies to be from Canterbury among a spread of finds from Merovingian tremisses through to a penny of Alfred. *EMC* extends this into the medieval period and includes three sceattas of Aldfrith (one pristine).

wool to woollens.[1077] Cultural material from the rest of the site does not indicate an economic discontinuity, despite the relatively early disappearance of *sceattas*—none of the later varieties is present. Their replacement by higher value pennies, eventually accompanied by *stycas*, may show that a bimetallic system evolved in the mid-ninth century, suggesting a strong need for exchange.

In common with Whitby, Flixborough has a paucity of bronze *stycas* and a relative abundance of blundered specimens, possibly from Æthelred's restoration—the earlier occurrence of this phenomenon. What significance, if any, this distribution has, is yet to be determined.

7.3.1.2 Numismatic Summary—Wolds West

Graph 8 illustrates the chronological dispersal of finds at the main sites. 'Site A' near Pocklington and Yapham have wider dispersals over all three phases of the coinage and South Newbald has solid representation from Eadberht's *renovatio* onwards. Other sites share a similar profile dominated by *stycas*.

A distinction can be drawn between the north of this area, including the cluster of sites around Pocklington, which have benefitted from diligent detecting, and the south, particularly South Newbald with its dominant local element. In the former, drawing a line, perhaps arbitrarily, at Market Weighton, *c.* 29 per cent of the coins are not local, compared to 1.5 per cent in the latter, *Dataset 17*.[1078]

However, bias against reporting common finds—such as the ineptly named 'porky'—may be apparent in the informal information from near Hayton, *Dataset 17, Hayton*. Were this accumulation brought into account, then 39 per cent of finds in the north of the area are non-local, almost entirely Continental. In conclusion, the regional generally was strongly engaged with non-local trade but South Newbald was a special-purpose, closely controlled location.

7.3.1.3 The Artefactual Dataset—Wolds West

Dataset 17, Categories tabulates 737 artefacts from 29 locations, 19 of which have also produced coins.[1079] A further five locations have produced coins but no recorded artefacts. Of the 12 locations with artefacts but no coins, there is a total of only 41 artefacts,[1080] such that these can be regarded as occasional losses.

The overwhelming majority, 86 per cent, of these 737 losses relate to personal items, mainly dress accessories, of which there are 26 different types; see *Dataset 17*. There are 24 items described as weights, which, were this attribution accurate,[1081] hints at commercial activity, or bullion exchange during the Viking period. Otherwise, the near absence of horse fittings, domestic articles, weapons, craft and industrial produce, waste and tools, may suggest that the populace were engaged solely in sheep-rearing and casting off clouts. Nevertheless, there are 50 different object types, demonstrating greater diversity than found in the lowlands. There is one stylus (and a whetstone) among 65 artefacts, predominately dress fastenings, from Welton.

However, PAS gives a partial view; there were clearly localized specialisms, as evident for example, by the numerous lead scraps and pottery sherds recovered from 'Site B' near Pocklington and elsewhere.[1082] Such discard is too abundant and commercially valueless for the vast majority of detectorists to record. Presumably, other occupations left little trace in the physical record.

The artefact distribution in the west Wolds correlates closely with the overall dataset, of which it constitutes 27.1 per cent.[1083] The overlap of coin- and artefact-rich locations is substantial, especially as two-thirds of artefacts arise from proven moneyed locations. This is a clear indication of monetization.

[1077] Archibald and others (2009, 406).

[1078] Only 12 of the 193 coins in the south are not from South Newbald.

[1079] I have associated the Newbald of the artefactual database with the South Newbald of the numismatic database.

[1080] Including pins, strap-ends and buckles—five of each—and 10 brooches.

[1081] Most are convincingly described others may be gaming pieces. The spread does not cluster around specific weights, as would be expected in a standardized system. See *fn.* 268.

[1082] *cf. c.* 7000 pieces of iron from Ryther.

[1083] *Dataset 17, Categories* compares fastener types across the Wolds, with the west favouring pins and strap-ends.

7.3.1.4 Illustrations—The Yorkshire Wolds West

Eadberht

Alchred with Ecgberht

Æthelred I: L: shrine issue of Cuthgils, R: rare 'double obverse'

Figure 90: Some early-penny finds from South Newbald.

Figure 91: Eardwulf by Cuthheard. Found 'Newbald side of Sancton'.

Figure 92: Hayton: radiate bust obverse with decorative serpent reverse. Artefact or *sceat*? (Courtesy Pirie archive)

Figure 93: Hayton, Merovingian *denier* of Martinus or Mariae, N. France.[1084] (Courtesy Ron Bude)

[1084] See also *EMC* 2015.0184.

Figure 94: Buttercrambe with Bossall, hoard. (Courtesy Portable Antiquities Scheme)

Figure 95: 'Site B' near Pocklington: coins. L: Unusual Eadberht/Ecgberht joint issue *sceat* with two croziers on reverse. R: 'Special motif' *styca* of Æthelred II by Leofthegn.

Figure 96: 'Site B' near Pocklington: artefacts an early Anglian gold and garnet cloisonné trapezoidal panel. (Courtesy Tony Laverack and Martin Moore)

Figure 97: Raven penny of Anlaf Guthfrithsson, Hiberno-Norse king of York, 939–41. Moneyer Adeler (N 537)

Figure 98: Exotic species from 'Site B' near Pocklington: L: W/N mule. R: Serpent type. (Courtesy Tony Laverack)

Figure 99: Pocklington: AR variety. (Courtesy Bonser archive)

Figure 100: Pocklington: Primary Continental and East Anglian *sceattas*. (Courtesy Martin Moore)

Figure 101: Pocklington: Unique mule of Series K and J, *SL*37–60,

Figure 102: 'Site A' near Pocklington: York gold shilling issued by Paulinus (Cii.1)

Figure 103: Yapham: copy of an imitative *Victory* type *tremisses*. (Courtesy Portable Antiquities Scheme)

Figure 104: North Cave find: Possibly imitating a Frankish *tremissis*.[1085] (Courtesy Portable Antiquities Scheme)

Figure 105: North Ferriby *sceattas*. L–R: Primary Series E, 'plumed bird' variety, 'Wodan' type, and a pristine specimen of Aldfrith. (Courtesy *EMC*)

Figure 106: Named-moneyer Northumbrian *sceattas* of Æthelred I from Sledmere. L: Tidwulf; R: 'Shrine issue', Cudcils.

[1085] PAS SWYOR-236F00

7.3.2. Wolds Central

7.3.2.1 Wolds Central

The northern sector of this undulating landscape is characterized by north-south droveways, coming up from the Vale of Pickering, intersecting with west-east trackways linking settlements. This communications network indicates a high level of economic activity and mobility.

Sledmere[1086]

Sledmere is in the centre of the Wolds about eight miles north-west of Driffield where the main north-south route from the Humber crossing to Scarborough intersects the east-west route from Bridlington to York. Crop marks date from the Bronze Age (including the Wold Entrenchments)[1087] and Roman period with little Anglian material recorded, other than the numismatic. Evidence of a *DMV* survives at Croom House.[1088]

In his 1997 article in *YN* 3, Bonser listed finds from an unidentified 'North of England' 'productive site'.[1089] In his final article,[1090] he identified this as Sledmere and catalogued 155 of the ostensible 1,000 coins extracted from the site, *Dataset 1* and *Dataset 15, Wic Comparison 2*.[1091] Metcalf's commentary provided a stark contrast to the composition of finds at South Newbald. Sledmere yielded only 17 Northumbrian Series Y *sceattas* (*Figure* 106), but is abundant in Series G and J—together nearly a third of all finds from the site.

However, the earliest specimens are two Merovingian *deniers* (*Figure* 107),[1092] *sceattas* from Series D and the primary phase of Series E. It is plausible that the economic stimulus was provided by incoming traders buying local produce in exchange for their Continental coins. There are seven English primary *sceattas* and an unusual number of exotic species—Æthiliræd, animal mask, *MONITASCORVM*, rosette, *SAROALDO* (*Figure* 108) and nine scarce varieties of ecclesiastical East Anglian Series Q (*Figure* 109). Curiously, there are more of the latter than the trading currency of East Anglia, Series R and secondary Frisian types are few, pointing to a possible redirection of trading relations. See *Graph* 10.2.

Overall this is an unusual assemblage leading Metcalf to speculate that Series J is perhaps the commercial currency of the region whereas Series Y is the regal coinage—just as East Anglian has Series Q and R (the former understood as ecclesiastical, the latter royal/commercial). This represents Sledmere as the commercial centre and South Newbald as regal—a *vicus regius* as is suggested for Rendlesham,[1093] another site with a rich mix of types. As there is no temporal overlap between Series Y and J, Metcalf's speculation is unsafe.

Arguably, the high level of exotic species at Sledmere should be discounted as metal detection was carried out by what Metcalf describes as 'two rough characters (or so they were described at the time; hopefully they have mellowed).'[1094] If the total finds are around one thousand coins, it is not surprising that these valuable 'eclectic' types were made available to collectors who subsequently reported them. There are 24 specimens for Periods N9–10c ranging from Eanred's 'Group A' moneyers to Æthelred II (*Figure* 110), Wigmund and Wulfhere—but no Eanbald II, Redwulf, or Osberht. There is no knowledge of subsequent issues so determining cessation of activity is speculative, but unlikely to be beyond the 860s.

How does Sledmere relate to Fishergate? One has to interpret Sledmere with care as the evidence has been reconstructed and there was no reliable local 'gatekeeper' to enhance the integrity of the data.[1095] However, overall the composition is not dissimilar to Fishergate though the volume of finds is very much greater at Sledmere and may well be indicative of the scale and range of losses that should be expected at a truly industrious site. There is only one specimen (the triquetras type) at Fishergate that could be described as an exotic species—an under-representation of the 'eclectic' types when compared to Sledmere and perhaps a further indication of the impoverished nature of Fishergate.

Cottam[1096]

Two sites, A, south, and B, north, joined by an ancient trackway, have been excavated. These touch the west of the Beverley-Driffield-Scarborough road and are served by dry valleys.[1097] Site A is a ladder settlement possibly for ephemeral grazing. Site B, closer to Cowlam *DMV*, is a Butterwick-type enclosure, seemingly disturbed by the Viking Great Army, with resettlement, as an Anglo-Scandinavian farmstead, a short distance northward.

1086 In compiling his corpus of finds and identifying the 'North of England 'productive site' as Sledmere, Bonser (2011, 159–80) opined that over 1,000 coins have been found and remarks on the surprisingly small proportion of local issues.

1087 http://www.pastscape.org.uk/hob.aspx?hob_id=1039123

1088 http://www.pastscape.org.uk/hob.aspx?hob_id=64700

1089 Bonser (1997, 43–44).

1090 Bonser (2011, 159–80).

1091 Detector information pinpoints the most prolific fields for *sceattas* on the right of Limekiln Hill, B1252, 1.1—1.3 miles south-east of Sledmere House.

1092 Unfortunately, the illustrations in Bonser (2011, 180, pl. 4b) are incorrectly captioned. The catalogue is correct.

1093 Leeds University IMS Open Lecture Series: Professor Christopher Scull, 'Rendlesham Re-Discovered: An East Anglian Royal Centre of the Time of Sutton Hoo', 7 October 2014.

1094 Bonser (2011, 161), implying that there may have been some disinformation. Detecting myth holds 'a silver 'plaque' had been found with an image of Archbishop Wulfhere or Wigmund on it' (*pers comm.* 01/07/15).

1095 Having personally contributed to this collation, I am not confident that the provenances given me by detectorists were reliable.

1096 Richards (1999a, 91, 2001a, 2001b, 2011a, 2013), the early papers pioneered the use of e-media in archaeology.

1097 Richards (1999b, 73, *Fig* 2).

The conclusion of two decade's work at these sites is that Cottam B and Cowlam were contemporaneous and, in the second half of the ninth century, these together with Cottam A were abandoned, around the same time.[1098] The *DMV* at Cottam may then have been set up and an Anglo-Scandinavian farmstead survived at Cottam B, for a further generation or two, on the trackway 100 metres to the north.

The Cowlam settlement migrated west along the trackway, where it developed, possibly under a new lord. This contrasts with, and may be a consequence of, the failing Cottam B.

Excavations at Little Westfield Farm of the continuation of the trackway 3 km south-east of Cottam B, showed the bulk of the pottery fill to be Anglo-Scandinavian Torksey ware in relatively good condition, and hence thought to have been recent and local, implying nearby Anglo-Scandinavian occupation activity.[1099]

Richards concluded that in early Anglo-Saxon times the Wolds were sparsely populated providing upland grazing for lowland settlements. Permanent settlements were established often as Butterwick-type enclosures, serving as 'sheep stations, hunting lodges, craft-working centres and foci for administration, and some developed as periodic market centres.'[1100]

Richards suggested that an élite, at the *villa regalis* of Driffield, controlled the distribution of prestige items. Settlements were dependencies of such estate centres, and may have developed specialisms. Scandinavian settlement disrupted land holding so that settlements became nucleated villages under new local lords, separated from their former estate centres.[1101]

Two stages are recognised in both the Anglian and Viking activity.[1102] The former identified, for the first time in England, the transition from eighth/ninth-century estate centre to a ninth-century market. It suggests that such sites may have acquired market functions during the ninth century. The Viking phase exhibits the critical evolution from raiding to settlement, the first such identification for a rural site, marking a significant development in land ownership.[1103]

In common with Ryther, Cottam shows what can be achieved by a dedicated detectorist working closely with a supportive archaeological professional in terms of demonstrating monetization.[1104] Over 80 coins of the period have been unearthed,[1105] including five *sceattas*—all Series Y representing Eadberht (*Figure* 111), Ælfwald, Æthelred I (second reign) and Æthelred I with Eanbald I—and one broad penny.[1106]

Eanred's silver-alloy coins are well represented, but the vast majority of finds are base *sceattas*, whose well-worn appearance is a sign of a healthy velocity of circulation (*Figure* 112). A *sceat* of Eadberht, is pecked, a rare phenomenon for *sceattas* and likely to be a Viking test-mark.[1107] See *Graph* 10.6.

The penny in *Figure* 113 was found in the pit at Cottam 'B' with the jaw-less female skull,[1108] probably a valediction by invading Vikings rather than indicative of economic continuity or a votive rite.

Cowlam[1109]

This site, at Cowlam Well near the *DMV*, to the north-east of Cottam, is close to the junction of the Driffield–West Heslerton track and Roman High Street, from Sledmere to Langtoft (joining the Driffield–Scarborough road), along which there are ancient burial mounds.

The four *sceattas* and 14 *stycas* recorded on the database held by ADS have been augmented by recent detector finds some of which are recorded on PAS.[1110] This assemblage includes three Series J *sceattas* (two of which are pristine) two secondary Series E[1111] and the now customary single specimen of Series Q (*Figure* 114) whose close affinities with the Series Y fantastic animal and rich iconography shows its propaganda rôle to be at least as important as the economic. There is one exotic species—a scarce runic bust/annulet cross type (*SL*14–20) and only one Northumbrian *sceat*, of Eadberht. This contrast with Cottam, which is graced with only Northumbrian *sceattas*, may not be of consequence in such a small sample but could be construed as reflecting a difference in site function.

There are three silver-alloy coins of Eanred (but no Eanbald II) and the base *stycas* include all the issuers of these. See *Graph* 10.5.

Burdale

Burdale is situated south of Wharram Percy, between two tributaries of the dry valley running from Thixendale to Fimber. We are, to too great an extent, reliant on what

1098 Richards and others (2013, 264–65).
1099 Hopkinson (2008).
1100 Richards and others (2013, 265).
1101 Richards and others (2013, 265).
1102 Haldenby and Richards (2016).
1103 Haldenby and Richards (2010 and 2016).
1104 In this case Dave Haldenby. Most detectorists are diligent; few are so meticulous in their reporting.
1105 From 20–30 centimetres of plough-soil.
1106 There is some confusion in the database as *EMC* lists Cowlam under Cottam. This possibly emanates from Pirie.
1107 Haldenby and Richards (2016, 10). Richards (2011b, 2013)
1108 See comments on a similar penny, found at Fishergate (99).
1109 See http://archaeologydataservice.ac.uk/archives/view/cowlam_york_2011/ Richards (2011, doi:10.5284/1000175, with coins catalogued by James Booth).
1110 Dave Haldenby (14 specimens) and Dave Hirst (7). *AJ* (**170**, 201–71).
1111 One of which was found at the DMV, *pers. comm.* Dave Haldenby, 19th March 2015.

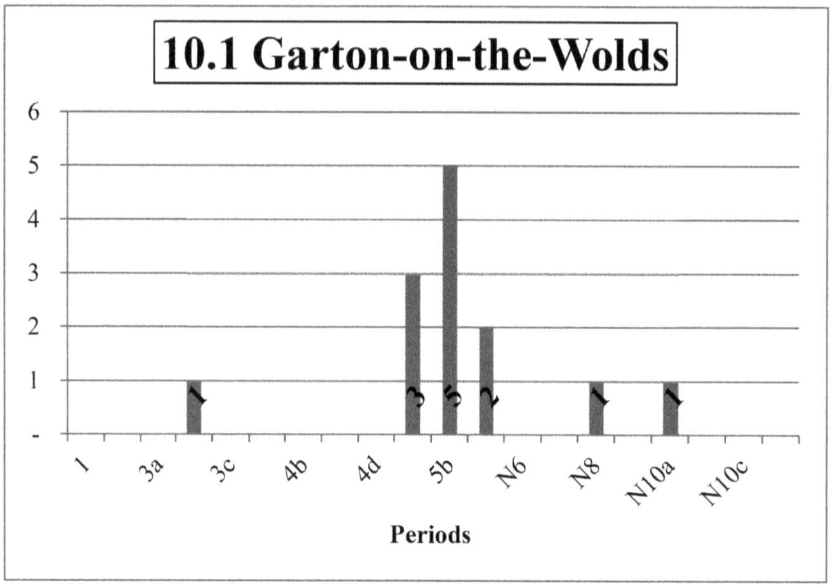
10.1 Garton-on-the-Wolds
6
5
4
3
2
1
-
1
3a
3c
4b
4d
5b
N6
N8
N10a
N10c
Periods
1
3
5
2
1
1

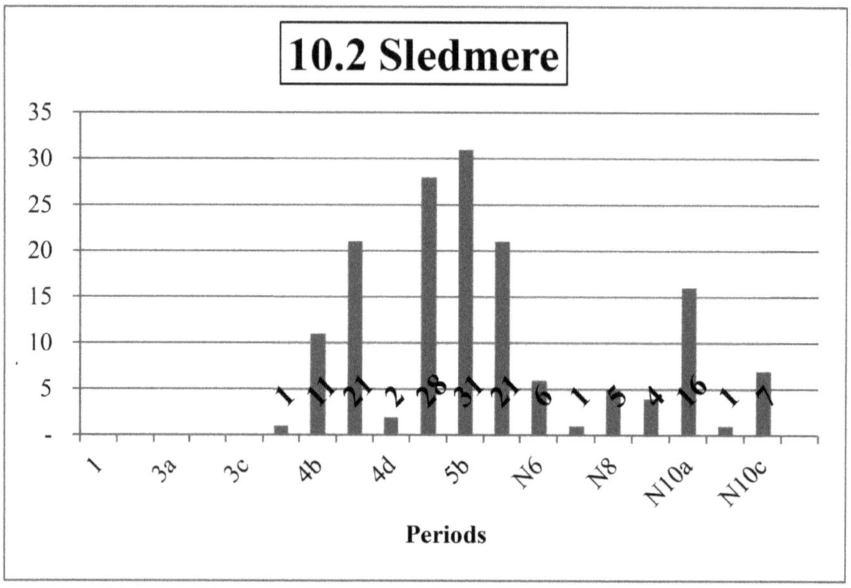
10.2 Sledmere
35
30
25
20
15
10
5
-
1
3a
3c
4b
4d
5b
N6
N8
N10a
N10c
Periods
1
11
21
2
28
31
21
6
1
5
4
16
1
7

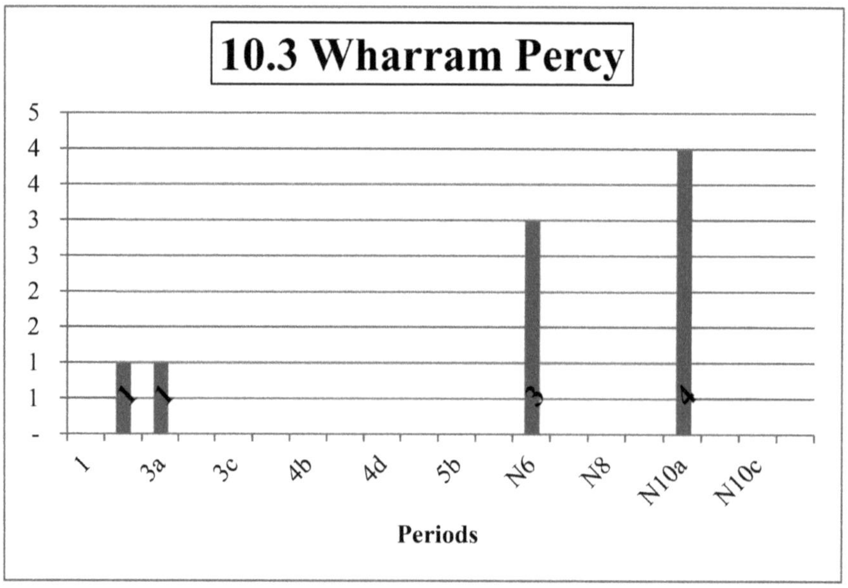
10.3 Wharram Percy
5
4
4
3
3
2
2
1
1
-
1
3a
3c
4b
4d
5b
N6
N8
N10a
N10c
Periods
1
1
3
4

Graphs 10

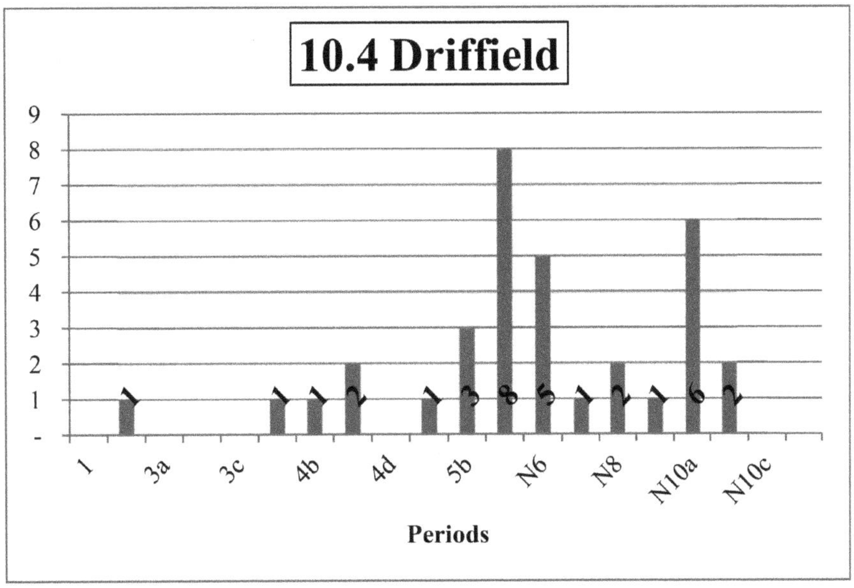

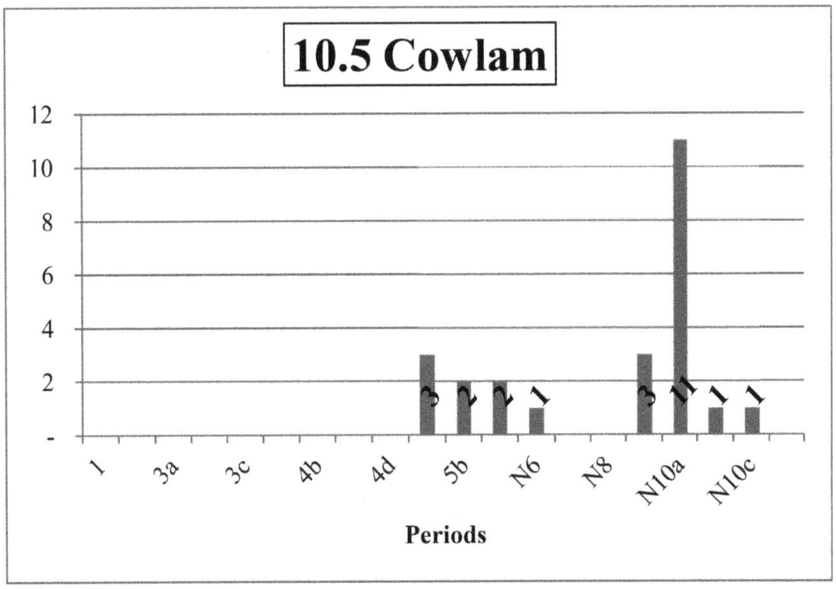

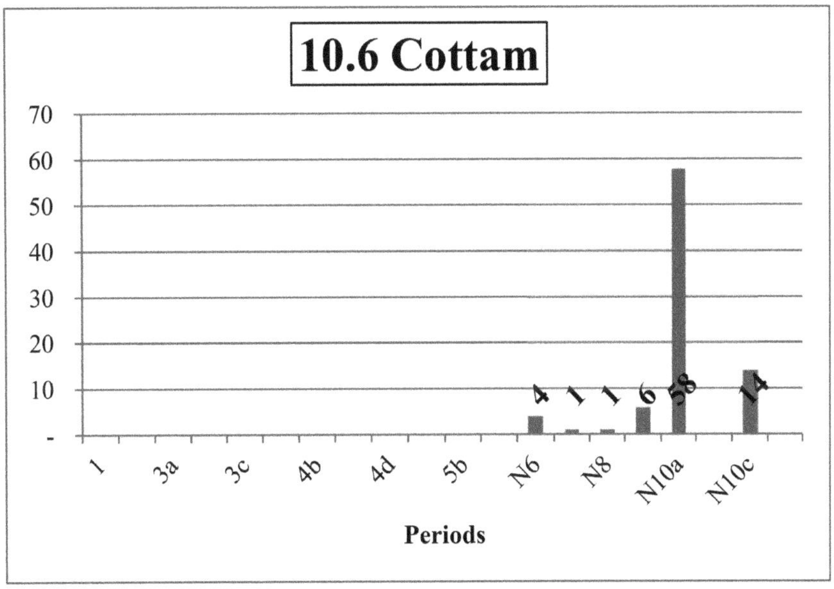

Graphs 10: Site finds by period arranged regionally by weighted average of peak activity, Wolds Central. Sources: *Datasets 1* and *8*. Numerical axis varies.

can be reconstructed of a rich site, after the depredations of illicit detecting activity over many years: most of the metal detecting has been illegal 'night-hawking', focussed on the eastern end of the valley away from Burdale House Farm. It is alleged,[1112] that 'this has produced material from the 1st century AD to the 8th century AD, including large numbers of Anglo-Saxon silver *sceattas*, a dispersed *styca* hoard, and Anglo-Saxon gold coins.'[1113] This loss to the formal record has been exacerbated by surreptitious disposal so that there is little informal data to be farmed. As regards the alleged gold coins: 'The illegal detecting was carried out by knowledgeable and proficient people…in the recent past something of significant importance has been unearthed.'[1114]

Anglian occupation seems to have commenced in the early eighth century before abandonment in the ninth. A worn Continental Primary phase *sceat* of Series D, type 2c, *c.* 700–15 is accompanied by a Stepped Cross (Primary Series E-related, *SL*91) in good condition to give an indicative start date of *c.* 710–20 (*Figure* 115), while a corroded, rather than worn, *styca* of Æthelred II is not *c.* 841–44 as reported, but by the restoration moneyer Eardwulf extending the likely dating up to *c.* 850. A fragmentary dirham (BUR07: sf27) from hacksilver signals Anglo-Scandinavian activity.[1115]

In common with other northern sites, the ceramic assemblage is modest but, here, the animal bone accumulation is considerable. Re-cut enclosures, including some of 'Butterwick-type', and *Grubenhäuser*,[1116] focussed in two groups, provide evidence of organised space and production, including metalworking with lead evident as at 'Site B' near Pocklington.

Anglian period finds include combs, tweezers, copper-alloy brooches and pins, and a range of craft-working knives. Ashby reported on the worked bone and antler, including 26 single- and double-sided composite combs, some of high quality.[1117] A bell and pins, similar to Coppergate finds from *c.* 930/5–*c.* 975, extend activity into the Anglo-Scandinavian period but changes in land-ownership with Scandinavian settlement may have disrupted what seems to be a close relationship with Wharram Percy, although Richards regarded Burdale as richer, based on quality of knife production.[1118]

Associating the high quality of both combs and knives, and the putative gold and silver coin finds and dispersed *styca* hoard, there is an implication that Burdale may have been higher in status than Wharram Percy in the Anglo-Saxon period; indeed, Burdale rather than Wharram Percy, could have been the main economic and trading centre in the estate.

Wharram Percy

This most famous of English *DMVs*[1119] was first surveyed by Captain Bayly of the Ordnance Survey in 1851 but its origins were identified by Maurice Beresford in 1948.[1120] He and John Hurst subsequently directed annual excavations of the site with its rectilinear 'tofts' and 'crofts'[1121] and surrounding furrows,[1122] which eventually stretched over four decades and formed an early attempt at an holistic approach to interpreting changes in the landscape from the scatter of pre-historic material, through the more substantial Iron Age and Romano-British workings to the early and late medieval settlement. The site is central to the north-east Wolds complex of Neolithic linear earthworks and trackside barrows and sits on a major north-south route.[1123]

One focus of Anglian activity, Area 10, enclosing Toft 10, provides evidence including pottery, bone, slag, timber structures and a single *sceat.*[1124] Black earth with unabraded sherds signifies a grassed area or orchard behind the toft.[1125] A smithy was located in the South Manor Area.[1126] While this is an intensively investigated site, with clear Anglian features (such as two *Grubenhäuser*[1127]), only 4 per cent of the total area has been excavated, and metal detection was not used during the excavation. The two *tremisses* (*Figure* 116) are taken to be metal-detected finds after archaeological investigations ceased and are presumed to be from outside the core area as the use of detectors is illegal within the scheduled area. In the absence of much early Anglo-Saxon material, the *Victory* type could be diagnostic in dating economic activity and identifying trading relationships. The pale-gold National Series *tremisses* shows that activity and contacts continued into the second half of the seventh century. However, it would be reasonable to expect such a site to be rich in *sceattas* and *stycas*. That the formal record amounts merely to three *sceattas* of Eadberht[1128] and four brass

[1112] Mark Ainsley *pers. comm.* 20 March 2007.
[1113] See http://archaeologydataservice.ac.uk/archives/view/burdale_york_2013/index.cfm
[1114] DOI Metal Detector Survey, by G. Bambrook, *Historia Detectum*, 2005 in Julian D Richards, Steve Roskams (2013) *Burdale: an Anglian settlement in the Yorkshire Wolds* [data-set]. York: Archaeology Data Service [distributor] (doi:10.5284/1021545).
[1115] http://intarch.ac.uk/journal/issue35/richards-roskams.html, Dating and Discussion.
[1116] Wrathmell (2012, 106, 164–68 and 178).
[1117] Ashby (2013).
[1118] Wrathmell (2012, 178).
[1119] Identified by 'suspiciously isolated or ruined churches as well as civil parishes (townships) without villages'. Beresford and Hurst (1990, 19).
[1120] Beresford (1954, 70–74).
[1121] Not the ladder pattern seen at West Heslerton.
[1122] Banham and Faith (2014, 131 and 287–88) suggested that ploughing here was a precedent for the open-field landscape of the Wolds.
[1123] Beresford and Hurst (1990, *figure* 63).
[1124] Beresford and Hurst (1990, *figure* 54).
[1125] Beresford and Hurst (1990, 77).
[1126] Wrathmell (2012, 154–62).
[1127] See Everson and Stoker (Wrathmell 2012, 164–68) for a discussion of *Grubenhäuser* and Butterwick-type features in the context of sheep rearing in the Wolds.
[1128] Wrathmell (2012, 143 and 147–48) noted a Series E sceat from the South Manor area.

stycas seems anomalous—especially when few northern sites can boast two early gold coins.[1129] The subsequent numismatic evidence (*Dataset 17, Site Finds by Issuer*) contributes little to the hypothesis of mid to late seventh-century resettlement.[1130]

There is a small number of Merovingian artefacts on the site, possibly contemporary with these *tremisses* and therefore suggesting direct trading links.[1131]

Of the Eadberht fantastic animal *sceattas*, one was found in disturbed graveyard soil, north of the north-east chapel, and another was found, with sherds of Tating ware,[1132] in the fill in the northern *Grubenhäuser*, with a triangular-backed comb of antler.[1133]

One of the two Forthred *stycas* comes from House 6,[1134] the Wigmund *styca* from the floor of the chancel and the Æthelred *styca* from fill of the 'charcoal' burial, south of the present chancel.[1135]

The sixth- and seventh-century gold coins, which display a reduction in precious metal content, and these few eighth-century silver and ninth-century base finds, mainly from around the church,[1136] could all be dismissed as stray trackway losses.[1137] Alternatively, the half dozen find-spots may be scattered farms or the site could be a 'small family monastic site'.[1138] Little weight is given to Everson and Stoker's view of Wharram at this time as a 'sheep-station and seasonal market'[1139] either by the modest numismatic assemblage, nor by Richardson's faunal analysis, which tempered the predominance of sheep with the 'broad, multi-faceted economy.[1140] The only coherent story told is monetary—the gradual reduction in denominational value over the centuries. Given the volume of nearby accumulations, the lack of coinage is not attributable to distance from the coast or York.[1141] Richards explained the contrast with the seemingly richer Burdale in terms of these adjacent locations falling under the same management as part of a 'multiple estate', where settlements would have complementary roles.[1142]

[1129] See *Graph* 10.3.
[1130] Wrathmell (2012, 99).
[1131] Wrathmell (2012, 147).
[1132] Which has ecclesiastical associations, Wrathmell (2012, 169).
[1133] Hurst (1979, 128–29, by A. McGregor). Beresford and Hurst (1990, *figure* 61, 83). Wrathmell (2012, 120, 139–62).
[1134] Directly uphill from the church. The cross fragment was also found here, perhaps indicating the site of an Anglian church, Beresford and Hurst (1990, 83 and *Fig* 62), Richards (1992, 93–94 and 2000, 200), Wrathmell (2012, 151).
[1135] Wrathmell (2012, 146).
[1136] Beresford and Hurst (1990, 73, illustration 54)
[1137] The terrace seems unused in the Anglo-Saxon period, Beresford and Hurst (1990, 82).
[1138] Beresford and Hurst (1990, 84).
[1139] Wrathmell (2012, 172).
[1140] Wrathmell (2012, 178)
[1141] Naylor (2004, 51).
[1142] Wrathmell (2012, 178).

Driffield

Driffield nestles in the crook of the Wolds at the junction of the Hull–Scarborough and York–Bridlington roads, on land well-served by natural springs, many of which arise around the *DMV* of Elmswell, near Little Driffield. There are Neolithic, Bronze Age and Roman remains. Possible Anglo-Saxon inhumations were found in 1820 and 1876, and a cemetery in 1882.[1143] King Aldfrith's memorial lies in St Mary's church in the south of Little Driffield.[1144]

Lovelock based Driffield's wealth on fertile land around the headwaters of the River Hull together with a local source of iron ore at Elmswell, with grave-goods providing evidence.[1145]

He cautioned that the medieval settlement of Driffield should not be equated too readily with the vill and estate visited by Northumbrian royalty. Far from such occasional visits implying that this was merely a periodic royal centre, Driffield was a permanent centre administered by a reeve.[1146]

Given the frequency with which detectorists attribute finds to the Driffield area, it is surprising that fewer than three dozen are recorded in *Dataset 1, Summary*. Presumably, the royal site is under the present town. Given the quality of high-status finds from Garton, there seems to be a clear connection.

The Lombardic *tremissis*, converted for secondary use (*Figure* 1),[1147], is a near Driffield find. This élite decorative piece marks the site as of high status.

Four primary period *sceattas* are recorded from this site, including, appropriately, one of Aldfrith (*Figure* 118) who died here, and two from the Low Countries. If genuine, the Series Z facing bust is of exceptional quality (*Figure* 119). Based on this specimen, the reverse should be interpreted not as a hound but as a foraging, long-snouted, curly-tailed wild boar, a feast animal held in some esteem in both Roman and Germanic cultures.[1148]

A specimen of the wide-spread Series G heads the secondary phase *sceattas*. There are seven secondary Series E *sceattas* such that the Continental proportion is high. A Series J coin is marked it out as imitative by the mirror-image reverse, though two others in crisp condition are reported (*Figure* 119). Southern *sceattas* show a good mix of Series K, N, Q and U; the last is in good condition, and of unusual style (*Figure* 122).

The Series Q *sceat*, found at Driffield (*Figure* 122), dates from the second quarter of the eighth century and

[1143] Mortimer and Sheppard (1905, 293–94).
[1144] http://www.pastscape.org.uk/hob.aspx?hob_id=79289
[1145] Lovelock (1996, 45).
[1146] Lovelock (1996, 43).
[1147] Courtesy of James Booth, *SCBI*69, 1074.
[1148] Smith, C. N. J. (2006, 108).

has much in common with contemporary, Northumbrian 'fantastic animal' types of Eadberht. The occurrence of single specimens of this series on northern sites as been noted previously. The bracteates from Kelleythorpe-Driffield and Hornsea illustrated design influences later reflected on coins. The presence of bracteates may provide evidence for élite sites whose high-status inhabitants were part of an international trade network sharing ideas and iconography.[1149]

The Northumbrian *sceattas* attributed to Driffield are quite exceptional in their rarity though small in number. Fantastic animal types of Eadberht, Alchred, Æthelred I and Ælfwald I are accompanied by three inscriptional coins of the highest rarity: a joint issue of Æthelwald Moll with Archbishop Ecgberht and no less than two specimens, of the nine known,[1150] of Eardwulf's *sceat* by Cuthheard (*Figure* 123).

This remarkable continuity is enhanced by a silver-alloy emission of Eanred by Cynewulf. There are no coins of Eanbald II but brass *stycas* are present for Æthelred II (*Figure* 124) and Wigmund and bronze coins, of Osberht and Wulfhere. However, finds are numerically far higher in the eighth than ninth centuries, *Dataset 1*, *Summary*, which contrasts with Bamburgh's absence of pre-ninth century coinage though a shift of the royal power base is unlikely.

Cessation of coinage activity, at least temporarily,[1151] has been marked at several other sites by the presence of a southern penny very plausibly lost by Viking visitors around the time of the fall of York. Here, a penny of Eadmund of East Anglia (855–69) is in that putative category.

Despite the lack of volume—and one senses this is the tastiest tip of the iceberg—'Driffield' presents a near full run of Northumbrian issuers supported by a good selection of southern and Continental specimens. The spread is wider than other Wolds sites including Sledmere, *Graph 10*. With all the caveats and constraints on interpretation, that this location is so rich in rare coinage, implies that Driffield was a site of special, not merely economic, significance, as would be expected for the final resting place of Aldfrith.

Garton-on-the-Wolds

This site is known for the relative wealth of inhumations with grave goods especially the high proportion of iron artefacts. Loveluck attributed this to the proximity of iron ore at Elmswell and the fertile local soils.[1152]

Garton has a high proportion of exotic species among the relatively few coin finds. Rigold reported as his Hoard VIII, *sceattas* of Series J (four), G (two), K/serpent (*SL*39–10), and an annulet cross type (*SL*14–10, *Figure* 125) similar to that found at 'Site C' near Wetherby.[1153]

Other local finds include a fine, well-centre, York gold shilling with a full if tantalising, *nomina sacra*, reverse inscription,[1154] a rare *sceat* of Eadberht with a swastika below the animal, a *sceat* of Æthelred I's restoration by Ceolbald and very rare *SEDE sceat* with its radiant, protective, serpent adding to the sense of a high-status location (*Figure* 127). Another singleton Q is present (*Figure* 128). This rich mix of finds for the seventh and eighth centuries suggests a location better characterized as high status than economically dynamic. See *Graph* 10.1.

Wetwang

Earthworks here form part of the Wold Entrenchment.[1155] This is also the site of a rock-cut cross below what is thought to be an Anglo-Saxon moot hill.[1156] Due to nighthawking, there are many more finds here, especially in 'Monument Field', than have been officially recorded. Illustrated at *Figure* 129 are some scarce types and one can assume that the detecting biases and deceptions described for Sledmere also relate to Wetwang.

Small Sites

In addition to the more productive sites there are again a significant number of sites yielding small numbers of silver and base coins. Duggelby, the Luttons, and Weaverthorpe are on the Gypsey Race before it runs eastward, through Burton Fleming and Rudston, reaching the sea at Bridlington. *Dataset 17, Small Finds ii) central* lists the small finds for the central Wolds.

I have tested, among informal sources, the rumour that the absence of Butterwick from the formal record is due to night-hawking. It is reported that *sceattas* of the Wodan type along with many Series Y coins of Eadberht and Æthelred I fantastic animal and rare named-moneyer types have been found (*Figure* 130).

7.3.2.2 Numismatic Summary—Wolds Central

While the central Wolds are graced with several highly important sites, my suspicion is that attributions to Weaverthorpe, Wetwang and Driffield, disguises numerous illicit finds from Sledmere. This contrasts with

[1149] Behr, Pestell and Hines (2014, 68). Hines (1997, 392–93).

[1150] As at April 2018.

[1151] Three Norman pennies, a cut-half and -quarter have been found at Driffield.

[1152] Loveluck (1996, 39–42) contrasted Garton with Kelleythorpe, also wealthy in base metals but not expressed in luxury, imported grave-goods. He attributed this to cultural differences. See also Loveluck (1996). 'Garton Station', *CA,* 9 (1987, 234–37).

[1153] Rigold (1960, 49 and pl. 4). Rigold and Metcalf (1984, 252).

[1154] Tentatively read by Mary Garrison (pers. comm.) as *Sancte via deus Eoforwic*, Holy God the way, reinforcing the ecclesiastical origins. Loveluck (2003, 168) took these to be 'manifestations of royal influence'.

[1155] http://pastscape.org.uk/hob.aspx?hob_id=61585

[1156] http://pastscape.org.uk/hob.aspx?hob_id=64545

the scrupulous treatment at Cottam and Cowlam. Despite these distortions, Sledmere with its substantial volume and rich mix, which vary over time but favour Series G and J, *Dataset 17*, dominates and demonstrates the economic vibrancy of the central Wolds. *Dataset 1*, shows the strength of imported coinage particularly in the Primary early-penny phase.

Graph 10 illustrates the chronological dispersal of finds at the main sites. Sledmere and Driffield display the greatest continuity but the former peaks earlier.

7.3.2.3 The Artefactual Dataset—Wolds Central

Of the artefacts in the dataset for the central Wolds, *Dataset 5*, 64.0 per cent emanate from Cottam and 31.3 per cent from Wharram Percy, with the other 10 locations contributing 32 recorded finds. All locations but Acklam (one brooch, one ingot), Birdsall (one book fitting) and Tibthorpe (one unidentified object) appear in the numismatic dataset—there are 17 coin find-spots in all. However, these statistics are unreliable as the artefactually underrepresented locations include Garton-on-the-Wolds, Wetwang and Sledmere all of which are known to be object-rich. Indeed, the last two are also grossly underrepresented on the numismatic dataset to which Haldenby has contributed conscientiously for Cottam and Cowlam. The latter distorts the object fingerprint, of 55 artefact types, such that pins and strap-ends are far more common than normal, whereas brooches, buckles, mounts and sleeve clasps are far fewer. Conceivably dress fashions or availability varied locally. *Dataset 17, Categories* shows that the central Wolds favour pins and strap-ends but not quite as much as the west and there are fewer brooches and buckles.

Weights are somewhat more common than the norm at Cottam, which may be indicative of a trading focus, the *micel here* period or detecting bias, but there is a near absence of domestic and industrial materials in the central Wolds. Local detectorists report of finds of four styli 'within ten miles of Driffield' (Elmswell?)

Despite the above caveats, the analysis is more significant than merely revealing varying fashions in dress accessories. At 75 per cent, *Dataset 3, Findspots, co-occurrence* for the central Wolds shows a convincing level of monetization. Moreover, Sledmere is shown to be a major centre of economic activity, Garton-in-the-Wolds and Driffield yield numismatically rich material showing their rôles to be socio-political more than economic, whereas Cottam demonstrates that coinage was used routinely in the ninth century. Were the diligence shown at the last location applied elsewhere, there would be little doubt that monetization would be proved to be ubiquitous in the Wolds in the ninth century.

7.3.2.4 Illustrations—The Yorkshire Wolds Central

Figure 107: Worn Merovingian *denier* from Sledmere.

Figure 108: Exotic species from Sledmere. Animal mask type (*SL*112–50); rosette type 68 (*SL*32–30); *SAROALDO* type 11 (*SL*7–40).

Figure 109: Sledmere, East Anglian Series Q, type 98 (*SL*63–90).

Figure 110: Eanred's Group A *stycas* from Sledmere. L: Moneyer Cunewulf; R: Moneyer Wulfheard.

Figure 111: Cottam: extremely rare *sceat* of Eadberht. (Courtesy David Haldenby)

Figure 112: Cottam: L: silver-alloy coin of Eanred R: *styca* of Æthelred II, 2nd reign. (Courtesy David Haldenby and Hull and East Riding Museum)

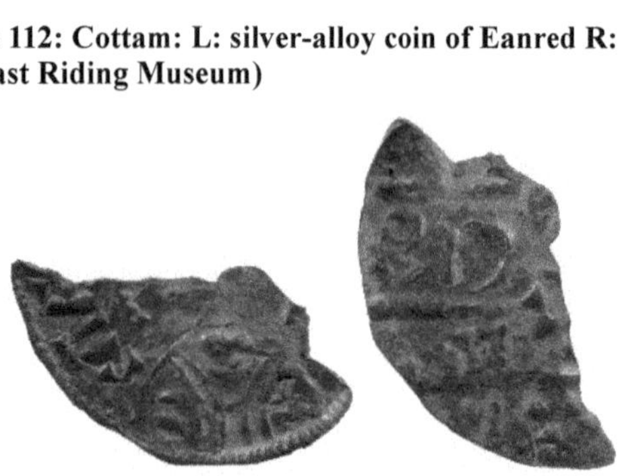

Figure 113: A penny of Æthelberht of Wessex (860–65), by the moneyer Wulfheard. (©Hull and East Riding Museum)

Figure 114: Cowlam: Series Q. (Courtesy Portable Antiquities Scheme)[1157]

[1157] PAS FAKL-166CD8), SL 64–110.

Figure 115: Burdale: Primary Continental *sceattas*, Series D, 2c and Stepped Cross. (Courtesy Archaeology Data Service)[1158]

Figure 116: Merovingian *tremisses* from Wharram Percy. L: Pseudo-Imperial *Victory* type, *c.* 650–80 (Belfort 5393var, Prou 17var). (Courtesy *EMC*)[1159] **R: National Series, Sacierge-Saint-Martin (Indre). Crude bust/cross pattée in circle, legend.**[1160]

Figure 117: Wharram Percy *Grubenhäuser* find: Eadberht *sceat* (*SL*70–150). (Courtesy Pirie archive)

Figure 118: *Sceat* of Aldfrith. Found Driffield (*EMC* 2006.0119). (Courtesy *EMC*)

Figure 119: 'Driffield', Series J, type 85. (Courtesy Alan Hunt)

Figure 120: Driffield: Series Z (*SL*102–20).

Figure 121: Series U. Found Driffield.

[1158] BUR07. Finds photos in Julian D Richards, Steve Roskams (2013) Burdale: an Anglian settlement in the Yorkshire Wolds [data-set]. York: Archaeology Data Service [distributor] https://doi.org/10.5284/1021543

[1159] *EMC* 2010.0172.

[1160] *EMC* 2010.0006. CR 2010, 49. *SCBI*69, 1087, *cf.* Belfort 1397-8 (obv.); Prou 1684 (obv.).

Figure 122: East Anglian, Series Q1H. Found Driffield.

Figure 123: Some rare finds attributed to Driffield. L: joint issue of Æthelwald Moll with Archbishop Ecgberht. R: of Eardwulf's *sceat* by Cuthheard.

Figure 124: *Styca* of Æthelred II by Vendelberht. Found Driffield.

Figure 125: Rigold: Garton-on-the-Wolds grave find. (Courtesy British Numismatic Society)

Figure 126: Garton-on-the-Wolds, Green Lane Crossing, pendant grave find. (Courtesy Chris Loveluck and Hull City Museums)[1161]

[1161] Loveluck (1996, plate 4). A gold, shell and garnet bulla pendant from Grave 7 at Garton 'Green Lane Crossing' originally described by Mortimer in his 1905 publication, now often referred to as Garton 2.

Figure 127: Garton-on-the-Wolds: some exotic species.

Figure 128: Series Q-related *sceat*. *EMC* 2003.0153 (*cf.* *SL*67–20). (Courtesy *EMC*)

Figure 129: Some scarce *sceattas* attributed to Wetwang.

Figure 130: Butterwick. L to R: Eadberht, fantastic animal *sceat*; *stycas* of Eanred by Wilheah and Redwulf by Coenred.

7.3.3 Wolds East

7.3.3.1 Wolds East

Kilham

This has been an active location from earliest times. It lies on the Roman Road from York to Bridlington in the Yorkshire Wolds, at the confluence of Old Gypsey and Beck Head, six miles north-east of Driffield. An inhumation cemetery possibly dates from the fifth century and was first excavated in 1814, then in 1953.[1162] Another may be later;[1163] there is also an Anglo-Saxon interment of a child with grave goods.[1164] Metal detection finds of *sceattas*

[1162] http://pastscape.org.uk/hob.aspx?hob_id=79461
[1163] http://pastscape.org.uk/hob.aspx?hob_id=910604
[1164] http://pastscape.org.uk/hob.aspx?hob_id=910830

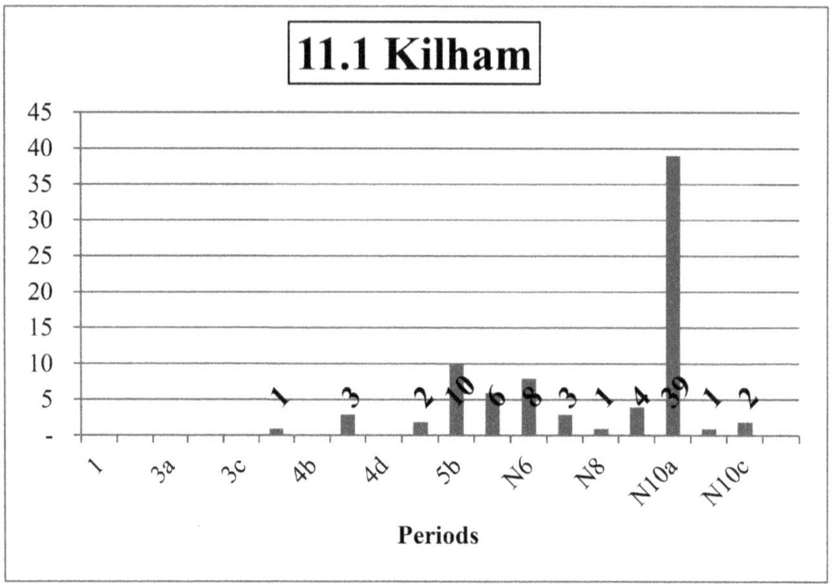

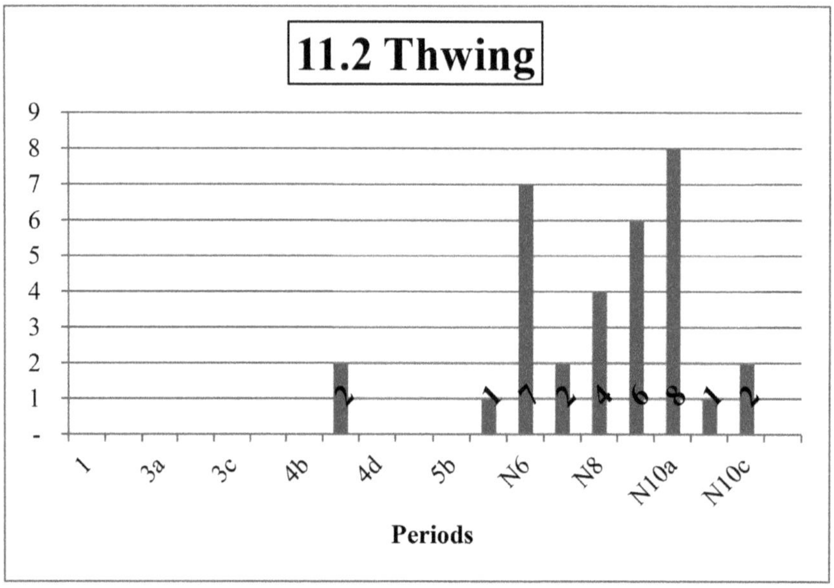

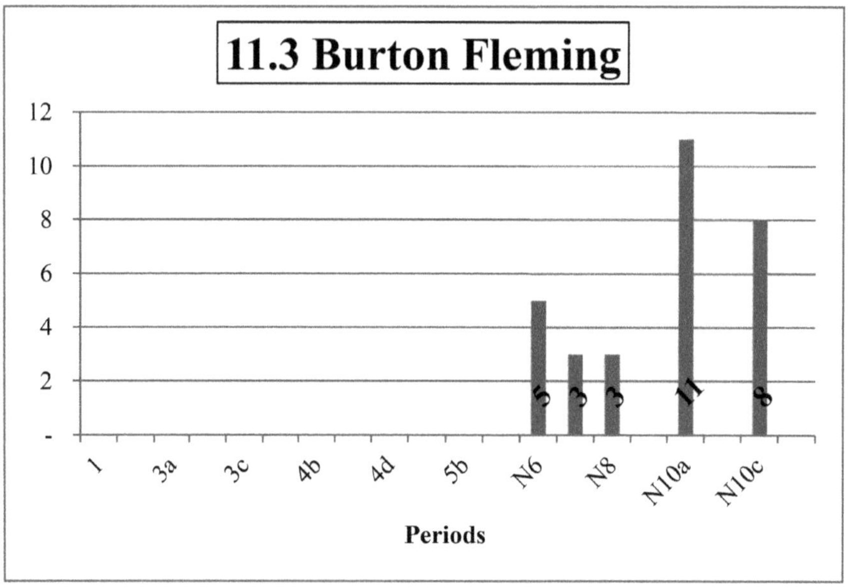

Graphs 11: Site finds by period arranged regionally by weighted average of peak activity, Wolds East. Sources: *Datasets 1* and *8*. Numerical axis varies.

and *stycas* surfaced in the 1990s. Trenching undertaken by YAT in September 2000 at Lowthorpe Beck, revealed settlement topography on gravelly chalk with a likely water source. A large animal bone assemblage seemed to have been deposited over a long period, but there are few artefactual finds.[1165]

However, the range and duration of the metal-detected coin finds indicate that this was a settlement of some importance. The data has been gathered from three sources—PAS entries by FLOs, *EMC* and informal input from a productive detectorist.[1166]

The earliest *sceattas* the site has yielded are a *sceat* of Aldfrith (*Figure* 131) and two primary phase Series E varieties probably dating to the late seventh century. The fine condition of the last two plausibly implies direct trade with the Low Countries. There is also a specimen of the ubiquitous Series G.

Of the secondary *sceattas*, two Series J varieties are worn. The other Southumbrian *sceattas*] show a pleasing diversity of types with representatives of Series K, N (two), O, U (two) and the accustomed solitary Q, implying broad trade with south-eastern, eastern and middle England. Continued healthy Continental export is indicated by the presence of four secondary *sceattas* from the Low Countries and one each from Ribe and, tentatively, Quentovic. A 'saltire' type takes activity to the end of the Southumbrian early-penny era and the presence of an exotic species, 'fleeing biped', confirms the legitimacy of this late, rare derivative variety.[1167]

Of the 34 *sceattas* reported, 13 are Northumbrian. The eight *sceattas* of Eadberht include one joint issue and both the early and late Booth Classes, but not the rarer Classes C, D or E. There are two more joint issues: one Æthelred I with Eanbald I and the other the second-known specimen of the patrician Æthelwald Moll with his heir apparent Æthelred (*Figure* 132).

While avoiding over-interpretation of the loss of such a rare coin, a plausible context would not diminish the dynastic propaganda heralded by the inscription. Its deployment in Kilham signifies a strategic political influence locally. This is corroborated by the volume of finds in this location—matching the total for the 26 inner York sites combined and exceeding the produce of Whithorn, Carlisle and Flixborough.

A scarce fantastic beast *sceat* of Alchred is present and an inscriptional coin of Æthelred I by Ceolbald taking the northern early-penny coverage into the 790s.

Continuity of activity, as best as it can be viewed through the prism of coinage, is demonstrated by the presence of four silver-alloy coins of Eanred. Save detecting bias, the pattern for brass *sceattas* differs from that seen elsewhere in that only two of the 42 finds are irregular, though even in these cases, 'illegible' would be a better description. Possibly, Kilham was more diligent in weeding out irregular *stycas*. The regular *stycas* include: Eanred (twelve), Æthelred 1st reign (fourteen), Redwulf (one), Æthelred II, 2nd reign (seven), Wigmund (five) and there is a solitary entry for Wulfhere. Osberht is absent, a pattern that is seen elsewhere. It is less likely that coin handlers would be sufficiently discerning to reject blundered, bronze *stycas* than there being a politico-economic cause for a lapse preceding the Viking invasion. See *Graph* 11.1.

Continued coin exchange is evidenced by two *deniers*—of Louis the Pious (814–40) and Charles the Bald (840–77) from Troyes.[1168] Again, the occurrence of two Carolingian coins at Kilham signifies its importance, duration and reach, despite the absence of southern pennies.

The contemporary artefactual finds have been of high status items (*Figure* 133). It is feasible that Kilham was something more than a place of refuge and sustenance between York (35 miles west) and Bridlington (10 miles east), though it is on no clear north-south route and has no obvious geographical advantages. Hopefully, this somewhat enigmatic site will be resolved by further finds.

Thwing (Paddock Hill)

Thwing rests between Bridlington (9m E) and Sledmere (9m W) in the eastern Wolds, overlooking the Great Wold Valley, four miles north of Kilham, and may have been a strategic location even though there is little to distinguish its location on current maps. The 120-metre diameter Bronze Age ringwork, which contains 132 tightly packed inhumations, many of high status, and was still in use to the early or mid-ninth century.[1169] There is evidence of timber structures, a palisaded enclosure, and a large *Grübenhaus*. Debris, dating up to the tenth century, included metalwork, animal bone, lava quernstone fragments, pottery (some Continental) as well as the coinage described below.[1170] Manby interpreted the site as an administration centre, possibly royal.

There are two well-circulated primary *sceattas* including a Series F now thought by Metcalf to be the emission

[1165] Two Constantinian *nummi* were found.

[1166] *Pers. comm.* Ian Bayles, 19th June 2010. The PAS entries are characteristically inaccurate. The bronze *styca* of Wulfhere is listed only in Pirie (2000, 129). Detectorist Stephen Reynolds is named in the YAT report as active in the 1990s.

[1167] *SL* 107–10. *cf.* Rendleham *EMC* 2011-0141. In November 2015, a mule of an early Series R obverse with *VICO* reverse (*SL* 12–10, second known) surfaced.

[1168] Pirie (2000, Appendix A 22–23).

[1169] http://www.pastscape.org.uk/hob.aspx?hob_id=79885

[1170] Manby (1985). Hall (2003, 176–77). Naylor (2004, 32).

of Theodore of Canterbury (d. 690) and his successor Berhtwald,[1171] and a Series D from the Low Countries. The only other Continental import is a well-preserved secondary Series E. There are 13 Northumbrian *sceattas* including fantastic animal reverses (six of Eadberht and an Alchred) two joint issues and four inscribed types covering Ælfwald I (by Cuthheard), Æthelred I (by Tidwulf and Cuthgils) and, exceptionally, Eardwulf (again by Cuthheard); this last being one of only nine known for this king (*Figure* 134). The numismatic evidence would point to a date for commercial activity commencing in the secondary early-penny phase but for the presence of the rare, probably early Primary, Valdoberhtus *sceat* (*Figure* 21).

The ninth century coins include six silver-alloy coins of Eanred and brass *stycas* of Eanred (three), Æthelred II (two of each reign), Redwulf (one) and a bronze *styca* of Osberht but no coins of the archbishops. However, cessation of activity prior to the arrival of the Viking *micel here* is unlikely in view of a recent find of a Viking penny.[1172] See *Graph* 11.2.

Many of the coin recoveries were 'as struck' according to Leahy,[1173] though Pirie's plate, be it of the same specimens, demonstrates this to be an overstatement.[1174] Undoubtedly, the site is strong in higher quality coins—fantastic animal *sceattas* and the silver-alloy coins of Eanred—with good continuity provided by specimens from Ælfwald I, Æthelred I and Eardwulf. This signals a high-status site, albeit short-lived.

Burton Fleming

Burton Fleming is on one of the parallel east-west routes through the northern Wolds running from North Grimston through several villages including Weaverthorpe and Wold Newton onto Bridlington. It lies in the Gypsey Race valley, seven miles west of Bridlington and north of Rudston and Thwing. Crop marks of uncertain prehistoric and Roman dated are scheduled.[1175] Pastscape suggests that Maiden's Grave may also have served as the *wapentake* meeting place, during the Early Medieval period.[1176] Should this suggestion be extended to include economic activity, then coin losses could be expected. The occurrence here of the first find of a *sceat* of king Eardwulf (*Figure* 135) may support this proposition.[1177]

All but one of the other 29 entries are from the concerted effort initiated by this then unique and significant find. All finds are Northumbrian. The 11 *sceattas* include five fantastic animal types: Eadberht (three), Æthelred I (one) and Ælfwald I (one) three different joint issues and three different inscriptional issues by the key moneyer Cuthheard. There are none of Eanred's initial issue but brass *stycas* of Eanred, Æthelred II and Wigmund and eight illegible specimens. The silver coins are a more representative selection than the base issues. See *Graph* 11.3.

Rudston

The Neolithic *cursus* monuments for which Rudston is famous lie close to the intermittent Gypsey Race in the Great Wold Valley, six miles west of Bridlington.[1178] The Roman villa is noted for its mosaics.[1179] A small number of coins finds include a *denier* of Lyon and a rare English version of the Interlace Cross type (*Figure* 136). A silver-alloy coins of Eanred was also detected (*Figure* 137).

That such a mix of coins should occur at this site is to be expected. The spectacular monolith in the church yard must have been a draw for inquisitive visitors from far afield over the centuries.

Boynton

Such travellers are very likely to have passed through Boynton, only 2.5 miles east of Rudston.

Crop marks indicate a likely enclosed settlement with finds of Roman and Anglian pottery.[1180] Inhumations with grave goods, discovered in 1951, could be early medieval.[1181] The site combines a mix of exotic *sceattas* (*Figure* 138) and some of the scarcer *stycas* (*Figure* 139) conjecturally indicating a special purpose location.

Small Sites

Langtoft, Nafferton and Bridlington (*denier* of Reims with facing heads and a C-bracteate, *Figure* 140 and a rare Wolf and Twins *sceat*, *Figure* 141) are among the lesser locations.

7.3.3.2 Grave Goods and Small hoards—Wolds East

Coins have been found in association with burials at Garton-on-the-Wolds (eight *sceattas*) and artefacts in association with human remains at Kilham. Small hoards have been unearthed at Buttercrambe (seventeen Primary *sceattas*), Everingham (eleven *stycas*) and Burdale (allegedly dispersed *styca* hoard). These are discussed in the respective site notes.

[1171] Metcalf (2014a, 54).
[1172] *Pers. comm.* A Gillis, 1st December 2015.
[1173] Leahy (2000, 72).
[1174] Pirie archive, Thwing plate.
[1175] For example, http://www.pastscape.org.uk/hob.aspx?hob_id=890202
[1176] http://www.pastscape.org.uk/hob.aspx?hob_id=79850
[1177] Pirie (1995a). *EMC* 1995.6001.
[1178] http://www.pastscape.org.uk/hob.aspx?hob_id=79482 and 79850
[1179] http://www.pastscape.org.uk/hob.aspx?hob_id=79473
[1180] http://www.pastscape.org.uk/hob.aspx?hob_id=81258
[1181] http://www.pastscape.org.uk/hob.aspx?hob_id=81243

7.3.3.3 Numismatic Summary—Wolds East

While the east Wolds may lack the volume and variety found elsewhere in the Wolds, the picture remains one of a healthy range of local and imported coin varieties. *Dataset 1* again shows the strength of imported coinages particularly in the Primary early-penny phase. *Graph 11* illustrates a healthy continuity.

7.3.3.4 The Artefactual Dataset—Wolds East

Two anomalies require explanations. First, the metal working debris at Rudston is associated with burials rather than industrial processing. This accounts for all but one item of metal working debris in the dataset—the other is a fragment of filigree-decorated gold sheet from Aldbrough, which would better have been classified as jewellery. Second, the hoard of 11 items from a burial at Kilham, seems also to be included in the PAS extract as individual items.[1182]

Of the dozen finds locations in the east Wolds, *Dataset 5*, the dominant two are Thwing (134 artefacts) and Rudston (112) contributing 71.9 per cent of the 342 artefacts; adding Kilham (41) takes this to 83.9 per cent. The latter is also the most prolific numismatically and only three locations, all minor (fifteen artefacts), have not produced coins. There are 10 coin find-spots in all, nine also producing artefacts. Forty-five object types are represented, though the distribution is skewed towards brooches rather than strap-ends with pins being well below norm. In common with neighbouring areas, this may be mere fashion and is again of less significance than *co-occurrence* of 75 per cent in the east Wolds, showing a consistently high level of monetization throughout the chalk upland.

7.3.4 Comparison to Normal Distribution—Wolds

As shown in *Dataset 1, Correlations*, the Wolds are very close to norm for the ninth century but the correlation for *sceattas* is weaker, especially in the central Wolds, due to the relative dominance of non-local *sceattas* in the Wolds, especially Sledmere.[1183] This is despite the exclusivity of local finds at South Newbald. Clearly, other than special-purpose sites, the Wolds are distinctively outward looking. Further analyses are detailed below.

[1182] YORYM-554033, Treasure Case 2011 T591 and 2012 T264, mainly brooches, strap-ends and the human remains. If this hoard is discounted and the metal working fragments from cremations at Rudston are regarded as eight finds rather than 34 fragments, the two dominant sites account for 71.9 per cent of 224 objects.

[1183] Correlations to 'F. Provenanced, not hoard' for single finds are west: 94 per cent, central (including Sledmere): 75 per cent, and east: 94 per cent. For sceattas alone, the west shows a strong correlation (92 per cent), central, no correlation, and east, moderate (82 per cent). The centre is anomalous due to the weighting of Sledmere. Basing computation on *Dataset 17*, strengthens the sceat correlation, by the inclusion of many more minor sites.

7.3.5 Comparison to Roman Finds – Wolds

The relatively greater economic importance of the Wolds in the Anglian period is demonstrated in *Dataset 7, Finds Comparison (Map 9)*. Whereas the Wolds' numismatic material accounts for over half the northern total in both eras (49 per cent Roman, 56 per cent Anglian), the artefactual material constitutes 22 per cent of Roman and 65 per cent of Anglian finds in the north. As noted above, the incongruous ratio of Roman coins to artefacts in the two periods requires further research. A possible explanation could be the reporting of Roman hoards as single finds.

7.3.6 The Artefactual Dataset—Wolds

Abandoning the artificial division between the west, central and east Wolds, the analysis for the whole region is summarized *Dataset 17. Artefacts—Summary*. Nearly two-thirds of the artefact dataset is attributable to the Wolds and covers 90 different types of artefact. Seventy percent of Wolds' sites with artefacts are monied with the centre and east the strongest. Coins are found at a further 14 sites. Variations are more likely to be a detection-reporting phenomenon, rather than real.

Given the dominance of the Wolds in the dataset, the functional distribution will be close to the norm as shown in *Dataset 17, Categories*. However, variations between the different parts of the Wolds arise particularly as regards dress fasteners. Given that the number of finds is not inconsiderable, this is more likely to be a real difference in local manufacture and usage than a detecting artifice. The east Wolds may prefer brooches to pins and strap-ends but it is the prevalence of knife blades and metal working debris that distinguish it from the west and centre, even though there is less diversity of artefacts types.[1184]

Wickham remarked: 'loom-weights are so common on settlement sites that every household could be assumed to have made its own clothes.'[1185] This should certainly be the case in the wool-producing Wolds. However, loom-weights do not feature as an artefact type in PAS. It is more likely that this is a recovery phenomenon, as they are non-metallic and escape metal-detection, rather than indicative of wool being shipped in a raw state with clothing imported.

Not only is the study area prolific in artefacts, but the coin mix, *Dataset 17. Coin Metal Mix*, shows that activity is significant throughout the early-penny and *styca* periods. Unlike the Central Lowlands, which seems to exhibit as much site migration as continuity, *Dataset 17, Coin Age Mix* shows that over two-thirds of the sites in the Wolds have longevity.

[1184] *Dataset 17, Artefacts—Details* gives the artefactual distribution in detail.

[1185] Wickham (2005, 807).

7.3.7 Conclusion

Based on the widespread and abundant distribution of both coins and artefacts and their close association throughout the Wolds, there can be no doubt about the routine and regular use of both *sceattas* and *stycas*. Imported coinages show the strength of trading relationships. In comparison to the more limited range in the Central Lowlands, Metcalf's suggestion 'that the Wolds were not fully under Eadberht's control'[1186] is endorsed. The resemblance of Vale of Pickering more to the Central Lowlands than to the Wolds is considered below.

7.3.8 Illustrations—The Yorkshire Wolds East

Figure 131: *Sceat* of Aldfrith. Found Kilham.

Figure 132: Æthelwald Moll with Æthelred. Found Kilham.

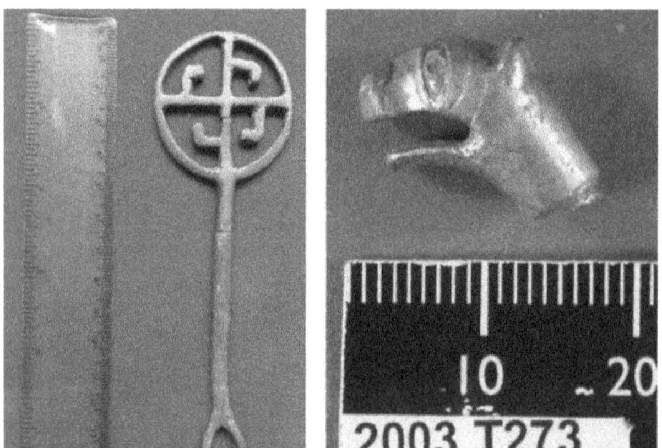

Figure 133: Two early Anglo-Saxon artefacts from Kilham. (Courtesy Ian Bayles)

[1186] Bonser (2011, 163).

Figure 134: *Sceat* of Eardwulf with a ligate initial in the moneyer's name on the reverse. Found Thirsk (Courtesy Ron Bude)

Figure 135: First known *sceat* of Eardwulf. *EMC* 1995.6001. (Courtesy British Numismatic Society)

Figure 136: Rudston: L: Merovingian *denier* of Lyon,[1187] R: interlaced cross type *sceat*.

Figure 137: Silver-alloy coin of Eanred by Wilheah.

[1187] Abramson 1245, *EMC* 2009.0018, *cf. MEC* (1986, 541), Prou (1892, 99–110). Similar in Cimiez hoard.

Figure 138: Boynton: *sceattas* of Series N, O and 'Wodan'.

Figure 139: L: Silver-alloy coin of Eanred. R: base *styca* of Æthelred II. L: Dægberht. R: Leofthegn.

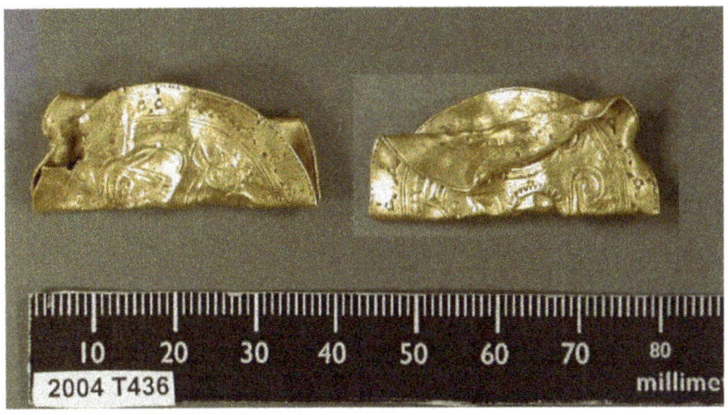

Figure 140: C-bracteate, Near Bridlington, typically associated with élite sites. Intentionally folded and probably a single grave deposit. (Courtesy Portable Antiquities Scheme)[1188]

Figure 141: Wolf and Twins *sceat*. Found near Bridlington.

7.4 Beverley (*Dataset 18*)

This episcopal settlement, between the Yorkshire Wolds and the River Hull, was founded in the early eighth century by the bishop of York, John of Hexham, later venerated as Saint John of Beverley.[1189] According to *VASLE* 'The site was interpreted by the excavators as the location of the monastery of *Inderauuda* 'in the wood of the men of Deira', where Bede says John of Hexham was buried in AD 721.'[1190] Beverley subsequently grew to some significance on the strength of the wool trade and construction of Beverley minster which is situated near the excavation site. Trenching in the intractable clays proved difficult and some anomalies of stratification occur. There was no metal detection. Some prehistoric and Roman finds show early occupancy.

In her 1991 paper on the Lurk Lane hoard, Pirie distinguishes between the great *styca* hoards accumulated over a lengthy period and '*purse-hoards…*savings on a more humble scale and veritable pocket money for current personal expenses.'[1191] Such was the recovery of 23 *stycas* compacted into a shallow pit near the occupation area. In common with the *stycas* at Flixborough, there are some irregular types absent from the great hoards, which leads Pirie to speculate on unofficial emissions.[1192] There has been a small number of other single finds of *sceattas* and *stycas*.

The earliest coin in the dataset, a secondary Series E,[1193] was found between Beverley and Woodmansey so may be more generally indicative of Frisian wool trade in the Wolds than diagnostic for Beverley. Three early Eadberht *sceattas* and a joint issue with Ecgberht mark the commencement of coin use at the site, possibly in the late 730s. While a fantastic animal *sceat* of Ælfwald is rare, the joint inscriptional issue of Æthelwald Moll with Ecgberht is one of only three known (*Figure* 142). It

[1188] PAS YORYM-58B842. Behr, Pestell and Hines (2014, 78).
[1189] Armstrong and others (1991, 1 and 243). Woodman (2012, 173–86).
[1190] http://intarch.ac.uk/journal/issue25/2/4.4.6.html
[1191] My italics
[1192] Pirie (1987, 127 and 1991). Archibald (2009, 417–18).
[1193] Metcalf (1993, 247).

would be conjectural to endow such a rarity with episcopal significance.

There is also an inscriptional *sceat* of Æthelred I by Tidwulf after which there is a considerable gap before two silver-alloy coins of Eanred reflecting a break in production of the order of 30 years after the 793 Viking attack, during which financial transactions would have been increasingly undertaken in commodity money. There are 14 brass *stycas* of Eanred, Æthelred II and Wigmund, three bronze *stycas* of Osberht (but none for Wulfhere) and 10 blundered specimens.[1194] This distribution does not support Armstrong's assertion of site abandonment *c.* 851.[1195] Traditionally, the minster is said to have been sacked by the Danes in 866/7 but there is no clear evidence of destruction. Five tenth-century pennies, three of the Vikings of York and two of the Kings of All England, demonstrate the resumed wealth of the site after the Viking incursions.

7.5 Holderness—East Yorkshire Coastal Plateau (*Dataset 18*)

Holderness is underlain by Cretaceous chalk, but this is disguised by heavy glaciation resulting in typical deposition features. This is largely a flat, treeless, fertile landscape of sizeable, exposed fields. Coastal erosion washes debris down to Spurn Head.

While the Doomsday Book records 45 freeholders in Holderness, it was probably largely undrained marshland in early Anglo-Saxon times. Other than at Beverley, finds are scarce; fifteen are shown in *Dataset 18*. The generally small cemeteries of the period probably represent the dispersed pattern of lowland settlement.[1196]

A York gold shilling, of variety C is recorded on PAS as from Flinton (*Figure* 143),[1197] an extraordinary finds for such a remote location with no obvious trading connections.

Bishop Burton, Kingston-upon-Hull and Roos have each produced a single *sceat* of Eadberht and Cottingham a joint issue with Ecgberht. Hornsea has yielded one of Æthelred I. The only Continental specimen is a primary Series E again from Bishop Burton.

The occurrence of the above *sceat* at Leconfield (*Figure* 144) probably results from traffic on the Beverley-Driffield road, which presumably carried goods transported across the Humber at Ferriby. Leconfield also supplied two brass *stycas* and single specimens are recorded for Skerne, Wansford, Skidby and Hornsea.

7.5.1 Comparisons to Norm and Roman Finds

Dataset 18, Beverley & Holderness—Site Finds by Issuer analyses the coin-rich sites of the area by period and issuer.

The comparably increased proportion of both coins and artefacts from the Roman to Anglian period are likely to be the consequence of better land usage and water management in the later period, probably reflecting the growing importance of Beverley.

Graph 12 illustrates the chronological dispersal of finds at the main sites. North Ferriby show early activity and Whitby shows good continuity, as does Beverley from the *renovatio* onwards.

7.5.2 The Artefactual Dataset

Dataset 18, Artefacts—Summary combines analyses of the Beverley area, Holderness and a scatter of northern and north-western locations.[1198] *Dataset 18, Categories* gives the artefactual analysis by functional categories. However, where dissimilar, these regions must be assessed separately. *Dataset 18, Accessories*—shows that the area preferred brooches above the norm.[1199]

Nine locations in the vicinity of Beverley have divulged 54 objects, but the assemblage is dominated by Beverley (Lurk Lane, 20 artefacts) and Bishop Burton (nineteen artefacts), *Dataset 5* and *Dataset 18. Artefacts—Summary*. Five of these locations have produced 42 coins, though 35 of these are from Beverley. As with the entire East Yorkshire extract from PAS, the artefact types are dominated by items of personal dress (70.3 per cent), including 10 brooches, which are more popular than pins, and a near absence of production artefacts.

There are 16 other sites in Holderness, from which 49 objects are recorded: 16 are from Paull (including five buckles) and 13 are brooches, again much favoured over pins in this region. Aldbrough, near the coast in Holderness, has produced a fragment of gold sheet with filigree decoration—classified as metal working debris. However, the numismatic evidence at these locations is scant—only two of these sites have produced coins—just a single *sceat* of Eadberht at Roos and a *styca* from Aldbrough. There are three more non-artefact coin find-spots, including Flinton, which produced a York shilling. In looking at the artefactual fingerprint and associations with coins, Beverley and Holderness may be analysed together.

Dataset 18. Artefacts—Summary shows the artefactual findings for Beverley, Holderness and other peripheral sites. While the Beverley area, with *co-occurrence* of 67

[1194] *Graph* 12.4.
[1195] Armstrong and others (1999, 1 and 243). Cessation of Lundenwic is similarly misattributed.
[1196] Van de Noort and Davies (1993, 82).
[1197] Naylor and Allen (2014, 157, C12).

[1198] Van de Noort & Davies (1993, 81, *figure* 3.13).
[1199] The detailed artefactual distribution is given at *Dataset 18, Artefacts—Details*.

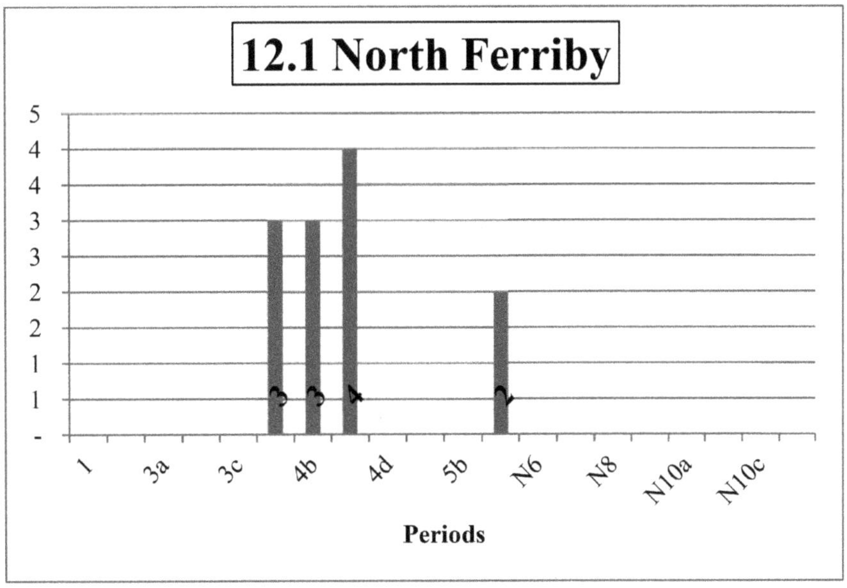
12.1 North Ferriby
Periods

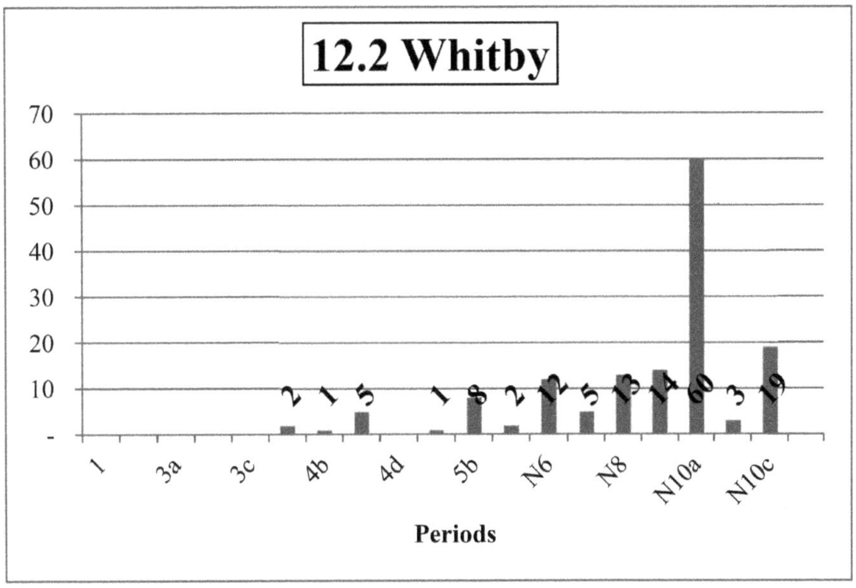
12.2 Whitby
Periods

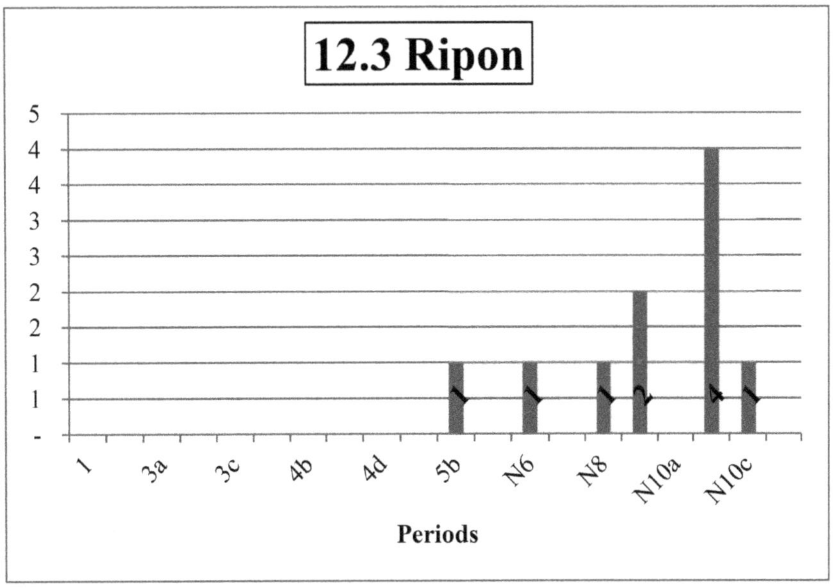
12.3 Ripon
Periods

Graphs 12

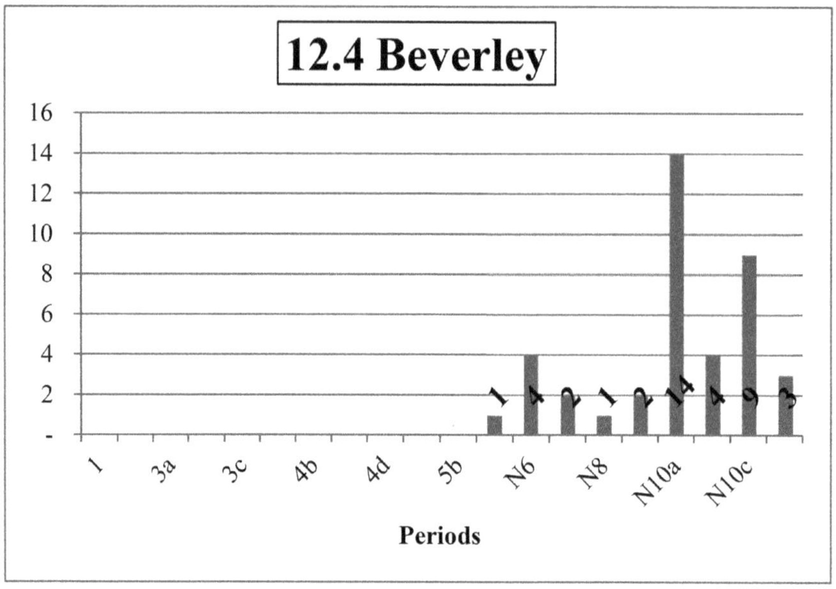

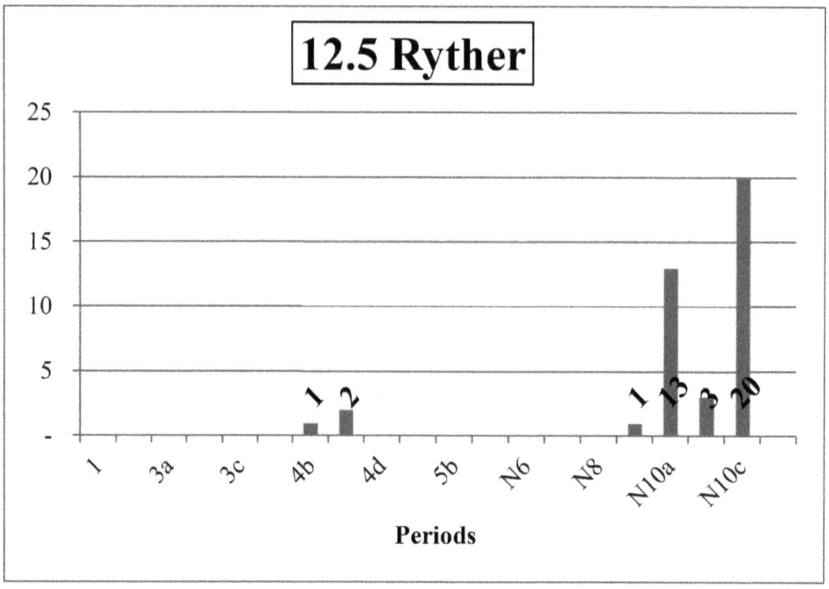

Graphs 12: Site finds by period arranged regionally by weighted average of peak activity, Deira. Sources: *Datasets 1* and *8*. Numerical axis varies.

per cent, is reasonably monetized, this is not the case for Holderness, which may well have been commercially remote.

The dominance of dress accessories in the artefactual assemblage exceed the norm as shown in *Dataset 18, Categories* and *Accessories*. In Beverley and Holderness, but more so in the northern regions, brooches are favoured over pins. On the west coast, Meols strongly favours pins.

Dataset 18, Coin Metal Mix shows that both early-penny and *styca* coinage circulated in Beverley and Holderness with artefacts. Though there are few finds and sites in Beverley and Holderness, the semblance of a pattern arises in *Dataset 18, Coin Age Mix* marginally, perhaps unexpectedly, favouring continuity over site migration.

7.5.3 Conclusion

In comparison to sites in the Wolds, Beverley starts late but does not suffer cessation of urban trading and manufacture on arrival of the *micel here.* Presumably, this resilience is due to its attractions as an Anglo-Scandinavian settlement.

Coin and artefact discoveries in coastal Holderness are less prolific than in the Central Lowlands or the Yorkshire Wolds but still present a picture of widespread use of coins in association with artefacts in the eighth and ninth centuries.

7.5.4 Illustrations—Beverley and Holderness

Figure 142: Beverley: *sceat* of Æthelwald Moll with Ecgberht. *EMC*1999.0019, *SL*76–10 (© Chris Rudd Ltd, www.celticcoins.com)

Figure 143: Flinton: York gold shilling (Ciii.3). (Courtesy Portable Antiquities Scheme)[1200]

Figure 144: Leconfield: *sceat* of Æthelred I by Ceolbald.

7.6 The Vale of Pickering (*Dataset 19*)[1200]

> 'it is noised abroad concerning some bishops, that they have no men of religion or continence near them; but rather such as indulge in laughter and jests, revellings, and drunkenness and other temptations of an idle life, and who rather feed their bodies with carnal food than their minds on the heavenly sacrifice.' Bede's letter to Ecgberht, 734, §4.

The Vale of Pickering is the catchment area of the River Derwent, enclosed by the Yorkshire Moors to the north and Wolds to the south, with the Howardian Hills to the west and the North Sea to the east.

The southern Roman road from York, passing through the Derwent Gap to Malton, skirts the Wolds to meet the coast at Filey. A northern route running from Ripon through Thirsk and Pickering reaches the coast at Scarborough. Fertile soils support intensive arable production in the former glacial Lake Pickering. There are diverse areas of undulating land, but woodland is largely absent. The coastal belt is a hillier landscape with glacial features.

In the south and north margins, starting from the spring-line near the lakeshore, 'elongated parishes',[1201] run to higher ground, taking in the spectrum of soil types and elevations—'river frontage, marshland, arable, water, upland grazing'[1202] implying transhumance and self-sufficiency.

Finds of Iron Age loom-weights and weaving combs, show that wool production was the foundation of a strong local economy. Ladder settlements followed the main trackways and it would have been straightforward for the Romans to exercise control from their forts at Malton and Scarborough, with minimal disruption. They introduced manufactured products and pottery kilns at Knapton, Norton and Crambeck. Coinage, and an improved plough, would have enhanced their tax revenue.[1203] Absence of Anglian coin and other artefactual evidence along the centre of the Vale suggests that marshy remnants of Lake Pickering persisted and the remains of a Roman flood barrier have been identified in extensive geophysics surveys in the Heslerton parish.[1204]

Morris illustrated the locations of early medieval religious houses, which are prolific in this region, with many on the straight Roman road between Hovingham and Malton.[1205] They are centrally located within each parish, many of which are elongated to include both marsh and carr landscapes.

7.6.1 Site Studies

7.6.1.1 Southern Routeway (now A64)

Coins have been found at most sites along this ancient routeway, including Malton, Norton, Rillington, West Heslerton, Sherburn, Binnington and Staxton, and although their density may have been exaggerated by a likely concentration of detecting along the modern road, these demonstrate that there was economic activity along the length of this ancient trackway.

Malton

This is the location of the Roman fort of Derventio and the Roman period is well-represented in artefacts, monuments and crop marks.[1206] Fragments of an Anglo-Saxon wheel-head crosses were preserved in the Priory Church.[1207]

1200 YORYM 78A342.

1201 Morris (1989, 144, *figure 32*) and (2012, 223).
1202 *Ibid.*
1203 Powlesland (2003, 27–28). Loveluck (2003, 154).
1204 Powlesland and May (2010), http://intarch.ac.uk/journal/issue27/2/3.html
1205 Morris (1989, 122).
1206 http://www.pastscape.org.uk/hob.aspx?hob_id=59791
1207 http://www.pastscape.org.uk/hob.aspx?hob_id=59846

At least two Merovingian *tremisses* have been attributed to the Malton area (*Figure* 145). These may be the gold coins referred to below as found near Rillington.[1208]

Of the 102 coins tabulated for the Vale of Pickering, *Dataset 19, Site Finds by Issuer*, 51 are ostensibly from 'near' Malton. This includes, two 'productive sites' and several single finds. However, the ticket of a very rare specimen[1209] found by Ian Postlethwaite at Binnington in mid-1997 records 'Binnington, situated at the Staxton end of the A64 heading towards Scarborough. The site is referred to by Bonser as 'Near Malton Site 1' in The Yorkshire Numismatist 3'. Moreover, Morris suggested that finds from West Heslerton had been disguised as 'near Malton'.[1210] Therefore, 'Near Malton Site 2' is assumed to be West Heslerton.[1211]

The remaining Malton single finds exhibit some continuity in the types represented. *Dataset 19, Site Finds by Issuer* shows three of the seven *sceattas* to be of Eadberht (two more come from neighbouring Norton) three to be different styles of Æthelred I plus a rare and noteworthy Eardwulf by Cuthheard. There is a silver-alloy emission of Eanred and seven base *stycas*. While lacking in volume, the spread of silver and copper alloy covers the period under review showing continued use of coin in economic transactions. *Graph* 13.2.

Indeed, marking the end-date of this study, there is evidence of the Viking bullion economy not only in the Malton area (*Figure* 146), but with the presence of fragmentary dirhams elsewhere, for example, at Burdale, showing temporary reversion to a more primitive medium.

Rillington

Rectilinear enclosures and field boundaries from the Roman period or earlier, lie either side of a trackway.[1212]

The three detector finds tabulated include an extremely rare variety of the *sceat* of Eadberht inscribed *ᚪЯ* on the reverse (*Figure* 150),[1213] presumably denoting episcopal authority albeit it a regal issue, and two silver-alloy coins of Eanred.

However, even more intriguing is a note in the Bonser archive reporting the finding of three gold coins, one a *thrymsa* of the LONDUNIV type, Viking hack-silver, weights and a dirham fragment, thought to be from the Scampston-Rillington area.[1214] While this is a small, and somewhat uncertain, accumulation, there is an implication of continual economic activity from the earliest coinage through to the return to a bullion system after the fall of York, though this is beyond the scope of the present study.

West Heslerton

Space permits only a résumé of this well-documented excavation. This project pioneered recording methods enabling over 300,000 artefacts to be digitally documented.[1215] These included, *inter alia*, ceramics, textiles, coins, imported lava stones,[1216] and shells—including a cowrie from the Red Sea from the early Anglo-Saxon period.

What emerged was a ladder of occupation, that was 'blurred and disjointed...structures, corrals, fence-lines, and ditches were periodically redefined as buildings wore out and patches of ground became rank.'[1217] The ladder ran continuously for six miles and continually, west to Hovingham, for over twenty, 'neither nucleated nor dispersed, but a filament of farms, a linear agricultural commune one building wide and tens of miles long',[1218] originating around 500 BC and occupied for more than a millennium.

This is far from the conventional perception of post-Roman demographic collapse,[1219] 'rewilding'[1220] and the imagined sequence of migrations, conquests and associated land clearance. The evidence from Heslerton undermines the conventional view that settlements were small and longevity limited. There may have been specific discontinuities—hand-made pottery replaced wheel-made pottery—and land-use may have changed, but this is likely to have been due to the expiration of Roman land-ownership presenting improved opportunities.

Morris noted the wide scatter of single early Anglo-Saxon coin finds: 'the tempo of economic activity they imply is brisk.'[1221]

Between the fifth and seventh centuries, Anglo-Saxons reused prehistoric sites—as in the case of the Heslerton cemetery over the Neolithic henge and Bronze Age barrows—but thereafter, churches such as Sherburn reserved control over burial.[1222] Heslerton shows zoned activity into the ninth century, and *Grubenhäuser*,[1223] of varying sizes, fulfil different functional, as opposed to domestic, rôles.

[1208] An entry in the Bonser archive for 7th December 1994 mentioned a Frisian gold coin of the National Series found in the Malton/Driffield area.

[1209] *SCBI*69, 452 *SL* 44–10. See *Figure* 35.

[1210] Richard Morris (*pers. comm.* 4th March 2015).

[1211] Were all disguises so effective this study would be rendered worthless. The Eboracum 'Ryedale' hoard, dated to *c.* 930–35, is from the Vale of York, see PAS YORYM-BC3AB2.

[1212] http://www.pastscape.org.uk/hob.aspx?hob_id=1433261

[1213] The only other specimen is from Pocklington (127).

[1214] Bonser no. 146, 11th March 1999.

[1215] Powlesland reported (2003, 43) that around a million animal bones were recovered from the site.

[1216] Possible sources include Norwegian mica-schist hone stones and Eifel Mountain lava quern stones (Sahlins, 2003, 38) and Niedermendig lava or mayan-basalt quern stones from the Rhine valley.

[1217] Morris (2012, 212).

[1218] Morris (2012, 222).

[1219] Powlesland (2003, 33–35).

[1220] Monbiot (2013).

[1221] Morris (2012, 218). Muir (1987, 110).

[1222] Morris (2012, 223).

[1223] Tipper (2004, 54–55).

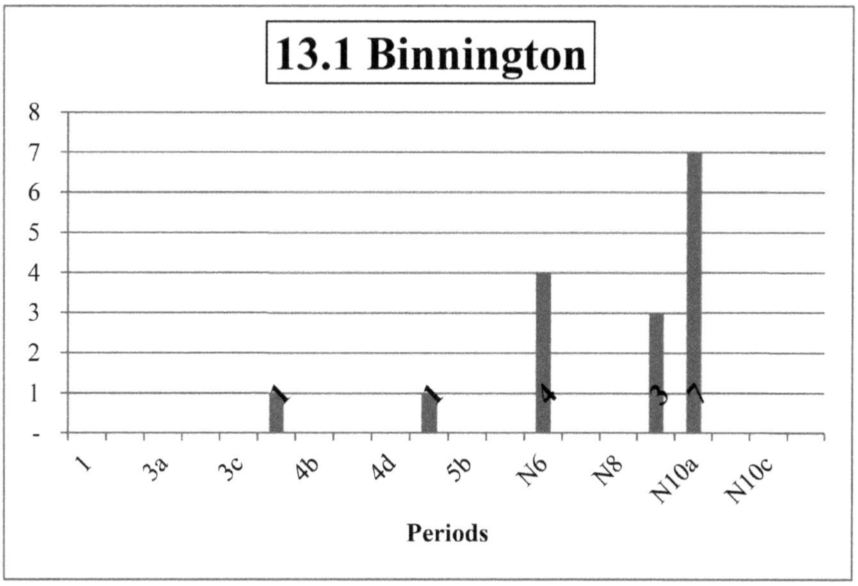
13.1 Binnington
8
7
6
5
4
3
2
1
-
1
3a
3c
4b
4d
5b
N6
N8
N10a
N10c
Periods

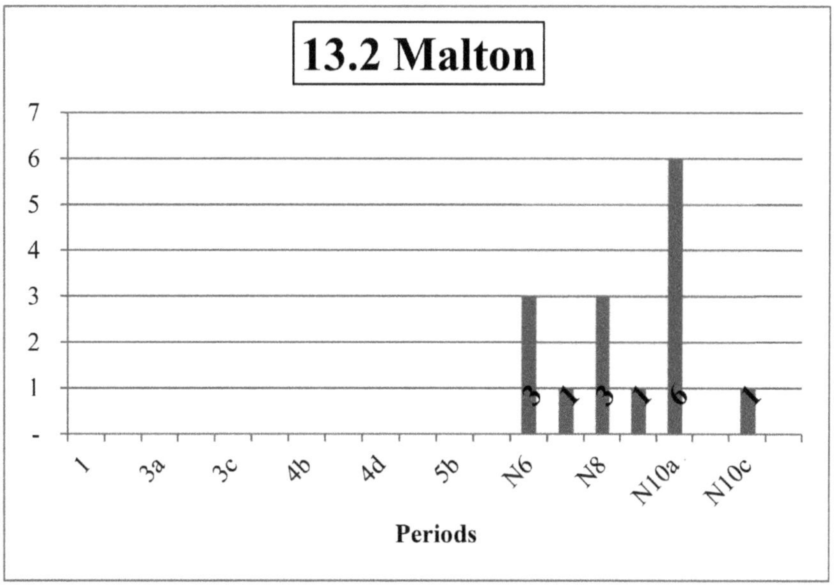
13.2 Malton
7
6
5
4
3
2
1
-
1
3a
3c
4b
4d
5b
N6
N8
N10a
N10c
Periods

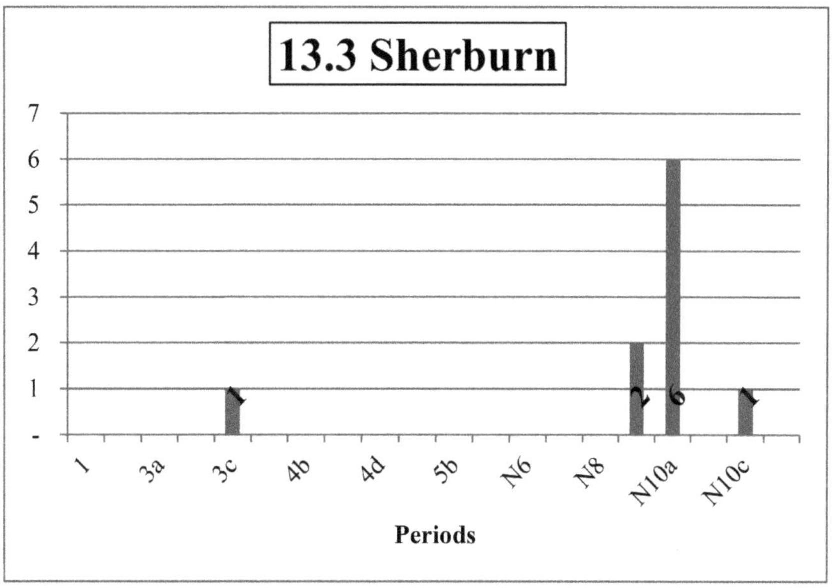
13.3 Sherburn
7
6
5
4
3
2
1
-
1
3a
3c
4b
4d
5b
N6
N8
N10a
N10c
Periods

Graphs 13

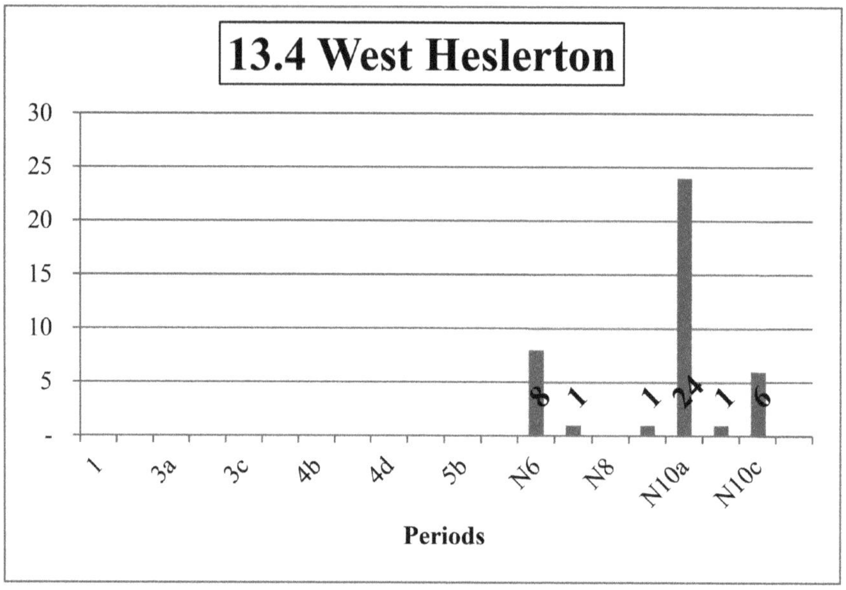

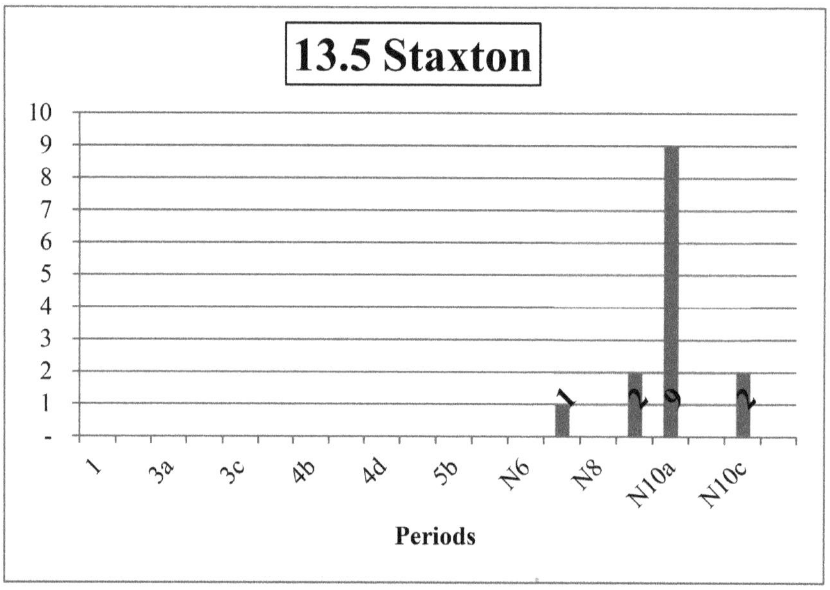

Graphs 13: Site finds by period arranged regionally by weighted average of peak activity, Vale of Pickering. Sources: *Datasets 1* and *8*. Numerical axis varies.

For the period *c.* 650 to *c.* 800, excavation produced a wealth of cultural material showing work in different materials—iron, bone, antler, ceramics and wood. There may have been exchanges of animals and textiles for German lava quern-stones. Pigs, fowl and geese were kept and Powlesland commented on the absence of cattle and sheep of 'market age' implying that these would have been traded or rendered as tax.[1224]

Rising groundwater, resulting from a wetter climate, may have caused a depopulation of the 'ladder' from around 850, according to numismatic evidence, with a move to West Heslerton village reflecting 'an evolution from late prehistoric society that Rome had ruled and exploited but not significantly altered.'[1225] The Anglo-Saxon site was absorbed into the open fields of the village. Morris saw 'not a systemic migration…but a bundle of sporadic episodes involving groupings of different size and varying composition.'[1226]

However, reminiscent of both Fishergate and Wharram Percy, the numismatic evidence is slender, especially here, in view of the intensive archaeological exploration of an unprecedentedly large area over many years. The dataset has a relatively modest 45 specimens, including 13 *sceattas*, four of which are Frisian Series E, divided equally between primary and secondary types. At least this implies North Sea trade, possibly indirect, as none

[1224] Powlesland (2003, 43–44).

[1225] Morris (2012, 227). Also see Powlesland (2003, 29–31).

[1226] Morris (2012, 233).

is pristine. The other *sceattas* are Northumbrian issues of Eadberht, Eadberht with Ecgberht and Ælfwald I and the brass *stycas* are all well-used including one bronze issue of Osberht. Bonser also listed early-penny specimens of Series G (Quentovic), and X (Ribe), J (two) and L (London), which are not in my database and lend the site a wider trading flavour.[1227] *Graph* 13.4.

The failure to metal detect this substantial site and a reluctance to co-operate as privately recorded by Pirie,[1228] causes a potentially serious omission from the numismatic and artefactual record, especially as night-hawking would have removed the prospect of repairing this deficiency.[1229] The presumption, based on the volume of visually detected coin finds by area, is that coins were largely absent rather than missed. Powlesland remarked on the self-sufficiency of the settlement;[1230] perhaps this was of such an extent that coinage was not a necessity here.

Sherburn

Given Sherburn is the site of a Roman period ladder settlement[1231] and an early medieval religious house (Anglian cross fragments were found in in Sherburn church[1232]) the scattering of ninth-century coins and discovery of a handsome and rare, partially runic, pale-gold portrait shilling of Pada (*Figure* 147) should be no surprise. The wonder is that the many minsters of the area are not so endowed, *Graph* 13.3.

A single find may be insufficient to validate the use of coin in long-distance trade in the Vale of Pickering in the final quarter of the seventh century, but it is certainly indicative.

Binnington

Now identified as Bonser's 'near Malton site 1',[1233] an intriguing spread of coins has been unearthed at Binnington, to the west of Staxton. *Sceattas* of Aldfrith, Eadberht, Alchred, and Æthelred I are enhanced by the first recognised[1234] specimen of the exotic species, now styled (by the author) the *fledgling type* for its graceful depiction of a running bird with an elaborately knotted tail (*Figure* 35). See *Graph* 13.1.

Morris associated the iconography with a story Bede's *Life of Cuthbert*,[1235] identifying the bird as an eagle, carrying a fish to sustain Cuthbert and his aide on their sojourn, as Cuthbert had prophesied. Of the 10 coins known for this type, five have northern provenances justifying tentative attribution as a northern emission.[1236] Ninth-century finds include the silver-alloy of Eanred but nothing later than Æthelred II's second reign.

Bonser also recorded six Series E (Frisian), specimens of Series J, K (Kentish) and N.[1237] These build on Metcalf's hypothesis of trade in wool as the driver of a prosperous local economy based on a fifth of all primary *sceattas* found in England being Frisian, focussing on sheep-rearing chalk uplands.'[1238]

Staxton

This site has evidence of an early Anglian farmstead and cemetery. The dataset includes 14 specimens including a joint-issue *sceat* of Æthelred I with Eanbald I. There are two silver-alloy coins of Eanred and specimens of both reigns of Æthelred II are divided by two *stycas* of Redwulf. See *Graph* 13.5. A York penny of the St Peter type, dating from 905–10, shows continuity of activity.[1239]

7.6.1.2 Southern Routeway—Conclusion

In conclusion, that little over a hundred coins are tabulated for an area which includes many minsters, and one of the most extensive excavations ever undertaken, is contrary to expectations and challenges the aphorism that coins are found where they are sought. As demonstrated below, under-reporting and lack of access are not convincing explanations, *Dataset 19, Site Finds by Issuer* and *Roman Coin Finds*.

7.6.2 Northern Routeway (the Modern A170)

Morris described the liminal location of many early religious houses, where the North York Moors descend into Ryedale.[1240] Blair painted a convincing picture of these being the nuclei of thriving local economies.[1241] Moreover, the Vale is better served by waterways than the dry Wolds. These factors hold much promise for rich findings.

From the west, local finds include single specimens at Kirkbymoorside (*sceat*, *Figure* 148), Snainton (brass *styca*), Seamer (a 'two-crozier' Eadberht/Ecgberht *sceat*, *Figure* 149 similar to that found at 'Site B' near

[1227] Bonser (1997, 42–43). I have discounted the possibility of duplication of data from the two main information streams, Pirie (archive) and Bonser (1997). The profiles of these sources are not dissimilar.
[1228] Pirie archive.
[1229] It is clear from Pirie's archives that only James Lyall co-operated in sharing information.
[1230] Powlesland (2003, 43).
[1231] http://www.pastscape.org.uk/hob.aspx?hob_id=1449251
[1232] http://www.pastscape.org.uk/hob.aspx?hob_id=64803
[1233] Bonser (1997, 42). This site is likely to have been detected by Ian Postlethwaite.
[1234] The 1986 specimen, appropriately from Bermondsey Abbey, was misunderstood by Metcalf (*BNJ*56, 3–4).
[1235] Ch. 12, see Marner (2000, pl. 15, 72).
[1236] The widespread southern findspots include White Colne, near. Colchester, Ewelme, Oxfordshire, Trimley St Martin, Suffolk and Harlington, Bedfordshire.
[1237] Bonser (1997, 42–43). This informal data is not in the formal Database. See fn. 1227.
[1238] Metcalf (2014, 244).
[1239] PAS YORYM-175630
[1240] Morris (2005, 3–21).
[1241] See ch. 2.

Pocklington) and near Scarborough (a secondary, cruciform Series E).

That so few early Anglo-Saxon coin have been disclosed—with nothing reported at Pickering or any of the minster sites—is wholly unexpected, particularly as the uncovering of other artefacts, *Dataset 5, Artefacts,* shows that access is not restricted.

There could be two causes; this is due either to recovery phenomena or social-economic agents. While the paucity of finds is stark for this north track, the contrast with the south track could be explained geographically. The south track serves the Wolds, economically active and demonstrated to be increasingly monetized throughout the study period, whereas the north track serves the North York Moors much of which is above the plough zone, inhibiting recovery, and the conditions are less conducive to agricultural development. Nevertheless, the outcome for both tracks is curious.

Adverse recovery factors could include restricted access, poor recording, soil conditions, ploughing practices and alluvium. None is entirely convincing other than the first in the immediate vicinity of minsters. At the time of loss, the soil and grassy pastures of the Vale would better conceal minute coins than would, say, the dry chalk Wolds.

Of the possible socio-economic explanations, the less appealing is that austere monastic practices inhibited the free flow of coinage. While there may have been some reserve on sacred ground, it would have been accepted that money lubricated the habitual transactions of daily life. Little more convincing is the proposition that the dominance of minsters in the region meant that goods were imported to support religious communities such that coinage flowed out. This would not prevent the loss of either coins or artefacts locally. Of possibly political explanations in the ninth century, it is inconceivable that Bernician influence or a continuing Celtic isolationism adversely affected the Vale, which was in the heart of Deira.

In the absence of adequate explanation, one must hope that future finds and improved access will show this discrepancy to be apparent not real. Until then, and given that 'the management for profit of church estates was a requirement of canon law',[1242] the 'minster hypothesis' lacks substantive economic evidence in Ryedale despite the prevalence of religious houses.

7.6.3 Comparison to Normal Distribution

For both eighth and ninth centuries, the Vale correlates closely (96 per cent, *Dataset 1*) with the numismatic norm. While the corpus is unexpectedly small it is not temporally skewed.[1243] *Graph 13* illustrates the chronological dispersal of finds at the main sites. While there are hints of early monetary activity, the dispersal is sparse with only Malton and West Heslerton suggesting continuity.

7.6.4 Comparison to Roman Finds

The relative proportions of finds for the Roman period are somewhat anomalous. With PAS showing over 850 coin finds for the Vale, including *c.* 130 from the Cawton area at the west end, this represents 7 per cent of over 17,600 Roman coin finds for the north,[1244] compared to 6.1 per cent for the Anglo-Saxon period, from a total of 1,168. Finds are well, and fairly evenly, spread throughout the north and south tracks in the Vale of Pickering, *Dataset 7, Finds Comparison.*

This demonstrates that in antiquity the Vale was undistinguished (by paucity) in its monetary activity and, more significantly, that Roman detecting finds are reasonably unrestricted in distribution—neither under-reporting nor denial of access should be an inhibition on finds from later periods,[1245] The numismatic proportions for the two periods are comparable and do not detract from the conclusion that the Anglian religious houses appear not to have enhanced local economic activity.

However, the artefactual pattern differs from the numismatic, *Dataset 7, Finds Comparison.* While Roman objects account for 6.6 per cent of the Roman corpus for the north, the proportion of early Anglo-Saxon artefacts is only 1.6 per cent.[1246] Access can be eliminated as an explanation. Furthermore, while slender shillings, *sceattas* and *stycas* are far harder to find than the bulkier Roman denominations, this is unlikely to hold for artefacts.[1247] Moreover, it is unlikely that there will be bias in reporting as typically the finder will lack chronological discrimination. Therefore, the Anglian artefactual paucity seems real.

7.6.5 The Artefactual Dataset

Although the sample in *Dataset 19, Artefacts—Summary* is too small to make safe assessments: there are 44 artefacts of only 14 types. Mounts, sleeve clasps, buckles and brooches are far more common than norm, and pins far less common. There are no strap-ends. Yet there seems to be a dominance of dress accessories and regional variation in fastener use. See *Dataset 19, Categories* and *Accessories.*

[1242] Smith (2006, 132).

[1243] Basing the computation on *Dataset 19* makes little difference as it is only slightly the more detailed.

[1244] As at December 2015.

[1245] Knowledgeable local detectorists, Tony Laverack (*pers. comm.* April 2015), and Andy Gillis (*pers. comm.* 3rd December 2015) agree that sites with Anglo-Saxon coins nearly always also produce Roman coins.

[1246] Though the correlation between coins and artefacts is significantly stronger in the later period, 97 per cent against 65 per cent for the Roman period (*Dataset 7, Finds Comparison*).

[1247] Logically the older artefacts are at greater depth.

The detailed artefactual evidence for the north and south tracks is shown in *Dataset 19, Artefacts—Summary*.

The PAS extract falls well short of comprehensive recording of finds, especially in view of the prolific material from West Heslerton. Nearly two-thirds of sites have produced three or fewer artefacts. *Co-occurrence* for the Vale is 53 per cent—more than half the sites with artefacts also have coins. This lies between the results for the Wolds (70 per cent) and the Central Lowlands (39 per cent). This statistical profile defines rather than resolves the anomalous situation in the Vale of Pickering. Just where one would expect to find the engine of economic growth there is a near void. The less fertile dry chalk Wolds are considerably more fecund economically.

Dataset 19, Coin Metal Mix shows transactions to have been settled with both *sceattas* and *stycas*. Even though this region is poorly represented numismatically, there is a convincing spatial and temporal proximity of coin and artefact finds to evidence monetization, though the sample is too small for statistical confidence. *Dataset 19, Coin Age Mix* is inconclusive regarding site mobility and stability.

7.6.6 Conclusion

In terms of periodic distribution of coinage, *Dataset 1* shows the Vale of Pickering to be close to the norm.

All early Anglo-Saxon coin finds, typically alongside more prolific Roman finds, are near the north and south routes, signifying either absence of contemporary commercial activity in the lower lying marshy Vale or restricted current access.

The quantum of recoveries of both artefacts and coins, separately and in association, fails to meet expectations that the Vale of Pickering, with its numerous religious houses, was a focus of economic activity as predicted by the minster hypothesis. Woods argued for strong royal connections to the Vale of Pickering, seeing its monasteries as playing a dominant rôle in Deira until the School of York developed.[1248] Powlesland warned of water-table problems, which may be a causal factor.[1249] Plausibly, lack of access is a recovery factor preventing accumulation of convincing evidence, but the distribution of Roman finds undermines this. How this picture compares to northern royal and minster locations is discussed below.

[1248] Wood (2008b, 18, 25).
[1249] Powlesland (1997, 102).

7.6.7 Illustrations—the Vale of Pickering

Figure 145: Malton finds of Merovingian *tremisses*. (Courtesy Spink & Son Limited)[1250]

Figure 146: Malton find: Abbasid, Caliph al-Mutawakkil or al Mustai'in, 854–64.

Figure 147: Pale-gold shilling of Pada, runic reverse. Found Sherburn.[1251]

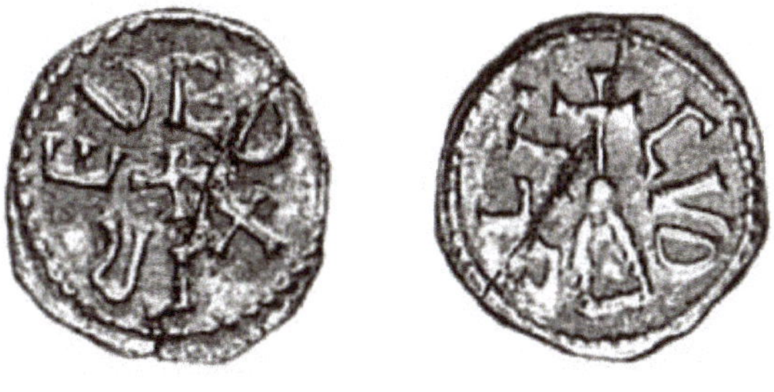

Figure 148: Kirkbymoorside: iconic 'shrine issue' *sceat* of Æthelred I (*EMC* 1997.8204). (Courtesy *SCBI*48, 204)

[1250] March 2014 auction 14004 lot 1337.
[1251] Abramson Pa02, CR 2011.77, *EMC* 2010.0248. *cf*.: the Finglesham Cemetery find. Rigold (*BNJ*1960, 51, PaIA2).

Figure 149: Seamer: rare 'two-crozier' joint issue *sceat*.

Figure 150: Rillington: rare 'AЯ' variety of Eadberht *sceat*.

7.7 Bernicia and the North

This is the final case study and considers the northerly regal and ecclesiastical sites: the royal palaces of Yeavering and Bamburgh first then the religious/minster locations of Whithorn, Whitby, and Lindisfarne.[1252] There are numerous other minster sites devoid of finds[1253] but to ensure that sites where no coins are present are considered, the unusual cemetery at Street House is described.

The Cheviots are a granite outcrop in the Borders with many peaks over 500 metres. Yeavering, presumed site of a Bernician royal palace, Bede's *Ad Gefrin* where Edwin met Paulinus in 627, is situated on the River Glen, near the twin-peak of Yeavering Bell, fortified in antiquity.

The North York Moors, largely above the plough-zone, present a complex Jurassic geology modified by repeated movement, inundation and glaciation. Water erosion has exposed the older rock both at the coast and in river valleys. The high moors are underlain by sandstone and the Tabular Hills by limestone. These infertile areas were largely deforested in the Bronze Age and were sparsely populated in early medieval period.

The historical and economic background is described at section 4.2.

7.7.1 Vicii Regius—Regal Sites

'It was aristocratic demand that mattered.'
Chris Wickham (2005, 824).

[1252] Manby, Moorhouse & Ottaway (2003, *Map* 1).
[1253] Such as Jarrow/Monkwearmouth.

Yeavering

According to Hope-Taylor it is the 'long series of correspondences between events recorded in history and the physical results of human activity on the site of *Ad Gefrin*'[1254] which give confidence to the conventional description of Bernician evolution. O'Brien summarized recent scholarship on Hope-Taylor's view of a hybrid culture.[1255] This is the site of the 'grandstand', or auditorium, from which Edwin addressed hundreds according to Bede.[1256] Other features include the palisaded Great Enclosure, The Great and Lesser Halls, and the inhumations including a battle cemetery.[1257]

Yeavering, more *Thing* than *villa regia*,[1258] lies a day's walk inland from Bamburgh and Lindisfarne. It was an early native British centre before the Romans built an *oppidum* on the Bell. Yeavering was abandoned in favour of Milfield, *Mælmin*.[1259] This occurred well before Bede recorded the abandonment in 731 and after the loss of a gold-washed imitation *tremissis* on copper core dated to the mid-seventh century

The identification as issuer of this imitation of Bertoaldus by Lafaurie, confirmed by Kent,[1260] is doubtful.[1261] Nor is Kent's argument that Bertoaldus issued in pale gold, such that his emissions date from the 630s or 640s, reliable in the case of a base, blundered, counterfeit. Lafaurie's date of *c.* 650–60 *may*, by chance, be more accurate. This is the only recorded coin find, though the site is pockmarked by night-hawkers. Assuming there are no other finds, this single Continental plated-gold find may re0

present élite gift exchange, albeit duplicitous, rather than early monetization, and early abandonment which contrasts to the absence of pre-ninth century coins at Bamburgh. The considerable interval abjures a settlement shift. No coins are reported from Milfield.

In the context of the number of Northumbrian sites where a specimen of East Anglian Series Q has been found, it is worth quoting Hope-Taylor: 'The idea of an East Anglian-Northumbrian political and cultural axis under Rædwald and Edwin is entirely in harmony with the historical facts: it could account for several remarkable

[1254] Hope-Taylor (1977, 277). Rollason (2003, 82–85). Alcock (2003, 238–56, 450). Higham and Ryan (2013, 135–37).
[1255] O'Brien (2011, 210–16).
[1256] Roebuck (2008, 121). Bede (1969, II, 14) described Yeavering as *villam regiam* and mentioned a *villa regia* and *basilicam* at *Campodunum* (Dewsbury) and a royal dwelling at *Loidis* (Leeds).
[1257] O'Brien (2011, 209–10).
[1258] O'Brien (2011, 211). Rollason (2003, 80–93), described three models and favoured conquest by Anglians.
[1259] Alcock (2003, 450). Higham and Ryan (2013, 136).
[1260] Hope-Taylor (1977, 183). See Belfort 1535.
[1261] The mint of Choae had several moneyers and this engraving is illegible. Belfort (1892–95, 432–41). Both the style of the bust and the Greek cross on the reverse, suggest that the original is the unusual runic tremissis of Huy, Belfort 1523, which has the only instance for Huy where the cross is not elaborate.

points of correspondence between the decorative arts of Rendlesham and Lindisfarne.'[1262]

In respect of Northumberland, Loveluck suggests that large enclosures may show that livestock as opposed to luxuries were 'a medium of expressing wealth and rank'.[1263] The implication here is that use of commodity money—livestock—obviated coinage.

Bamburgh

Din Guardi, ancient capital of the Brythonic kingdom of Brynaich, was taken by Anglian forces, led by Ida, around 547. As Bebbanburgh, renamed for Æthelfrith's wife Bebba, it was the capital of Bernicia, which was merged with Deira in 634, to form Northumbria with its capital at York.[1264] Bamburgh regained some importance when York fell to the Vikings in 867. The ancient royal Bamburgh Castle occupies a well defended dolerite coastal prominence.[1265]

Were one to judge from the material in *EMC*, consisting of the 67 single finds from Hope-Taylor's excavations of 1960–61 and 1970–74 and a few stray finds since, one would form the opinion that the 72 well-used coins recovered from this site comprise an undistinguished group balanced between brass (thirty-five) and blundered/illegible (thirty-seven) *stycas* separated by a single bronze specimen of Wulfhere. The silver-alloy coins of Eanred and Eanbald II, the brass *stycas* of Redwulf and the bronze of Osberht, are not represented. In summary, this modest and unexceptional accumulation of finds shows activity restricted to perhaps only 20 or so years before, say, the mid 850s.[1266] There is no case for Bamburgh as a mint and little sign of commercial,[1267] ecclesiastical or even royal endeavour. However, the hoard of 312 coins subsequently found by local metal-detectorists need to be assessed.[1268]

As *Dataset 20, Bamburgh* shows the chronology is confirmed rather than widened by this new material, which is again well used; a sole representative of Eanred's silver-alloy coinage cannot be taken as diagnostic, though the presence of more bronze *stycas* corroborates deposition relatively early in the reign of Osberht. A single specimen of Redwulf has no bearing on the date of deposition or site use. The higher than normal proportion of unidentifiable coins may merely reflect corrosive soil conditions. Pirie noted that several other sites exhibit early evidence of cessation—Wearmouth, Jarrow, Newcastle Black Gate,[1269] Lindisfarne, Dunbar and Aberlady.[1270] It could well be that all suffered related insecurity.

Recent archaeology has unearthed a further hoard of 77 fused and corroded *stycas* with residues of both vegetable fibres and textiles.[1271] Only around 40 of the coins have been identified, the others being blundered or uncertain. Æthelred II (twenty-six) predominates with seven coins attributable to each of Eanred (*Figure* 151) and Wigmund. There are no certain coins of Osberht or Wulfhere suggesting a deposition date, subject to further identifications, in the 840s rather than the 850s as suggested by the Treasure Report. This neither disturbs the chronology of *Dataset 20, Bamburgh* nor suggests the hoard was brought by the *micel here*.

In summary, while the brief duration of the coinage at Bamburgh is perhaps unexpected given its royal status, it is the very ordinariness of the coinage and lack of diversity which are positive indications of monetization, albeit brief. The absence of any type of imported Southumbrian or Continental coinage demonstrates that the site was a closely controlled military stronghold, rather than engaged in secular or religious activity. That there is a relative abundance of coinage must be viewed in the context of the high proportion (84 per cent) of hoard coins, reinforcing the control rather than economic function of the site.

Conclusion

These sites again emphasise the contrast between Bernician and Deiran locations. Bamburgh and Yeavering show that Bernician finds are largely the result of formal excavations with access to other areas inhibited, rather than the absence of stray finds being attributable to low occupancy. The Roman finds distribution, *Map 4*, confirms the paucity of finds in the north, other than along Hadrian's Wall.

Yeavering's lack of Anglo-Saxon coinage contrasts with Bamburgh's abundance of *stycas*, whereas the relatively prolific early-penny finds at the other royal palace, Driffield, are typical for the Wolds. Wood advocated a rôle for the cluster of minsters in the Lower Tyne from the late seventh century,[1272] but numismatic evidence for this is absent from the coin record discussed below.

Street House Cemetery

This unique, high status, square cemetery, between Redcar and Whitby, is rich in Kentish-influenced grave-goods (*Figure* 152) with over a hundred inhumations surrounding the bed-burial of a princess in a *Grübenhaus*. Other than two Iron Age coins, the absence of later coinage is notable

[1262] Hope-Taylor (1977, 321).
[1263] Loveluck (1996, 46). Banham and Faith (2014, 85).
[1264] Alcock (2003, 447).
[1265] Alcock (2003, 198–99).
[1266] *Graph* 6.1.
[1267] Pirie recorded a balance.
[1268] In 1999 (parcel A, 249) and 2002 (Parcel B, 63). The latter have an average weight of 0.99g compared to a database average of 1.06g.
[1269] *Graph* 6.2.

[1270] Pirie (2004, 74). Her speculations on 'Vinred' as a newly-discovered Northumbrian king (Eanred) and the blundered 'Antedi' as revival of a Celtic name in a society recalling its British heritage, are both misguided. *Graph* 5.3.
[1271] https://finds.org.uk/database/artefacts/record/id/279980
[1272] Wood (2008b, 25).

in such an élite site, especially in view of the Kentish influence.

Occasional finds (*Figure* 153) indicate long distance contacts but out of context and without accompanying material, all that can be concluded is that Continental merchants travelled widely and beyond recognised *wics*.

7.7.2 Ecclesiastical Sites

> 'Scot-free the Poets drank and ate;
> They paid no taxes to the State!'
>
> John Wolcot, *Odes of Condolence*, 1792.[1273]

In chapter 2, the rôle of minsters, largely as expounded by Blair and Foot, were discussed in broad terms. Three northern, coin-rich, monastic sites, Whithorn, Whitby, and Lindisfarne,[1274] all subjected to formal excavations, will now be contrasted to the paucity of sites in the Vale of Pickering. No separate study of western Northumbria has been made but artefact finds are discussed below.[1275]

Whithorn

Background

> 'The Whithorn finds make a vital contribution to the study of Northumbrian coins.'
>
> Peter Hill, The Whithorn Excavations (1990b, Supplement, 12).

Excavations at Whithorn were carried out mainly between 1984 and 1990 on the south slope of a small hill which is topped by the medieval church.

It is thought that the origin of the name Whithorn, *Candida Casa*, has ancient roots, connected with lime-washed buildings,[1276] which predate the arrival of St Ninian in the late fourth century.[1277] The site of the earliest Christian church in Scotland, as attested by the *Latinus* stone found in the 1880s,[1278] was under the influence of Bernicia by the sixth and seventh centuries.[1279] Whithorn grew into a full monastic community with Irish contacts as signified by pottery and glass finds, burial practices, double-walled wattle buildings and some elements of church architecture (though others have a wider currency,[1280] and the greatest influence is Northumbrian[1281]). Despite the defeat at Nechtansmere, Northumbrian influence seems to have continued as, by the time of Bede's *Ecclesiastical History* (*c.* 731), a Northumbrian bishopric, under Pecthelm, had been established to administer western domains.[1282]

The Isle of Whithorn afforded a natural harbour and the Galloway hinterland provided the site with raw materials including red deer antler, leather, iron and lead. These were worked locally[1283] and traded with merchants from Gaul and the Mediterranean for glassware, bronze pins, soapstone and whetstone.[1284] Later, Whithorn became a Hiberno-Norse trading post and place names reveal limited Norse settlement.[1285]

The periodic sequence of coin finds corresponds neatly with the stratigraphy.[1286] A children's graveyard within the precinct signifies a lay population alongside the monastery, which was probably also a shrine to St. Ninian. Food debris is interpreted as evidence that the royal entourage visited to collect renders. Archaeology from the Northumbrian period is well preserved but the settlement is far from fully explored. There is little penetration of coinage rurally, just a few finds of Northumbrian coins at Barhobble (Mochrum) and Luce Sands,[1287] possibly a beach market similar to Meols.[1288] However, the impressive volume of coin recoveries should not be interpreted solely as market activity, but probably also as cultic.

Moreover, as Brooke said: 'The Christian settlement at Whithorn has now to be seen, not as a retreat for contemplation and personal soul-saving, but as a resolute intrusion into the religious core of a tribal society.'[1289] Pagan practices are represented by nearby rock carvings.

As remarked earlier,[1290] the conflation of such a horned deity into the Northumbrian leonine crest may be intentionally ambiguous (*Figure* 154). Brooke added: 'How benign was that compromise between the new faith and the old religion.'[1291] The tenacity of cults should not be underestimated.

Coinage

Given the antiquity of the site and the clear indications of early trading activity, the absence of any coinage before Period 5 is a little surprising. Possibly, this is due to the relatively restricted excavation, so that early finds are yet to be discovered. The earliest specimen, in excellent condition (*Figure* 155L), lends weight to a northern source for Series J. This sits comfortably alongside the regal and ecclesiastical issues of York, present here in numbers. The

[1273] 'Scot-free' equates to 'free of dues', dues being the original meaning of *sceat*.
[1274] In addition to Beverley (152) already discussed.
[1275] Clark (2011).
[1276] In the tradition of St Martin of Tours signifying a Gallic connection.
[1277] *EH* (III, 4). Alcuin received a copy of *Miracula Nynie Episcopi*, St Ninian's life in verse.
[1278] Thomas (1992, 1–13).
[1279] Toop (2011, 103). Clark (2011, 114–15).
[1280] Cramp (1995, 15).
[1281] Cramp (1995, 16).
[1282] Cramp (1995, 13).
[1283] There is little evidence of manufacture in the immediate vicinity, Hill (1990, 21) but Mote of Mark was an industrial *atelier* (Alcock, 2003, 94–95, also 217–25 and 450).
[1284] Alcock (2003, ch. 8).
[1285] Hill (1990, 22).
[1286] Hill (1990, 8).
[1287] Pirie (2000, 64 and 214). Hill and Cowie (2001, 98–99).
[1288] Cramp (1995, 12). Hill and Cowie (2001, 99).
[1289] Brooke (1999, 21).
[1290] *Fn.* 577.
[1291] Brooke (1999, 21).

sceattas of Eadberht are well represented showing the rich variety of types. Conditions vary, demonstrating the replenishment of well-worn specimens; a joint issue *sceat* of Eadberht and Ecgberht is beautifully preserved (*Figure* 155R).

The contemporary *sceat* of King Beonna is a remarkable and territorially distant survivor of this typically tightly-distributed East Anglian coin.[1292] The scarce successor emissions of the fantastic beast type are represented only by a *sceat* of Alchred, showing continuity into the economically difficult third and early fourth quarters of the eighth century. A joint issue *sceat* of Æthelred I with Archbishop Eanbald I (790–96) and four specimens of Æthelred I's named moneyer issues carry coin use into the late eighth century. The latter cover three of the five moneyers, all are rare varieties including a unique new type for Tidwulf.[1293]

The impression of this precious mix of rare types, particularly the *sceat* of Beonna, is enhanced by the presence of no less than 22 specimens of silver-alloy—including a strikingly rare Tidwine—many in an excellent state. Perhaps this impressive assemblage is related to the healing cult of St Ninian and the payment of tribute in coin[1294] may have afforded some artefactual conspicuous consumption.[1295] Coincidentally, there are also 22 base *stycas*.[1296] *Dataset 1* shows that, in the normal distribution, the brass *stycas* substantially exceeded the silver-alloy coins.[1297] However, Whithorn has a unique and short profile and, given that there is only one bronze *styca* of Osberht[1298] the site clearly suffered a marked reversal, at least in terms of coin circulation, early in the period of Eanred's production of brass coins.[1299] Perhaps, a scatter of medieval pennies defines the delay in recovery—the mix is noteworthy: two of these are Hiberno-Norse (995–1150), one Scottish (1124–53) and two southern (Edgar and Cnut). The archaeological report appropriately describes this period as 'The Hidden Years (*c.* 850–1250)' after which activity is more evident.[1300]

Discussion

Several theories can be advanced for Whithorn's decline. First, could there have been the Anglian settlement shift which seems to occur elsewhere—from Heslington Hill to Fishergate,[1301] and North Ferriby to Newbald?[1302] Candidates include Barhobble (Mochrum) and Luce Sands. The former, a monastic site, has produce only one coin—a *sceat* of Eadberht and the latter, 13 coins consisting of Periods N8, N9, N10a and N10c. The latter is a more typical profile but there is nothing here to suggest a settlement shift. Indeed, at a slightly later date, the reverse seems to be the case—the clergy of Lindisfarne arrived in Whithorn around 882 or 883.[1303] Looking further afield, the periodic profile of Carlisle is closer to the norm and may disguise a shift of commercial activity from Whithorn.[1304]

It speaks volumes for the rich diversity of the Northumbrian coinage when a site as limited and mundane in its numismatic material as Carlisle, is able to produce a brace of recorded, but seemingly unremarked, unique specimens: a new variety of the joint issue of Æthelred I and Eanbald I with the cross within the legend, and a *styca* by Wilheah with a runic initial *wynn* in the reverse inscription (*Figure* 156).[1305]

While the phasing of the Carlisle material dovetails neatly with Whithorn, the nature of the finds contrasts. Carlisle's coin assemblage—there is the familiar Series Q singleton (*Figure* 157), but 85 per cent are base *stycas* belonging to Period N10—shows every sign of heavy use, whereas that at Whithorn is earlier, distinctive and well-preserved. One would struggle to argue with conviction that a shift in activity from one site to the other has occurred. However, describing the Carlisle finds as *mundane* is indicative that monetization has taken place—as with the single finds in inner York, although the absolute number may be modest, the widespread urban distribution shows that *stycas* were widely used, spatially and societally.[1306]

The weakness of the settlement shift argument is that this would be a symptom when we are seeking a cause. Might a second, better explanation for the apparent decline at

[1292] Pirie 'The early medieval coins' no. 62 in Hill (1996). Archibald, Fenwick and Cowell (1995, 15, C13). Might there be a connection with the lead trial piece of Beonna's interlace type recently found not far from Ripon Cathedral? Abramson Sylloge, *SCBI*69 (2018, 961b).

[1293] *SL* 80–80, 80–90, 83–10 and for the new Tidwulf variety, 82–50.

[1294] Alcock (2003, 224).

[1295] Davies (1998, 6–7). Or the coins may be an example of liminal 'self-shaping', Clark (2011, 114).

[1296] The period N10a material comes from a confined area outside the inner precinct and, were this a scattered hoard, it should be excluded from the comparison with the normal distribution, thus increasing the skew even further.

[1297] For non-hoard material, the ratio is usually around 7:1. The correlation for *stycas* is a mere 53 per cent.

[1298] There are three blundered specimens of unknown period.

[1299] *Graph 5, no. 28.*

[1300] Hill (1990, 22). Hill (1997) referred to 'The Missing Years'.

[1301] See *fn.* 895.

[1302] Leeds (1913, 15–16). Beresford (1954). Arnold (1977, 309–15; 1988, 37–49). Arnold and Wardle (1981, 145–49). Hodges (1989, 80–92). Welch (1985, 13–25). Hodges (1989, 43–68). Hamerow (1991, 1–17). Hines (1997). Hansen and Wickham (2000). Moreland (2000b, 82–84). Hoggett (2010, 132–35). Higham and Ryan (2013, 199). Blair (2014, *CA* 291, http://www.archaeology.co.uk/articles/features/exploring-anglo-saxon-settlement.htm), gives a summary of 'grey literature'.

[1303] Dumville (1997, 24). Presumably they brought the cult of St Cuthbert as 'Kirkcudbright' is derived from 'kirk of St Cuthbert'.

[1304] The road between presumably was a pilgrim route given the proximity of the famous crosses of Hoddom, Ruthwell and Bewcastle (Rollason, 2003, *Map* 3, 29).

[1305] Stewart Lyon (*pers. comm.* 20th December 2014) pointed out that *CKN*462 from Coppergate may be similar. Pirie had discussed these pieces (archive, Carlisle, July 1981, unpublished) and another from the 1695 Ripon hoard.

[1306] *Styca* finds at excavations in Carlisle, according to Pirie 2000 (200–09) occur at Abbey Street (1) Blackfriars Street (3), Annetwell Street (Tullie House, 13, including the runic-initialled Wilheah), Castle Street (11), Scotch Street (3), Sewerworks (3), Town Dykes Orchard (1), The Lanes: Keays Lane (2), Laws Lane (1) Lewthwaites Lane (1) (Pirie noted that The Lanes finds are well-worn, well east of the main ninth century settlement and residual [archive, Carlisle, 22nd August 1991]) and at the Cathedral (unstratified deposits generally in better condition than other

Whithorn be a diminution in, rather than a transfer of, trade, possibly as a consequence of hostile Viking incursions in the 830s? To quote Dumville: 'Colonisation...was unlikely to be a peaceful process and raiding was an essential stage in probing, softening up, or dislodging the indigenous inhabitants of a potential settlement area.'[1307] He also spoke of a 'monastic thessalocracy' in the Western Isles from 550 to 800, referring to the sea-borne piratical empire of the Vikings and the consequent insecurity and disruption.[1308] Whithorn would have been a poorly-defended 'honey pot' just as was Lindisfarne.

Gallgoídil is a term used for what may have been 'Gaels' influenced by, or racially mixed with, Scandinavians. This seems to be the origins of the term Galloway which came into use as Northumbria was fading after York fell to the *micel here.*[1309] But perhaps Northumbrian support for Whithorn had failed well before this, either as a consequence of the attack on Lindisfarne or, plausibly, with power ceded under the 829 settlement at Dore. The growing powers in southern Scotland were the Picts and the Strathclyde Britons, though the former suffered a catastrophic defeat by the Vikings at northerly Fortriu in 839 before being attacked by Cináed mac Ailpín (Kenneth MacAlpine).[1310]

There are two hoards of the period, both on the inland route to Whithorn, no doubt deposited as a consequence of such upheavals. The Lochar Moss hoard is likely to have been the source of material gifted in 1782 to the Edinburgh Museum.[1311] This seems to have included southern *sceattas* or pennies and fifteen *stycas*, though such mixed hoards are most unusual. A silver crucifix found in the same leather bag is now lost but may hint at a cleric travelling to or from Whithorn, some 66 miles away. Another mixed hoard, only 23 miles from Whithorn, was 'salvaged from a cottar's peat fire in 1912'[1312] at Talnotrie (now Talnotry) included a mix of decorated pins and strap-ends of English origin, Viking-style weights (such as unearthed at Whithorn), fragments of a *Christiana Religio denier* of Louis the Pious and of dirhams, six *stycas*, four Southumbrian pennies of Burgred including one which has been mounted. Archibald dated the deposition to 'the early or mid-870s' and Graham-Campbell surmised this hoard to be the property, from several sources, of a native Northumbrian metalworker rather than Viking hack-silver.[1313] Metcalf facilitated this attribution by explaining that incoming Carolingian coins were destined for the melting pot,[1314] the presumed intention of the hoard-maker. Certainly, the historical context is one of Viking predation in Scotland and the archaeological context of peat cuttings suggests burial for safe-keeping and later retrieval.

In this context, two contemporary coins found at the Churchyard Holm field, Hoddom, near Ecclefechan, Dumfries and Galloway, 80 miles to the east of Whithorn on the road to Carlisle, merit consideration.

One is a brass *styca* of Æthelred the other a fragmentary, but almost pristine, *denier* of Lothar I (840–55) (*Figure* 158),[1315] minted in Pavia, Italy, again suggestive of contact with the Continent,[1316] perhaps in preference to Southumbria.

There is a small scattering of *sceattas* and *stycas* on the roads leading east and south. At Castle Douglas 25 miles west of Whithorn there is an illegible *styca* three more at Ribblehead, four finds at Settle—Æthelred I *sceat* by Cuthheard, a silver-alloy coin, and three Æthelred II *stycas*. Malham has yielded a *sceat* of Eadberht and two brass *stycas* of Eanred. Not so obviously in the direction of York are four coins from Dacre: a silver-alloy coin a *styca* of Æthelred and two illegible specimens. Grange-over-Sands has a *styca* of Eanred, three of Æthelred II and two illegible. One may surmise that all are conceivably losses by traders, travellers or pilgrims whose routes are marked by monumentality.[1317]

A third alternative or contributory cause of the apparent decline of Whithorn may be the watershed event separating archaeological phases II and III, namely, the destruction by fire of the church and burial chapel. The extent and impact of this catastrophe is difficult to gauge.

While the precise reasons for the perceived and sudden decline of Whithorn are obscured, one can assume that the continuing, and better documented, attacks on Iona were probably widespread and far from conducive to ecclesiastical tranquillity. However, as a destination for pilgrims to the healing cult of St Ninian,[1318] a change in sentiment or loss of enthusiasm may be a more likely, if intangible, fourth explanation for decline rather than anything more concrete or objective.

This presumed cultic activity[1319] contributes to an assessment of the extent of monetization. In Whithorn's heyday, pilgrims, probably from elsewhere in Northumbria if not further afield, paying tribute, or seeking personal redemption or healing, were clearly sufficiently confident in the status of a coinage conveying clear theological attributes, that its use would not jeopardise their mission. Whilst this elevated status for the silver coinage of the

local finds, including: 1 sceat of Æthelred I with Eanbald I, 17 *stycas*, and 1 enigmatic uniface piece showing a standing, robed, crowned bishop). The sole Southumbrian sceat, unsurprisingly, is an East Anglian Series Q1G, *SL*63–100, *EMC* 1977.0014, which has clear religious iconography.

1307 Dumville (1997, 4).

1308 Dumville (1997, 17–18).

1309 Dumville (1997, 29).

1310 Dumville (1997, 34).

1311 Graham-Campbell (2001, 20).

1312 Archibald in Webster and Backhouse (1991, 248 (f)). Graham-Campbell (2001, 21–23) related that on complaining to the Chancellor of the Exchange, Lloyd George, the finder, a Mr Thomas Gordon had the consideration doubled—to two pounds!

1313 Graham-Campbell (2001, 20).

1314 Metcalf (1998b, 175–76).

1315 Not Louis the Pious as thought by Pirie (1991, archive).

1316 Or a bullion economy.

1317 Toop (2011, 86).

1318 Toop (2011, 103).

1319 With coin finds in and around the church, Hill (1990a,14).

eighth century is perhaps too precious for a denomination fit for commonplace exchange, it is a vital steppingstone to the eventual wider penetration of a baser circulating medium.

Whitby

> 'Time, which subverts and destroys the greatest works of mankind,
> hath an equal property of bringing things to light.'
> Francis Drake, antiquary, in *Eboracum*, 1747.

The earliest settlement at Whitby probably grew around the bridging point of the River Esk as it enters the North Sea. The river mouth and harbour are on a geological fault resulting in steep cliffs either side and affording natural advantages. The double monastery of Whitby, founded by Oswy in 657, served as the venue for the highly significant Synod of 664. Oswy's niece Hild was the first abbess and it is likely that wattle and daub remains mark her foundation at *Strenæshalch* prior to more permanent and extensive stone construction, possibly in her lifetime.[1320]

At 9:00am on Wednesday 16th December 1914, Rear Admiral Hipper's squadron of five battlecruisers launched an unprovoked attack on Whitby, having earlier attacked Hartlepool and Scarborough.[1321] It is no compensation to the fatalities that restoration of damage to Whitby Abbey, by the Office of Works commencing in 1920, led to the excavation of an open field area north of the Abbey in 1923–25, and the recovery of artefacts.[1322] In 1923–24 a large central area was uncovered (Area A) and in 1924–25 a series of trenches were dug to the east and west (Area B).[1323] The numismatic material seems to have been transferred to the British Museum at the outbreak of hostilities in 1939, but by this time the record had lost integrity, some of which Pirie was able to restore.[1324] Area A included a purse-hoard of 22 brass *stycas* found on the north side of the north transept on seventh March 1924, which Pirie tentatively re-assembled based on 'condition, toning and surface accretion', *Dataset 20, Whitby.*[1325]

While there remains some difficulty in reconciling various listings,[1326] this need not detain us as the *EMC* content now supersedes previous *corpora*. The material from both areas A and B and the hoard differ little. In fretting over the minutiæ of the somewhat inadequate record-keeping and the attribution of *stycas*, Pirie fails to report on the non-Northumbrian *sceattas*.[1327]

For the primary periods, the site produces seven *sceattas*—two each of the local Aldfrith type, from the Low Countries, Series D and E. The sole Southumbrian representative is a Series BZ a fairly exotic species with religious iconography. All are heavily worn so there is no direct evidence that coinage arrived before *c.* 710. For the secondary periods, the mix is wide, if lacking depth—there is also a single specimen of the putative northern Series J single *sceattas* of Series H (a unique variety, *SL*49–10), K, L, Q, R, U in addition to a couple of exotic types—a possibly unique Celtic cross (*SL*28–30, *SCBI*63 no. 543) and a K/N mule (*SL*37)—and imported from the Continent, an E and a G.

For the Northumbrian *sceattas*, the site is strong in Eadberht with 10 examples, and a further four for the joint issue with Ecgberht. There is a single fantastic beast type for Ælfwald I and one joint issue of Æthelred I with Eanbald I. The inscriptional type for Æthelred I is again strong, with 14 specimens. This is matched by the silver rich emissions of Eanred and Eanbald II before substantial growth in coinage volume in the period of the brass *styca*. There are three *stycas* recorded for Osberht but this cannot be verified, and none for Wulfhere.

More recent excavations were carried out between 1993 and 2014. Wilmott reported that only two Anglian period coins surfaced, both from the area of the southern cemetery. This included a Series E *sceat* from the fill of a primary grave, though not placed and a base *styca* of Eanbald II (or possibly Redwulf)[1328] from the upper fill of the cemetery boundary ditch. See *Graph* 12.2.

This assemblage reveals a healthy picture of a site both active in the local economy and widely connected with Southumbria and the Low Countries in the first half of the eighth century—the assemblage represents Kent, London, East Anglia, the Thames Valley, and Frisia. The usual third quarter recession is marked by a dearth of specimens before a revival during Æthelred I's second reign. The post-Lindisfarne recovery is strong in the ninth century with vigorous use of the circulating medium, denoting the progress of monetization. This is exactly what may be predicted for a monastic coastal site with a natural harbour, a productive hinterland and fisheries, subject to the vagaries of early medieval political life. As Leahy said:

1320 Rahtz (1976). Further limited site investigation was carried out by Rahtz in 1958, which showed evidence of Saxon settlement outside the Abbey grounds.

1321 Pickup (2012, 311).

1322 The Finds Register noted 1,136 items between 8th November 1920 and 30th May 1928.

1323 Pirie (1991–92). Leahy (2000, 72), attributed recovery of coins at Whitby to 'the payment of *baksheesh*'.

1324 Roman finds, including 11 coins, are described in Kitson (Pirie archive, 1935, 138–39), who recorded Chief Inspector of Ancient Monuments Sir Charles Peers' report that two Constantinian coins were found in a hoard of *stycas* at Whitby (see also Allan, 1943 and Metcalf, 1960, 53), which may raise issues about the integrity of the hoard as much as the possibility of such anachronistic intrusions. The non-numismatic material has fared little better. Stopford made the case for reopening archaeological investigations.

1325 Pirie (1991–92, Appendix A).

1326 Allan (1943), R&M (1984), Booth (1984) and Pirie (1986a and 1991–92). *EMC* includes 10 coins attributed to Whitby rather than Whitby Abbey. The eighth century *sceattas* include two unidentified, a Series U, three Eadberht, one more with Ecgberht and one of Æthelred I, second reign. One ninth century coin is from Eanred's silver-alloy period [N9] and one *styca* is unidentified.

1327 To be fair, Archibald (*corr.* 18th October 1991) had requested initially a corpus of just the Northumbrian coins in the BM Whitby cabinet. Allan (*Archaeologia* 89, 1943, 85–86.) took a broader, if brief, view.

1328 Not seen.

'Seen in terms of an extra-mural market, this is precisely what would be expected.'[1329] The mix of coins could be interpreted more as of a secular, commercial nature rather than conveying much in terms of ecclesiastical power or iconography, although the Celtic cross *sceat* mentioned above is exceptional (*Figure* 159). Its portrayal of a cowled, female, figure with long cross pommée either side, standing in a celestial boat, makes a particularly apt *imprimatur* for St. Hild. Even though there are very few other Southumbrian *sceattas* from this site, it must be coincidence rather than selective use, that brings a further two showing similar standing figure reverses and a third, a Series Qiv (*Figure* 160), which recalls the ecclesiastical ties between York and East Anglia through use of an animal reminiscent of, but much later than, Aldfrith's beast.

Clearly, other artefactual finds of this period indicate activity associated with the monastery, particularly incised stone crosses and styli,[1330] but also items of a domestic and personal nature, contemporary with the coinage, such as a comb, probably no later than eighth or early ninth century, with runic inscription '...God look on us, God Almighty help (the) kindred spirit...'[1331]

The paucity of coins for Osberht and absence of those for Wulfhere is interpreted as an abandonment of the site in the early 850s, possibly related to the general vulnerability of this coastal site to Viking attack rather than directly as a result of the later activities of the *micel here.* Such abandonment may not have been short-lived as there are no pennies—or other artefacts—to indicate a restoration of activity until after the Norman Conquest.

Lindisfarne[1332]

> '...fiery dragons were seen flying in the sky.'
>
> *ASC*, 793.

Lindisfarne is a tidal island of 400 hectares, across the bay from Bamburgh.[1333] Under the auspices of Oswald, Aidan of Iona founded the monastery around 634. The episcopal succession of Finian, Cuthbert and Eadfrith in the seventh century and Eadberht in the eighth, ensured that this was the base for conversion activity in the north of England with missions travelling far afield. Though Wilfrid gained possession on Cuthbert's death in 687, the community of St Cuthbert was resilient, even to the Vikings.[1334]

In view of this, the dearth of coins at this high-status site would be unexpected, if not for the recovery constraint provided by its protected status. The monastic farming site at Green Shiel in the north of the island, possibly related to vellum production,[1335] divulged 17 coins: one of silver-alloy and 16 brass *stycas*. Issuers include only Eanred, Æthelred II and Wigmund, denoting a brief period of activity in the second quarter of the ninth century, given that only the two brass *stycas* of Æthelred II's restoration moneyer Eardwulf are in fine condition. There are a mere four coins not from the Green Shiel site: single fantastic beast *sceattas* of Eadberht and Æthelred I and two brass *stycas*. No images are available for the Æthelred I *sceat* but the Eadberht coin is much worn, signifying loss long after issuance.[1336]

What may be concluded from such slender evidence is that Lindisfarne recovered from the disastrous Viking plunder of 793 but what, presumably, was an austere regime discouraged economic activity within the *vallum monasterii*. While coin production was clearly deferred for decades, Eardwulf's seemingly trivial output notwithstanding, it is likely that coin use diminished over time.

7.7.3 Comparison to Normal Distribution

For Bernicia, single finds in the eighth century correlate 92 per cent to norm but in the ninth are closer at 98 per cent, possibly signifying a higher degree of monetization after the introduction of the lower denomination *styca*, reflecting its better revenue raising potential.

Graphs 7 and 8 illustrate the chronological dispersal of finds at the main sites. Yeavering is an anomaly with only a counterfeit *tremissis*. Whithorn, and in the later stages, Carlisle, are the only sites to show any continuity.

7.7.4 Comparison to Roman Finds

The relative proportions of Roman and early Anglo-Saxon coin finds in Bernicia and the north-west, taken together are similar at *c*. 16 per cent, *Dataset 7, Finds Comparison*, even though the distributions focus on markedly different locations of economic activity. However, as might be expected in view of the provisioning needs of the military defences along Hadrian's Wall, the associated supply routes and fortifications elsewhere, Roman artefactual material in the northern region, accounts for a quarter of all northern non-numismatic Roman finds, whereas Anglian finds are *c*. 10 per cent, again showing the lack of correlation between the period for the two finds categories.

7.7.5 The Artefactual Dataset

Twenty-three outlying, northern and western locations, composed of four on the north-east edge of the North York

[1329] Leahy (2000, 78).
[1330] Rahtz (1967). Cramp (1976). http://www.pastscape.org.uk/hob.aspx?hob_id=7835
[1331] Found Whitby, 1867 (Whitby Museum).
[1332] English Heritage (2009).
[1333] Holdsworth (1995, *figure 14*).
[1334] Woodman (2012, 12). Also, Alcock (2003, 450).

[1335] David Petts, Durham University, lecture, 18th November 2015, 'Early Medieval Lindisfarne', York Seminar Series. The claim of Bruce-Mitford (1967, 2) that Ceolfrith's three bibles, written at Wearmouth and Jarrow, needed skins from 1,550 calves, exemplifies the scale of animal rearing.
[1336] *Graph* 5.4.

Moors, nine in Northumbria, four in Cravendale,[1337] three near Carlisle, two in Cumbria and one on the Wirral, have produced a total of 221 artefacts.[1338] These are included as likely communications routes between the great ecclesiastical centres such as York, Whitby, Carlisle and Whithorn.

A cruciform pendant (*Figure* 161) links Redcar with several other finds locations on what could well have been a route between Whitby and Whithorn. These include Loftus, Newby, Croft, Stapleton, Moulton, East Layton and Whorlton. The route probably then followed the River Greta from Bowes to Brough. There are no associated coin finds other than those excavated at Whitby.

The PAS database for County Durham reveals one further artefact, a fine scabbard mount from Gainford,[1339] and one coin, a worn *sceat* of Eadberht from Hawthorn. It seems a reasonable claim, therefore, that Bernicia, beyond the major excavated sites, is deficient in coinage.

7.7.6 Conclusion

The established ecclesiastical centres were routine users of both silver and base coins and stray finds show regular travel between these central places. It seems likely that the paucity of finds in the more northerly hinterlands is due to recovery factors, particularly restricted access, given the small quantum of Roman finds, *Map 4*. What can be concluded is that there is a difference in coin use patterns between Bernicia and Deira.[1340] The former, including western Northumbria, is represented by concentrations of finds around established sites whereas the latter has a diffuse usage, with the iceberg revealed in many specific locations of evident economic activity. However, it is not possible to separately characterize regal and ecclesiastical sites by their coin volume, density or mix. Where coins appear in numbers, typically as a result of trade, types associated with royal or church emissions are thoroughly mixed.

This concludes the case studies. Detailed application of the analytical tools for each region, at the parish level, has illuminated differences in trading and settlement patterns and facilitated distinctive economic characterization, especially contrasting the Wolds and surrounding lowlands. The numismatic and artefactual material has enabled conclusions to be drawn in addressing the major questions raised in chapter one.

7.7.7 Illustrations—Bernicia and the North

Figure 151: Bamburgh: silver-alloy coin of Eanred by Wulfheard (Pirie, 2004, A1). (Courtesy Pirie archive)

Figure 152: Street House: pendant grave finds. (Courtesy Stephen Sherlock)[1341]

Figure 153: Burton-in-Kendal: Dronrijp *tremissis*. (Courtesy Portable Antiquities Scheme)[1342]

[1337] Craven has been a distinctive region from ancient times. Loveluck (2003, 158).
[1338] This includes the Irish Sea/Merseyside location of Meols, from which single finds of artefacts and coins have been recovered—including Byzantine *nummi*.
[1339] Alcock (2003, 153) noted weapon burials at Greenbank (Darlington) and Norton.
[1340] Perhaps the austerity of the Irish educated Oswald had long-term influence. Bede (1969, III, 3).

[1341] http://antiquity.ac.uk/projgall/sherlock/index.html
[1342] PAS LANCUM-3E51D8

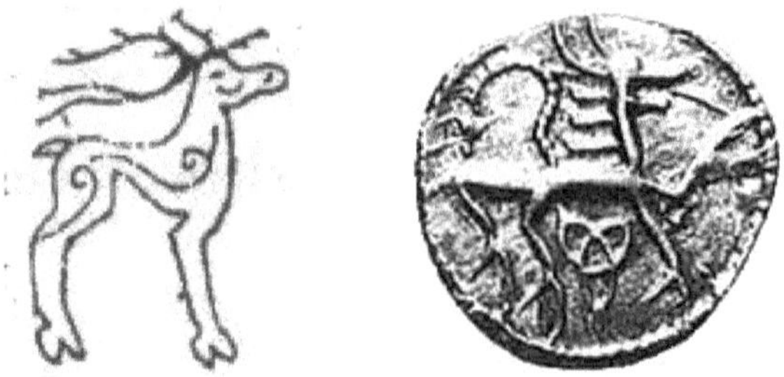

Figure 154: L: Carvings from Eggerness Peninsula. (Courtesy of the Whithorn Trust) R: *Sceat* of Eadberht, Whithorn (*EMC*1997.0404).[1343]

Figure 155: Whithorn, *sceattas*. L: Series J, 85. R: Eadberht with Ecgberht, 737–58. *EMC* 1997.0461 and 0406 (Whithorn 61 and 6).

Figure 156: Unique varieties from Carlisle. L: joint issue sceat, *EMC* 1997.8207. R: styca of Eanred, *EMC* 1997.8622, reverse only. (Courtesy *SCBI*48, 207 and 422)

Figure 157: Carlisle: *Sceat* of East Anglian Series Q1G. *EMC* 1977.0014, *SL*63–100. (Courtesy British Numismatic Society)

Figure 158: Carolingian *denier*, Hoddom (*EMC* 2001.0445). (Courtesy Galata Print Limited)[1344]

1343 Image left: Brooke, 1999, fig. 2B. Horned Cernunnos, 'Father of the Gods' in Celtic terms is shown on the Gundestrup cauldron next to a horned stag (Ellis, 1998) close in style to a unique sceat of Series Q (SL64–80) and similar to the fantastic animal of Northumbrian Series Y. (Ross, 1967, 418–23). Higham (1993, 26) also mentions the Carvetti — 'deer people' — of Cumbria. Sceat image courtesy Sutton Publishers (Hill, 1990).
1344 Pirie (2000, 77).

Figure 159: A possibly unique Celtic cross *sceat* bearing an apt imprimatur for St. Hild. (Courtesy *EMC*)[1345]

Figure 160: Reverses of *sceattas* found at Whitby. *EMC* 1977.0097, 1977.0099 and 1977.0100.[1346]

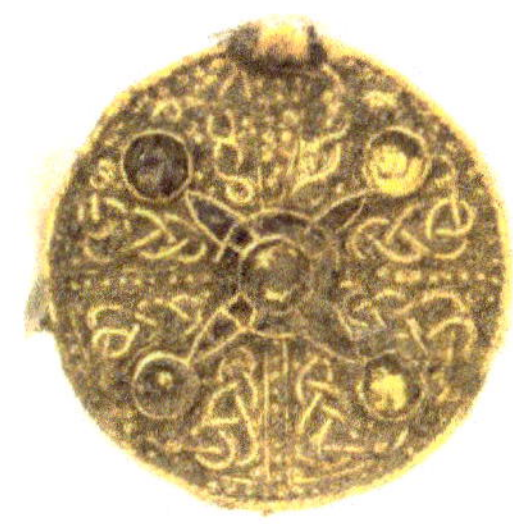

Figure 161: C7th Gold pendant. Found Street House Anglo-Saxon cemetery, Redcar. (Courtesy Portable Antiquities Scheme)[1347]

[1345] *SL*28–30, *SCBI*63 no. 543, *EMC* 1977.0098

[1346] First image courtesy of the British Numismatic Society, others courtesy of the Royal Numismatic Society, Hill (1953, nos. 20, 36)

[1347] PAS NCL-A09134, 2007T498 (Annual Report 2007, no. 184), found with fragments of a gold chain, gold and glass beads, a chatelaine (?) and small sherds.

8

Conclusions

'What is not surmise is conjecture',
Christopher Challis, BANS seminar, 1997.

The broader conclusions on monetization are now summarized, and the subsidiary questions raised in chapter one are also addressed. This covers the evolution of the coinage, balance of power, expropriation of surplus, regional comparisons and settlement patterns.

The findings of this study of co-occurrence of coins and artefacts, builds significantly on previous work in both numismatic and artefactual material. In particular, by removing the obstacle to *styca* studies injudiciously created by Pirie, the way has been cleared for the 'enormous potential' envisaged by Metcalf. Moreover, the under-utilization of *VASLE* must be a disappointment to those who invested so much effort in creating it. The use of that data here certainly builds directly on those endeavours in arriving at the conclusions given below. This study is not heavily reliant on data drawn directly from PAS, but nevertheless parallels recent work based on that resource. Further studies which may reduce some of the limitations of the current work are suggested as future research at section 8.3.

In broad terms, I conclude that monetization and fiscal efficacy increased as the denomination fell, the political acuity of the archbishops of York deflected dynastic friction into a cultural *renaissance*, the *styca* was a small enough denomination to facilitated expropriation relatively painlessly, counter-intuitively the Wolds show greater enterprise than the more constrained lowlands, and that the pattern of finds can reveal changes such as settlement shift.

8.1 Monetization

In chapter four, the core attributes of Northumbrian monetization were described. How this evolves over time and differs between regions is now discussed in light of the numismatic findings from the dataset analyses and case studies.

In this essentially practical study built on recorded data, a pragmatic rather than philosophical characterisation and definition of monetization is preferred. The relative extent of monetization can be assessed by comparison with the Roman data recorded by the PAS.[1348] As noted above, as of December 2015, *c.* 228,000 single coins and 377 hoards were registered on PAS; in Roman Britain coinage was ubiquitous. As Naismith commented: 'It is figures such as these which are essential for keeping the monetization of the eighth and ninth centuries in perspective. Substantial it may have been, but total or even large by the yardstick of ancient or modern monetary systems it was not.'[1349]

However, this must not detract from the transformation in our perception of the early medieval period following the discovery of the volume of Anglo-Saxon coins as a result of widespread metal-detecting.[1350] Even if Metcalf's computations of Low Countries early-penny production can be challenged, tens of millions of metrologically uniform and interchangeable coins circulated in a defined trading zone. Once the threshold of coin use for everyday transactions is crossed, monetization has been achieved, irrespective of absolute volume. Moreover, Roman monetization served a more populous urban and martial economy, so the rural comparison is less stark, though all Anglo-Saxon coin sites also produce Roman coins. The volume of English hammered coinage did not exceed the Anglo-Saxon period until the thirteenth century,[1351] though coins were in everyday use in the intervening years.

As regards artefacts, dress accessories dominate numerically, *Dataset 5, Summary*. Generally, artefacts are unsophisticated but, for example, garnet-encrusted gold jewellery evinces an aristocratic presence. Fashions in dress fasteners vary regionally but of greater importance is the distribution and diversity of artefact types, especially the relative paucity of work/craft related materials, tools and produce, and horse fittings. While it is the close association of artefacts and coins that is here taken to be indicative of monetization, the frequency of cosmetic items over industrial artefacts does not comply with the expected economic model, although this could be the result of detecting bias. Overall, the volume and mix of artefacts follows the same regional patterns as the coinage, mirroring the process of monetization.

In characterising monetization, a device, *co-occurrence*, has been used as a measure for the extent to which coins are found in association with artefacts, demonstrating routine valuation of goods in the circulating denomination. *Co-occurrence* is healthy in the Wolds but relatively depressed in the lowlands of the north where coins exhibit a thin but wide distribution. It is not merely a viable volume of currency that characterizes monetization, but its widespread dissemination, an increasing and managed

[1348] This is for comparative scale only as there were many finds before the establishment of PAS in 1997 and many others escape the regime.

[1349] Naismith (2012, 285).

[1350] Abramson (2008).

[1351] Allen (2015, 404–24). Allen and Oddie (2015, 238–56). Peak *styca* production was possibly not exceeded before mechanisation.

element of *fiat* currency and the presence of counterfeiting. The penetration of coinage was inversely related to denomination, increasing as the denomination gradually fell, even if progress was stratified—gold for the seventh-century élite, silver for eighth-century traders and base coin in the ninth century, throughout Northumbria.

This research has built on the work of Lyon, Pirie, Metcalf, Blackburn and Naylor, but has attempted to take a more holistic approach and draw upon a greater volume of data to considered northern monetization, a topic not previously studied *per se*. In chapter one, several supplementary questions relevant to assessing monetization were raised: coinage evolution, balance of power, regional differences, expropriation, and settlement patterns. The conclusions on these topics are now summarized.

8.1.1 Evolution

> 'Coinage was not one of the three vital innovations in the evolution of money'
>
> John Maynard Keynes, A Treatise on Money (1930, 10)[1352]

The objective was to establish whether the evolution of the Northumbrian coinage was steady or erratic, and to assess the relationship between the advancement of Northumbrian coinage and political and economic developments.

My periodization of *Database 1*, originally created by digitization of Pirie's corpus of *stycas*, augmented from other sources, has facilitated, through statistical analysis, several observations on the composition, distribution and use of the northern coinage. The analytical tools created include the normal distribution by period, *Dataset 1, Summary,* the regional density of finds, *Dataset 5, Density,* the metal mix by long period, *Dataset 5, Coin Metal Mix* and the coin age mix, *Dataset 5. Coin Age Mix.*

The phased decline in intrinsic worth evident in the evolution of English coinage from gold shilling to *styca*, from noble to base metal, at all phases a sole denomination of uniform size, is characterized by increasing volume as the use of coin penetrated more deeply and widely into economic activity. *Stycas* were deployed in satisfying increasingly small and varied transactions, well beyond enabling peasants to pay church dues.[1353] The expansion of monetization is analogous to a step from coin use in mercantile wholesaling to communal retailing.

While it is analytically convenient to compartmentalize this coinage, this disguises the gradual increase in user confidence which permits a stealthy softening of intrinsic worth such that there is a growing element of *fiat* currency.[1354] While *stycas* have been denigrated for generations, until recently, as a 'token coinage', it is precisely this attribute which signifies their success.

Allowing for continued, if declining, coin use in the absence of coin production, the sporadic nature of northern minting, *Table 2*, is suggestive of a slow, almost long-term, recovery from adversity, though nearer a 15–25 year *swing* than a 45–60 year *wave*.[1355] A cyclical pattern is discernible, with alternate phases marked by: the gold shilling, Aldfrith's *sceat*, Eadberht's fantastic animal issue, the third quarter eighth-century recession, the sharp post-Lindisfarne decline, the discontinuity between Eanred's two issues, and the post-*micel here* reversion. At each discontinuity, rebuilding confidence could take decades; even so the periods of local mint activity are much shorter than the absences/importations. The politico-economic causes of sporadic production are complex—Nechtansmere immediately preceded the first northern *sceat*; in contrast, Lindisfarne was followed by a long depression. Albeit in staccato fashion, issuers provided the potential for monetization but varying local conditions exacerbated the erratic nature of the process, both temporally and spatially.

Despite the absence of historical record, the archaeological evidence, such as at the Cottam/Cowlam complex, supports increasing economic activity linked with greater use of coinage. Use of metal detection alongside geophysical survey and excavation have facilitated refinement of the artefactual typology and chronology, which, together with the numismatic evidence, has enabled identification of transitions, showing a shift of focus from Anglian settlement to market, and Viking looting to Anglo-Scandinavian settlement.[1356] Specifically, the finds associated with the Butterwick-type enclosure at Cottam B, combined with the absence of settlement evidence around the ninth-century focus slightly to the north, indicate that occupation continued in the enclosure whilst the adjacent commercial site evolved. This may have wider implications, setting a precedent for the evolution of 'productive sites' as markets in the context of increasing monetization. Such evolution is not apparent in southern sites and, together with the paucity of finds around Ryedale's religious houses, detracts from Blair's minster hypothesis.

It is also possible that informal credit played an alternating rôle with coinage, compensating for both denominational and production deficiencies, especially during the periodic hiatuses, *Table 2*. It is likely that this applied to both smaller scale, shorter term, informal credit between private individuals and more substantial, longer term, credit from moneylenders, though, conceivably, sources

[1352] By which Keynes meant that the state controls *commodity* money and *managed* money. *Representative* money can be issued either by the state or (central) bank. Coinage and *fiat* money are subsets of these that merely differ in form from other types of money.

[1353] They are found in association with a greater variety of artefact types than *sceattas*.

[1354] *cf.* Van Arsdell (1989, 49).

[1355] These are recognized cyclical periods in economic theory but are capitalist constructs.

[1356] Haldenby and Richards (2016), http://intarch.ac.uk/journal/issue42/3/6.html

of credit differed between the managed estates of the Central Lowlands and the seemingly more enterprising Wolds. The nature and structure of credit[1357] in the early medieval economy is little understood and the relationship of landholding to monetization in Anglian Northumbria is a topic where future research is needed.

8.1.2 Power

'kings make coins and coins make kings'
Leslie Alcock (2003, 92)

The objective was to describe how Northumbrian coinage reflected the exercise and balance of power, specifically between church and state.

I have established that the York gold shilling was an episcopal emission. Moreover, the joint issues of *sceattas*, the gold *solidus* of Archbishop Wigmund and the heavy involvement of the bishops as *styca* issuers, are interpreted as indicative both of the balance of power favouring the church and of the bishops exercising greater political acuity. To collect renders, the king was peripatetic, while the archbishop remained in his power base, issuing coins when he chose, not exclusively for monetary reasons but to support his congregation and estates and to promote the cultural blossoming of Northumbria, collecting dues by faith not force—and, were church dues imposed in coin, monetization would be catalysed.

Specifically, in the case of Ecgberht, both his authority and the status of his See were enhanced during the reign of Eadberht's predecessor (and cousin) Ceolwulf, by receipt of both the *pallium* and Bede's famous letter on affairs of state. Ecgberht's much earlier arrival in office, and far greater tenure, in contrast to Eadberht's retirement to a monastic life, hint at the former's seniority in both achievement and age. Ecgberht's succession of joint issues demonstrate an astute political approach.[1358]

In Bernicia, it is not possible to distinguish royal and church sites from their coin profiles. In both Bernicia and Deira, where coins appear in sufficient numbers to indicate trade, types linked to regal or ecclesiastical sources are comprehensively mixed.

Abercrombie, Hill and Turner argued that, before capitalism, the theocracy imposed its élite identity through a horizontal division of society predicating 'feudalism'.[1359] Early-penny evidence may support horizontal stratification; both the southern iconography of the Conversion Period and the more conservative Northumbrian designs, apparently issued only with archiepiscopal approval, may have been aimed at an élite mercantile class. The currency has a substantially larger rôle than as a mere medium of exchange—the early-penny iconography of the Conversion Period provided powerful, even mystical, propaganda. However, the relation of church to state is inevitably complex. Church involvement in coinage is visible at the start and end of the circular flow—in coinage production and fiscal extraction. Apart from the enduring iconographic message, church activity is less visible at the transactional stage of commerce, as discussed below.

The symbolism of coinage in the context of power politics is ripe for future research. The *styca* was clearly a mass denomination penetrating deep into society, whether by design or serendipity. Social reciprocity declined as monetization penetrated all levels of society and all transaction types.

It is argued that there is no binary choice between formalism and substantivism, nor between gift and commodity economies. The reality is always more complex than portrayed by reductionist theorising. Indeed, neither the 'ideology of primitivism'[1360] nor the social stratification of 'ranked spheres of exchange'[1361] is appropriate to the current discussion. By analogy, perhaps one could postulate 'ranked spheres of reciprocity'. At the highest level this would have involved hierarchical reciprocity on the Germanic model,[1362] whereby the chieftain distributed wealth to retain the *fealty* of the warrior aristocracy. Such positive inducement was reinforced by negative sentiment towards the common enemy.[1363] This balance of privileges and obligations co-existed with the institutions of religion as the theocracy strengthened and 'bookland' proliferated. The reciprocal relationship between church, monarchy and society was multi-faceted. The episcopacy not only gave sanctuary in the turmoil of eighth- and ninth-century dynastic feuding but often intervened to avoid instability, by condoning or condemning a prospective successor.[1364] The monarchy provided physical security and a great deal of land. To the people, the church gave spiritual succour and pastoral care in exchange for unquestioning commitment to faith and, indeed, fiscal support. The complexity of these arrangements, albeit here oversimplified, obviates reductionist theories. In the early Anglo-Saxon world, the invisible hand of faith[1365] eclipses that of the market.

[1357] Sehgal (2015, ch. 3).
[1358] Security of tenure *may* show where power lay: from king Aldfrith to Ælle (685–867), 19 reigns averaged 9.6 years while from Ecgberht to Wulfhere (732–900), six Archbishops averaged 28-year tenures.
[1359] Abercrombie, Hill and Turner (1986). See p. 16.

[1360] Thomas (1994, 10).
[1361] Bohannan (1957).
[1362] Hedeager (1992, 121–31) quoted in Moreland (2000a, 14–17).
[1363] Samson (1991, 91) referred to this as 'negative reciprocity'—a binding relationship of feud and vendetta against the enemy. Charles-Edwards (1997, 172).
[1364] Woodman (2012, 38–42).
[1365] 'the unknowable unknown', Stanley (1975, 122). Whitmarsh (2015).

8.1.3 Regional Differences

'We are...only at the beginnings of our understanding of these regional differences.'

Chris Wickham (2000, 354).[1366]

The objective was to expose significant regional differences, and metro-centricity, in coin use.

Dataset 1 provides analysis of regional coin finds by site and period. In particular, *Dataset 1. Analysis* enables comparison of the progression of monetization, from which several conclusions can be drawn. Based on sites with five or more finds, coinage volumes for the Wolds are equally divided between the eighth and ninth centuries, but for the Central Lowlands, Vale of Pickering and Bernicia 70–80 per cent of finds are ninth century. York falls between these with 60 per cent in the ninth century. Monetization for the Wolds is earlier and deeper. Bringing into account all sites, *Dataset 1. Summary*, it is evident that smaller sites predominate in the Central Lowlands, Beverley and the Vale of Pickering, whilst the Wolds presents a more balanced picture. This again points to a veneer of finds in the lowland areas. Beverley is monetized before its hinterland, but in the Central Lowlands and Vale of Pickering the small sites are earlier than the larger ones.

It may well be that the types of detecting bias described by Robbins are responsible for the paucity and distribution of reported finds from the north of the study area. Only nine locations are included in *Dataset 2* for Northumberland and these are clustered not far from the Great North Road in the narrow coastal plain between Bamburgh and Hexham. The absence of finds from key Bernician sites and concentration in others, for both the Roman[1367] and early Anglo-Saxon periods, contrasts sharply with Deira, with its widespread pattern of associated coins and artefacts, though both typically feature evidence of long-distance trade. *Graphs 6–8* also show Bernician coin usage to be later than Deira.

The contrast suggests something more than detecting bias, possibly a structural difference in social organisation.[1368] Deira offers greater social and economic empowerment of the populace through widespread use of currency, especially the *styca*, whereas Bernician over-lordship is more stratified. The concentration of finds in controlling regal centres, Bamburgh and Yeavering, and ecclesiastical sites, Carlisle, Whithorn, Whitby and Lindisfarne suggests a more regulated regime, discouraging social and spatial mobility. Indeed, these mainly coastal locations are the only ones where coins have been found in numbers, presumably in connection with long distance trade. Possibly rural Bernicia was sparsely populated. The huge *styca* hoard from the more inland Hexham does not signify trade or travel but safe deposit of a significant, presumably ecclesiastical, fiscal treasury of 'widow's mites',[1369] demonstrating that paucity need not imply poverty. A greater proportion of the populace could now be taxed, and pay church dues, in coin.

Fishergate and the central Wolds have a far higher proportion of work artefacts than other areas. However, Fishergate does not stand comparison to the southern wics in terms of the volume, range and mix of coinage, which is regarded as fundamental in demonstrating the diverse and long-term relationships characteristic of an emporium, *Dataset 15, Wic Comparison* and *Dataset 20*. An economic definition of a *wic* is favoured: a topographically favoured, non-agrarian, trading location, under the auspices of a controlling authority, providing sufficient commercial, fiscal, monetary and judicial mechanisms to enable buyers and sellers to exchange goods securely and for specialised craft and manufacture to develop.[1370] *Sceattas* catalysed this process. The prevalence of each of these attributes varied between *wics* according to local conditions. Economic activity also took place on sites lacking some of these attributes and more dedicated to processing or redistribution.[1371] Fishergate had a restricted commercial function, not as a full-blown *wic*, though one must have existed in such a wealthy metropolis and cannot have been far away.

The veneer of single finds in York and the Central Lowlands have a similar thin, dispersed profile suggesting a similar controlling, land-owning, regime. Central governance seems to have been effective despite the rich diversity, and porous borders, of the hinterland. The spatial frequency of artefact and coin finds in the main areas of this study are assessed in *Dataset 5, Density*. Excluding hoards and finds from York eliminates metro-centricity, as monetization requires widespread use in rural areas.

Assuming similar caveats affect all locations, the picture presented is one of considerable contrasts. Volumes, densities and diversity of types in the Wolds are considerably greater than elsewhere. The sheer number of locations in the Central Lowlands is impressive though 84 per cent of both artefact and coin locations produced three finds or fewer. Locations in the Wolds were significantly more productive, averaging 33 artefacts and 13 coins per location. As with *co-occurrence*, the Vale of Pickering falls between these two regions for the number of locations with three or fewer finds but is much closer to the Central Lowlands in terms of densities and has far less variety of types. Beverley shows a considerably higher level of activity of the two, with Holderness comparable to the other lowlands—a pattern replicating that in York and the Central Lowlands.

[1366] Wickham suggested regional differences may be due to 'a zone where urban and rural exchange was slowly becoming more integrated and hierarchical' and 'other areas where artisanal activity tended to be relatively simple and localised.'

[1367] *Map 4*.

[1368] http://intarch.ac.uk/journal/issue25/2/3.3.1.1.html

[1369] Alcock (2003, 93)

[1370] Scull (1997, 271–74).

[1371] See Rumble (2001, 1–2) for linguistics, origins and usages.

Throughout the period studied, Northumbria is clearly metro-centric as shown by the comparative artefactual fingerprints. While York (and the monasteries) dominated very large territories, the evidence is not yet available (accepting that Fishergate is not the emporium) to compare it to the southern *Vicii Regius*, such as Rendlesham, with their evident wealth. The accumulations at York, Yeavering and Bamburgh differ significantly, reflecting weaker Bernician monetization. Yeavering seems to have been abandoned before monetization and Bamburgh is very well endowed, but only late, with base, especially blundered, *stycas*.

Assuming that the regions studied are not mere chance but have some internal cohesion, the contrast between the lowlands and Wolds suggests that monetization is related most closely to the freedoms that the populace enjoyed, whether granted by design or taken through neglect. Essentially, this refers to freedom of enterprise, but also, ironically, the church did not favour manumission.[1372]

8.1.4 Expropriation

> DENNIS: Anarcho-syndicalism is a way of preserving freedom.
> WOMAN: Oh, Dennis, forget about freedom. Now I've dropped my mud.
> Monty Python and the Holy Grail (1975)

The objective was to examine the role of coinage in surplus expropriation by the authorities.

While the quest for present and future security, both physical and psychological, motivates behaviour, satisfying immediate needs is an innate imperative, irrespective of possibly adverse longer-term consequences, such as habitat degradation or unsupportable reproduction. Planning for the future, whether defensive or offensive, is accomplished through innovation—language, belief, technology, hierarchy and exchange.[1373] In applying rational judgements retrospectively to historical cause and effect, archaic priorities, perceptions and motivations are almost inevitably misunderstood, often failing to recognise that surrender to belief seems hardwired into the human psyche.[1374] People have a predisposition to be cossetted by their communal belief for spiritual security, facilitating an unopposed, even cynical, exploitation by the theocracy.[1375] Certainly, substantial ecclesiastical fiscal treasuries are evident. Typically, strong regimes may enhance stability, but often pursue regressive, usually veiled, redistribution, from poor to rich, so that their subjects' horizons are short, their resistance and expectations limited. Moreover, the 'widow's mite' was not too great an imposition on the populace and was easily extracted.

[1372] Pelteret (1995, 255).
[1373] Cribb (2005–09) as summarised in Abramson (2012b, 122–25).
[1374] Dawkins (2006, 200–01).
[1375] *cf.* Abercrombie and others (1986).

The Marxist view was given by Saunders: 'emporia were settlements specialising in the production and exchange of prestige goods. They regulated trade in luxury items for the exclusive usage of the tributary ruling élite and were thus divorced from the rural economy.'[1376] While, the residents were susceptible to both autocratic and theocratic exploitation in the Conversion Period, as evident from the lack of diversity in the diet at Fishergate, the conclusion developed by Saunders that: 'Emporia, therefore, cannot be conceived as a dynamic force in Anglo-Saxon society'[1377] is contrary. The return to labour was expropriated—*quid novi?*—how rapaciously cannot be determined.

Urbanism facilitates specialisation, attracting workers skilled in artefact manufacture and crafts. It is more likely that such skilled workers operated from a workshop rather than being peripatetic, though their skills were mobile.[1378] These artisans are valued by the élite not just for their skills but for their ability to bear taxation. Urban craft specialism is not what Polanyi meant as *disembedded*, though specialism implies some sacrifice of self-sufficiency. His context was capitalism, when embeddedness and monetization are inversely related. During the period of study, early medieval artisans remained socially engaged but the situation was fluid and economic characterisation as a binary choice between substantivism and formalism is a false dichotomy.

Moreover, application of formalism to the early medieval period is not only anachronistic but also over-presumptuous about the sophistication of the price mechanism in resolving central micro-economic issues: the allocation of scarce resources and optimisation of returns to the factors of production. Macro-economic objectives of stability, growth, employment and fiscal and trade balances could, at best, only be seen in political terms. Besides, it was the victors and clerics, such as Bede, who recorded their partial version of historical events.[1379]

8.1.5 Settlement Patterns

> 'For better or worse the whole saga of human achievement and vigour,
> stupidity and greed is etched in the landscape'
> Richard Muir, *Old Yorkshire* (1987, 21)

The objective was to investigate how the varying mix of coins indicates different trading and settlement patterns and networks.

Measures of the interaction of coinage in the northern economy involve assessing and comparing the mix of both coin metallurgy and age. The mix of metals, *Dataset 5, Coin Metal Mix,* here a surrogate for the denominational value of the single circulating type, shows that the three lowland

[1376] Saunders (1991, 278).
[1377] Saunders (2001, 12).
[1378] See for example, Ashby (2011 303–19 and 2015, 193–208).
[1379] Wolf (1982, 5).

areas have a similar profile, with *stycas* predominating. The Wolds have a distinctly different pattern with much greater representation of the silver *sceat* in the eighth century, a higher proportion of Eanred's silver-alloy issue but copper-alloy *stycas* accounting for only just half of the local coinage. The distinctive profile of the Wolds is also clear from the correlations in *Dataset 1, Correlations*.

The Wolds also show substantially greater site longevity, *Dataset 5, Coin Age Mix,*[1380] with more than two-thirds of the locations continuing from the eighth to the ninth centuries, suggesting permanent long-term occupation. *Graphs 7* and *8* show uniformity of mix and, therefore, healthy circulation between sites on the Wolds. The lowland areas seem more prone to settlement-shift, which may be due to waterlogging and soil exhaustion in these arable areas. The *gleys* of the Central Lowlands, for instance, have restricted fertility and drainage[1381], whereas pastoral farming in the Wolds is less dependent on soil fertility. Higham considered that the Wolds had advantageous conditions during the poor climate of sixth- to ninth-century Britain.[1382]

Incremental extensions to ladder settlements in the Wolds, perhaps when land became compacted and stale (*cf.* p. 158), are too small scale to show in my settlement-based analysis. *Dataset 1, Stability—Coin Sites* shows the stability of individual sites having both coins and artefacts and suggests a dozen prospective settlement shifts in the Central Lowlands. Several possible settlement-shifts are mentioned: Heslington Hill to Fishergate, North Ferriby to Newbald, Cottam B northwards and Yeavering to Milfield.[1383] This has a bearing on the long-running discussion on the origin of settlements.[1384] Presumably, settlement-shift occurs when incremental shuffling, as in a ladder settlement, would be unproductive. Hodges advocated positive reasons for settlement-shift, specifically improvement in location may have helped meet fiscal obligations.[1385]

The relative abundance of coinage in the Wolds, compared to the lowlands, seems more emancipated—an enterprising, rather than exploited, tenancy. The pattern for the Vale of Pickering is also anomalous. There is a dearth of coins and artefacts relative to the Wolds,[1386] although the minster hypothesis predicts a focus of economic activity. The density of finds, *Dataset 5, Density*, for low-lying Northumbria is significantly lower than the Wolds; causes may include underdeveloped hydrological management, settlement-shift (*Dataset1, Stability—Coin Sites*), and the land-management regime. Wickham's insightful 'it was simply the level and stability of aristocratic demand that mattered for exchange networks, not the total subjugation of peasant neighbourhoods' is apposite.[1387]

Presumably, the aristocracy domiciled in the Vale of Pickering, economically active in the Wolds, was shrewd enough not to despoil their own doorsteps with mercenary commercialism. Bede's letter to Ecgberht may support this: 'having gained possession of farms and villages, they free themselves from every bond, both human and Divine.'[1388] Bede included here their obligations to the king, but begs the question of how otherwise the king was fiscally and militarily supported. Presumably, the tax- and draft-dodgers were a minority.

Mobility is an attribute of enterprise and the elongated parishes, which indicate transhumance from the Wolds into the Vale of Pickering, reflect the seasonal movement of livestock, and routinely of those engaged in economic activity.

The question posed in chapter two is whether the numismatic evidence validated the dendritic system of nodes and hubs. Detecting bias obscures the picture and it may be premature to endorse the Hodgian model. Well before Hodges, classical economic theory demanded structured markets, but sustained discovery is required before a clear economic profile crystalizes. These caveats aside, both the Central Lowlands and the Wolds were composed of non-nucleated farmsteads[1389] with nodal points at locations such as Sledmere, South Newbald and Kilham, and acted as distributed networks of settlements.

O'Connor discussed the polyfocal nature of York with foci at the *principia* and Fishergate, later Coppergate; he concluded 'In strictly substantivist terms, it is a change from a redistributional system to one of exchange.'[1390] But evidence is being shoe-horned to corroborate theory and certainly Skre's post-substantivist approach favoured a more site-specific interpretation.[1391] His synthesis is commended: substantivism prevailed in relatively primitive economies, possibly using commodity money, with formalism foremost in developing economies generating a surplus, facilitating specialization and complex transactions exercising the fuller functions of money.[1392]

[1380] There are no discernible trends for gold in *Dataset 5, Coin Metal Mix*, as numbers are inadequate.

[1381] Soil compaction from occupation exacerbates low porosity. Monbiot (2013, 153–66).

[1382] Higham (1987, 35–44) and *VASLE* §3.3.1.

[1383] And, less certainly, Whithorn (170).

[1384] See *fn.* 1302. Discussion of the 'Middle Saxon shuffle', ably summarised by Moreland (2000b, 82–87), related chiefly to seventh-eighth century transformations to more fertile land. Nucleation integrating cemeteries into coalesced permanent settlements is typically accompanied by the presence of Ipswich ware.

[1385] Hodges (1989, 63).

[1386] And of artefacts relative to Roman times (81).

[1387] Wickham (2005, 813).

[1388] https://tenthmedieval.wordpress.com/2010/03/18/from-the-sources-v-Bedes-letter-to-egbert/ 734, §12. Also see §3–5, 7, 9, 11, 14 and 16.

[1389] Haldenby and Richards (2016, 2).

[1390] O'Connor (1994, 146).

[1391] Skre (2008, 333–35). See ch. 2.

[1392] Skre (2008, 333–35).

8.2 Impact

A major impact of the current work lies in my digitization of Pirie's corpus of *stycas*, now available for others to use. Moreover, the periodization is specifically based on numismatic chronology.

The most significant numismatic finding arising is undoubtedly my identification and dating of the Paulinus shilling. Not only has this significance for the chronology of early Anglo-Saxon coinage and the Anglian history of York but it supports the argument made here regarding the balance of power in Northumbria to favour the episcopacy. The premises for that conclusion include the joint issues of *sceattas* and the church accumulations of *stycas* in hoards. Moreover, this identification has opened discussion of the unique theological iconography of the series.

Other numismatic findings are summarized in chapter six.

The clear contrast drawn between the manifestations of enterprise in the Yorkshire Wolds and the various lowlands demonstrates that where people are able to take the initiative they will endeavour to improve their circumstances, often by trading their surpluses.

The progress of monetization in Northumbria shows that once the élite had relinquished its preference for gold coin for largely non-monetary purposes, monetary momentum built as the face value of the sole denomination fell.

8.3 Future Research Directions

There are several areas in which further research would clarify current findings. While the study is based on the association of coin and artefact finds, a more inclusive approach, building on the data here provided, would include studies of:

- The metallurgy of *styca*s to give better definition to significant changes in alloy.
- The relationship of landholding, tenure and episcopal sees to monetization in Anglian Northumbria.
- The distribution and frequency of Roman coinage in the region and the anomalous regional artefactual correlation.
- Assessment of bio-archaeology and detecting discard on coin/artefact-rich sites.
- The iconography of the York gold shillings.

Digitizing Pirie's corpus has illuminated a significant facet of early medieval economic history. Hopefully, putting this in the public domain, eventually to be populated with images, will facilitate further research.

> 'I know nothing whatsoever about Dark Age trade, or at any rate no more than befits a gentleman'
> Professor Middleton in Wilson, *Anglo-Saxon Attitudes* (1956, 37)

Bibliography

Abdy, R. (2006) After Patching: Imported and Recycled Coinage in Fifth- and Sixth-Century Britain. In *Archibald Festschrift*, pp.75–98.

Abdy, R., and Williams, G. (2006) A Catalogue of Hoards and Single Finds from the British Isles, *c.* AD 410–675. In *Archibald Festschrift*, pp.11–74.

Abercrombie, N., Hill, S., and Turner, B. S. (1986) *Sovereign Individuals of Capitalism.* London: Allen & Unwin.

Abramson, T. (2002) A Second Wolf Head/Running Fledgling Sceat. *SNC.* 110, p.335.

Abramson, T. (2006) *Sceattas: An Illustrated Guide.* King's Lynn: Heritage.

Abramson, T. (ed.) (2008) Two Decades of Discovery. In *SiEMC.* Volume 1.

Abramson, T. (ed.) (2008–14) *Studies in Early Medieval Coinage.* 3 Volumes. Woodbridge: Boydell & Brewer; London: Spink.

Abramson, T. (ed.) (2011) New Perspectives. In *SiEMC.* Volume 2.

Abramson, T. (2012a) The Roman Influence on Early Anglo-Saxon Coinage. *YN.* 4, pp.73–104.

Abramson, T. (2012b) Sceats: How Do We Assess their Success? *YN.* 4, pp.105–34.

Abramson, T. (2012c) The Lorin Kay Collection of Northumbrian *Stycas*. *YN.* 4, pp.305–09.

Abramson, T. (2012d) *Sceatta List: An Illustrated and Priced Catalogue of Sceats for Collectors.* Wakefield: Anglo-Saxon Coinage. [with *Stycas Simplified* supplement]. 2nd ed. Spink, London. 2017.

Abramson, T. (2012e) *Anglo-Saxon Counterfeits: Fakes, Forgeries & Facsimiles,* AD *600–1066.* Fakenham Magna: Anglo-Saxon Coins.

Abramson, T. (ed.) (2014) Sifting the Evidence. In *SiEMC.* Volume 3.

Abramson, T. (2018) *The Abramson Collection: Coins of Early Anglo-Saxon England and the North Sea Area.* SCBI. 69. London: Spink.

Abramson, T. (2019) England's Earliest Coinage, with Particular Reference to the York Group of Gold Shillings. *BNJ.* 89.

Agar, B. (2011) A Preliminary Note on the Artefacts from the Vale of York Viking Hoard. In *SiEMC.* Volume 2.

Alcock, L. (2003) *Kings & Warriors: Craftsmen & Priests in Northern Britain,* AD *550–850.* Edinburgh: Society of Antiquities of Scotland.

Allan, J. (1943) The Saxon Monastery of Whitby. *Archaeologia.* 89, pp.85–86. [Pirie archive].

Allen, M. (2015) *Mints and Money in Medieval England.* Cambridge: CUP.

Allen, M., and Oddie, G. (2015) Revised Estimates of the English Silver Currency, 1282–1351. *BNJ.* 85, pp.238–56.

Andrews, P. (ed.) (1988) *The Coins and Pottery from Hamwic.* Southampton: Southampton City Museums.

Archibald, M. M. (1985) The Coinage of Beonna in the Light of the Middle Harling Hoard. *BNJ.* 55, pp.10–54.

Archibald, M. M. (2007) The Evidence of Pecking on Coins from the Cuerdale hoard. Summary version. In *SEVA*, pp.49–53.

Archibald, M. M., Fenwick, V., and Cowell, M. R. (1995) A Sceat of Ethelbert I of East Anglia and Recent Finds of Coins of Beonna. *BNJ.* 65, pp.1–19.

Archibald, M. M., Pirie, E. J. E., Wastling, L. M., Panter, I., and Rogers, N. (2009) The Anglo-Saxon Coins, Mensuration Weights and Ingots. In Evans and Loveluck (eds.) (2009), pp.402–24.

Armstrong, P., Tomlinson, D., and Evans, D. H. (1991) *Excavations at Lurk Lane, Beverley, 1979–82, Report 1.* Beverley: Humberside Archaeology Unit.

Arnold, C., and Wardle, P. (1981) Early Medieval Settlement Patterns in England. *Med Arch.* 25, pp.145–49.

Ashby, S. P. (2011) A Study in Regionality: Hair Combs and Bone/Antler Craft in the Northern Danelaw. In *EMN*, pp.303–19.

Ashby, S. P. (2013) The Worked Bone and Antler from Burdale. [Online]. Available from: http://archaeologydataservice.ac.uk/archives/view/burdale_york_2013/downloads.cfm?group=8

Ashby, S. P. (2015) Making a Good Comb: Mercantile Identity in 9th- to 11th-century England. In Ten-Harkel, L. and Hadley, D. M. (eds.) *Everyday Life in Viking Towns: Social Approaches to Towns in England and Ireland, c. 800–1100.* Oxford: Oxbow Books, pp.193–208.

Attenborough, G. B. (2012) *The Laws of the Earliest English Kings.* London: Forgotten Books. [Originally published 1922. Cambridge: CUP.]

Bailey, R. N. (1974) The Anglo-Saxon Metalwork from Hexham. in Kirkby, D. P. (ed.) *Saint Wilfrid at Hexham* Newcastle upon Tyne: Oriel Press, pp.141–67. [Pirie archive].

Banham, D., and Faith, R. (2014) *Anglo-Saxon Farms and Farming.* Oxford: OUP.

Banting, H. M. J. (1989) *Two Anglo-Saxon Pontificals.* Woodbridge: Boydell.

Barrow, G. W. S. (1969) Northern English Society in the Early Middle Ages. *NH.* 4, pp.1–28.

Bautier, R.-H. (1971) *The Economic Development of Medieval Europe.* Translated by Karolyi, H. London: Thames and Hudson.

Bede (1896) *Historiam ecclesiasticam gentis Anglorum; Historiam abbatum; Epistolam ad Ecgberctum una cum Historia abbatum auctore anonymo.* Edited by Plummer, C. 2 Volumes. Oxford: Clarendon Press.

Bede (1969) *An Ecclesiastical History of the English People.* Edited and Translated by Colgrave, B., and Mynors, R. A. B. Oxford: Clarendon Press.

Behr, C., Pestell, T., and Hines, J. (2014) The Bracteate Hoard from Binham: An Early Anglo-Saxon Central Place? *Med Arch.* 58, pp.44–77.

Belfort, A. de (1892–95) *Description générale des monnaies mérovingiennes.* 5 Volumes. Paris: Au siège de la Société française de numismatique.

Beresford, M. (1983) *The Lost Villages of England.* Gloucester: Sutton. [Originally published 1954. London: Lutterworth.]

Beresford, M., and Hurst, J. G. (1990) *English Heritage Book of Wharram Percy: Deserted Medieval Village.* London: Batsford.

Bevan, A. (2012) Spatial Methods for Analysing Large-Scale Artefact Inventories. *Antiquity.* 86, pp.492–506.

Birbeck, V., Smith, R. J. C., Andrews, P., and Stoodley, N. (2005) *The Origins of Mid-Saxon Southampton: Excavations at the Friends Provident St Mary's Stadium, 1998–2000.* Salisbury: Wessex Archaeology Salisbury.

Blackburn, M. A. S. (ed.) (1986) *Anglo-Saxon Monetary History.* Leicester: Leicester University Press.

Blackburn, M. A. S. (1989) Single-Finds as a Measure of Monetary Activity in the Early Middle Ages. *Prace i Materiały, Muzeum Archeologicznego i Etnograficznego w Łodzi. Seria Numizmatyczna i Konserwatorska.* 9, pp.67–85.

Blackburn, M. A. S. (1993) Coin Finds and Coin Circulation in Lindsay, *c.* 600–900. In Vince, A. (ed.) *Pre-Viking Lindsey.* Lincoln: City of Lincoln Archaeology Unit, pp.80–90.

Blackburn, M. A. S. (1994) A Variant of the Seventh-Century 'York' Group of Shillings Found in Lincolnshire. *NC.* 154, pp.204–08.

Blackburn, M. A. S. (1998) A New Coin of King Eadbald of Kent (616–40). *Chris Rudd List.* 34, pp.2–4.

Blackburn, M. A. S. (2003) Productive Sites and the Pattern of Coin Loss in England, 600–1180. In *P&U.* pp.20–36.

Blackburn, M. A. S. (2004) The Coinage of Scandinavian York. In Hall, R. A., and others (eds.) *Aspects of Anglo-Scandinavian York.* AY. 8.4. York: CBA, pp.325–49.

Blackburn, M. A. S. (2006) Two New Types of Anglo-Saxon Gold Shillings. In *Archibald Festschrift,* pp.127–40.

Blackburn, M. A. S. (2007) Gold in England during the 'Age of Silver' (Eighth–Eleventh Centuries). In *SEVA,* pp.55–98.

Blackburn, M. A. S. (2011) Coinage in its Archaeological Context. In Hamerow, H., and Hinton, D. (eds.) *A Handbook of Anglo-Saxon Archaeology.* VI. Trade, Exchange, and Urbanization, 30, Oxford: OUP.

Blackburn, M. A. S., and Bonser, M. (1986) Single Finds of Anglo-Saxon and Norman Coins, 3. *BNJ.* 56, pp.64–102.

Blackburn, M. A. S., and Dumville, D. N. (eds.) (1998) *Kings, Currency and Alliances: The History of Southern England in the Ninth Century.* Woodbridge: Boydell and Brewer.

Blair, J. (2005) *The Church in Anglo-Saxon Society.* Oxford: OUP.

Bland, R., and Johns, C. (1993) *The Hoxne Treasure: An Illustrated Introduction.* London: BM.

Bloch, M. (1961) *Feudal Society.* Translated by Manyon, L. A. Chicago: University of Chicago Press.

Blunt, C. (1960) Presidential Address. *NC* 6th ser. 20, pp.iv–vii.

Bohannan, P. (1957) *Justice and Judgement among the Tiv.* Oxford: OUP.

Bonser, M. (1997) Fifteen Years of Coin Finds from Productive Sites. *YN.* 3, pp.39–45.

Bonser, M. (2011) The 'North of England' Productive Site Revisited. In *SiEMC.* Volume 2, pp.159–80.

Booth, J. (1984) Sceattas in Northumbria. In *BAR128,* pp.71–111.

Booth, J. (1987) History vs Numismatics: Sceattas and *Stycas. SNC.* 95, p.6. [Pirie archive].

Booth, J. (1997a) *Northern Museums: Ancient British, Anglo-Saxon, Norman and Plantagenet Coins to 1279.* SCBI. 48. Oxford: OUP.

Booth, J. (1997b) Northumbrian Coinage and the Productive Site at South Newbald. *YN* 3, pp.15–38. Also in Geake, H., and Kenney, J. (eds.) (2000) *Early Deira: Archaeological Studies of the East Riding in the Fourth to Ninth Centuries AD*. Oxford: Oxbow Books, pp.83–97 and plates 7.4, 7.5.

Booth, J. (2011) Notes on the Keith Chapman Collection of Northumbrian Silver Sceats, *c.* 700–*c.* 788. In *SiEMC*. Volume 2, pp.193–216.

Booth, J. (2014) When Did the Western Roman Empire End? In *YNS Newsletter*. (January), pp.3–7.

Booth, J., and Blowers, I. (1983) Finds of Sceattas and *Stycas* from Sancton. *NC*. 143, pp.139–45.

Breeze, A. (2009) The Name of Bernicia. *The Antiquaries Journal*. 89, pp.73–79.

Brindle, T. (2013) Making the Most of PAS Data: Macro- and Micro-Level Studies of Romano-British Settlement. *Landscapes*. 14, pp.73–91.

Brindle, T. (2014) *The Portable Antiquities Scheme and Roman Britain*. London: BM.

Brooke, D. (1999) *Saints and Goddesses: The Interface with Celtic Paganism*. Whithorn Lecture. 7. Whithorn: Friends of the Whithorn Trust. [Pirie archive].

Brooks, N. (1987) Epilogue. In *BAR180*, pp.397–401.

Brown, E. (1974) The Tyranny of a Construct: Feudalism and Historians of Medieval Europe. *American Historical Review*. 79, pp.1063–68.

Bruce-Mitford, R. L. S. (1967) *The Art of the Codex Amiatinus*. Jarrow: Parish of Jarrow.

Bruce-Mitford, R. L. S. (1975) *The Sutton Hoo Ship Burial*. Volume 1. London: British Museum.

Bude, R. (2014) The Class E Sceattas of Eadberht: The Work of 'Retrograde Man'. In *SiEMC*. Volume 3, pp.18–28.

Bude, R. (2016) The joint coinage of Ecgberht and Eadberht of Northumbria. *BNJ* 86, pp. 118-139.

Burnett, A. M. (1984) Clipped Siliqua and the End of Roman Britain. *Britannia*. 15, pp.163–68.

Carver, M. O. H. (ed.) (1995) *Excavations at York Minster: From Roman Fortress to Norman Cathedral*. London: HMSO.

Charles-Edwards, T. (1997) Anglo-Saxon Kinship Revisited. In Hines (ed.) (1997a), pp.171–210.

Chester-Kadwell, M. (2009) *Early Anglo-Saxon Communities in the Landscape of Norfolk*. B. A. R. British Series. 481. Oxford: BAR Publishing.

Chick, D. (2010) *The Coinage of Offa and his Contemporaries*. Edited by Blackburn, M. A. S., and Naismith, R. BNS Special Publication. 6. London: Spink.

Clark, F. H. (2011) Thinking about Western Northumbria. In *EMN*, pp.113–28.

Cloke, H. J., and Toone, L. (2015) *The London Mint of Constantius & Constantine*. London: Spink.

Collins, R. (1991) *Early Medieval Europe, 300–1000*. Basingstoke: Macmillan Education.

Cook, B., and Williams, G. (eds.) (2006) *Coinage and History in the North Sea World, c. AD 500–1250: Essays in Honour of Marion Archibald*. Leiden: Brill.

Coupland, S. (2003) Trading Places: Quentovic and Dorestad Reassessed. *Early Medieval Europe*. 11, pp.209–32.

Coupland, S. (2007) *Carolingian Coinage and the Vikings: Studies on the Power and Trade in the 9th Century*. Aldershot: Ashgate.

Coupland, S. (2010a) Boom and Bust at 9th-Century Dorestad. In Willemsen, A., and Kik, H. (eds.) *Dorestad in an International Framework: New Research on Centres of Trade and Coinage in Carolingian Times*. Turnhout: Brepols, pp.95–103.

Coupland, S. (2010b) Carolingian Single Finds and the Economy of the Early Ninth Century. *NC*. 170, pp.287–319.

Cowie, R., and Blackmore, L. (2012) *Lundenwic: Excavations in Middle Saxon London, 1987–2000*. London: Museum of London Archaeology.

Cramp, R. (1976) Analysis of Finds Register and Location Plan of Whitby Abbey. In *AASE*, pp.453–57. [Pirie archive].

Cramp, R. (1995) *Whithorn and the Northumbrian Expansion Westwards*. Whithorn Lecture. 3. Whithorn: Friends of the Whithorn Trust. [Pirie archive].

Creeke, A. B. (1905) The Regal Sceatta and Styca Series of Northumbria. *BNJ*. 1, pp.65–96.

Cribb, J. (2005–09) 'Money as Metaphor': The President's Address to the Royal Numismatic Society. *NC*. 165(2005), pp.417–38. 166(2006), pp.493–518. 167(2007), pp.361–96. 169(2009), pp.461–530.

Dale, G. (2010) *Karl Polanyi: The Limits of the Market*. Cambridge: Polity.

Dark, K. R. (2000) *Britain and the End of the Roman Empire*. Stroud: Tempus.

Daubney, A. J. (2016) *Portable Antiquities, Palimpsests, and Persistent Places: A Multi-Period Approach to Portable Antiquities Scheme Data in Lincolnshire*. Leiden: Sidestone Press.

Davies, G. (1994) *A History of Money: From Ancient Times to the Present Day*. Cardiff: University of Wales Press.

Davies, W. (1998) *Whithorn and the World*. Whithorn Lecture. 6. Whithorn: Friends of the Whithorn Trust. [Pirie archive].

Dawkins, R. (2006) *The God Delusion*. London: Bantam.

Dobney, K., Hall, A., and Kenward, H. (2000) The Bioarchaeology of Anglo-Saxon Yorkshire: Present and Future Perspectives. In Geake and Kenny (eds.) (2000), pp.133–40.

Dolley, R. H. M. (ed.) (1961) *Anglo-Saxon Coins: Studies Presented to F. M. Stenton on the Occasion of his 80th Birthday*. London: Methuen.

Dolley, R. H. M. (1976) The Coins. In *AASE*, pp.349–72.

Drew, K. F. (1991) *The Laws of the Salian Franks (Pactus legis Salicae)*. Philadelphia: University of Pennsylvania Press.

Dumville, D. (1989) The Tribal Hidage: An Introduction to its Texts and their History. In Bassett, S. (ed.) *Origins of Anglo-Saxon Kingdoms*. Leicester: Leicester University Press, pp.225–30.

Dumville, D. N. (1997) *The Churches of North Britain in the First Viking Age*. Whithorn Lecture. 5. Whithorn: Friends of the Whithorn Trust. [Pirie archive].

Durliat, J. (1980) La valeur relative de l'or, de l'argent et du cuivre dans l'empire protobyzantin (IVe–VIIIe siècle). *RN*. 6(22), pp.138–54.

Einzig, P. (1949) *Primitive Money in its Ethnological, Historical and Economic Aspects*. London: Eyre & Spottiswoode.

Ellis, P. B. (1998) *The Ancient World of the Celts*. London: Constable.

English Heritage (2009) *Holy Island, Northumberland Extensive Urban Survey*. Morpeth: Northumberland Conservation.

Esty, W. W. (2006) How to Estimate the Original Number of Dies and the Coverage of a Sample. *NC*. 166, pp.359–64.

Evans, D. H., and Loveluck, C. (eds.) (2009) *Life and Economy at Early Medieval Flixborough*. Oxford: Oxbow.

Faith, R. (2009) Forces and Relations of Production in Early Medieval England. *Journal of Agrarian Change*. 9, pp.23–41.

Fennell, W. (1849) On a Hoard of Northumbrian *Stycas*, Discovered in Yorkshire (The Collection of William Fennell, Antiquarian from Wakefield, West Yorkshire, England). *JBAA*. 4, pp.127–32.

Fenton-Thomas, C. (2005) *The Forgotten Landscapes of the Yorkshire Wolds*. Stroud: Tempus.

Feveile, C. (2008) Series X and Coin Circulation in Ribe. In *SiEMC*. Volume 1, pp.53–67.

Foot, S. (2006) *Monastic Life in Anglo-Saxon England, c. 600–900*. Cambridge: CUP.

Fossier, R. (ed.) (1989) *The Cambridge Illustrated History of the Middle Ages, 350–950*. Cambridge: CUP.

Gaimster, M. (2007) Viking Economies: Evidence from the Silver Hoards. In *SEVA*, pp.123–33.

Gannon, A. (2003) *The Iconography of Early Anglo-Saxon Coinage, Sixth to Eighth Centuries*. Oxford: OUP.

Gannon, A. (2016) Series X and its International Framework: An Art Historical Contribution to the Study of Early-Medieval Coinage. In Willemsen, A., and Kik, H. (eds.) *Proceedings of the Second Dorestad Congress 2014. Leiden, Rijksmuseum van Oudheden, 2-5 July 2014*. Turnhout: Brepols, pp.71–77.

Garmonsway, G. N. (trans.) (1953) *The Anglo-Saxon Chronicle*. London: Dent & Sons.

Garrison, M. (1999) 'Send More Socks': On Mentality and the Preservation Context of Medieval Letters. In Mostert, M. (ed.) *New Approaches to Medieval Communication*. Turnhout: Brepols, pp.69–99.

Garrison, M. (2001) Alcuin of York and his Continental Context. In Hogarth, S., and Wallace, V. (eds.) *Yorkshire People and Places: A Millennium Celebration*. York: Yorkshire Philosophical Society, pp.15–28.

Gaunt, G. D., and Buckland, P. C. (2003) The Geological Background to Yorkshire's Archaeology. In Manby, Moorhouse, and Ottaway (eds.) (2003), pp.17–23.

Geake, H. (1997) The Use of Grave-Goods in Conversion-Period England, c. 600-c. 850. BAR. 261. Oxford: BAR.

Geake, H., and Kenny, J. (eds.) (2000) *Early Deira: Archaeological Studies of the East Riding in the Fourth to Ninth Centuries AD*. Oxford: Oxbow Books.

Gilmore, G. R. (1987) Metal Analysis of the Northumbrian *Stycas*. In *BAR180*, pp.159–73.

Gilmore, G. R., and Pirie, E. J. E. (1988) Consistency in the Alloy of the Northumbrian *Stycas*: Evidence from Redwulf's Short Reign. In *BAR180*, pp.175–85.

Graham-Campbell, J. (ed.) (1994) *Cultural Atlas of the Viking World*. New York: Facts on File.

Graham-Campbell, J. (2001) *Whithorn and the Viking World*. Whithorn Lecture. 8. Whithorn: Friends of the Whithorn Trust. [Pirie archive].

Graham-Campbell, J. (2011) *The Cuerdale Hoard and Related Viking-Age Silver and Gold from Britain and Ireland in the British Museum*. London: BM.

Graham-Campbell, J., Sindbæk, S. M., and Williams, G. (eds.) (2011) *Silver Economies, Monetisation and Society in Scandinavia, AD 800–1000*. Aarhus: Aarhus Universitetsforlag.

Graham-Campbell, J., and Williams, G. (eds.) (2007) *Silver Economy in the Viking Age.* Walnut Creek: Left Coast Press.

Grantley, Lord (1911) Saint Cuthbert's Pennies. *BNJ.* 8, pp.49–53.

Gräslund, B., and Price, N. (2012) Twilight of the Gods? The 'Dust Veil Event' of AD 536 in Critical Perspective. *Antiquity.* 86, pp.428–43.

Grierson, P. (1951) The Gold Solidus of Louis the Pious and its Imitations. *JMP*. 38, pp.1–47.

Grierson, P. (1959) Commerce in the Dark Ages: A Critique of the Evidence. *TRHS* 5th ser. 9, pp.123–40.

Grierson, P. (1962) The Authenticity of the York 'Thrymsas'. *BNJ.* 31, pp.8–10. [*MEC*: 'reprinted in *DAN*, [no. VIII,] with an additional note publishing 1.1481 which had come to light since the original article'].

Grierson, P. (1967) The Volume of Anglo-Saxon Currency. *EcHR* 2nd ser. 20, pp.153–60.

Grierson, P. (1975) *Numismatics.* Oxford: OUP.

Grierson, P. (1979) *Dark Age Numismatics: Selected Studies.* London: Variorum.

Grierson, P., and Blackburn, M. A. S. (1986) *Medieval English Coinage, Cambridge, I: The Early Middle Ages (5th–10th Centuries).* Cambridge: CUP.

Griffiths, D. (2003) Markets and 'Productive' Sites: A View From Western Britain. In *P&U*, pp.62–72.

Guest, P. (1997) Coin Hoards and the End of Roman Britain. in Bland, R., and Orna-Ornstein, J. (eds.) *Coin Hoards from Roman Britain.* Volume 10. London: BM), pp.411–23.

Gunn, J. D. (ed.) (2000) *The Years without Summer: Tracing AD 536 and its Aftermath.* B. A. R. International Series. 872. Oxford: BAR Publishing.

Haldenby, D. (1990) An Anglian Site in the Yorkshire Wolds. *YAJ.* 62, pp.51–63.

Haldenby, D. (1992) An Anglian Site on the Yorkshire Wolds, Continued. *YAJ.* 64, pp.25–39.

Haldenby, D. (1994) Further Saxon Finds from the Yorkshire Wolds. *YAJ.* 66, pp.51–56.

Haldenby, D., and Richards, J. D. (2009) Settlement Shift at Cottam, East Riding of Yorkshire, and the Chronology of Anglo-Saxon Copper-Alloy Pins. *Medieval Archaeology*. 53, pp.309–14.

Haldenby, D., and Richards, J. D. (2010) Charting the Effects of Plough Damage Using Metal-Detected Assemblages *Antiquity*. 84(326), pp.1151–62.

Haldenby, D., and Richards, J. D. (2016) The Viking Great Army and its Legacy: Plotting Settlement Shift Using Metal-Detected Finds. *Internet Archaeology.* 42. [Online]. Available from: http://dx.doi.org/10.11141/ia.42.3

Haldenby, D., and Richards, J. D. (forthcoming) The Anglo-Saxon/Anglo-Scandinavian Transition: Plotting Settlement Shift Using Metal-Detected Finds.

Halkon, P. (2003) Researching an Ancient Landscape: The Foulness Valley, East Yorkshire. In Manby, Moorhouse, and Ottaway (eds.) (2003), pp.261–74.

Halkon, P., and Millett, M. (eds.) (1999) *Rural Settlement and Industry: Studies in the Iron Age and Roman Archaeology of Lowland East Yorkshire.* YAHS Report. 4. Leeds: YAHS.

Hall, C. (1774) illustrations of Saxon coins. In Withy, R., and Ryall, I. (1774) *Coins of the Heptarchy.* London, plate 1.

Hall, R. A. (1988) York, 700–1050. In Hodges, R., and Hobbley, B. (eds.) *The Rebirth of Towns in the West, AD 700–1050.* CBA Research Report. 68, pp.125–32.

Hall, R. A. (1996) *Book of York.* London: English Heritage.

Hall, R. A. (2003) Yorkshire, AD 700–1066. In Manby, Moorhouse, and Ottaway (eds.) (2003), pp.171–80.

Hall, R. A., Paterson, E., and Mortimer, C. (1999) The Ripon Jewel. In Hawkes and Mills (eds.) (1999), pp.268–80.

Hall, R. A., and Whyman, M. (1996) Settlement and Monasticism at Ripon, North Yorkshire, from the 7th to 11th Centuries AD. *Med Arch.* 40, pp.62–150.

Hamer, R. (ed. and trans.) (1970) *A Choice of Anglo-Saxon Verse.* London: Faber.

Hamerow, H. F. (1991) Settlement Mobility and the 'Middle Saxon Shift': Rural Settlements and Settlement Patterns in Anglo-Saxon England. *Anglo-Saxon England.* 20, pp.1–17.

Hann, C., and Hart, K. (2011) *Economic Anthropology: History, Ethnography, Critique.* Malden: Polity Press.

Hansen, I. L., and Wickham, C. (eds.) (2000) *The Long Eighth Century.* Leiden: Brill.

Härke, H. (1997) Early Anglo-Saxon Social Structure. In Hines (ed.) (1997a), pp.125–70.

Hawkes, J., and Mills, S. (eds.) (1999) *Northumbria's Golden Age.* Stroud: Sutton.

Hedeager, L. (1992) The Creation of the Germanic Identity: A European Origin-Myth. In Brun, P., van der Leeuw, S. E., and Whittacker, C. R. (eds.) *Frontièrs d'empire: Nature et signification des frontières romaines.* Nemours: Editions de l'Association pour la promotion de la recherce archéologique en Ile-de-France, pp.121–31.

Heywood, B. (1995) York in the Roman and Early Medieval Periods: A Context for the Excavations, Part

1: From the Foundations of York to the End of the Roman Period. In Carver (ed.) (1995), pp.1–8.

Higham, N. J. (1986) *The Northern Counties to AD 1000.* London: Longman.

Higham, N. J. (1987) Land Use and Landscape in Northern England: A Survey of Agricultural Potential, *c.* 500 BC–AD 1000. *Landscape History*. 9, pp.35–44.

Higham, N. J. (1993) *The Kingdom of Northumbria, AD 350–1100.* Dover: Sutton.

Higham, N. J. (1997) The Convert Kings, Power and Religious Affiliation in Early Anglo-Saxon England. Manchester. Manchester University Press.

Higham, N. J. (1999) Imperium in Early Britain: Rhetoric and Reality in the Writings of Gildas and Bede. In *ASSAH*. 10, pp. 31–36.

Higham, N. J., and Ryan, M. J. (2013) *The Anglo-Saxon World.* New Haven: Yale University Press.

Hill, D., and Cowie, R. (eds.) (2001) *Wics*: *The Early Mediaeval Trading Centres of Northern Europe.* Sheffield: Sheffield Academic Press.

Hill, D., and Metcalf, D. M. (eds.) (1984) *Sceattas in England and on the Continent: The Seventh Oxford Symposium on Coinage and Monetary History*. B. A. R. British Series. 128. Oxford: B. A. R.

Hill, P. (1953) Uncatalogued Sceattas in the National and Other Collections. *NC, sixth series, volume* 13, pp.92–114.

Hill, P. (1990a) *Whithorn 3: Excavations at Whithorn Priory, 1989–90.* Whithorn: Whithorn Trust. [Pirie archive].

Hill, P. (1990b) *The Whithorn Excavation: 1990 Supplement.* Whithorn: Whithorn Trust. [Pirie archive].

Hill, P. (1996) *Whithorn and St Ninian: The Excavations of a Monastic Town, 1984-91.* Stroud: Sutton.

Hines, J. (ed.) (1997a) *The Anglo-Saxons from the Migration Period to the Eighth Century: An Ethnographic Perspective.* Woodbridge: Boydell.

Hines, J. (1997b) Religion: The Limits of Knowledge. In Hines (ed.) (1997a), pp.375–410.

Hines, J., and Bayliss, A. (eds.) (2013) *Anglo-Saxon Graves and Grave Goods of the 6th and 7th Centuries AD: A Chronological Framework.* London: SMA.

Hines, J. (2010) Units of Account in Gold and Silver in Seventh-Century England: Scillingas, Sceattas and Pæningas. *Antiquaries Journal* 90, pp.153–73.

Hines, J. (2014) The Hunting of the Sceatt. In *SiEMC*. Volume 3, pp.7–17.

Hinton, D. (2011) Weland's Work: Metals and Metalsmith. In Hyer, M. C., and Owen-Croker, G. R. (eds.) *The Material Culture of Daily Living in the Anglo-Saxon World.* Exeter: University of Exeter Press, pp.185–200.

Hirth, K. G. (1978) Interregional Trade and the Formation of Prehistoric Gateway Communities. *American Antiquity*. 43, pp.35–45.

Hodges, R. (1988) *Primitive and Peasant Markets.* New York: Blackwell.

Hodges, R. (1989a) *The Anglo-Saxon Achievement: Archaeology and the Beginnings of English Society.* Ithaca: Cornell University Press.

Hodges, R. (1989b) *Dark Age Economics*: *The Origins of Towns and Trade, AD 600–1000.* 2nd ed. London: Duckworth.

Hodges, R. (2004) Goodbye to the Vikings? *History Today*. 54(9).

Hodges, R. (2008) Fifty Years after Dunning: Reflections on Emporia, their Origins and Development. In *SiEMC*. Volume 1, pp.113–18.

Hodges, R. (2012) *Dark Age Economics: A New Audit.* London: Bristol Classical Press.

Hodges, R., and Cherry, J. (1983) Cost-Control and Coinage: An Archaeological Approach to Economic Change in Anglo-Saxon England. *Research in Economic Anthropology*. 5, pp.131–84.

Hodges, R., and Waterhouse, D. (1983) *Mohammed, Charlemagne and the Origins of Europe: Archaeology and the Pirenne Thesis.* London: Duckworth.

Hoggett, R. (2010) *The Archaeology of the East Anglian Conversion.* Woodbridge: Boydell.

Holdsworth, P. (1995) Post-Roman Pottery. In Carver (ed.) (1995), pp.468–80.

Hooke, D. (1997) The Anglo-Saxon in England in the Seventh and Eighth Centuries: Aspects of Location in Space. In Hines (ed.) (1997a), pp.65–100.

Hope-Taylor, B. (1977) *Yeavering: An Anglo-British Centre of Early Northumbria.* London: HMSO.

Hopkinson, G. (2008) Little Westfield farm, Cottam Site report (Client Copy), Unpublished Report. *Archaeoscope*. [Online]. Available from: http://www.archaeoscope.org/report.php?ID=10

Howgego, C. (1995) *Ancient History from Coins.* London: Routledge.

Hunter Blair, P. (1948) The Northumbrians and their Southern Frontier. *AA*. 26, pp.98–126.

Hunter Blair, P. (1956) *An Introduction to Anglo-Saxon England.* Cambridge: CUP.

Hurst, J. G. (ed.) (1979) *Wharram: A Study of Settlement on the Yorkshire Wolds. Volume 1: Domestic Settlement.* London: SMA.

Hutcheson, A. R. J. (2009) The Origins of East Anglian Towns: Coin Loss in the Landscape, AD 470–939. Unpublished PhD thesis. University of East Anglia.

Hyer, M. C., and Owen-Crocker, G. R. (eds.) (2011) The Material Culture of Daily Living in the Anglo-Saxon World. (Exeter: University of Exeter Press).

James, E. (1995) Part 2: The Post Roman Period to 1066. In Carver (ed.) (1995), pp.9–12.

Jersey, P. de (1997) Cast Away Riches: Estimating the Volume of Celtic Coinage Found in Britain. *YN*. 3, pp.1–13.

Jevons, W. S. (1875) *Money and the Mechanisms of Exchange*. New York: D. Appleton.

Jones, T., and Ereira, A. (2006) *Barbarians*. London: BBC Books.

Keary, C. F. (1887–93) *A Catalogue of English Coins in the British Museum, Anglo-Saxon Series*. 2 Volumes. London: Longmans & Co.

Kelleher, R. M. (2012) Coins, Monetisation and Re-Use in Medieval England and Wales: New Interpretations Made Possible by the Portable Antiquities Scheme. Unpublished PhD thesis. University of Durham.

Kemp, R. L. (1996) *Anglian Settlement at 46–54 Fishergate*. AY. 7. York: CBA.

Keynes, S. (1994) *The Councils of Clofesho*. Vaughan Papers in Adult Education. 38. Leicester: University of Leicester.

Keys, D. (1999) *Catastrophe: An Investigation into the Origins of the Modern World*. London: Arrow.

Kirby, D. P. (1991) *The Earliest English Kings*. New York: Routledge.

Kitson, C. M. (1935) A Gazetteer of Roman Remains in East Yorkshire. *Antiquity*. 11(43), pp.381–82. [Pirie archive].

Kjølbye-Biddle, B. (1995) Iron-Bound Coffins and Coffin-Fittings from the Pre-Norman Cemetery. In Carver (ed.) (1995), pp.489–521.

Lang, J. T. (1995) Pre-Conquest Sculpture. In Carver (ed.) (1995), pp.433–67.

Lang, J. T. (1999) The Imagery of the Franks Casket: Another Approach. In Hawkes and Mills (eds.) (1999), pp.247–55.

Leahy, K. (2000) Middle Anglo-Saxon Metalwork from South Newbald and the 'Productive Site' Phenomenon in Yorkshire. In Geake and Kenny (eds.) (2000), pp.51–82.

Leeds, E. T. (1913) *The Archaeology of the Anglo-Saxon Settlements*. Oxford: Clarendon Press.

Lendinara, P. (1997) The Kentish Laws. In Hines (ed.) (1997a), pp.211–44.

Leonard, A. (2015) Nested Negotiations: Landscape and Portable Material Culture in Viking-Age England. Unpublished PhD thesis. University of York.

Levison, W. (1946) *England and the Continent in the Eighth Century*. Oxford: Clarendon Press.

Liebermann, F. (ed.) (1903–16) *Die Gesetze der Angelsachsen*. 3 Volumes. Halle a. S.: Niemeyer.

Lipsey, R. G., and Lancaster, K. (1956) The General Theory of Second Best. *Review of Economic Studies*. 24, pp.11–32.

Loveluck, C. (1996) The Development of Anglo-Saxon Landscape, Economy and Society 'On Driffield' East Yorkshire, 400–750 AD. *ASSAH*. 9, pp.25–48.

Loveluck, C. (2003) The Archaeology of Post-Roman Yorkshire, AD 400 to 700: Overview and Future Directions for Research. In Manby, Moorhouse, and Ottaway (eds.) (2003), pp.151–70.

Loveluck, C., and Tys, D. (2006) Coastal Societies, Exchange and Identity along the Channel and Southern North Sea Shores of Europe, AD 600–1000. *Journal of Marine Archaeology*. 1, pp.140–69.

Loyn, H. R. (1981) *Anglo-Saxon England and the Norman Conquest*. London: Longman.

Lyon, S. (1957) A Reappraisal of the Sceatta and Styca Coinage of Northumbria. *BNJ*. 28, pp.227–42.

Lyon, S. (2016) *The Lyon Collection of Anglo-Saxon Coins*. SCBI. 68. Oxford: OUP.

Lyons, A. W., and Mackay, W. A. (2007) The Coinage of Æthelred I (865–871). *BNJ*. 77, pp.71–118.

Mackay, W. (2004) A New Early Secondary Sceatta Type Linking Series W and Series N. *SNC*. 112, pp.159–60.

Mainman, A. J. (1993) *Pottery from 46–54 Fishergate*. AY. 16. London: CBA.

Mainman, A. J., and Hall, R. (2015a) *Eoforwic: Post-Roman and Anglian York, 410–866*. York Archaeological Trusts.

Mainman, A. J., and Hall, R. (2015b) *York, British Historic Towns Atlas*. Barnsley: Oxbow Books for the Historic Towns & York Archaeological Trusts.

Malinowski, B. (1922) Argonauts of the Western Pacific: An Account of Native Enterprise and Adventure in the Archipelagoes of Melanesian New Guinea. London: Routledge and Kegan Paul. See also Enhanced Edition (2013). Long Grove: Waveland Press.

Manby, T. G. (1985) Thwing Excavation and Field Archaeology in East Yorkshire. *YAS Prehistory Research Section Bulletin*.

Manby, T. G., Moorhouse, S., and Ottaway, P. (eds.) (2003) *The Archaeology of Yorkshire: An Assessment at the Beginning of the 21st Century*. Leeds: Yorkshire Archaeological Society.

Marner, D. (2000) *St Cuthbert: His Life and Cult in Medieval Durham*. London: British Library.

Marsden, J. (1992) *Northanhymbre Saga: The History of the Northumbrian Kings of Northumbria.* London: Kyle Cathie.

Mauss, M. (1970) *The Gift: Forms and Functions of Exchange in Archaic Societies*. Translated by Cunnison, I. (London: Routledge & Kegan Paul).

Mayr-Harting, H. M. R. E. (1967) Paulinus of York. In Cuming, G. J. (ed.) *Studies in Church History IV: The Province of York.* Leiden: Brill, pp.15–21.

McCarthy, M. R. (1990) *A Roman, Anglian and Medieval Site at Blackfriars Street, Carlisle: Excavations, 1977–9.* Kendal: Cumberland and Westmorland Antiquarian and Archaeological Society. [Pirie archive].

McCarthy, M. R. (1993) The Lanes Project, Carlisle: Background and Guidance for Specialists. Carlisle Archaeological Unit. [Pirie archive].

Metcalf, D. M. (1960) Some Finds of Medieval Coins from Scotland and the North of England. *BNJ.* 30, pp.88–123.

Metcalf, D. M. (1965) How Large Was the Anglo-Saxon Currency? *EcHR* 2nd ser. 18, pp.475–82.

Metcalf, D. M. (1967) The Prosperity of Western Europe in the Eighth and Ninth Centuries. *EcHR* 2nd ser. 20, pp. 344–57.

Metcalf, D. M. (ed.) (1987) *Coinage in Ninth-Century Northumbria: The Tenth Oxford Symposium on Coinage and Monetary History*. B. A. R. British Series. 180. Oxford: B. A. R.

Metcalf, D. M. (1993–94) *Thrymsas and Sceattas in the Ashmolean Museum, Oxford.* RNS Special Publication. 276. 3 Volumes. London: RNS.

Metcalf, D. M. (1995–99) Viking Age Numismatics. *NC*. 155(1995), pp.413–41. 156(1996), pp.399–428. 157(1997), pp.295–335. 158(1998), pp.345–71. 159(1999), pp.395–530.

Metcalf, D. M. (1998a) *An Atlas of Anglo-Norman Coin Finds, c. 973–1086.* London: RNS.

Metcalf, D. M. (1998b) The Monetary Economy of Ninth-Century England South of the Humber: A Topographical Analysis. In Blackburn and Dumville (eds.) (1998), pp.167–97.

Metcalf, D. M. (2003) Variations in the Composition of the Currency at Different Places in England. In *P&U*, pp.37–47.

Metcalf, D. M. (2009) Betwixt Sceattas and Offa's Pence: Mint-Attributions, and the Chronology of a Recession. *BNJ.* 79, pp.1–33.

Metcalf, D. M. (2011) English Money, Foreign Money: The Circulation of Tremisses and Sceattas in the East Midlands and the Monetary Role of 'Productive Sites'. In *SiEMC*. Volume 2, pp.13–46.

Metcalf, D. M. (2014a) Merovingian and Frisian Gold in England: Was There a Money Economy in the Sixth and Seventh Centuries? In *SiEMC*. Volume 3, pp.47–67.

Metcalf, D. M. (2014b) The Archbishop's Hat: A Suggested Attribution for the Sceattas of Series F. *BNJ.* 84, pp.52–71.

Metcalf, D. M. (2014c) Thrymsas and Sceattas and the Balance of Payments. In *EMMH*, pp.243–56.

Metcalf, D. M., and Northover, J. P. (1987) The Northumbrian Royal Coinage in the Time of Æthelred and Osberht. In *BAR180*, pp.187–233.

Metcalf, D. M., and Op den Velde, W. (2014) The Cothen Hoard of Porcupine Sceattas and Merovingian Deniers. *JMP*. 101, pp.27–51.

Monbiot, G. (2013) *Feral: Searching for Enchantment on the Frontiers of Rewilding.* London: Allen Lane.

Moorhead, S., and Walton, P. (2014) Coinage at the End of Roman Britain. In Haarer, F. K., Collins, R., Fitzpatrick-Matthews, K. J., Moorhead, S., and Petts, D. (eds.) *AD 410: The History and Archaeology of Late and Post-Roman Britain.* London: Society for the Promotion of Roman Studies, pp.99–116.

Moreland, J. (2000a) Concepts of the Early Medieval Economy. In Hansen and Wickham (eds.) (2000), pp.1–34.

Moreland, J. (2000b) The Significance of Production in Eighth-Century England. In Hansen and Wickham (eds) (2000), pp.69–105.

Morris, R. K. (1986) Alcuin, York, and the *Alma Sophia.* In Butler, L. A. S., and Morris, R. K. (eds.) *The Anglo-Saxon Church: Papers on History, Architecture, and Archaeology in Honour of Dr H. M. Taylor.* London: CBA, pp.80–89.

Morris, R. K. (1989) *Churches in the Landscape.* London: Dent.

Morris, R. K. (2005) 'Calami at Iunci': Lastingham in the Seventh and Eighth Centuries. *Bulletin of International Medieval Research.* 11, pp.3–21.

Morris, R. K. (2011) Local Churches in the Anglo-Saxon Countryside. In Hamerow, H., and Hinton, D. A. (eds.) *A Handbook of Anglo-Saxon Archaeology.* Oxford Handbooks in Archaeology. Oxford: OUP, pp.174–99.

Morris, R. K. (2012) *Time's Anvil: England, Archaeology and the Imagination.* London: Weidenfeld & Nicholson.

Morris, R. K., and Stocker, D. (1987) *Recording Worked Stone: A Practical Guide*. Practical Handbooks in Archaeology. 1. London: CBA.

Mortimer, J. R., and Sheppard, T. (1905) *Forty Years' Researches in British and Saxon Burial Mounds of East Yorkshire, Including Romano-British Discoveries, and a Description of the Ancient Entrenchments on a Section of the Yorkshire Wolds*. London: A. Brown.

Muir, R. (1987) Old Yorkshire: The Story of the Yorkshire Landscape and People. London: Michael Joseph.

Myers, A. R. (1986) *England in the Late Middle Ages*. 8th ed. Harmondsworth: Penguin Books.

Myhre, B. (1993) The Beginning of the Viking Age: Some Current Archaeological Problems. In Faulkes, A., and Perkins, R. (eds.) *Viking Revaluations*. London: Viking Society for Northern Research, pp.182–204.

Naismith, R. (2011) *The Coinage of Southern England, 796–865*. 2 Volumes. London: Spink.

Naismith, R. (2012) *Money and Power in Anglo-Saxon England: The Southern English Kingdoms, 757–865*. Cambridge: CUP.

Naismith, R. (2014a) Gold Coinage and its Use in the Post-Roman West. *Speculum*. 89, pp.273–306.

Naismith, R. (2014b) Money of the Saints: Church and Coinage in Early Anglo-Saxon England. In *SiEMC*. Volume 3, pp.68–121.

Naismith, R. (2014c) Review of: 'Abramson, T. (2012) *Sceatta List: An Illustrated and Priced Catalogue of Sceats for Collectors, with Stycas*. Wakefield: Anglo-Saxon Coinage'. *BNJ*. 84, pp.275–77.

Naismith, R. (2015) *Spending Power, Money and Power Relations in Early Medieval Europe*. Uppsala University Coin Cabinet Working Papers. 16. Uppsala: Uppsala University Coin Cabinet.

Naismith, R. (2017) Medieval European Coinage, with a Catalogue of the Coins in The Fitzwilliam Museum, Cambridge. 8: Britain and Ireland, c. 400–1066. Cambridge: CUP.

Naismith, R., Allen, M., and Screen, E. (eds.) (2014) *Early Medieval Monetary History: Studies in Memory of Mark Blackburn*. Farnham: Ashgate.

Naylor, J. D. (2002) An Archaeology of Trade in Eastern England, *c.* 650–900 CE. Unpublished PhD thesis. University of Durham.

Naylor, J. D. (2004) *An Archaeology of Trade in Middle Saxon England*. B. A. R. British Series. 376. Oxford: BAR Publishing.

Naylor, J. D. (2006) Mercian Hegemony and Series J Sceattas. *BNJ*. 76, pp.159–70.

Naylor, J. D. (2007) The Circulation of Early-Medieval European Coinage: A Case Study from Yorkshire, *c.* 650–*c.* 867. *Med Arch*. 51, pp.41–61.

Naylor, J. D. (2012) Coinage, Trade and the Origins of the English Emporia, *c.* AD 650–750. In Gelichi, S., and Hodges, R. (eds.) *From One Sea to Another: Trade Centres in the European and Mediterranean Early Middle Ages*. Turnhout: Brepols, pp.237–66.

Naylor, J. D. (2016) Emporia and their Hinterlands in the 7th to 9th-Centuries AD: Some Comments and Observations from England. *Revue du Nord*. 24, pp.59–67.

Naylor, J. D., and Allen, M. (2014) A New Variety of Gold Shilling of the 'York' Group. In *SiEMC*. Volume 3, pp.153–58.

Naylor, J. D., and Richards, J. D. (2005) Third-Party Data for First Class Research. *Archeologia e calcolatori*. 16, pp.83–91.

Newman, J. (2008) Sceattas in East Anglia: An Archaeological Perspective. In *SiEMC*. Volume 1, pp.17–22.

North, J. J. (1994) *English Hammered Coinage*. 3rd ed. London: Spink.

Nuttgens, P. (1976) *York: The Continuing City*. London: Faber.

O'Brien, C. (2011) Yeavering and Bernician Kingship: A Review of Debate on the Hybrid Culture Thesis. In *EMN*, pp.207–20.

O'Connor, T. P. (1994) 8th–11th-Century Economy and Environment in York. In Rackham (ed.) (1994), pp.136–47.

O'Connor, T. P. (2001) On the Interpretation of Animal Bone Assemblages from *Wics*. In Hill and Cowie (eds.) (2001), pp.54–60.

Oliver, L. (2002) *The Beginnings of English Law*. Toronto: University of Toronto Press.

O'Neil, B. H. St. J. (1935) The South Ferriby Theodosian Hoard. *NC*. 15(60), pp.254–74.

Op den Velde, W., and Metcalf, D. M. (2003) The Monetary Economy of the Netherlands, *c.* 690–*c.* 715 and the Trade with England: A Study of the Sceattas of Series D. *JMP*. 90, pp.1–211.

Op den Velde, W., and Metcalf, D. M. (2009–10) The Monetary Economy of the Netherlands, *c.* 690–*c.* 760 and the Trade with England: A Study of the 'Porcupine' Sceattas of Series E. *JMP*. 96–97, pp.1–506.

Op den Velde, W., and Metcalf, D. M. (2014a) The Hexagram ('Herstal') Type Sceattas. In *SiEMC*. Volume 3, pp.122–40.

Op den Velde, W., and Metcalf, D. M. (2014b) The Cothen Hoard of Porcupine Sceattas and Merovingian Deniers. *JMP*. 101, pp.27–51.

Orton, F., Wood, I., and Lees, C. A. (2007) *Fragments of History: Rethinking the Ruthwell and Bewcastle Monuments*. Manchester: Manchester University Press.

Ottaway, P. (1992) *Anglo-Scandinavian Ironwork from 16–22 Coppergate*. AY. 18.1. London: CBA.

Ottaway, P. (2004) *Roman York*. Stroud: Tempus.

Oxford Archaeology (2009) *Nighthawks & Nighthawking: Damage to Archaeological Sites in the UK & Crown Dependencies Caused by Illegal Searching & Removal of Antiquities. Strategic Study and Final Report.* Oxford: English Heritage.

Pagan, H. E. (1987) Some Thoughts on Hoard Evidence for the Northumbrian Styca Coinage. In *BAR180*, pp.147–58.

Pagan, H. E. (1990) The Anglo-Saxon Coins. In McCarthy, M. R. (ed.) *A Roman, Anglian and Medieval Site at Blackfriars Street, Carlisle, Excavations, 1977–9.* Kendal: Cumberland and Westmorland Antiquarian and Archaeological Society, pp.180–81.

Pagan, H. E. (1993) Andreas Fountaine *eques auratus* A.A.A.F III Vir. *BNJ.* 63, pp.114–22.

Pagan, H. E. (1997) Review of: 'Pirie, E. J. E. (1996) *Coins of the Kingdom of Northumbria, c. 700–867 in the Yorkshire Collections: The Yorkshire Museum, York, the University of Leeds, the City Museum, Leeds.* Llanfyllin: Galata'. *NC* 1997, 274-282.

Page, R. I. (1972) *Life in Anglo-Saxon England.* London: Batsford.

Pelteret, D. A. E. (1995) *Slavery in Early Medieval England.* SASH. Woodbridge: Boydell.

Perring, D. (2002) *Town and Country in England: Frameworks for Archaeological Research.* York: CBA.

Pestell, T., and Ulmschneider, K. (eds.) (2003) *Markets in Early Medieval Europe: Trading and 'Productive' Sites, 650–850.* Macclesfield: Windgather.

Petts, D., and Turner, S. (eds.) (2011) *Early Medieval Northumbria: Kingdoms and Communities, AD 450–1100.* Turnhout: Brepols.

Pickup, D. (2012) Remember Scarborough. *YN.* 4, pp.311–44.

Pirenne, H. (1939) *Mohammed and Charlemagne.* Translated by Miall, B. New York: W. W. Norton. [Reprinted 2001, Mineola: Dover Publications.]

Pirie, E. J. E. (1975) *Coins in Yorkshire Collections: The Yorkshire Museum, York, the City Museum, Leeds, the University of Leeds.* SCBI. 21. London: OUP.

Pirie, E. J. E. (1982) The Ripon Hoard, 1695: Contemporary and Current Interest. *BNJ.* 52, pp.84–103.

Pirie, E. J. E. (1986a) Finds of Sceattas and *Stycas* in Northumbria. In Blackburn, M. A. S. (ed.) *Anglo-Saxon Monetary History: Essays in Memory of Michael Dolley.* Leicester: Leicester University Press, pp.67–90. [Pirie archive].

Pirie, E. J. E. (1986b) *Post-Roman Coins from York Excavations, 1971–81.* AY. 18.1. London: CBA.

Pirie, E. J. E. (1987) Adamson's Hexham Plates. In *BAR180*, pp.257–327.

Pirie, E. J. E. (1988) Early Northumbrian Orthography and the Problem of Convention. *YN.* 1, pp.1–8.

Pirie, E. J. E. (1991) The Northumbrian Coins: Single Finds and the Purse-Hoard. In Armstrong, Tomlinson, and Evans (1991), pp.164–67. [Pirie archive].

Pirie, E. J. E. (1991–92) Excavations at Whitby Abbey, Yorkshire, 1920–6. Unpublished, prepared for BM. [Pirie archive].

Pirie, E. J. E. (1992a) *Excavations at Whithorn, Wigtownshire, 1984–91.* Unpublished. [Pirie archive].

Pirie, E. J. E. (1992b) The Seventh-Century Gold Coinage of Northumbria. *YN.* 2, pp.11–15.

Pirie, E. J. E. (1994) *The York Hoard, 1831.* Llanfyllin: Galata.

Pirie, E. J. E. (1995a) Earduulf: A Significant Addition to the Coinage of Northumbria. *BNJ.* 65, pp.20–31.

Pirie, E. J. E. (1995b) Post-Roman Coins. In Carver (ed.) (1995), pp.527–30.

Pirie, E. J. E. (1996) *Coins of the Kingdom of Northumbria, c. 700–867 in the Yorkshire Collections: The Yorkshire Museum, York, the University of Leeds, the City Museum, Leeds.* Llanfyllin: Galata.

Pirie, E. J. E. (1997) London MoLAS Excavations, 1989–96: Royal Opera House, 1996, Together with Leicester Square, 1989 and Bull Wharf, 1990. In Malcolm, G., Bowsher, D., and Cowie, R. (eds.) *Middle Saxon London: Excavations at the Royal Opera House, 1989–99.* London: Museum of London Archaeology Service. [Pirie archive].

Pirie, E. J. E. (2000) *Thrymsas, Sceattas and Stycas of Northumbria: An Inventory of Finds Recorded, to 1997.* Northumbrian Numismatic Studies. 2. Llanfyllin: Galata.

Pirie, E. J. E. (2003) *The Bamburgh Hoard in the Museum of Antiquities, Newcastle-upon-Tyne, Parcel A – 1999, Parcel B – 2002: A Check-List.* Newcastle: Museum of Antiquities, Department of Archaeology, University of Newcastle upon Tyne.

Pirie, E. J. E. (2004) The Bamburgh Hoard of Ninth-Century Northumbrian Coins. *AA* 5th ser. 33, pp.65–75.

Polanyi, K. (1977) *The Livelihood of Man.* New York: Academic Press.

Polanyi, K. (2001) *The Great Transformation: The Political and Economic Origins of our Time.* Boston: Beacon Press.

Powlesland, D. (1997) Early Anglo-Saxon Settlements, Structures, Form and Layout. In Hines (ed.) (1997a), pp.101–24.

Powlesland, D. (2003) *Twenty-Five Years of Archaeological Research on the Sands and Gravels of Heslerton.* Yedingham: Landscape Research Centre.

Powlesland, D., and May, K. (2010) *DigIT: Archaeological Summary Report and Experiments in Digital Recording in the Field.* [Online]. Available from: http://intarch.ac.uk/journal/issue27/2/index.html

Prou, M. (1892) *Catalogue des monnaies françaises de la Bibliothèque nationale: Les monnaies mérovingiennes.* Paris: C. Rollin & Feuardent.

Quiggin, A. H. (1949) *A Survey of Primitive Money.* London: Methuen.

Rackham, J. (ed.) (1994) *Environment and Economy in Anglo-Saxon England: A Review of Recent Work on the Environmental Archaeology of Rural and Urban Anglo-Saxon Settlements in England.* York: CBA.

Rackham, J. (1995) Animal Bone from Post-Roman Contexts. In Carver (ed.) (1995), pp.533–58.

Rahtz, P. A. (1967) Whitby, 1958. *YAJ.* 40, pp.604–18.

Rahtz, P. A. (1976) Whitby, 1958, Site Two. In *AASE*, pp.459–62. [Pirie archive].

Ramm, H. (1978) *The Parisi.* London: Duckworth.

Reece, R. (1987) *Coinage in Roman Britain.* London: Seaby.

Reece, R. (1991) *Roman Coins from 140 Sites in Britain.* Cirencester: Cotswold Studies.

Reece, R. (2002) *The Coinage of Roman Britain.* Stroud: Tempus.

Reynolds, S. (1974) *Fiefs and Vassals: The Medieval Evidence Reinterpreted.* Oxford: OUP.

Richards, J. D. (1992) Anglo-Saxon Settlement at Wharram Percy: A General Introduction. In Milne, G., and Richards, J. D. (eds.) *Wharram: A Study of Settlement on the Yorkshire Wolds. 7: Two Anglo-Saxon Buildings and Associated Finds.* York: Department of Archaeology, University of York, pp.89–94.

Richards, J. D. (1999a) Cottam: An Anglian and Anglo-Scandinavian Settlement on the Yorkshire Wolds. *AJ.* 156, pp.1–110.

Richards, J. D. (1999b) What's So Special about 'Productive Sites'? Middle Saxon Settlements in Northumbria. *ASSAH.* 10, pp.71–80.

Richards, J. D. (2000) Anglo-Saxon Settlements and Archaeological Visibility in the Yorkshire Wolds. In Geake H., and Kenny, J. (eds.) *Early Deira: Archaeological Studies of the East Riding in the Fourth to Ninth Centuries AD.* Oxford: Oxbow Books, pp.27–39.

Richards, J. D. (2001a) Anglian and Anglo-Scandinavian Cottam: Linking Digital Publication and Archive. *Internet Archaeology.* 10. [Online]. Available from: http://dx.doi.org/10.11141/ia.10.4

Richards, J. D. (2001b) *Burrow House Farm, Cottam: An Anglian and Anglo-Scandinavian Settlement in East Yorkshire,* York: Archaeology Data Service. [Online]. Available from: http://dx.doi.org/10.5284/1000339

Richards, J. D. (2011a) *Cottam A: A Romano-British and Anglian Settlement in East Yorkshire*, York: Archaeology Data Service. [Online]. Available from: http://dx.doi.org/10.5284/1000132

Richards, J. D. (2011b) *Cowlam: Anglian Settlement in East Yorkshire*, York: Archaeology Data Service. [Online]. Available from: http://dx.doi.org/10.5284/1000175

Richards, J. D., and Naylor, J. D. (2009) The Real Value of Buried Treasure: VASLE. In Thomas and Stone (eds.) (2009), pp.167–80.

Richards, J. D., and Naylor, J. D. (2011) Settlement, Landscape, and Economy in Early Medieval Northumbria: The Contribution of Portable Antiquities. In *EMN*, pp.129–50.

Richards, J. D., and others (2013) Cottam, Cowlam and Environs: An Anglo-Saxon Estate on the Yorkshire Wolds. *AJ.* 170, pp.201–71.

Rigold, S. E. (1960) The Two Primary Series of Sceattas. *BNJ.* 30, pp.6–53.

Rigold, S. E. (1988) Coins Found in Anglo-Saxon Burials. In Reece, R., and Casey, J. (eds.) *Coins and the Archaeologist.* 2nd ed. London: Seaby, pp.201–05.

Rigold, S. E., and Metcalf, D. M. (1977) A Check-List of English Finds of Sceattas. *BNJ.* 47, pp.31–52 [MEC: 'list superseded by Rigold and Metcalf 1984, but illustrations of finds remain useful'].

Rigold, S. E., and Metcalf, D. M. (1984) 'A Revised Check-List of English Finds of Sceattas. In *BAR128*, pp.245–68.

Robbins, K. J. (2012) From Past to Present: Understanding the Impact of Sampling Bias on Data Recorded by the Portable Antiquities Scheme. Unpublished PhD thesis. University of Southampton.

Roebuck, D. (2008) *Early English Arbitration.* Oxford: Holo Books.

Rogers, N. S. H. (1993) *Anglian and Other Finds from 46–54 Fishergate.* AY. 17. London: CBA.

Rollason, D. (2003) *Northumbria, 500–1100: Creation and Destruction of a Kingdom.* Cambridge: CUP.

Rollason, D., Gore, D., and Fellows-Jensen, G. (1998) *Sources for York History, to AD 1100.* York: YAT.

Roosevelt, T. (1910) Man in the Arena Speech (Citizenship in a Republic). The Sorbonne, Paris, France, 23 April 1910.

Roskams, S. (2001) *Excavation.* Cambridge: CUP.

Roskams, S., Neal, C., Richardson, J., and Leary, R. (2013) A Late Roman Well at Heslington East, York: Ritual or Routine Practices? *Internet Archaeology.* [Online]. Available from: http://intarch.ac.uk/journal/issue34/5/toc.html

Ross, A. (1967) *Pagan Celtic Britain: Studies in Iconography and Tradition.* London: Routledge & Paul.

Rostow, W. W. (1963) *The Economics of Take-Off into Sustained Growth.* London: Macmillan.

Rumble, A. R. (2001) Notes on the Linguistic and Onomastic Characteristics of Old English Wic. In Hill and Cowie (eds.) (2001), pp.1–2.

Sahlins, M. (2003) *Stone Age Economics*. 2nd ed. London: Routledge.

Salzman, L. F. (1970) *English Industries of the Middle Ages*. Rev. ed. London: H. Pordes.

Samson, R. (1991) Economic Anthropology and Vikings. In Samson, R. (ed.) *Social Approaches to Viking Studies.* Glasgow: Cruithne, pp.87–96.

Saunders, T. S. A. (1991) Marxism and Archaeology: The Origins of Feudalism in Early Medieval England. Unpublished DPhil thesis. University of York.

Saunders, T. S. A. (2001) Early Mediaeval Emporia and the Tributary Social Function. In Hill and Cowie (eds.) (2001), pp.7–13.

Sawyer, P. (1981) Fairs and Markets in Early Medieval England. In Skyum-Nieben, N., and Lund, N. (eds.) *Danish Medieval History: New Currents.* Copenhagen: Museum Tusculanum Press, pp.153–68.

Sawyer, P. (2013) *The Wealth of Anglo-Saxon England.* Oxford: OUP.

Schumpeter, J. (1942) *Capitalism, Socialism and Democracy.* New York: Harper.

Scott, E. (2012) *Mohammed & Charlemagne Revisited: The History of a Controversy.* Nashville: New English Review Press.

Scull, C. (1990) Scales and Weights in Early Anglo-Saxon England. *AJ.* 147, pp.183–215.

Scull, C. (1997) Urban Centres in Pre-Viking England. In Hines (ed.) (1997a), pp.269–97.

Scull, C., and Naylor, J. (2016) Sceattas in Anglo-Saxon Graves. *Med Arch.* 60(2), pp.205–41.

Sear, D. (1983) *Roman Coins and their Values.* London: Spink.

Sehgal, K. (2015) *Coined: The Rich Life of Money and How its History Has Shaped Us.* London: John Murray.

Sindbæk, S. M. (2007) Networks and Nodal Points: The Emergence of Towns in Early Viking Age Scandinavia. *Antiquity*. 81, 119–32.

Skre, D. (2008) Post-Substantivist Towns and Trade, AD 600–1000. In Skre D. (ed.) *Means of Exchange: Dealing with Silver in the Viking Age.* Aarhus: Aarhus Universitetsforlag, pp.327–42.

Skre, D. (2011) Commodity Money, Silver and Coinage in Viking-Age Scandinavia. In *SEMSS*, pp.67–91.

Skre, D. (2015) Post-Substantivist Production and Trade: Specialized Sites for Trade and Craft Production in Scandinavia *c.* 600–1000 AD. In Barrett, J. H., and Gibson, S. J. (eds.) *Maritime Societies of the Viking and Medieval World.* Leeds: Maney Publishing, pp.156–70.

Smart, V. (1997) A Problem of Convention: A Belated Reply. *YN.* 3, pp.69–72.

Smith, A. (1950) *The Wealth of Nations*. Edited by Cannan, E. London: Methuen. [Originally published 1776, London: Strahan and Cadell.]

Smith, C. A. (ed.) (1976) *Regional Analysis 2: Social Systems.* New York: Academic Press.

Smith (née Holas-Clark), C. N. J. (2006) The Economic History of Anglian Deira, 700–870. Unpublished PhD thesis. University of York.

Spratt, D. A., and Harrison, B. J. D. (eds.) (1989) *The North York Moors: Landscape Heritage.* Newton Abbot: David & Charles.

Spufford, P. (1988) *Money and its Use in Medieval Europe.* Cambridge: CUP.

Stahl, A. M., and Oddy, W. A. (1992) The Date of the Sutton Hoo Coins. In Farrell, R., and de Vegvar, C. N. (eds.) *Sutton Hoo: Fifty Years After*. American Early Medieval Studies. 2. Oxford, OH. 1992.

Stanley, E. G. (1975) *The Search for Anglo-Saxon Paganism.* Cambridge: D. S. Brewer.

Steedman, K. (1994) Excavation of a Saxon Site at Riby Cross Roads, Lincolnshire. *AJ.* 151, pp.212–306.

Stewart, B. H. I. H. (1978) Anglo-Saxon Gold Coins. In Carson, R. A. G. and Kraay, C. M. (eds.) *'Scripta Nummaria Romana, Essays Presented to Humphrey Sutherland',* (London). pp.143–72.

Stiglitz, J. E. (2002) *Globalization and its Discontents.* London: Penguin.

Stocker, D. (1999) *The College of the Vicars Choral of York Minster at Bedern: Architectural Fragments*. AY. 10.4. York: CBA.

Story, J. (2003) *Carolingian Connections: Anglo-Saxon England and Carolingian Francia, c. 750–870.* Aldershot: Ashgate.

Sugden, K. F., and Warhurst, M. (1979) An Unrecorded Parcel from the Hexham Hoard of 1832. *NC.* 139, pp.212–17. [Pirie archive].

Sutherland, C. H. V. (1948) *Anglo-Saxon Gold Coinage in the Light of the Crondall Hoard.* London: OUP.

Sutherland, C. H. V. (1955) *Art in Coinage.* London: Batsford.

Tapsell, R. F. (1987) *Monarchs, Rulers, Dynasties and Kingdoms of the World.* London: Thames and Hudson.

Thomas, C. (1992) *Whithorn's Christian Beginnings*. Whithorn Lecture. 1. Whithorn: Friends of the Whithorn Trust. [Pirie archive].

Thomas, N. (1994) *Entangled Objects: Exchange, Material Culture, and Colonialism in the Pacific*. Cambridge, MA: Harvard University Press.

Thomas, S., and Stone, P. G. (eds.) (2009) *Metal Detecting and Archaeology*. Woodbridge: Boydell.

Tipper, J. (2004) *The Grübenhaus in Anglo-Saxon England: An Analysis and Interpretation of the Evidence from a Most Distinctive Building Type*. Yedingham: Landscape Research Centre.

Toop, N. J. (2011) Northumbria in the West: Considering Interaction Through Monumentality. In *EMN*, pp.85–111.

Tweddle, D. (1986) *Finds from Parliament Street and Other Sites in the City Centre*. AY. 17.4. London: CBA.

Tweddle, D., and Moulden, J. (1992) Seventh-Century Gold Coins from York. *YN*. 2, pp.17–20.

Tweddle, D., Moulden, J., and Logan, E. (eds.) (1999) *Anglian York: A Survey of the Evidence*. AY. 7.2. York: CBA.

Tye, R. (2001) *Gyges Magic Ring? The Origins of Coins*. South Uist: Robert Tye.

Ulmschneider, K. (2000) *Markets, Minsters, and Metal-Detectors: The Archaeology of Middle Saxon Lincolnshire and Hampshire Compared*. *BAR*. 307. Oxford: BAR.

Van Arsdell, R. D. (1989) *Celtic Coinage of Britain*. London: Spink.

Van de Noort, R., and Davies, P. (1993) *Wetland Heritage: An Archaeological Assessment of the Humber Wetlands*. Edited by Ellis, S. Kingston upon Hull: Humber Wetlands Project, University of Hull.

Van de Noort, R., and Ellis, S. (eds.) (1999) *Wetland Heritage of the Vale of York: An Archaeological Survey*. Kingston upon Hull: Humber Wetlands Project, University of Hull.

Veblen, T. (1899) *The Theory of the Leisure Class: An Economic Study in the Evolution of Institutions*. New York: Macmillan.

Vegvar, C. N. de (1999) The Travelling Twins: Romulus and Remus in Anglo-Saxon England. In Hawkes and Mills (eds.) (1999), pp.256–67.

Verhulst, A. (2000) Roman Cities, *Emporia*, and the New Towns (Sixth–Ninth Centuries). In Hansen and Wickham (eds.) (2000), pp.105–20.

Verhulst, A. (2002) *The Carolingian Economy*. Cambridge: CUP.

Vince, A. (1994a) Saxon Urban Economies: An Archaeological Perspective. In Rackham (ed.) (1994), pp.108–19.

Walbers, B. (2012) Number and Measurement in Anglo-Saxon Christian Culture: Editions and Studies of Numerical Notes in Eight Anglo-Saxon Manuscripts, *c.* 800–*c.* 1150. Unpublished PhD thesis. University of York.

Walton, P. (2011) Rethinking Roman Britain: An Applied Numismatic Analysis of the Roman Coin Data Recorded by the Portable Antiquities Scheme. Unpublished PhD thesis. University College London.

Walton, P., and Broughton, D. (2009) The Portable Antiquities Scheme in the North. In Thomas and Stone (eds.) (2009), pp.147–52.

Webster, L., and Backhouse, J. (eds.) (1991) *The Making of England: Anglo-Saxon Art and Culture,* AD *600–900*. London: BM.

Webster, L., and Brown, M. (eds.) (1997) *The Transformation of the Roman World,* AD *400–900*. London: BM.

Welch, M. (1985) Rural Settlement Patterns in the Early and Middle Anglo-Saxon Periods. *Landscape History*. 7, pp.13–25.

Whitelock, D. (ed.) (1979) *English Historical Documents: Volume 1, 500–1042*. 2nd ed. London: Methuen.

Whitmarsh, T. (2015) *Battling the Gods: Atheism in the Ancient World*. London: Faber and Faber.

Wickham, C. (2005) *Framing the Early Middle Ages*. Oxford: OUP.

Wiechmann, R. (1998) Souvenirs aus England, Zwei northumbrische '*Stycas*' gefunden in Schleswig-Holstein. In Wesse, A. (ed.) *Studien zur Archäologie des Ostseeraumes, von der Eisenzeit zum Mittelalter. Festschrift für Michael Müller-Wille*. Neumünster: Wachholtz, pp.453–60. (Hamburg) [Pirie archive].

Williams, G. (2006) The Circulation and Function of Coinage in Conversion-Period England, *c.* AD 580–675. In *Archibald Festschrift*, pp.145–92.

Williams, G., and Hook, D. (2013) Analysis of Gold Content and its Implications for the Chronology of the Early Anglo-Saxon Coinage. In Gannon, A. (ed.) *British Museum, Anglo-Saxon Coins I: Early Anglo-Saxon Gold and Anglo-Saxon and Continental Silver Coinage of the North Sea Area, c. 600–760*. SCBI. 63. London: BM, pp.55–70.

Wilson, A. (1956) *Anglo-Saxon Attitudes*. New York: The Viking Press.

Wilson, D. M. (ed.) (1976) *The Archaeology of Anglo-Saxon England*. London: Methuen.

Withy, R., and Ryall, I. (1756) *Coins of the Heptarchy*. London: Hogarth Head. Reissued 1774, London:

Charles Hall, incorporating three plates of Saxon coins engraved.

Wolf, E. R. (1982) *Europe and the People without History.* Berkeley: University of California Press.

Wood, I. (1987) Anglo-Saxon Otley: An Archiepiscopal Estate and its Crosses in a Northumbrian Context. *NH.* 23, pp.20–38.

Wood, I. (1997) Before and after the Migration to Britain. In Hines (ed.) (1997a), pp.41–64.

Wood, I. (ed.) (1998) *The Transformation of the Roman World,* AD *400–900.* Leiden: BM.

Wood, I. (2000) Before or after Mission: Social Relations across the Middle and Lower Rhine in the Seventh and Eighth Centuries. In Hansen and Wickham (eds.) (2000), pp.149–66.

Wood, I. (2007) Review Article: Landscapes Compared. *Early Medieval Europe.* 15, pp.223–37.

Wood, I. (2008a) Thrymsas, Sceattas and the Cult of the Cross. In *SiEMC.* Volume 1, pp.23–30.

Wood, I. (2008b) Monasteries and the Geography of Power in the Age of Bede. *NH.* 45, pp.11–25.

Woodman, D. A. (ed.) (2012) *Charters of Northern Houses.* Anglo-Saxon Charters. 16. Oxford: OUP.

Woolf, A. (2006) Dún Nechtain, Fortriu and the Geography of the Picts. *The Scottish Historical Review.* 85(220), pp.182–201.

Wormald, P. (2006) *The Times of Bede, 625–865: Studies in Early English Christian Society and its Historian.* Malden: Blackwell.

Wrathmell, S. (2003) Regional Frameworks for Medieval Rural Settlement. In Manby, Moorhouse, and Ottaway (eds.) (2003), pp.363–68.

Wrathmell, S., Harding, C., Marlow-Mann, E., and Wrathmell, S. (eds.) (2010) *Wharram: A Study of Settlement on the Yorkshire Wolds. Volume 12: The Post-Medieval Farm and Vicarage Sites.* York: Department of Archaeology, University of York.

Wrathmell, S. (ed.) (2012) *A History of Wharram Percy and its Neighbours. Wharram: A Study of Settlement on the Yorkshire Wolds. Volume 13.* York: Department of Archaeology, University of York.

Yorke, B. (1990) *Kings and Kingdoms in Early Anglo-Saxon England.* London: Seaby.

Websites

Abramson, T., Early Anglo-Saxon Coinage, http://www.anglo-saxon-coinage.co.uk/

Archibald, M. (2011) *Specialist Report: Coins from the Ipswich Excavations* http://archaeologydataservice.ac.uk/archives/view/ipswich_parent_2015/

Ashby, S. (2013) The Worked Bone and Antler from Burdale http://archaeologydataservice.ac.uk/archives/view/burdale_york_2013/downloads.cfm?group=8

Bambrook, G. (2005) Metal Detector Survey. In *Historia detectum.* http://archaeologydataservice.ac.uk/archiveDS/archiveDownload?t=arch-1596-1/dissemination/pdf/metal_detector_survey/BURDALE_metaldetecting_report_1.pdf

Blair, J. (2014) Exploring Anglo-Saxon Settlement. *CA.* 291 www.archaeology.co.uk/articles/features/exploring-anglo-saxon-settlement.htm

Corpus of Anglo-Saxon Stone Sculpture www.ascorpus.ac.uk/index.php

Corpus of Early Medieval Coin Finds http://www-cm.fitzmuseum.cam.ac.uk/dept/coins/projects/hoards/

Corrosionpedia www.corrosionpedia.com/definition/638/hot-shortness

DigIT: Archaeological Summary Report and Experiments in Digital Recording in the Field Powlesland, D., and May, K. (2010) http://intarch.ac.uk/journal/issue27/2/index.html

Distribution Mapping Software www.dmap.co.uk/

Early Medieval Corpus www.fitzmuseum.cam.ac.uk/coins/emc/

English Heritage www.english-heritage.org.uk/

Google Maps www.google.com/fusiontables/DataSource?docid=1Olx-waa2UBfq02PgLq23ecgCmxSt7eRIpYb8MQLB

Haldenby, D., and Richards, J. D. (2016) The Viking Great Army and its Legacy: Plotting Settlement Shift Using Metal-Detected Finds. *Internet Archaeology.* 42. http://dx.doi.org/10.11141/ia.42.3

Hayton www.southampton.ac.uk/archaeology/research/projects/landscape_archaeology_of_hayton.page

Historic England's Pastscape https://www.pastscape.org.uk/

Historic Environment Records www.algao.org.uk

Hopkinson, G. (2008) Little Westfield Farm, Cottam Site Report (Client Copy), Unpublished Report. *Archaeoscope.* http://www.archaeoscope.org/report.php?ID=10

Jarret, J. *A Corner of Tenth-Century Europe.* https://tenthmedieval.wordpress.com/2010/03/18/from-the-sources-v-bedes-letter-to-egbert/

Landscape and Soil Types http://publications.naturalengland.org.uk/

Macnab, N., and McComish, J. *28–29 High Ousegate, York, UK* www.iadb.co.uk/waterstones/intro.htm

Matthew, H. C. G., and Harrison, B. (eds) (2004) *Dictionary of National Biography*. New ed. Oxford: OUP. www.oxforddnb.com/

McComish, J. Roman, Anglian and Anglo-Scandinavian Activity and a Medieval Cemetery on Land at the Junction of Dixon Lane and George Street, York. www.iadb.co.uk/i3/item.php?ID=IADB:1307:U71

PastScape http://pastscape.org.uk/hob.aspx?hob_id=61387

Portable Antiquities Scheme Finds Database http://finds.org.uk/

Prosopography of Anglo-Saxon England www.pase.ac.uk/index.html

Residuality www.york.ac.uk/archaeology/strat/pastpub/95ch2.pdf

Richards, J. D. (1999a) Cottam: An Anglian and Anglo-Scandinavian Settlement on the Yorkshire Wolds. *AJ*. 156, pp.1-110. http://dx.doi.org/10.1080/00665983.1998.11078904

Richards, J. D. (2001a) Anglian and Anglo-Scandinavian Cottam: Linking Digital Publication and Archive. *Internet Archaeology*. 10. http://dx.doi.org/10.11141/ia.10.4

Richards, J. D. (2001b) *Burrow House Farm, Cottam: An Anglian and Anglo-Scandinavian Settlement in East Yorkshire*. York: Archaeology Data Service. http://dx.doi.org/10.5284/1000339

Richards, J. D. (2011a) *Cottam A: A Romano-British and Anglian Settlement in East Yorkshire*. York: Archaeology Data Service. http://dx.doi.org/10.5284/1000132

Richards, J. D. (2011b) *Cowlam: Anglian Settlement in East Yorkshire*. York: Archaeology Data Service. http://dx.doi.org/10.5284/1000175

Richards, J., and Roskams, S. (2013) Burdale: An Anglian Settlement in the Yorkshire Wolds. *Internet Archaeology*. 35. http://dx.doi.org/10.11141/ia.35.8.

Richards, J. D., Naylor, J. D., and Holas-Clark, C. N. J. (2008) Anglo-Saxon Landscape and Economy: Using Portable Antiquities to Study Anglo-Saxon and Viking Age England. *Journal*. http://intarch.ac.uk/journal/issue25/2/toc.html

Richards, J. D., Naylor, J. D., and Holas-Clark, C. N. J. (2009) Anglo-Saxon Landscape and Economy: Using Portable Antiquities to Study Anglo-Saxon and Viking Age England. *Internet Archaeology*. http://intarch.ac.uk/journal/issue25/2/toc.html

Roskams, S., Neal, C., Richardson, J., and Leary, R. (2013) A Late Roman Well at Heslington East, York: Ritual or Routine Practices? *Internet Archaeology*. http://intarch.ac.uk/journal/issue34/5/toc.html

Schmandt-Besserat, D. (2008) *Reckoning before Writing*. http://en.finaly.org/index.php/Reckoning_before_writing

Scull, C., and Naylor, J. (2016) Sceattas in Anglo-Saxon Graves. *Med Arch*. 60(2), pp.205–41. http://dx.doi.org/10.1080/00766097.2016.1221262

Sherlock, S., and Simmons, M. *Street House Cemetery*. http://antiquity.ac.uk/projgall/sherlock/index.html

Smith, C. N. J. (2006) The Economic History of Anglian Deira, 700–870. Unpublished PhD thesis. University of York. http://yorsearch.york.ac.uk/44YORK:44YORK_ALMA_DS21202548930001381

Tunstall, P. (trans. 2005) *The Tale of Ragnar's Sons*. http://www.germanicmythology.com/FORNALDARSAGAS/ThattrRagnarsSonar.html

UK Detector Finds Database www.ukdfd.co.uk/

University of Hull http://www2.hull.ac.uk/student/archaeology/research/hayton.aspx

University of York Archaeological Data Service, http://archaeologydataservice.ac.uk/

Vince, A. (1994b) Approaches to Residuality in Urban Archaeology. In Shepherd, L. (ed.) *Interpreting Stratigraphy*, City of Lincoln Archaeological Unit, pp.9–14: www.york.ac.uk/archaeology/strat/pastpub/95ch2.pdf

Whyman, M., and Howard, A. J. (2005) *Archaeology and Landscape in the Vale of York*. York: YAT: www.yorkarchaeology.co.uk/resources/voy-web.pdf.

York Archaeological Trust www.yorkarchaeology.co.uk/resources/publications

Maps

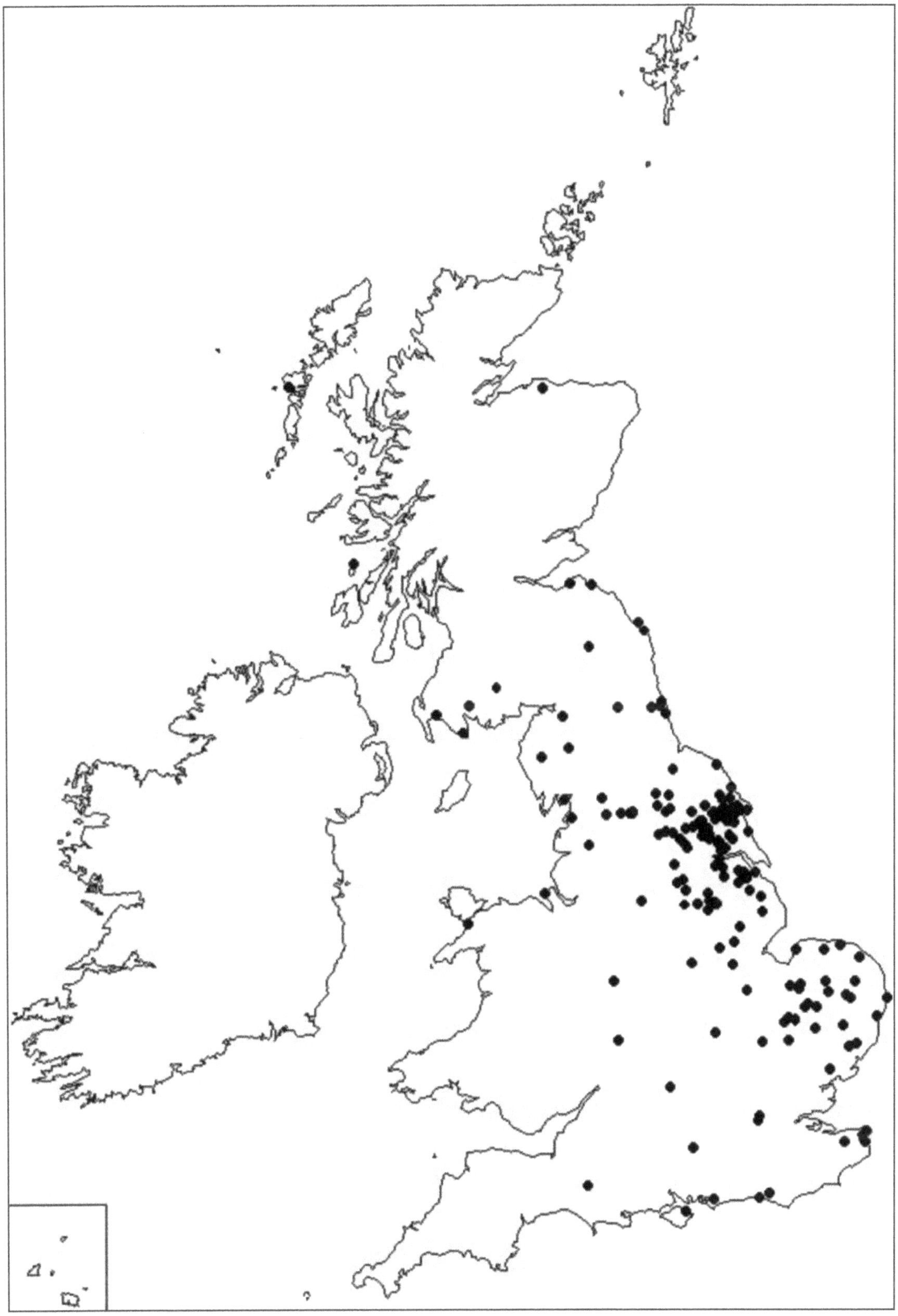

Map 1: Stycas included in *Database 1*, showing location of known styca finds, excluding hoards. Source: *Database 1*, using mapping from http://www.dmap.co.uk/.

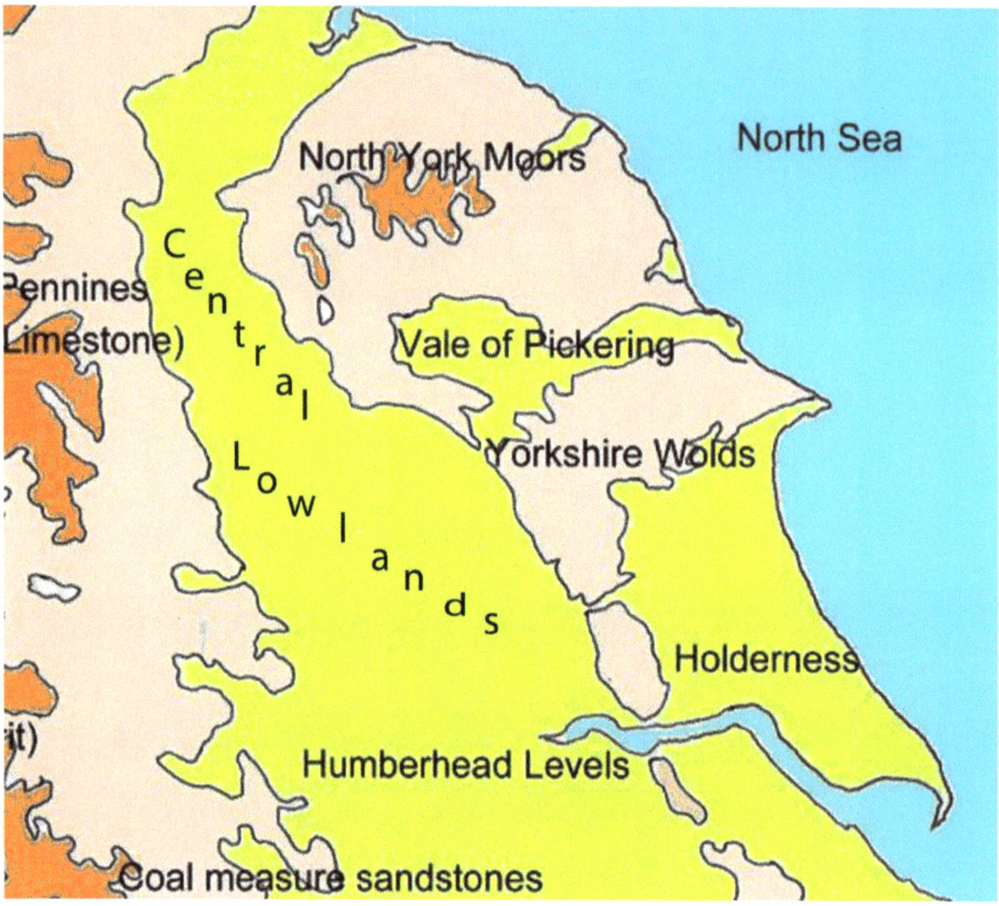

Map 2: A simplified topography of Yorkshire. Source: http://e.wikipedia.org/ user: Harkey Lodger, 18 June, 2007. This work is licensed under the Creative commons Attribution-ShareAlike 3.0 License.

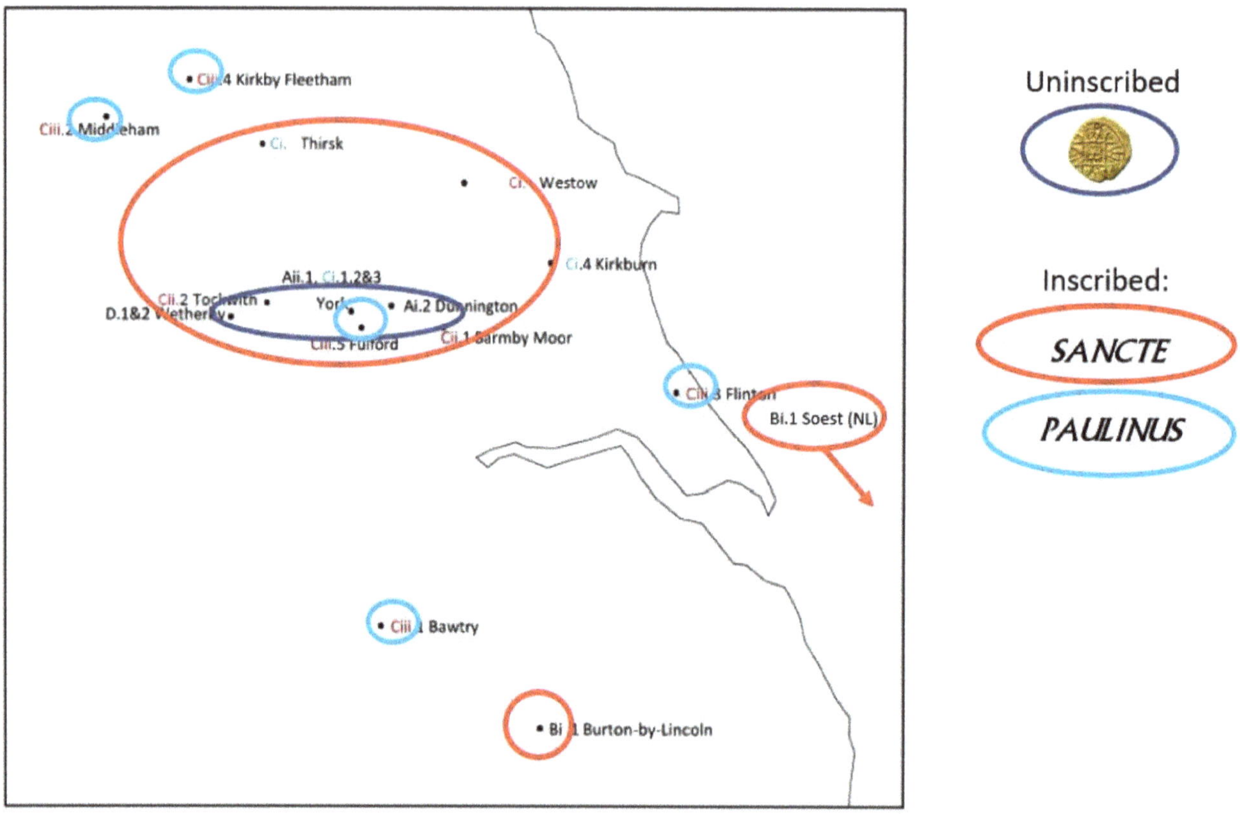

Map 3: Distribution of seventeen provenanced finds of York gold shillings from a corpus of twenty-too. Source: Abramson (2009).

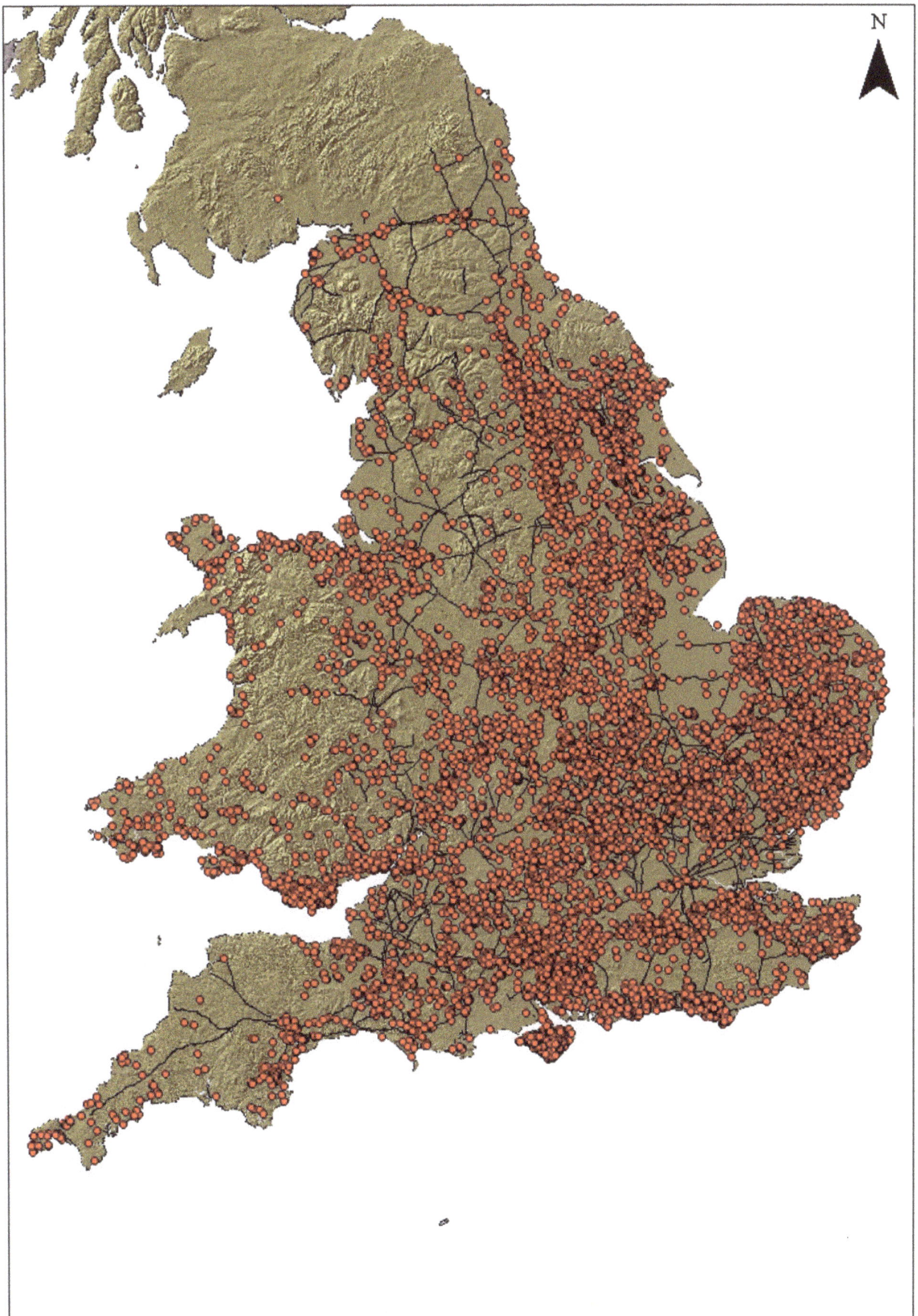

Map 4: Roman coin finds. Source: Portable Antiquities Scheme until the end of 2012, E Philippa Walton.

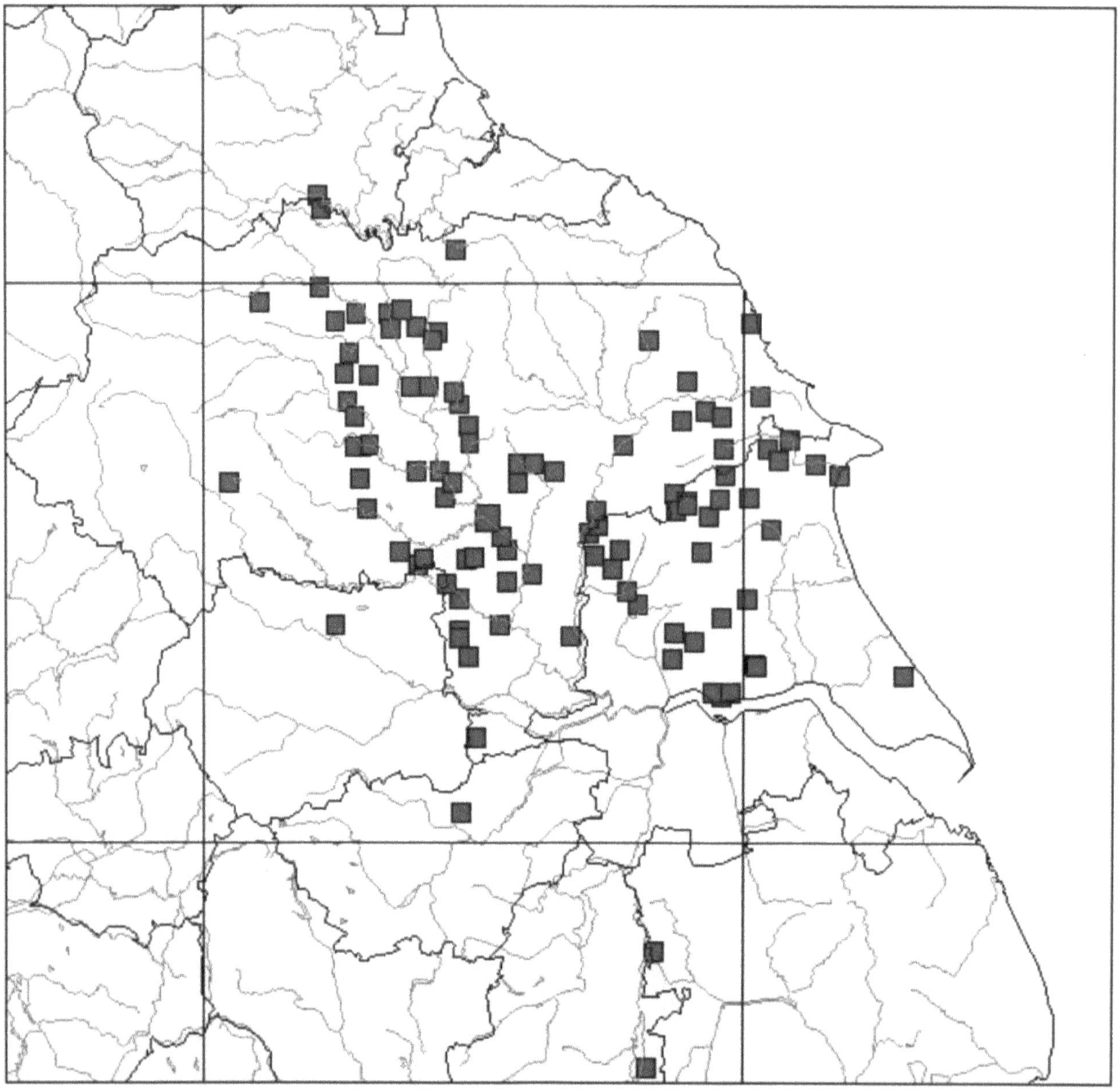

Map 5: Locations of artefacts recorded in the PAS database. Source: *Database 8* Early Medieval Yorkshire – Artefacts, using mapping from http://www.dmap.co.uk/.

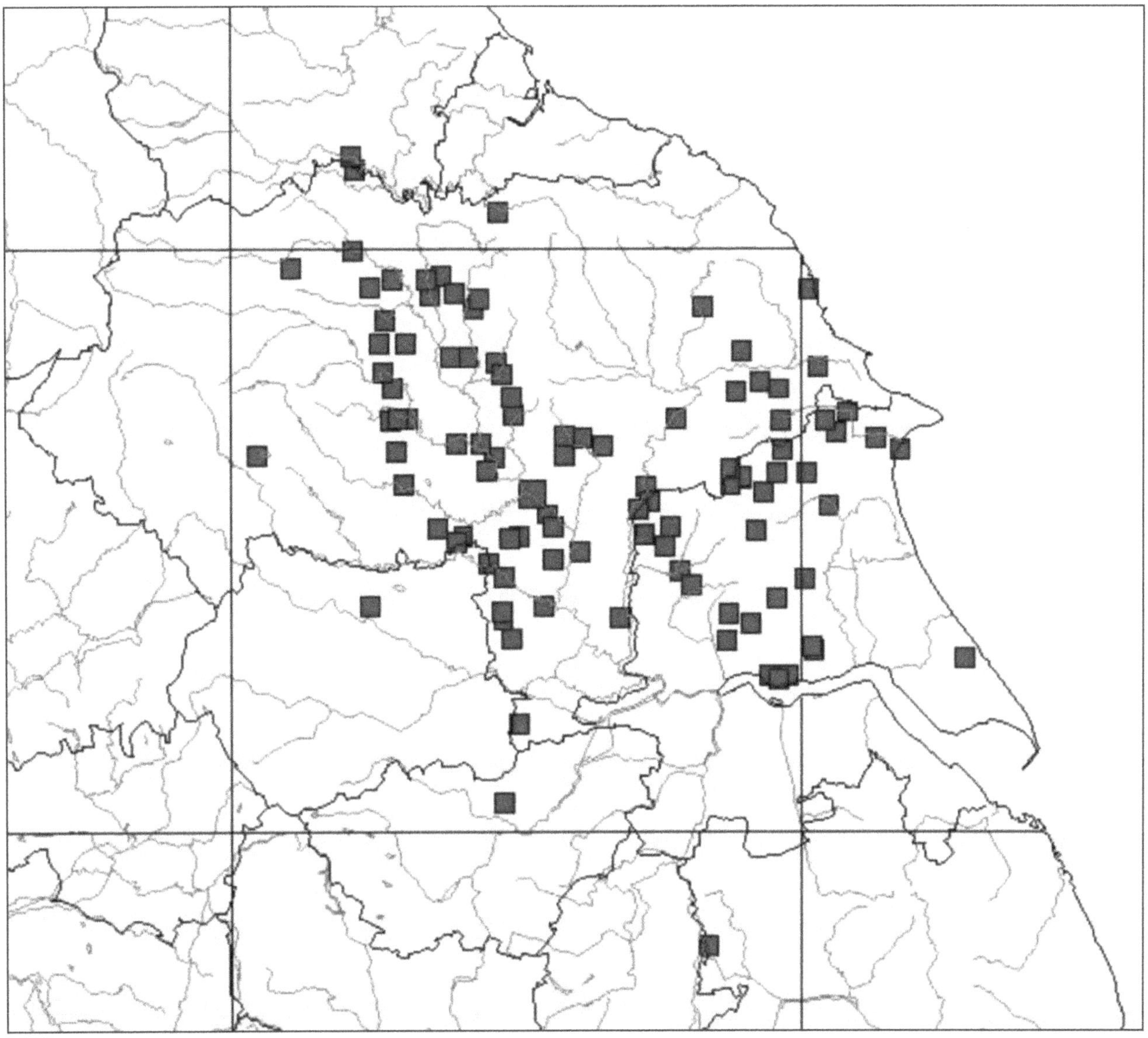

Map 6: All coin findspots. Source: *Database 1*, using mapping from http://www.dmap.co.uk/.

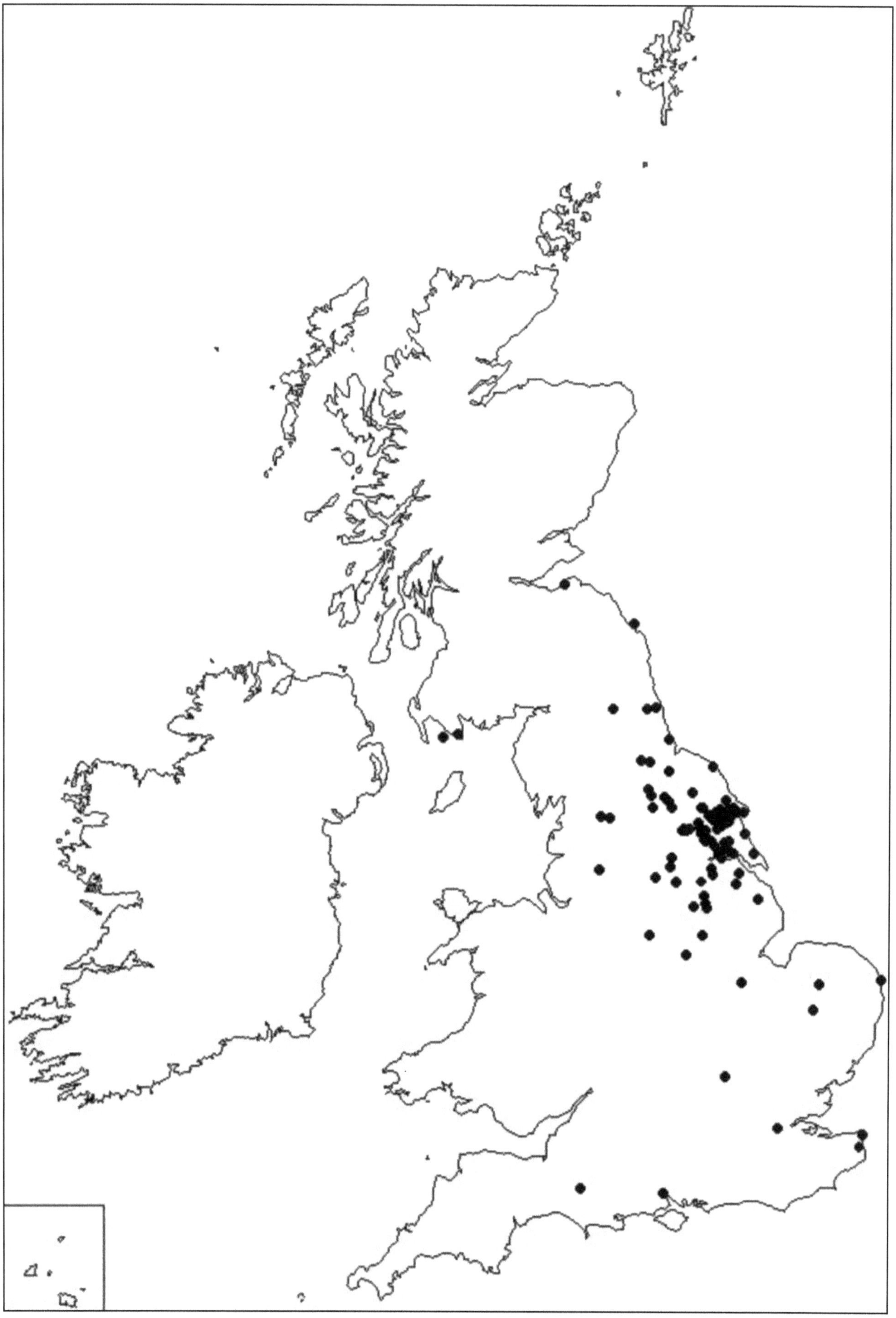

Map 7: Northumbrian *sceattas* included in *Database 1*. Source: *Database 1*, using mapping from http://www.dmap.co.uk/.

Map 8: Southumbrian *sceattas* found in Northumbria included in *Database 1*. Source: *Database 1*, using mapping from http://www.dmap.co.uk/.

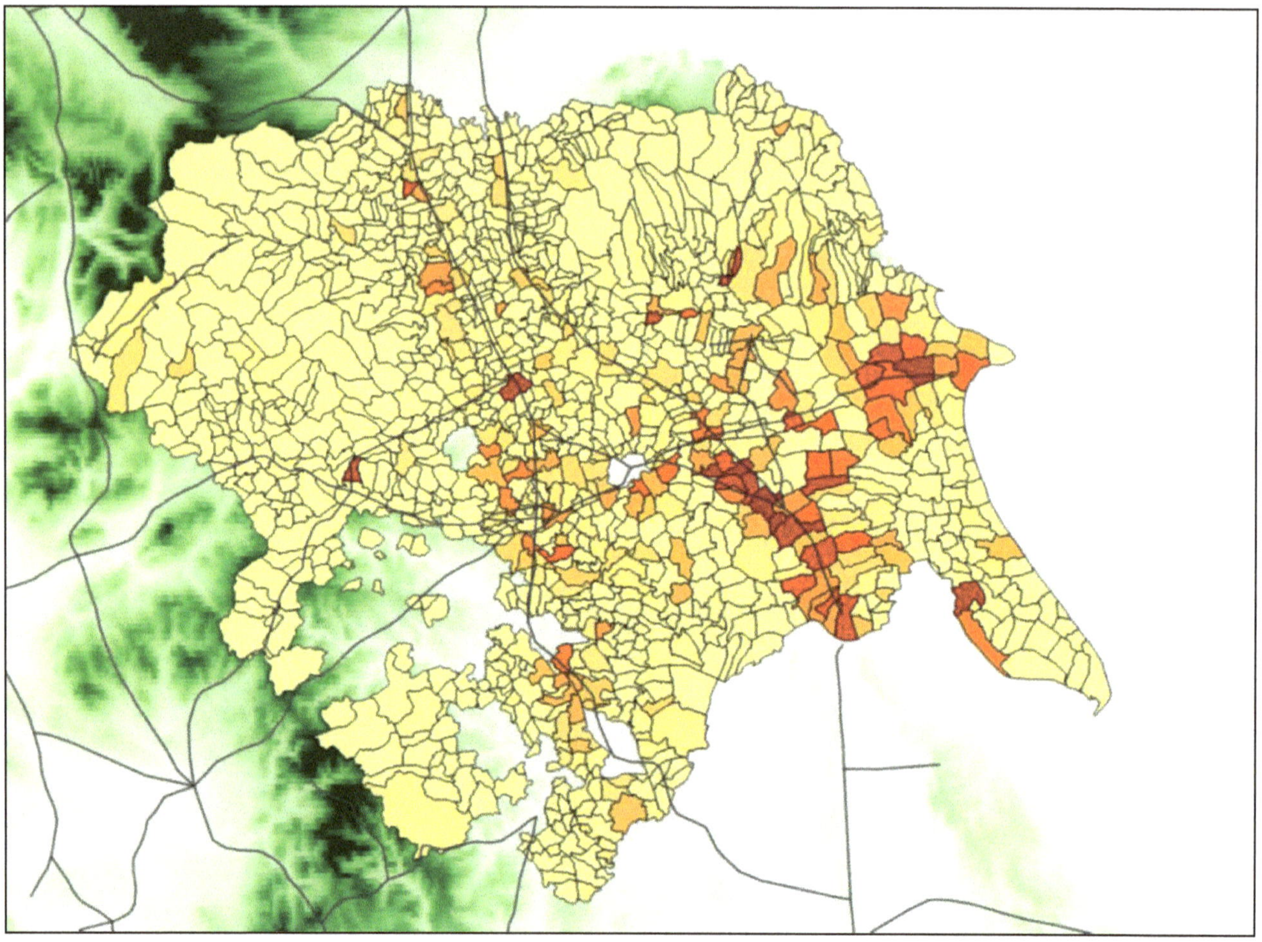

Map 9: Roman finds density by parish. Source: Andrew Woods, March 2016.

Index of Site Studies

www.ingramcontent.com/pod-product-compliance
Lightning Source LLC
LaVergne TN
LVHW072253300926
849160LV00018B/1653